Democracy Unrealized

Documenta11_Platform1

Democracy Unrealized

Documenta11_Platform1

Edited by
Okwui Enwezor
Carlos Basualdo
Ute Meta Bauer
Susanne Ghez
Sarat Maharaj
Mark Nash
Octavio Zaya

Hatje Cantz

This volume contains all contributions to
Documenta11_Platform1, "Democracy
Unrealized," a series of conferences and lectures,
held in Vienna, Academy of Fine Arts, March
15– April 20, 2001, and in Berlin, House
of World Cultures, October 9–30, 2001.

Managing Editor: Gerti Fietzek

Editing: Philomena Mariani

Translations: Jefferson Chase, Vincent Martin

Visual Concept and Typography: Ecke Bonk

Typesetting: Weyhing digital, Ostfildern-Ruit

Printed by Dr. Cantz'sche Druckerei,
Ostfildern-Ruit

© 2002 documenta und Museum
Fridericianum-Veranstaltungs GmbH, Kassel,
Hatje Cantz Publishers, and authors

Photo credits:
pp. 212–219 © 2000 Francesco Jodice;
pp. 315–317 Courtesy archive Vladimir Paperny

Published by
Hatje Cantz Publishers
Senefelderstrasse 12
73760 Ostfildern-Ruit, Germany
www.hatjecantz.de

Distribution in the USA
D.A.P., Distributed Art Publishers, Inc.
155 Avenue of the Americas, 2nd Floor
New York, NY 10013, USA
www.artbook.com

ISBN 3-7757-9082-9

Printed in Germany

Die Deutsche Bibliothek – CIP-Einheits-
aufnahme
A catalogue record for this book is available from
Die Deutsche Bibliothek

The first part of Platform1 was organized in
collaboration with the Academy of Fine Arts
Vienna/Institute for Contemporary Art; the
second part was organized in collaboration with
the House of World Cultures and DAAD
(Deutscher Akademischer Austauschdienst –
German Academic Exchange Service), Berlin.

Project advisors and research:
Oliver Marchart and Charity Scribner

Organization: Markus Müller and Angelika Nollert

Lounge Vienna:
Seminar "Theory (Un)realized": Oliver Marchart
Film workshop/seminar "Imagining
Democracy": Hito Steyerl
Interior design: class of Heimo Zobernig

Thanks to:
Carl Pruscha, Rector, Academy of Fine Arts Vienna
Team Academy of Fine Arts Vienna:
Jessica Beer, Ruth Lackner
Pirmin Blum, Maja Grafe, Doris Guth,
Roland Kollnitz, Wolfgang Meisinger,
Sonja Parzefall, Andreas Spiegl, Christina Werner,
Ingeborg Wurzer

Peter C. Seel, Director, Department of
Literature, Society, Science, House of World
Cultures, Berlin
Michael Thoss, Director, Department of Fine
Arts, Film/Video, House of World Cultures,
Berlin
Susanne Sporrer, Director, Department of Public
Relations, House of World Cultures, Berlin
Friedrich Meschede, Director, Department of
Visual Art, Artists-in-Residence Programme,
DAAD, Berlin

Platform1 was realized with the generous
support of:
Bundeskanzleramt, Sektion II –
Kunstangelegenheiten, Vienna
Bundesministerium für Bildung, Wissenschaft
und Kultur, Vienna
DAAD, Berlin
House of World Cultures, Berlin

Contents

Outlook: The Political Discourse of Democracy

It is now commonplace to declare that the world changed with the spectacular and traumatizing events of September 11, 2001. What the change represents, however, is still hard to define, given how deeply such change is also seen to be caught in the proliferating processes of globalization. A teleological reading of September 11 positions it in a sort of flawed cause-and-effect representation. That it marks a deep cleavage in the ways one thinks of political Islam is certain, but whether this should mean that all responses to it should be understood from the point of view of the pre- and post-syndrome that has overtaken all discussions around it, especially in the United States, is quite another matter.

Even if we cannot deny that the events of September 11 and its aftermath in the war in Afghanistan have significantly widened the political horizon of democratic and juridical discourses of our time, they could hardly be pronounced the central ground on which the struggle to overcome Westernism and imperialism is being waged. September 11 represents one of the most radical and terrible visions of the conflict of values that has attended the slow dismantling of imperialism. It is also a sanguine lesson for late modernity, and has launched debates worldwide – from Palestine, Pakistan, Saudi Arabia, Iran, and the rest of the Islamic world to the United States, France, England, the North Atlantic Treaty Organisation alliance, and Russia – on themes of fundamentalism (religious and secular), concepts of governance and political participation, juridical interpretations of civil society, ethical principles of terrorism as a tool of radical political struggle, peace, security, and other secular and theocratic themes. Whatever the outcome of these debates, the commonplaces we all share are to be found in the very features of global instability and insecurity that explode the triumphalist conceit of "a new world order." Not since the end of World War II and then the collapse of communism in the Soviet Union have there been such demands for such radical rearticulations and reinterpretions of the basic principles of universal political rights.

What is to be done? This popular refrain, heard so often in these tense times, is a measure of the incertitudes that have suddenly arisen to make deeper demands on the sunny projections of globalist progress. Such incertitudes mark another kind of critical procedure, namely the analogous idea that globalization and the political discourse of terrorism have a common root in fundamentalism, whether secular or theocratic, in that they respectively hegemonize the markets and religion with limited participation from other sources.

The series of conferences, public debates, and film and video projects from which the first four books of Documenta11's five Platforms are drawn were planned and begun more than two years before the events of September 11 brought a new urgency to the political and philosophical debates that form the focus of our wider project – debates on democracy, justice, cultural and religious difference, and new spatial arrangements. Nonetheless, the contributions to these volumes share a common assumption in the fact that each is an attempt by the author to illuminate the epistemological texture and complexity of the present political and cultural climate.

Beginning in Vienna on March 15, 2001, and ending in Kassel on September 15, 2002, the Platforms, based on the conceptual initiative of Documenta11, unfolded over the course of eighteen months. The first four Platforms were constituted as collaborations between Documenta11 and the Prince Claus Fund for Culture and Development, The Hague; the India Habitat Centre, New Delhi; the Academy of Fine Arts Vienna; the House of World Cultures, Berlin; DAAD (Deutscher Akademischer Austauschdienst – German Academic Exchange Service), Berlin; CODESRIA (Council for Development of Social Science Research in Africa), Dakar; and the Goethe Institute, Munich and Lagos. For the present volume, Documenta11, the Academy of Fine Arts Vienna, the House of World Cultures, and the DAAD have worked closely at every stage of the realization of the Vienna and Berlin conferences.

These collaborations not only highlight the larger scope of Documenta11's intellectual project based on the principle of shared research interests, they inscribe within Documenta11's exhibition project a critical interdisciplinary methodology that is to be distinguished from interdisciplinarity as a form of exhibitionism. The interdisciplinary dimension that forms part of our common association is also a manifestation of a central concern of Documenta11 from the very beginning, namely the idea that the space of contemporary art, and the mechanisms that bring it to a wider public domain, require radical rethinking and enlargement.

Such an enlargement has both spatial and temporal consequences. In a kind of counterprocedure, it represents a limit and a horizon. The limit specifies the point of Documenta11's beginning, that is, the articulation of the exhibition dimension of the project; while the horizon points to the intellectual and artistic circuits that make up aspects of the exhibition project's drive toward the production of knowledge, through a gesture of open contestation, debate, and transparent processes of research. The framework within which this takes place has both political and aesthetic objectives. But rather than subsume the concerns of art and artists into the narrow terrain of Western institutional aesthetic discourses that are part of the current crisis, we have conceived of this project as part of the production of a common public sphere. Such a public sphere, we believe, creates a space whereby the critical models of artists, theorists, philosophers, historians, activists, urbanists, writers, and others working within other intellectual traditions and artistic positions could productively be represented and discussed. The public sphere imagined by these collaborations is to be understood, then, as a constellation of multifaceted Platforms in which artists, intellectuals, communities, audiences, practices, voices, situations, actions come together to examine and analyze the predicaments and transformations that form part of the deeply inflected historical procedures and processes of our time.

If there is a politics of any kind to be deduced from the above, it is a politics of nonambiguity, and the idea that all discourses, all critical models (be they artistic or social, intellectual or pragmatic, interpretive or historical), emerge from a location or situation, even when they are not defined or restricted by it. In proposing the five Platforms that make up our common public sphere, we have above all else been attentive to how contemporary artists and intellectuals begin from the location and situation of their practice. The objective of all five Platforms has been to bring all the forces emanating from these disciplinary departures and conjunctions into an enabling space of productive intellectual and artistic activity.

Okwui Enwezor
Artistic Director, Documenta11

Boris Groys
Rector, Academy of Fine Arts Vienna

Hans-Georg Knopp
Secretary General House of World Cultures, Berlin

Ulrich Podewils
Director, Artists-in-Residence Programme DAAD, Berlin

As the ideological forces of the "New World Order" recede and those of institutions of global economics and politics become entrenched values, there have emerged a number of powerful questions about the fate of democracy at the beginning of the new millennium. Though these questions have preoccupied intellectuals, institutions, and thinkers of all stripes for more than half a century, it was only in the waning moments of the 20th century that the full meaning of the political fragmentation that attended the dissolution of the Soviet empire made issues of democracy more pronounced. Several factors have contributed to the current wave of reassessments of the ideological hegemony of democracy, namely: the scale and penetration of global capitalism in determining every facet of cultural and political life around the world; the rise of nationalisms and fundamentalisms of every imaginable kind as responses to the neoliberal globalist onslaught; the widened horizon of notions of citizenship produced by large-scale displacements and immigration that today are reshaping the face of once stable societies; and finally, the emergence of the postcolonial state as it grapples with the imperfect legacy of imperialism and colonialism.

Within all these transformations, crucial to the narration of modernity in our time and the formation of subjectivity (ethnic or national, individual or collective), an important qualification needs to be made, which is the extent to which current tendencies of democratic governance are inherited from, and connected to, the traditions of Western conceptions of democracy. Because it cannot be denied that the state of democracy around the world today has become more varied and flexible, we are moved to question whether the notion of democracy can still be sustained only within the philosophical grounds of Western epistemology. What are the possible ways to imagine democracy today as method and praxis available to both governors and governed, nation and subjects alike?

Even if democracy has been the watchword for different kinds of participatory governance and political systems of the last half century, to a large degree it remains a project under constant reinvention. The notion *unrealized* alluded to in the title of this project is a way to interpret the varied modifications that the ethic of democracy and its institutional forms have undergone and continue to undergo today, making democracy a fundamentally unrealizable project – or, put another way, a work in progress.

As an example, we may recall the subversion of democratic logic by far right extremists, nationalist parties, and xenophobes sweeping through Europe today, or the conditions of democracy within totalitarian governments in the former communist countries, dictatorships in Africa, Asia, and Latin America. On the opposite side of the spectrum, the appropriation of the democratic ethic recently enacted by the reformist movement in Iran calls for a fresh examination of the fundamental concept of democracy as essentially a secular endeavor. Equally, the history of the independence movements and decolonization in Africa, Asia, and the Middle East testifies to the extreme topicality attained by the idea of democratic politics. This has led not only to structural changes in those societies in which democracy and its institutions form part of the heritage of the former colonial state, but also in the political culture itself. These associations have been reinforced since the collapse of the USSR at the end of the 1980s and the ensuing, apparently "natural," co-dependence between liberal democracy and global capitalism.

In the last twenty years, the structure of a powerful ideological discourse has crystallized in the West that emphasizes the mutual belonging of these two components. This is a model of democracy that emphasizes individual rights above any form of collective action. Meanwhile, in the "developing" world, a search for an alternative paradigm is producing sober reassessments. Activists, thinkers, artists, and cultural producers both from Western and non-Western contexts have sought to resist and contest these assumptions. Entirely new uses and possible forms of democratic contestation have also been articulated, at the core of which lies an interpolation of the traditional Western European conception of democracy and the appropriation of its rhetorical methods in the service of other agendas. Notions such as "representation," "hegemony," and "popular participation" have been refined by different groups in an attempt to elaborate new forms of resistance to the pervasive neoliberal ideology and ascendant right-wing extremism that characterizes late capitalism in the West.

To fully appreciate the debates on democracy within this project, a few issues require consideration.

Exploring the Term "Unrealized"   The central impetus of this project is to discuss how liberal democracy has been presented in the post–Cold War setting – not only as the best of all systems but as a totally realized, essentially completed project. From this rather triumphal, post–Cold War perspective, if democracy is to be described as a finished project, it means that no structural changes are conceivable or necessary, that it is complete in all its foundational features – only small technical adjustments and minor tinkering may be needed in future. The logic of this argument can be seen as the technocratic interpretation of the term *unrealized*, which is seen as fine tuning of democratic procedural methods and due processes that have already been largely settled. This has been the way in which the main Western democracies view themselves – at best, as "incomplete implementations" of equality and justice on which modern democracy is based, rather than limits, flaws, dead-ends, and problematics inscribed in the principles themselves. In reaction to this presumption, we start from the idea that Democracy Unrealized is a matter of bringing to light what liberal democracy promises but fails to deliver. The emphasis, then, is on the potential for revision, revaluation of values, extension, and creative transformation to keep in step with 21st-century globalizing processes – the idea of an ever-open, essentially unfinishable project that in principle has fallen short of its ideals.

The End of History, Emergent Democracies, Unstable Democracies Against the backdrop of the Soviet Union's meltdown in the early 1990s, Francis Fukuyama, in *The End of History and the Last Man* (1992), spelled out what would become virtually a post–Cold War doctrine – that liberal democracy is tied to the marketplace. According to Fukuyama, the end of communism conclusively demonstrated that no other system could match, supercede, or improve upon liberal democracy. Hence his claim that liberal democracy marks the "end of history" – not in the sense that everyday events and developments have come to a halt, but in that no further structural development beyond the framework of contemporary liberal democracy is possible. Today one can say that no viable alternatives appear, or will present themselves, on the contemporary horizon. Liberal democracy, bound up with global market economics, represents a limit case of the development of political life, "the end point of mankind's ideological evolution," as he asserts. A part of Fukuyama's thesis depends on, not an analysis of rational factors or economics, but a master/slave metaphor. In this analysis, liberal democracy emerges and evolves from the idea of the recognition of the master (aristocracy, bourgeoisie) into a form of universal recognition. But is the recognition available to citizens of contemporary liberal democracies completely satisfying? The long-term future of liberal democracy, and the alternatives to it that may one day arise, depend above all on the answers to this question.

We may have already arrived at the point when such alternatives need careful examination. The various forms of democratic processes that have engulfed the emergent countries of Eastern Europe, the struggle to align democracy to the theocratic, authoritarian political institutions of present-day Iran, or, in the case of Africa, the sheer futility of asking postcolonial African regimes to reform the former colonial state's institutions, mark the ontology of forms of democratic governmentality that are irreconcilable with the principles propagated in the West.

Equally pressing in this evaluation are the dynamics of what emerges as the dialectics of fundamentalism and liberalism as played out in Algeria, Turkey, and the ex–Soviet Union; the violence enacted in former Yugoslavia; China's "One Country, Two Systems" policy. Whatever one may make of these democracies, their very contradiction calls for an analysis of democracy from both inside and out in order to form a coherent picture of the present system of global transition.

Tolerance   With issues of tolerance, we see most strikingly the construction and exclusion of difference and otherness, the burden of assimilation placed on immigrants and outsiders, and the delegitimation of other ways of living and knowing. All of these mark the limits of tolerance in liberal democracies. Tolerance itself implies looking outward from a ready-made body of values to which others are expected to conform, as opposed to ethical encounters and engagements with difference, mutual exchange, or transformation. What are the implications of the construct of tolerance in our present global society?

In this forum on democracy's ethical and epistemological blind spots, we are confronted with forms of lived experience and knowledge that are not acknowledged or provided for; limits revealed as Western liberal democracies encounter new categories of citizens: economic immigrants, political refugees, asylum seekers, *sans papiers*, and other excluded groups, whose pressing demands for recognition, presence, and participation have increasingly exposed the limits of tolerance, the limits of notions of civil rights and the universality of human rights. From the foregoing, it seems necessary to re-engage and examine how narratives and testimonies of marginalized groups, especially how their struggle to overcome their sense of exclusion, pressures democracies to examine their ethical and epistemological limits, sometimes forcing them to extend and forge new spaces and provisions for difference.

Work Ethic   The claim that democracy can only be realized and operate when its prerequisite – the work ethic – is strongly established is the argument put forward for the basis of liberal democracies in the West and Japan. In the United

States, it is attributed to Protestant culture; this argument is similarly wielded against places that, through colonialism, are struggling to develop alternative forms of governance. Is the work ethic, then, the instrument of conversion? What are the counter-narratives that question whether democracy can only truly secure itself when a work ethic is inculcated and institutionalized?

Development Ethics, Globalization, and Democracy   Since the end of World War II, "development" has been a catchword of modernization, the great leap forward toward sustainability and self-sufficiency. It has equally been the directive from a range of global institutions of creating democratic societies within the confines and on the fringes of Western capitalism. By grafting an economic structure onto the rhetoric of democracy, rigid practices of developmental institutions such as the World Bank and IMF have in fact disrupted societies in the process of transition. The ethics of such globalization have been bitterly debated from inside the countries which are "to be developed," offering alternatives to the polarization of tradition and modernity and the simultaneous conflation of development with progress.

Okwui Enwezor
Carlos Basualdo
Ute Meta Bauer
Susanne Ghez
Sarat Maharaj
Mark Nash
Octavio Zaya

**Democracy Unrealized:
Alternatives, Limits, New Horizons**

Democracy, Globalization, and Difference

Stuart Hall

One is tempted to say of democracy what, according to an essay by Immanuel Wallerstein, Mahatma Gandhi said of Western civilization. "What do you think of Western civilization, Mr. Gandhi?" someone asked him. To which he replied, "It would be a good idea." The organizers of Documenta11 were wise to recognize that, in relation to the conditions of existence of artistic practice today, few topics are more significant than the fate and future of democracy. Art today is increasingly "democratic" in a loose sense: more people, from wider conditions of life, are able to practice it, and its subject matter has been radically democratized – whatever invisible symbolic frame the artist is able to weave around a subject makes it count as "a work of art." On the other hand, the "art world" remains a highly exclusive "club," its discourse precious and rarified and more than ever penetrated through and through by money and the market. Documenta11 calls for a timely inventory of democracy's unrealized potential, but I want to kick off by talking about democracy's present vicissitudes. For an inventory of its possibilities is difficult to undertake without immediately encountering its opposite – democracy's *impossibility*. At the end I may try, briefly, to say why this *impossibility* may be democracy's saving grace. But before we make this redemptive move, let me stare its down-side in the face.

I understand its impossibility in two senses, one practical, one more conceptual. The meaning of the word *democracy* is now so proliferated, so loaded down with ideological freight, so indeterminate where it stands at the nexus on different, often mutually exclusive paradigms – liberal democracy, participatory democracy, popular democracy – that it is virtually useless. So unstable that it often cannot sustain meaningful dialogue, so that it is questionable whether it is any longer "good to think with." Increasingly emptied of real content, as the gap between real and ideal widens, it is progressively weighed down by the plentitude of its unfulfilled promises. It is simultaneously too empty and too full. It can only be used in its radically deconstructed form. It is, to coin a phrase, under deep *erasure*.

The second aspect relates to this gap between real and ideal. The discourse of democracy is, to use the language of spectrality, haunted by the ghost of its ideal. The problem is that the gap between any actually existing system of democracy and its status as a universal regulative idea is read teleologically. So that each manifestly inadequate historical example is seen as another stage in the inevitable onward march toward its full realization – a moment of Hegelian reconciliation between democracy's "real" and democracy's "reason." To the contrary, I want to argue that this "lack" is not contingent but constitutive of the democratic idea, which can only function as what Ernesto Laclau calls "a horizon" – without specific, transhistorical content: a necessarily empty signifier. According to Laclau, a horizon is that "which establishes, at one and the same time, the limits and the terrain of constitution of any possible object – and that, as a result, makes impossible any 'beyond.'"[1] I will return to this idea at the end.

The spirit animating democracy through its many actual forms is that legitimate government must rest on the incorporation and the active consent and participation of all, and this "all" implies a radical equality between the totality of its subjects, carrying with it the promise of the leveling of power. When in the historical world has such a system been constructed in any way but across its manifest *lack*? Athenian democracy – small enough to give the appearance of transparency – existed in a tiny circle of light supported by the invisibility of forced labor and surrounded by the immense darkness of the barbarian other. The Lockean ideal enshrined in the American Constitution was the privilege of propertied men, not the poor, women, the enslaved or indigenous people. The "freedom" of this exclusion was recently once again vividly demonstrated in the US Electoral College, which legitimated the passage of the presidency to the candidate who had lost the popular vote. The Declaration of the Rights of Man and the Citizen, an inspirational democratic document worldwide, could not ensure that the Assembly would recognize the inalienable rights to freedom of black Haitian slaves – the "Black Jacobins" who, paradoxically, had been inspired precisely by the Abbé Reynal, the *philosophes*, and *liberté, égalité, fraternité*. The popular democracies, in a Brechtian move, elected the Party in place of the People. In Western democracies, the long struggle to reform and expand the franchise inched forward to assimilate a wider and wider tranche of adult men, but fiercely resisted the enfranchisement of women and could not universalize democracy's ideal even to its own poor and powerless citizens. In T. H. Marshall's historicist reading of citizenship, the progressive movement – first, equality before the law, then the franchise, then the "amelioration of class" through

1 Ernesto Laclau, *Emancipation(s)* (London: Verso, 1996), p. 102.

the welfare state – comes to a shuddering halt before the frontier of giving socioeconomic rights any deep content: a threshold the international doctrine of human rights found impossible to encompass.[2]

This should not be taken as meaning that the subject of democracy is no longer worth pursuing. It remains a powerful idea animating radical demands everywhere, and a critical idea to bring to bear against and to lever open the actually existing structures of power: though, probably, more in its adjectival sense – the "democratization of social life" – than in its substantive form. These days, when I hear "democracy" I am pretty certain that I am already launched on the treacherous seas of some deep and complex ideological maneuver. This does not mean that it has some already given actual historical content toward which it is always "tending" which one day will be completed in its already known forms. Nor does it mean that its efficacy is limited to the West, though we may have to radically rethink the conditions of existence it may require to become strategically operative in societies where the other conditions of existence in which it has become embedded in the West are not present. Ideas are not limited to their place of origin, though we should expect their radical transformation as they begin to "travel": increasingly so, as cultures cease to be autonomous, self-sustaining, enclosed entities, writing the scripts of their members from birth to death and entering the cosmopolitan condition where ideas, images, as well as forms of life flow across boundaries and begin to indigenize – a topic to which I will also return.

Nevertheless, despite this more qualified optimistic note, the limited inventory I want to offer as a way of starting this investigation is less about democracy's potential, "unrealized" possibilities, and more about its actually existing realization in the contemporary setting. And here my argument is that in recent years, the balance in what we may call the relations of democratic forces has decisively swung against the democratic tide. The gap I referred to earlier between the stuttering incompleteness of its forms of empirical realization and its onward march as transhistorical ideal has been hegemonized. The ideas circulating within democracy's wider frame have been condensed into "liberal democracy," and liberal democracy reduced to the system that now prevails in the Western developed "democratic capitalist" world. This form of democracy is said to have reached such a close approximation to its ideal that it is, for all practical purposes, complete. It may require tinkering here and here, and the sort of regular motor maintenance check to make sure the engine is running smoothly. But generally, in its sublating movement of supercession, the system is close to

2 See T. H. Marshall, *Citizenship and Social Class* (1950; London: Pluto Press, 1991).

the complete "exhaustion" of its potential through its "realization"; bringing us, as Francis Fukuyama has argued, at last, face to face with "The End of History," in the sense that there are no great political conceptions of freedom and equality to come, no profound ideological work remaining to be done, no new political goals that are not already within our empirical grasp. Liberal democratic Man is The Last (natural) Man. This is the quasi-Hegelian conflation that underpins Fukuyama's vision of liberal democracy as "the only coherent political aspiration that spans different regions and cultures around the globe."[3]

Fukuyama explicitly connects this completion of the liberal democratic dream *within* the West to its new, *global* mission. The link is secured by the fact that, as Fukuyama puts it, "A liberal revolution in economic thinking has [everywhere] sometimes preceded, sometimes followed, the move toward political freedom around the globe."[4] In short, as Derrida notes acerbically, "The alliance of liberal democracy and of the free market" – their absolute and ultimate interdependence – is "the good news of this later quarter century."[5] It is this couplet that has made liberal democracy the political advance guard of the tremendous avalanche of neoliberal orthodoxy now sweeping the post–Cold War world with evangelical zeal. Fukuyama does not altogether deny liberal democracy's "dark side," nor that, here and there, the system may need a little light renovation. But these are assigned to the side of the contingent – "the empirical flow of events in the second half of the century."[6] Their accumulation in no way refutes, qualifies, or undermines the ideal, which remains "perfect" – the only coherent global aspiration to freedom. What Derrida calls "the telos of a progress that [has] the form of an ideal finality."[7]

Of course, the interchangeability of liberal democratic conceptions of political freedom and market freedom is not new. The conjunction of two, mutually qualifying terms – *liberal* and *democracy* – already marks the site of this fateful convergence. But in more reformist times, each was supposed to qualify and in some way limit the other. "Liberal" recognized that the market remained the best "impartial" allocator of economic resources, and one could go only so far in interfering with its "logic": that capital accumulation provided the economic basis of living standards and prosperity, and imposed its limits on how far economic power could be "democratized." Liberal also implied the full panoply of other liberal relations that constituted the conditions of existence of actually

---

3 Francis Fukuyama, *The End of History and the Last Man* (London: Penguin, 1992), p. xiii.
4 Ibid.
5 Jacques Derrida, *Specters of Marx: The State of the Debt, the Work of Mourning, and the New International*, trans. Peggy Kamuf (New York: Routledge, 1994).
6 Ibid., p. 70.
7 Ibid., p. 57.

existing liberal democracy: individual autonomy; an abstract-equivalent notion of the citizen; a formal not a substantive conception of equality; a neutral, culture-blind state ("veiled in assumed ignorance," as they say); and representative government. But "democracy" promised the constitution of public political spaces in which private interests would be required to take account of a wider set of "public" interests. It recognized that government could not be conducted without acquiring the consent of its citizens; that institutions should somehow be "accountable" not only to their owners or governors but to wider social interests; that the power of capital and the inequalities of power, everywhere the inevitable consequence of capitalist market societies, should enter a trade-off against the power of one person—one vote. I am not suggesting that this ideal-typical picture – liberal democracy as the best of all possible shells for the development of market capitalism, Lenin might have said – ever prevailed in practice. But I am pointing out the room for struggle, contestation, and negotiation produced by the necessary interdependency but mutually limiting effect of this heavily compromised formation. These are indeed the only spaces in which genuine social reforms have been won.

It is by taking this best-possible reading of liberal democracy and contrasting with it recent developments in three spheres that I constitute my provisional inventory. It is, then, something radically new – we are in a radically new conjuncture – when the two terms are positively advanced, not as an articulation, but as linked by an internal necessary within a single, self-sealing totality. From this perspective I want to discuss, first, the hollowing out of democracy at the very moment of its so-called apotheosis; second, the way the transnational diffusion and flow of power, in contemporary forms of Western-dominated economic, financial, and cultural globalization, short-circuits and undermines even the limited countervailing powers won in the nation-state era; and third, how the emergence of "difference" in every sphere of life subverts and undermines the basic but unspoken assumption of cultural and social homogeneity that underwrites optimal definitions of liberal democracy, piercing the very heart of the concept.

Pluralization and fragmentation of the social and political field are well-advanced features of late modern Western societies. This does not mean that there are no centers of power or that the great inequalities of power, resources, and privilege that used to pass under the general category of "class" have ceased to exist. In most Western societies, the inequality gap between the haves and the have-nots has widened significantly even in the most recent period of sustained economic growth. This is now a constitutive feature of Western "success," and has occurred, of course, in tandem with a parallel trend on the global stage. But the complexities of modern technology, the specialization of labor markets, the

advanced character of the division of labor, the expansion of "the political" mul-
tiplying the sites of antagonism and diffusing the centers where the operative
decisions that affect our lives are taken, are not only, to different degrees in different developed societies, the fate of "late modernity" but have deep consequences for the "settled" forms of citizenship and democratic participation
arrived at by the middle of the 20th century. The pluralization of social antagonism and the production of new subjects have, we would argue, positive potential for the struggles to widen political participation and for the deepening of
democratic life. But their immediate effect is dislocating: the loss of effectivity
and distinctiveness by the old ideologies that articulated different social interests
and hegemonized the ideological field, and the waning or ossification of the
political parties that were the principal articulating points of mediation and
contestation between popular consent in a representative system and the system
of governmentality.

   Though by no means concluded, I would argue that not the deepening of
democratic contestation but the *hollowing out* of liberal democracy has been its
principal tendency. In the absence of more developed political ideologies, populism, the market, and different versions of nationalism provide, in principle,
articulating grounds. Populism – the use of "the people" as an empty signifier to
conflate into a single "big tent" interests that are different and antagonistic – is,
of course, especially attractive because it simultaneously replicates *and* supplants
the more democratic alternative it replaces. The people and the popular are such
near-cousins, such seductive synonyms, that the sleight of hand involved is
hardly perceptible. The second articulating principle is the way market freedom
now condenses metonymically every kind of freedom. Why bother with the difficult process of articulating alliances, constructing subjects, and winning political representation when, in our detotalized individuality, we can instantly participate through immediate consumption, or even by a mouse click, in the big
"free" bazaar of life? One tiny indicator of the growing "marketization" of social
life in Britain, which must here be my main source of examples, is the way the
specification of professions, knowledge, expertise, and role is dissolved by the
acid of equivalence of "the consumer." We no longer have teachers and students,
doctors and patients, social workers and clients, local administrators and citizens, but the all-encompassing *consumer*. My prime minister, confronting the
crisis in public education – a "democratic" issue if ever there was one – declared
all public-sector workers, including teachers, to be "the forces of conservatism,"
then, in a more positive vein, encouraged them to boost their confidence by
thinking of themselves as "social entrepreneurs" and to acquire something of the
status currently enjoyed by "businessmen." This is a telltale symptom of that
larger movement which has brought about the collapse of the very idea of "the

public," the cynicism which greets the idea that economic ministers making judgments about "competition" should take a wider "public interest" into account, and of course the remorseless drive to "privatization."

The evidence of what we call the short-circuiting of democratic contestation and accountability is overwhelming: the centralization of executive power, even within the so-called parliamentary system, coupled with the erosion of local government and local democracy; the managerialist style of governance, with the country run like a private corporation with the prime minister as its CEO and elections as occasional meetings of an emasculated body of shareholders; the expansion of an entrepeneurial style of governance, where government functions and departments are increasingly "outsourced" or converted into agencies, with no clear line of accountability, and public servants are recommended to entrepreneurialize their practice and "take ownership" of policy.

Critics who question whether the neoliberal revolution initiated by Mrs. Thatcher in Britain had real practical effects on the governance of the country rarely take account of the role played by American-style management ideology as "the vanishing mediator" in the relay between ideology and practice. Then there is the "mediatization" of politics which, in the present era, has reached a new intensity. I refer to the massive manipulation of public opinion and consent by the swollen echelon of political public relations and focus-group polling; the way special-interest lobbying outweighs the cumbersome practices of public argument; the consistent adaptation of policy to the agendas of the media, which become a more authentic ventriloquizing "voice" for "the people" than the people themselves; and, in the UK certainly, the obsessive use of "spin," which some regard as a mere surface affliction, but which, in the context of the Third Way – determined to square every circle and triangulate every social interest – is profoundly endemic to the system. Finally, there is the drift of liberal, democratic politics to the "radical center," a vacuous concept in itself as even Third Way supporters themselves can see, with its Third Way commitment to a politics "beyond left and right," a politics, as Chantal Mouffe has argued, without antagonism, without enemies – that is to say, a politics without politics: politics as a management technology. Despite various strategies of social amelioration and redistribution by stealth, my government is remorselessly opposed, ideologically, to redistribution *as an idea* – and hence cannot provide a range of deprived and dispossessed groups more generally with an articulating theme or construct a constituency for it.

All of this is, to a very real extent, the consequence internally of the new-liberal orthodoxy as a so-called public philosophy and the advance of transnational global techno- and financial capitalism. It is underpinned by the profound belief that neoliberal forms of globalization are "inevitable": like Fate, they can only be obeyed. The role of government is, therefore, to help create the conditions for private capital to prosper, to pursue at home those privatizing and deregulative strategies calculated to make the nation more competitive in the global environment, to ease the path of transnational capital, and, most particularly, to educate and tutor its citizens to adapt to the new cold climate, to adapt to the logic of market forces, by removing the "disincentives" posed by universal forms of welfare; to encourage the two-thirds who *are* prospering to make private provision for life's vicissitudes – birth, parenting, education, health insurance, insurance against redundancy in "flexible" labor markets, retirement, care in old age, and death – and to drive down to its lowest level the threshold of the "residuum," who must be rigorously means-tested to receive aid and are invited, US-style, as rapidly as possible, to wean themselves from the infantilism of "welfare dependency." I know that the UK's favoring of the American model of what Michael Walzer calls Liberalism 1 over the more European social-market model, while of course wanting to "play its full part in Europe" – the Third Way always wants to have its cake *and* eat it – may distort my perspective. Things may not yet be so bad in your neck of the woods, but I am sure this is a nightmare coming your way.

I want to say less, because more is known and more already said, about the impact on liberal democracy as "the only coherent conception of political freedom around the globe" of what the Documenta11 briefing calls "the neoliberal globalist onslaught" and the forces of transnational global capitalism. I focus on one aspect – some consequences for democracy unrealized.

One can see why a Western-driven globalization prefers to operate where liberal democracies have been established. Foreign investment, the transnational movement of finance capital, technology, and corporate bases work best where there is stability of sociopolitical conditions, and where governments that are required to collaborate and be complicit with global penetration have the legitimacy of popular consent. Dictatorships are notoriously unstable; human rights abuses by authoritarian regimes give the international corporations that are taking competitive advantage of divergent labor market conditions a bad name and can stimulate international mobilization. New technologies, labor patterns, cultural models work best where there is a sympathetic basic value orientation toward change, innovation, and modernity: they work best where societies have political systems whose orientation, modes of operation, and basic values are symbiotic with Western ones. Modern mass production and mass marketing on a global scale require indigenization: the local settings must be ones in which the logic of market forces has been socially embedded and culturally internalized. Where nonliberal democratic forms of popular mobilization occur – ultranationalist, theocratic, ethnic, racial, or charismatic – they tend to be anti-Western, antimodernity, and opposed to globalization's free play. In the drive to transform society in Eastern Europe, liberal democracy and the market have been indivisibly linked, dismantling both authoritarian forms of politics and state-oriented economics. In the developing world, the neoliberal tide requires the dismantling of barriers and regulative checks once considered protectively essential to the project of nation-building that characterized the first phase of the postindependence and postcolonial projects.

Increasingly, the transnational exercise of economic and cultural power is beyond the reach of democratic systems limited by the nation-state and has effectively escaped democratic regulation at the global level. How can relatively weak and hard-pressed new nations bargain, with any semblance of equality, with the overdeveloped Western powers, the bases from within which transnational global capitalism operates? How can developing nations, whose futures depend on acquiring the technology and "know-how" of the New Economy and finding a niche in increasingly free-trade, unregulated financial, commodity, service, media, and cultural markets, find the space to work out some balanced solution between "tradition" and "modernity" in their respective cultures, in the face of the homogenizing cultural assault? I am not so cynical to believe that all international organizations are merely a convenient cover for the free play of American imperializing interests. I know that some developing countries have tried to use what muscle they have in these global forums to win some advantages for the poorer peoples of the earth. But, far from constituting an embryonic transnational regulatory system, they have been dominated by Western interests and the engines driving through a particular version of globalization – deregulating and dismantling the barriers and inhibitions to technological and cultural penetration, imposing structural adjustment programs that intervene directly in the balance of social forces, insisting on free-trade terms that expose fragile markets, using advanced technologies and the Western patent system to destroy local enterprise and social-service provision, for instance, making subsistence farmers totally dependent for seed on Western agrobusiness and blocking the distribution of cheaper generic drugs to poor peoples devastated by HIV and other diseases and chronic infections.

I want to comment on only one aspect of this scenario. Liberal democracy took root in and remains embedded within what David Held calls "a fixed and bounded territorial conception of political community"[8] – the nation-state. Of course, as we have all learned from Immanuel Wallerstein, capitalism as a world-system benefited from the extraordinary interdependence and complicated ten-

---

8 David Held and Anthony McGrew, with David Goldblatt and Jonathan Perraton, *Global Transformations: Politics, Economics, and Culture* (Cambridge: Polity Press, 1999).

sions between the growing international capitalist market and the nation-states, and the trend toward national autonomy and the trend toward globalization are *both* rooted in modernity. Liberal democracy took advantage of this tension to win space and reforms within the political arena of particular nation-states which could not at that stage be generalized across the world-system. Until very recently, it has been within nation-states that the struggles to expand the sphere of representation have been conducted, and the nation-state, not primarily international law, that has been the guarantor of civic and citizens rights. It is rarely recalled that Article 3 of the Declaration of the Rights of Man and the Citizen (1789) reads, "The principle of all sovereignty lies essentially in *the nation*; no group, no individual may have any authority that does not expressly proceed from it."

However, as power increasingly flows "across, around, and over territorial boundaries," "the neat correspondence between national territory, sovereignty, political space, and the democratic political community" is disrupted.[9] It is not (yet) the case that the powerful nation-states are disappearing. It is hard to see any strengthening of the international regulatory system which does not have nation-states as key players in the process of reform. However, their "reach" has been curtailed, their capacity to insulate themselves from the cold winds of global forces and influences is greatly diminished, their capacity to sustain sovereign national economies, polities, cultures uncontaminated by global power is profoundly transformed. In addition, they are busy reorienting themselves, their political structures and economic goals, toward success within a wider globalizing horizon. Even within the serious limits of liberal democracy, this is the source of a growing "democratic deficit" on a world scale.

Here I want only to note a troubling ambivalence, which brings us to our last main area. In his recent overview of the logic of globalization, Fredric Jameson notes that although "nation-states today remain the only concrete terrain and framework for political struggle," any temptation to secede from the global system in order to protect oneself from its worst effects seems to provide a counterpoint "where a nationalist politics might rear its head."[10] In fact, as we have hinted, the many varieties of nationalism, racism, xenophobia, and fundamentalism that have reemerged center stage to global politics are often, in part (though I would argue not exclusively) responses to – reactions against, even – the pressure of a modernizing globalization. Many are the symptoms of a failed nationalist project in hostile international circumstances or of a failed

---

9 Ibid.
10 Fredric Jameson, "Globalization and Political Strategy," *New Left Review* (July–August 2000), p. 64.

modernization. Many are not all entirely antimodernity but instead, Janus-like, mix past and future in highly unstable amalgamations – combining a search for mythic origins in an invented tradition with a ruthless competition to secure nation-state status in the global power stakes at the very moment when the star of the nation-state is waning. This is the case with Balkan nationalisms and, for example, in the way modernism and traditionalism are combined in the current claims of the Hindu fundamentalists in India. But this would be to suggest that every form of resistance which has to make use of the nation-state space is by definition backward and reactionary – which is to suggest that it has a universally fixed political content, itself a form of "funda-mentalism." Also, it implies the binary contrast between "them," who are still prey to irrational and antimodern impulses, and "us," who are thoroughly "modern." I cannot hope to resolve the complex issues of strategies of resist-ance here. I have only to say that when, during the Asian crisis, President Mahatia of Malaysia suspended all currency exchanges, or if the president of South Africa were now to consciously break international drug-patent law in the name of national survival, these are "nationalist" reprises I can live with. And to note, on the other hand, in the advanced democracies the resistance to a more cosmopolitan outlook – to the increasingly mixed character of our populations and more culturally diverse claims on citizenship – that frequently takes the form of a profoundly "fundamentalist" reaction, an attempt to demonize the strangers in our midst, to close the doors of the culture and to climb back into an embattled and defensive little nationalism, with its clear racist, xenophobic, and culturally differential supplements. This is now evi-dent everywhere in Europe, and is the underlying source of that gut-Europho-bia that now afflicts the British soul.

Globalization is not directly responsible for what the Documenta11 briefing calls "the large-scale displacements and immigration that today are reshaping the face of once stable societies" and the "widened horizon of notions of citizen-ship" this has produced. But it is one of globalization's unintended conse-quences, in a larger sense. Postwar, it begins with the movements of national independence and wars of national liberation that triggered decolonization; and has been greatly intensified by the unofficial opening up of borders and bound-aries due to a host of factors: globalization itself and the push and pull of eco-nomic opportunities; poverty, immiseration, unemployment, and structural underdevelopment; political and military coups, tribal and ethnic conflicts, civil wars; natural disasters or environmental catastrophes like drought, floods, ero-sion, global warming, and climate and ecological change; more recently "ethnic cleansing," racism, and xenophobia; and across all that, the unsponsored move-ment of peoples in search of better times.

I want to consider briefly two ideal-typical responses to the demands for, on the one hand, equality, social justice, and inclusion, and on the other hand, for inclusion and the recognition of difference. The first response is essentially *assimilationist*. This can be practiced in weaker and stronger forms, with a tolerant acceptance that the process will take time or the aggressive insistence that foreigners and strangers must either conform to the majority culture and embrace the universal liberal values of modernity or "go back home." But either way, the idea that national identity is not fixed eternally in the myths of historical time but is always a moving feast, constantly being historically redefined, or the recognition that the presence of multicultural differences obliges a society to expand, transform, and enlarge the boundaries and definitions of citizenship and the national community, are strongly resisted. Mr. Hague, the leader of the opposition in the UK, recently described a Britain that is strongly integrated into Europe, hospitable and open to foreigners, welcoming to refugees and asylum seekers, and willing to renegotiate the boundaries of national belonging as fast becoming "a foreign country," alienated from itself. A profound assimilationism is the foundation stone of the revival of nationalist and racist movements and sentiment in Europe, providing the silent legitimation for widespread, if less vocal, forms of national exclusionism, racism, and cultural differentialism, which are more popular today than politicians are willing to acknowledge. The second response is what its enemies call *multiculturalism*, though we know in fact that this is a highly contested term and that there are many varieties which conceive difference in more open, inclusive, and interdependent ways. I am referring to the strongly pluralist conception of difference we find in some versions of "multiculturalism," which not only acknowledge the world significance of different cultural and religious traditions and recognize the strength of religious, cultural, linguistic, and other differences, but regard these as making "cultures" into organic, indivisible "wholes," which saturate entire communities, subordinating individuals to communally sanctioned forms of life exclusively on the basis of their membership within, as it were, a hierarchically arranged pecking order.

One sees here two extreme cases of the struggle between universalism and particularism which has a special salience for the debate about liberal democracy as a global project. The values of liberalism have historically been aligned with those of "modernity." As such, though they were deeply embedded in particular cultures and historical circumstances, they have been re-presented as the sign of universality itself and, in that form, used to insist on assimilation, "trumping" all cultural particularisms. The surmounting of the particularist threshold is often represented as liberal democracy's principal achievement and it is on that basis that it is seen as the necessary precondition for global modernization.

From this perspective, all those who resist its universal appeal are represented as permanently mired in tradition and particularity. Thus the world struggle for liberal democracy assumes the form of a sacred struggle between the universalism of the West as the new global orthodoxy and the particularism of the rest.

But as Ernesto Laclau has cogently argued in *Emancipation(s)* and elsewhere, a logic of pure difference is only a viable strategy where an identity wants nothing from, and is not constitutively related to, any other identity. This is logically difficult to sustain, since all identity is constituted with reference to a lack – to that other which is not the same, from which "sameness" must differentiate itself. One cannot, as Laclau says, affirm an identity without also affirming the wider context which establishes the ground of its difference, or without the constitutive role of power which effects the exclusion that at any point marks off the sameness of an identity from the difference of its others. This of course entails a very particular conception of difference: not the binary of fixed difference that treats ethnicities or cultures as integral "wholes," but what Derrida calls the "logic of *différance*" – "the playing movement that 'produces' ... these differences, these effects of difference," the weave of differences that refuse to separate into fixed binary oppositions, where "every concept [or meaning] is inscribed in a chain ... within which it refers to the other, to other concepts, by means of the systematic play of differences."[11] Identity can only be conceived through difference – present, as it were, only differentially, through its absence. As Laclau puts it, "all differential identity will be constitutively split; it will be the crossing point between the logic of difference and the logic of equivalence."[12] It is difficult to claim equal rights if one is only different from other groups and does not also share something with them which is the basis for the expansion of the claim. A pure logic of equivalence is the abolition of all difference. A "pure logic of difference" can be the basis only of a system of social apartheid and ethnic cleansing. To avoid this, the right to difference "has to be asserted within the global community – that is within a space in which that particular group has to coexist with other groups," which could not be possible "without some shared universal values, without a sense of belonging to a community larger than each of the particular groups in question."[13] If this is not to restore a universalism of the liberal variety, which zooms down from outer space and trumps every particular, it can only be by the recognition of the necessity of living with difference; by continually expanding *the opening to the other* – a reaching from within

---

11 Jacques Derrida, *Margins of Philosophy*, trans. Alan Bass (Chicago: University of Chicago Press, 1982), p. 11.
12 Laclau, *Emancipation(s)*, p. 53.
13 Ibid., p. 32.

the particular toward some wider horizon, without the consolidation of some final closure. Universalization in this open sense "condemns all identity to an unavoidable hybridization, but hybridization does not necessarily mean decline through the loss of identity; it can also mean empowering existing identities through the opening of new possibilities."[14] We are dealing with an indeterminate notion of identity and what Chantal Mouffe has called an "agonistic" conception of democracy.

Laclau has argued that, for a minority group to affirm only the identity that it has at that moment, is to confirm its permanent marginalization: "If, on the other hand, it struggles to change its location within the community and to break with its situation of marginalization, it has to engage in a plurality of political initiatives" which not only expands the political field of contestation radically, but transforms that identity itself, taking it "beyond the limits defined by its present identity."[15] If the spheres of antagonism and democratic contestation are widened and multiplied, "universalism as a horizon is expanded at the same time as its necessary attachment to a particular content is broken."[16] That is why – though I cannot replicate the complexities of Laclau's argument here – he insists that democracy as a horizon has no specific or fixed content, since its content and field will change as it is expanded with each attempt to generalize or "universalize" it to wider spheres of application. Like the universal, it is "an always receding horizon resulting from the expansion of an indefinite chain of equivalent demands."[17] Since its role is to bring about this agonistic mediation between particularity and universalism, "there is no content that is a priori destined to fill it and it is open to the most diverse articulations. But this means that the 'good' articulation, the one that would finally suture the link between universal task and concrete historical forces, will never be found and that all partial victory will always take place against a background of an ultimate unsurpassable impossibility."[18] This is democracy's status as what Laclau calls "an empty signifier."

Democracy in either its liberal or more radical varieties has traditionally counterposed equality to difference, and political theory has been fixated by the impassable barrier between them. What the new situation seems to require is the development of a new articulation, a new political logic. The presence of the stranger presents democracy with this radically new double demand: for equality and social justice *and* for the recognition of difference, neither existing in a

14 Ibid., p. 65.
15 Ibid., p. 49.
16 Ibid., p. 34.
17 Ibid.
18 Ibid., p. 63.

pure state, both qualifying and modifying the other in a ceaseless struggle. Far from marking the apotheosis of democracy itself, this eruption of difference at its center points to the depth of the transformations democracy – the promise of freedom and equality – has yet undergone and the struggles to come.

I am aware that I have altogether neglected to address how these considerations bear on the issues that most preoccupy Documenta11. I want to do so but only in a concluding footnote. I have spent the recent months working on the text for a selection of photographic images produced by forty contemporary photographers from the margins of the West. They are part of a dynamic creative drive that emerged in the mid-1980s from outside the cultural and artistic mainstream, fueled by the demand to bring their objective conditions and subjective experiences into the frame, to give the invisible visibility and to open a "third space" in cultural representation. This work, which is intensely varied, does not explicitly address political questions, but is preoccupied with its own "differences" and was driven by what was called at the time "the search for identity." What is quite extraordinary about this work is that it is *not* the product of what one might call "identity politics": it is about, and at the same time subverts, identity. It recognizes that we all come from somewhere, speak from some place, are multiply positioned and in that sense "located." But in its many different ways, it refuses to be rendered motionless by place, origin, race, color, or ethnicity. It knows that identity is always constructed within, not outside, representation and uses the symbolic space of the image to explore, construct, and at the same time go beyond identity. It is in some radical sense postidentity without being beyond the reach of its effects. It arises at the overdetermined space where different differences overlap and intersect. It is preoccupied with staging the self only in a way that is "open to the other." It represents a new kind of "vernacular cosmopolitanism." It eschews – thank goodness – any reference to political theory. But within its own symbolic time and space, it anticipates what Julia Kristeva calls the recognition of the fact that we are always "strangers to ourselves."

Identity, Relativism, and the Liberal State

Akeel Bilgrami

Strange to say, there is health in hostility. For centuries the relations between European Christendom and Islam, vilifying in word and violent in deed, nevertheless displayed a respect for one another, trading in diverse material products, and engaged in a prolonged and most fruitful mutual intellectual and artistic collaboration and influence; all of which, when viewed from the thoroughly revised circumstances of modernity, can only seem enviably robust and healthy. For those many hundred years prior to the consolidation of Western colonial rule, both cultures were feudal and pastoral, and, despite local differences in religious doctrine, which was in large part the avowed ground of the antagonism, there were shared intellectual premises that governed these differences. In fact, paradoxically, it is really the *shared* element which was the indirect source of the hostility. The more ancient religions of the East, such as Hinduism and Buddhism, were not only more removed in space, but were intellectually too remote to be palpably threatening to Christianity, in the way that Islam, with its many shared assumptions, was. The Crusades were thus fought less in the cause of recovering the Cross for Palestine from some *altogether foreign* emergence, but more to eradicate the *heresy* represented by the Muslims in Arabian lands.

Napoleon's invasion of Egypt and the British conquest of India, however, gradually gave rise to an era defined by a quite different tone of relations. Hostility was of course still there on both sides, but it was not the key to future relations. It was the new tenor of colonial domination that mastery required attitudes of condescension, and were felt to be so by the subject people, breeding not so much a robust sense of hostility, but one of alienation and resentment. This new psychology that accompanied colonial relations was of course undergirded by an altering of the material relations which had held for centuries. The growing mercantile and industrial forces of the most powerful Christian lands were, as we know, steadily destroying the pastoral societies in their own terrain, but their effect on the lands and economies of their colonial subjects was altogether different. What feudal structures it destroyed to recreate new and vibrant economies in its own midst, it left well alone in these other lands, taking only that which was necessary for its mercantile and industrial requirements. By transforming its own political economy while extracting surpluses but leaving structurally unchanged its conquered lands, European colonialism thereby laid the foundation for an abiding material differential, which would continue until today to be the underlying source of the ideological rhetoric of superior progress, not only material but also civilizational. The health of hostility by more or less equal foes had by these material agencies now deteriorated to the alienating effects of condescension and defensive resentment among increasingly unequal ones.

Decolonization, though it once seemed an achievement, did not do much to change these relations, since it was followed by political domination and manipulation by the superpowers as well as substantial economic control of one salient commodity by foreign companies and the elites of client states such as Saudi and Kuwait.

More interestingly, since decolonization, the same set of problems began to be transplanted.

Islam's theological vision had always presented itself as a *world* religion. And the Ottoman empire had set out with considerable success to give that theological vision substantial practical instance for a very long period. But after World War II, Islam began to be a world religion in a quite different sense, one which made a vital difference to the life and politics of European nations. In the long aftermath of the war, many of these nations were reconstructing economies devastated by it. Initially the rebuilding of the industrial base and the service sector was able to absorb the population, but as the base grew and services needed fuller replenishment, there was a seriously growing labor shortage in these countries, most especially in the more menial services to which local populations turned last or not at all. It was during this period, the 1950s and '60s, that Britain, France, and Germany threw open their doors to immigration in order to cope with this shortage, and naturally the largest numbers of immigrants for the jobs that most needed filling were from the ex-colonies or, in the case of Germany, from Turkey, where economic conditions did not always absorb their own local populations into fruitful employment. Very large sections of these immigrants were Muslims and by the 1970s, this immigration was quite substantial. And since the immigration to a large extent consisted of illiterate and semiliterate populations from the countryside of these ex-colonies seeking to be absorbed elsewhere than the glutted metropoles in their own countries, and since they were finding employment in the least desirable jobs in the European nations, it became apparent that even after almost total decolonization, something rather similar to colonial relations between the same peoples was being replicated, only now *inside* of European nations, and not by conquest but by immigration. The psychology of these relations became entrenched when, once the labor shortages eased, local populations often resisted allowing the full and equal assimilation of migrant workers. So to many immigrants it seemed as if history had brought no progress: the colonized remained colonized, their masters too remained masters, it is just that the latter were now the natives and the former the outsiders.

I have rehearsed these familiar historical points to bring out why Islam seems a renewed source of dignity and autonomy not only in Muslim nations but also for Muslim populations in Europe, where their marginalization and failure to be assimilated have reinforced those feelings of vulnerability. Identities are formed most strongly when the source of identity promises dignity and self-respect in the face of such a long and continuing sense of defeat, and the present rise of absolutist elements of Islam in Europe as well as of course in the Middle East and elsewhere is to a very large extent explained by this.

Let us explore this very theme within one specific context: the long and continuing aftermath of the publication of Rushdie's *The Satanic Verses*.[1] All those who have witnessed the episode and written about it have testified to how it mobilized toward Muslim identity not just in Britain but elsewhere in Europe. Let us put aside the *fatwa*, which was preposterous even by the tenets of Islamic Law, which gives no sanction for passing a death sentence on a denizen of Dar-ul-harb or non-Muslim land. Terrifying as it must have been and must be for the author, it is a red herring as far as the deeper issues are concerned. It is enough to consider the more domestic and domesticated European phenomenon of Muslims in Britain and elsewhere in Europe in very large numbers demanding that the book be banned.

What issue does this raise? Of course it raises the issue of the first freedom, the right to speech and writing. But the complicating factor is that it does so in the context of liberal states in nations where there are vast immigrant populations demanding that a liberal principle of free speech be put aside. What Rushdie unintentionally succeeded in doing was to galvanize large numbers of Muslims, who for two decades at least had sought, unsuccessfully, to integrate themselves into British society, to start saying that it is precisely integration that they did *not* now want. They began to demand that the Muslims in Britain be allowed to live under their *own* laws, and deal with blasphemy as *their* laws see fit. In fact, interestingly, they were demanding a revival in reverse of the legal policies of the Ottoman state, under what was called the *millet* system, where, for example, communities of Greek and Russian Orthodoxy were allowed to live

---

1 Salman Rushdie, *The Satanic Verses* (London: Viking, 1988).

under their own system of laws by their Muslim rulers. European nations, as militant British Muslims now envisioned it, could continue to be governed by liberal states, but they demanded that there be a special twist to the liberal states' own idea of minority rights, whereby such rights should now precisely permit Muslim minorities to live by their own *sharia* or legal code on a range of issues of importance to them. Islamic identity in Europe therefore raises a familiar basic paradox at the heart of the European liberal ideal. It is this. The liberal ideal of minority rights can grant status to minorities (say, immigrant Muslims) in forms that are susceptible to minorities demanding the right to various laws and practices and customs to live by which can, as it turns out, amount to *il*liberalism in various respects, ranging from the banning of books to practices reflecting gender injustice in the details of marriage, divorce, alimony, and inheritance.

Now one may think that allowing such illiberal outcomes within liberal doctrine is a harmless paradox, easily resolved even if one granted such a right to Muslims, because if it led, say, to gender injustice for Muslim women in one or other respect, then all one needed to do was to grant to Muslim women who were affected by a particular circumstance of injustice *the right to exit* from their communities and its personal law. The paradox thus would be resolved by a certain nesting of rights, that is, by supplementing minority rights that grant autonomous laws to communities with a further embedded right, the right to exit to individuals within those communities whenever they felt the illiberalism and the injustice of those laws. This is a most inadequate response. The fact is that such a solution – the right to exit – is academic and nominal. The idea that a traditional Muslim woman may just up and exit her community if confronted with an unjust law is absurdly unrealistic, since traditional women have well-known material and other sources of inhibition that tie them to family and community. It is utterly unrealistic for women in the first generation of immigration, and not obviously realistic for second-generation women either.

Failing this facile solution, there seems to be no easy way for the liberal states of Europe to accommodate this particular formulation of the idea of minority rights that surfaced so strongly in the aftermath of the Rushdie crisis. Even so, all sorts of theorists, not just philosophers, have argued that liberal theory and practice must now transform itself to accommodate this new phenomenon. Much of this discussion has gone on in a more general vein under the label of "communitarianism" and a number of political theorists have made an extensive critique of standard liberal theory from a position bearing that name. I will focus on one particular argument raised by the anthropologist Talal Asad because it focuses on the particular context of the liberal reaction to Rushdie's book. However, what Asad has to say echoes in much detail what is often said in general by "communitarians" and much of what I have to say in response will obviously be relevant to that general position.

In his conceptual and historical study of Europe's experience of Christianity and Islam, called *Genealogies of Religion*,[2] Asad closes by speaking directly to the effects of the Rushdie crisis on European liberalism, arguing that Britain and other liberal states in Europe have congratulated themselves on making many superficial concessions to Islamic dress, cuisine, and even school curricula in the name of "multiculturalism," but as soon as their religious tradition began to get *politicized* in the wake of the Rushdie crisis, the liberal state cracked down on the grounds that this was now transgressive of British liberal and secular identity. Asad questions this as an unfair exercise of *state* power in the name of *liberalism* which will not give to immigrants more than a nominal concession to their ways of life and thought. It is important, as we shall see, to understand this as criticism of both liberal doctrine and the liberal *state*, which these critics of the Enlightenment see as highly integrated.

I have now, in very broad stroke, set up the hard issue – I should say "a" hard issue – of identity in the context of an integrated conceptual framework spanning (liberal) politics and (colonial) history and (immigrant) culture. What might a philosopher contribute to this issue? One thing a liberal theorist might do is to accept Asad's advice and fashion a liberal doctrine that embraces his conception of minority rights. Something like that is indeed the communitarian's response. This seems to me and others to offer up a liberalism that is so concessive to the communitarian tendency exemplified in Asad's work that it is hardly recognizable as continuous with the original doctrine. So I want to give a methodological diagnosis of how we have come to this pass, and explore how, if at all, we may cross it.

We can begin by noticing that Asad's argument fails to notice a gap in its own steps. It is a gap that allows two separate questions to be compatibly raised together, but which in fact Asad does not raise because he fails to notice the gap. The first question which arises for any European liberal in the context of our present discussion is how to defend his or her liberal commitments, whether to free speech or gender justice: in other words, how to refuse the argument from minority rights which demands diverse communitarian legal codes that may clash with liberal principles. And the second question is, how to refuse this while at the same time assuring these Muslim voices that liberal principles are *not* nonnegotiable givens of the Enlightenment tradition, which they must either accept or leave. I think that there are theoretical resources and practical

2 Talal Asad, *Genealogies of Religion: Discipline and Reasons of Power in Christianity and Islam* (Baltimore: Johns Hopkins University Press, 1993).

efforts possible by which both these tasks can be attempted. The first question is about how a liberal can retain the substance of her liberal position. The second question is about how such a substantive liberalism can be established without being subject to Asad's charge against the liberal state that it has failed to respect the fact that the Muslims have their own point of view which may not on matters of substance (particular legal issues) conform to the substance of liberal laws. But why should one assume that one could not defend one's own commitment to substantive liberal principles (such as, say, free speech or gender justice) and repudiate Muslim hostility to these things in particular European contexts, without respecting the Muslim point of view? This question does not even so much as occur to Asad and to some others who take his sort of position.

To respect someone else's point of view is not necessarily and always to capitulate to *all* their particular substantive commitments. One can still be respecting another's point of view if we try and get them to capitulate to *one's* commitments by appealing to some of *their* own commitments. I will, following Bernard Williams, call this *internal* argument or internal reasoning.[3] It is perfectly possible for a liberal state to adopt such an attitude toward antiliberal elements in a community within its purview. Now, I do not doubt that Asad is right when he says that European states, including Britain, may have failed to respect the point of view of its Muslim immigrants in the aftermath of the publication of Rushdie's book. The gap in his own argument that escapes Asad's notice is that the fact that liberal states in Europe may have actually failed to respect the Muslim point of view in answering the first question (i.e., in trying to retain one's substantive liberal position against Muslim opposition) does not amount to saying that it is *built into* the nature of anyone wanting to retain such a substantive liberal position that they *cannot but* fail to respect the Muslim point of view. Only an impoverished conception of the philosophical options would lead one to think so.

A first stab at doing better than Asad might be to say this. The liberal state in Europe must retain its laws and principles via a negotiation with its Muslim communities. In order to do this it must provide arguments for its principles which have appeal even to Muslims, arguments, that is, which are internal to Muslim values and commitments, rather than external arguments which simply appeal to the grand liberal tradition of the Enlightenment into which the immigrant Muslims have landed, and so which they must now accept.

The word *negotiation* here is fraught with the possibility of misunderstanding and it will become clear at the very end of this paper that I do not necessar-

---

3 Bernard Williams, "Internal and External Reasons," in his *Moral Luck: Philosophical Papers, 1973–1980* (Cambridge: Cambridge University Press, 1981).

ily have in mind anything like entering into some sort of canonical across-the-table discussion with a view to providing such internal arguments. Communities do not usually have a structure of representation such that its "representatives" could enter into such dialogues and "negotiations," in some *strict* sense of that term. And besides, as I will argue, those among Muslims who take the line that Muslims should be governed by the *sharia* are not in any case, even loosely speaking, the most representative of the community at large. The idea of a "negotiated" secular liberalism in the context of these clashes is, rather, the much broader idea of how the state can get the Muslims to autonomously see from some aspects of their own value commitments the point of not insisting on the illiberal aspects of their own legal codes. How exactly that autonomous perception on the part of Muslims is brought about by the state is a matter worth discussing in far greater detail than I will be able to do here, though I will say something about it at the very end. And I believe it is a matter that is unusually neglected in political theory. But the point for now is that it does not have to be achieved by negotiation in the strict sense in order to be a negotiated liberalism in this broad sense of the term. In any case, a liberal secularism so arrived at could not possibly be subject to Asad's criticism that liberal states simply impose secular liberalism on communities on the grounds either that that is how we live here (Margaret Thatcher) or that it is the more demonstrably and objectively true doctrine.

Attempts at a sort of archimedean philosophical demonstration of the truth of liberal principles are familiar in the classical liberal tradition from Mill[4] to Rawls[5] and after. In this paper, I shall assume what I have tried to argue elsewhere,[6] that these demonstrations have a philosophical fault line which makes them quite incapable of coping with a philosophically rigorously defined notion of identity. But these difficulties with classical liberalism need not lead to Asad's communitarian version of minority rights. The constant conceptual oscillation between the postures of the British liberal state and Asad's position, consolidated theoretically in the oscillation between classical liberalism and communitarianism, is as intolerable as it is uncompulsory. Philosophy should have rich enough resources in this region to help us halt this pendulum swing.

Let me begin with a simple diagnosis and complicate it in stages. The simple thought is that the resources needed here may need to be only as rich as those needed to repudiate a certain recognizable version of cultural relativism. For, it

---

4 John Stuart Mill, "On Liberty," in *Three Essays* (London: Oxford University Press, 1975).

5 John Rawls, *A Theory of Justice* (Cambridge, Mass.: Harvard University Press, 1971).

6 See my "Secularism and the Moral Psychology of Identity," in *Muticulturalism, Liberalism, and Democracy*, ed. Rajeev Bhargava, Amiya Kumar Bagchi, and R. Sudarshan (New Delhi: Oxford University Press, 1999).

is a concealed and confused commitment to something like relativistic assumptions which gives Asad the impression that if there are no archimedean or external arguments that will show the Muslim denial of free speech to be wrong, then a nonoppressive liberalism should allow Muslims to live by their own laws. And Asad's impression is recoverable, I am saying, as an echo of a philosophical one, i.e., if, following Williams, we say that there is no external argument that will ever show one party in a moral or evaluative disagreement to be wrong, this gives philosophers (the "classical liberals," as I have labeled them) the impression that in some sense relativism would have to be true. That impression is wrong. If relativism is true, then two inconsistent-seeming value judgments would not be inconsistent because they could be seen as judged relative to certain points of view. Nothing I say in this paper commits me to denying that, of two contradictory value judgments, only one can be true. But I will insist that to say only one can be true, to say there is a fact of the matter as to which is true, is of no help in the matter of reasons and reasoning since we still have to give reasons to those with whom we are in conflict. To that extent, issues about truth and issues about reasoning are separable issues whether in morals or in science. I will say a word more about this later, but for now, putting abstract points about truth aside as not directly relevant, a question might arise in someone's mind as to what the philosophical equivalent of relativism would be for reasoning rather than truth. I am not sure that I can quite make sense of this question, but let me pretend for a moment that I do. I would still answer it by saying that Williams's claim that internal reasoning is all we have is not sufficient to erect what would be philosophically equivalent to relativism in the matter of reasoning. What more is needed to erect it?

At least this: relativism would hold of reasons not merely because internal reasoning and argument is the only reasoning there is, but because of that plus the further claim that internal argument is impossible. I say "impossible" and mean it. It will not be enough to point to cases of disagreement in which internal argument is difficult at a given time. Relativism is, after all, a philosophical position, not a vague pointer to how conflict sometimes can prove to be a very hard problem for politics and morals. It would be foolish for any philosopher to deny that the moral and political life throws up hard cases of disagreement. But it would be equally foolish of her to assume that such difficulty generates a conceptual position in which we have to say that moral values are relative to points of view in a way that reasoning is inapplicable. This latter claim defines relativism as a philosophical position. And such a position is only generated if it is demonstrable that it is impossible not merely difficult, and difficult at the moment, to provide internal arguments. It is a recognizable mistake of a common sort in the writings of some anthropologists to fail to see this point. Their sentimental reification of difference is precisely this recognizable mistake. What I am claiming, then, is that relativism is a threat to liberalism *only* to the extent that *internal* argument over values with another (say, with immigrant Muslims) is *impossible*. But why should we think that to be so?

Let us take the problem first as a general one in philosophy and ask: What in general would have to be the case such that one would be forced to say that internal argument with someone with whom one disagrees about some values is impossible?

To answer this question, let me set up just a bit of apparatus. Let us terminologically stipulate for the moment that a person's or group's values are a subset of her desires. (This is a harmless, analytic philosopher's way of talking – thus one can desire that one work for social justice as much as one can desire that one drinks a glass of water.) Our question, then, is about the scope of rationality, of the possibility of giving reasons, in the realm of desires. In a person's or group's psychological economy there are both desires and beliefs. The relations between beliefs have been widely studied in philosophy and we are fully aware of the codified forms in which these relations constitute various forms of rationality (deductive rationality, inductive rationality...). The relations between desires and beliefs have also been widely studied in philosophy, initially in Aristotle's practical syllogism, and then in subsequent recent refinements of Aristotle in decision theory and surrounding disciplines. What is much less studied is the relations between desires themselves. Part of this neglect is due to the fact that both of two highly influential opposing positions which have dominated the study of rationality (Kantian and Humean positions) have been skeptical that any rationality can attach to relations between desires. Holding beliefs steady for the moment, let us ask all the same: are there relations between desires themselves which are of interest to those interested in reason-giving and rationality?

First of all, there could be consistency and inconsistency among desires. This is hardly controversial, and even Humeans and Kantians could hardly deny it. But if that was all that rationality between desires amounted to, that would not be interesting or particularly useful for our purposes. After all, consistency among desires merely requires that they be mutually implementable. Two desires may be consistent with one another in this sense and have nothing to do with one another in a psychological economy. My desire for tea happens to have nothing to do with my desire to do philosophy, and they are both mutually implementable. But it is surely arguable that there may be a richer relation between desires that might lead to a richer notion of rationality regarding desires than that they be consistent rather than inconsistent. Take the following pair of desires: my desire to do philosophy and my desire to be respected by my intellectual peers. These are (in my case) related by more than mere consistency, they are more than merely mutually implementable. We can label this further relation as "reinforcement." These two desires reinforce each other. However, though reinforcement is in this way more than mere consistency, it ought not to be confused with another relation between desires, which is the means/end or instrumental relation. Reinforcement is not a means/end relation because if I were asked whether I pursue my desire to do philosophy *in order to* fulfill my desire to be respected by my peers my answer might well be "no."

I am spending some time on this point because it is an important one to make against those who think that any serious and intrinsic conception of rationality is not applicable to such things as desires, but is restricted only to beliefs. As I said, despite their well-known antagonism, both Humean and Kantian traditions of thinking about human behavior and moral psychology (for very different reasons) share such a skeptical attitude about allowing desires to be the subject of a rich notion of rationality. And since so much of current thinking about this subject sees itself as broadly influenced by one or other of these two opposing traditions, this skeptical attitude is very widespread. According to this widespread picture, desires may be subject to an instrumental rationality but they do not possess any *intrinsic* rationality except for the very thin notion of consistency among desires (which, as I said earlier, amounts only to their mutual implementability). The notion of reinforcement, by contrast, brings with it a thicker conception of rationality and allows us to think of desires (and not just beliefs) in terms of a coherentist conception of rationality, where coherence is something stronger than consistency. That is why the idea of reinforcement allows us to get beyond the narrowing Kantian idea that our moral rationality cannot traffic in anything so contingent and nonuniversal as desires, at the same time as it surpasses the equally narrowing Humean idea that the only rationality to which motivating states (what he called the "passions") are subject is instrumental.

The crucial bit of apparatus that needs to be added to these simple points is this. If there can be reinforcement among desires, there can also be the lack of it. The opposite of the relation of reinforcement between desires is, let us call it, the relation of "infirmity" between them. Infirmity stands to reinforcement as inconsistency stands to consistency. Just as desires may be inconsistent with other desires, so they may be infirmed by their relations with other desires. And thus we may find a person irrational not only if one finds his desires inconsistent but also, more interestingly, if one finds some of them infirm.

Now, with all this in place, we can return to our question: What would have to be the case for us to be forced to say that internal argument with another is impossible? Or, in particular, that internal argument with Muslims in Europe is impossible? Internal argument, remember, is the idea that we can give reasons to another from within his own point of view for adopting a value (free speech, say) which he presently shuns but which we embrace. For such internal argument to happen, there would obviously have to be some conflict within the other's evaluative economy. That is to say, for this to happen some of the desires in his evaluative economy will have to stand in *infirming* relations to his commitment to shun free speech. If that were so, we could appeal to those desires to construct an argument to persuade him to come around to embracing free speech. We can now answer our question as follows. Internal argument would be *im*possible only if we thought that Muslims' psychological economy (which contains the desire to ban certain sorts of publications) is totally and perpetually without conflict. And with our apparatus in place, we now know that the notion of conflict is not only to be characterized as simple inconsistency within values (which may be harder to find) but infirmity as well, which is very much more likely to be found in most groups and individuals. So to the extent that we think that Muslims, like any community, are not monsters of consistency *and coherence*, so long as we do not think of them as some sort of rational automata, to that extent there is always scope for internal conflict within them which leaves scope for liberals to engage in internal argument with them. To the extent that this is possible, relativism is held at bay. Relativism is only plausible under the very unlikely scenario that two individuals (or groups) who are in disagreement both have psychological economies which are made up of perfectly consistent and *maximally* "reinforced" desires. Anyone who has followed what I meant by "reinforcement" would have gotten the point that it is unlikely in the extreme that creatures, such as human beings anyway, possess desires that are maximally reinforced in some perfect equilibrium.

As I threatened, the picture is more complicated than this simple one. I have said that Asad rightly criticizes European liberal states for appealing only to the values and arguments of their Enlightenment tradition, which they take to be established by philosophical argument. But I am resisting any effort to conclude from these criticisms, as he does, that these states should capitulate to the demands of Muslim minorities on the matter of free speech or gender justice by granting them minority rights to live by their own laws on questions such as blasphemy, etc. Why does Asad not see that it is resistible? I have just discussed the ersatz and hidden relativism in the thinking which makes him blind to the possibility of resisting it. But there is another closely related blind spot, which Asad and others like him simply inherit from a recent critique of Enlightenment thinking. This is a deep, almost *a priori* hostility to the modern state as a coercive institution. What is the close relation between these two blind spots? One way of bringing it out is to invoke certain ideas of Foucault.[7] Foucault's notion of "governmentality," for instance, is introduced by him centrally to make a critique of a certain conception of sovereignty revolving around the modern state. It is well known that for Foucault, the state assumes a position of authority and power issuing from an archimedean Enlightenment conception of Reason, i.e., of what is rational and universal in politics. And so the Foucauldian advice to communities would generally be to resist entering the discursive space of reasons where the technologies of governmentality operate. As one recent Foucauldian has memorably put it: "The only way [for a community] to resist submitting to the powers of sovereignty is to literally declare itself *unreasonable*."[8] The picture here is quite simply that if the archimedean arguments for liberal principles are unconvincing to those holding communitarian commitments (say, Muslims in European nations), then there are *no* arguments possible and so, from the point of view of communities, the state must necessarily – not as a matter of fact in contemporary Britain and Europe – but *necessarily* become something coercive because it is *incommensurate*. That is the deep connection between the relativism and the antistatism of Foucault's thinking, and it is precisely what surfaces in Asad's communitarian response to the issues we have been discussing.

But notice a curious thing. There is a crucial assumption that is *shared* here by the bitterest of dialectical foes – the liberal of the classical tradition and his Foucauldian critic. Because of their dialectical opposition, the shared assumption will get expressed differently by each of them, each with different rhetoric putting the blame on the other. But that should not hide the fact that the deeper common assumption exists. From the point of view of the classical liberal, the assumption is expressed as: "If there were no external and universal and archimedean points of reasoning which justify Liberal principles (which we believe there are), then nothing will justify a secular liberalism, and we can expect nothing but communitarian mayhem." From the point of view of the critic of the Enlightenment, the same assumption gets expressed as: "If there are no archimedean points of reasoning which will justify secular liberal principles (which we believe there are not), the Liberal state is founded on a false ideal and revealed to be the coercive institution it really is." The common assumption is clear and evident. Both sides, despite their bitter opposition to one another, believe in common that it is "External Reasons or Bust!" No doubt, descriptions like "communitarian mayhem" and "coercive Liberal state" will be found by their respective targets to be tendentious. And no doubt these hostile descrip-

---

7 Michel Foucault, "Governmentality," in *The Foucault Effect*, ed. Graham Burchell, Colin Gordon, and Peter Miller (Chicago: University of Chicago Press, 1991).
8 Partha Chatterji, "Secularism and Toleration," *Economic and Political Weekly* (July 9, 1994), pp. 1768–1777.

tions reflect genuine disagreement with one another on important issues in politics and the philosophy that underlies it. But none of that cancels the fact that this disagreement is the disagreement it is only because there is agreement on a philosophical issue which could in the end matter a great deal more to the politics of state and its relation to community than the disagreement itself. For a quite new and liberating politics in this domain could be generated by questioning that common assumption since to question it would be to question an entrenched disjunction between state and community. It is this common assumption that makes for the endless oscillation between classical liberalism and communitarianism that I am seeking to halt. And it would seem that there is no way to halt it but to question the shared assumption. That is what I have been trying to do in trying to show that it is possible for the *state* to engage in *internal* reasoning with communities. (I emphasize both "state" and the "internal" here deliberately and will return to the significance of this in a moment.) A state which did so would not fall prey to the charge of governmentality as Foucault deploys it. And if it succeeded in this internal reasoning, it need make no concessions to any substantive communitarianism of the sort that goes deeply against liberal principles (such as free speech, for instance, or gender justice).

Internal reasoning, I have said, is always possible so long as disagreement is not between maximally "reinforced" systems of value. And systems of values to which human agents are likely to subscribe are most likely not to be such. Their desires and values are often in internal conflict, and certainly they are permanently in *potential* internal conflict since agents and communities live in an environment that is changing, and such changes will often inject conflict into their values. This is just what Hegel called History and the dialectic it engenders. If we keep firmly in mind the cautionary anti-Whiggish point that there is nothing historically inevitable about liberalism or any other consummation, one very useful way of reading Hegel's primary insight here is precisely to see History as the movement and sway of internal reasoning in society, with the State as the moral agent which is the seat and source of such reasoning. What Foucault fails to see, despite some extraordinarily acute specific historical diagnoses of various social institutions, is that the success of these historical analyses yield him his heated relativist conclusions in political philosophy only because he is deaf to this Hegelian insight about History.

There is a further point of nuance that needs to be added at this stage of the argument. It is an implication of antistatist communitarian conclusions which are drawn by Asad and others influenced by Foucault, that something like free speech cannot be insisted upon by the British government in the aftermath of the Rushdie crisis. So if Muslims came to accept free speech they should do it by reforming internally among themselves and it is not something that should issue from the state. But the use of the word "internally" in the last sentence is *not* what I have in mind by "internal" in internal reasons and internal argument. To say that communities must change their conceptions only internally is a communitarian conclusion. To say what I have been saying, viz, that *the state* can give internal reasons to a community to change, is not a communitarian conclusion because it insists on the agency of the state in coming to liberal conclusions; it just says that the state should reason with the communities along *internalist* lines. This is a more nuanced distinction than we have made so far but it is essential to the point I want to make about the possibilities for a substantive liberalism, which is not communitarian. The communitarian sees "internal" liberalization and reform as meaning reform coming from within the agencies of the community. The liberal picture that I am offering as an alternative to both archimedean liberalism and communitarianism has as central to it the idea that liberal reform takes place on a statist site but it does so via internal reasoning with the community. To put it paradoxically, on my liberal picture *internal* reform of a community happens not necessarily *within* a community on intra-community sites alone, but also can and should happen on a *statist* site. (An aside: Not that I think that it is a bad thing if it happens within the community alone by internal change. I am only disputing that it must happen that way and must not happen by the agencies of the state. In other words, I am disputing the neurotic antistatism of the critique of the Enlightenment which goes from observation of particular wrongs of particular states of the modern period to erecting antistatism into a *philosophical* doctrine issuing from its critique of an Enlightenment conception of Reason working itself out in politics. For me the wrongs done by the modern state lead to the instruction: Let us struggle to improve the state! For the Foucauldian critique of the Enlightenment, that instruction is necessarily bogus.) To see things this way is to see the liberal state as being able to provide a field of force of internal reasons addressing different communitarian perspectives from within their own internal substantive commitments and unsettling them into awareness of their own internal inconsistencies so as to eventually provide for a common secular outcome, each on different internal grounds.

Such a theoretical view of the liberal state is of course dramatically different from the way in which the liberal state appears in Rawls and Mill. That much is perhaps obvious. But it is not merely different from the classical tradition, it is also measurably different from the face-saving retreat of recent political theorists such as Steven Lukes, who in the face of communitarian attack take all the content out of liberalism in order to save some of its universalism. Thus for instance, pointing out that even the communitarians talk in the idiom of rights when they demand rights for minorities, they find in this idiom a universalist discourse that is essentially liberal, even if not the full prestige of secular liberalism. It is liberal in the sense that it is minimally neutral between the different contested claims of ethnic and communal identity.

But why should we allow the difficulties raised by identity to cause us to abandon full secular outcomes for such manifestly skimpy universals in liberal politics? To see the state as a possible field of force for internal reasons is precisely not to adopt the strategy of retreating to thinner and thinner neutral ground that all communities and particular identities must minimally share. It is, rather, precisely not to rest with a base of *neutral* common agreement which is likely to be necessarily thin gruel in a multicommunal society, and instead for the state to seek for the thicker brew of a fully secular outcome via a signing up of communities to such a thick secular-liberal agenda for different, and therefore nonneutral, reasons given by the state from within the communities' own very different substantive value economies. To put it in terms I have set up here, the power of the strategy of internal reasons is to get to a thick secular-liberal ideal by looking for different "infirmities" in the different communities' antiliberal commitments, and thereby internally transforming their commitments to more liberal ones. It is worth repeating here that the very fact that it can be for *different* reasons (coming from within different communitarian perspectives) that various communities may agree on a common secular outcome is proof that the grounds for secular liberalism need *not* be neutral.

I would add here that this idea, which is one way to read Rawls's later idea of an overlapping consensus – as I have argued elsewhere, Rawls himself is much too unclear about what he has in mind by this idea – has within it the ingredients to characterize an ideal of pluralism that makes no concession whatsoever to the highly influential but theoretically incoherent remarks one finds about pluralism in the much-admired writings of Isaiah Berlin.[9] Berlin speaks of pluralism as a philosophical doctrine about value which respects value-conflict to the extent that it theoretically allows for contradictory evaluative judgments among different groups to be unthreatening to the very idea of value judgment. But in this he is simply wrong. Values are no different from cognitive states, even scientific beliefs, in this respect, and no one should deny the idea that of two imperatives (all things considered imperatives, of course) which are inconsistent, only one can be true. So pluralistic tolerance should not make reckless theoretical concessions. What pluralism nevertheless could define itself as is the ideal (not perhaps always achievable, but in that it is like all ideals) that when a state embraces a doctrine or point of view, its tolerance consists not in admitting

9 Isaiah Berlin, *Four Essays on Liberty* (London: Oxford University Press, 1969).

that there may be conflicting true doctrines, but rather in promoting what it takes to be the true doctrine as something that recalcitrant groups must be brought around to embracing by providing reasons from within *their* values. Such a sane notion of pluralism should be brought to center-stage in any liberal ideal coping with the sort of identities we are discussing.

Before I bring this very abstractly made claim to an end, let me return to what I started this paper with and say something a little more concrete about the case of Muslims.

Here is a plain empirical fact. Everywhere in the world, whether in Bradford or Kreuzberg, or even in Tehran, the majority of Muslims are either against the fundamentalist or absolutist elements in their society or too busy with their occupations or preoccupations to be anything more than indifferent to them. It is only a shrill minority in any Muslim community anywhere that has absolutist Islamist commitments. Yet it is this minority which seems to everyone to be the representative voice of the community. The failure of the liberal state therefore has been its inability to establish to the community itself that this shrill minority is precisely that, a *minority*, an *un*representative voice in the community, most of whose members are either against or indifferent to Islamic fundamentalism. In a word, the failure of the liberal state in Europe has been *its failure to democratize* its immigrant communities, so that the representative voices are the voices of its overwhelming majority of ordinary Muslims, who have no particular developed absolutist commitments.

In the polarity between the classical liberal on the one hand and Asad and other communitarians on the other (both sides of which I have opposed here), there is grotesque theoretical neglect of the possibilities of the liberal state to democratize the communities in its midst. Ever since the authoritarian aftermath of the French Revolution, the possibilities of the state to be the agent of democratization have raised the specter of mass movements that has so filled liberal theorists with reticence that potentially a whole field of theoretical possibilities has passed unnoticed. Given the ubiquitous empirical fact which I mentioned at the beginning of the last paragraph, how to theorize the possibilities of such democratization without the descent into Jacobin-style authoritarianism ought to be a theme of the highest importance and urgency in political theory, if the subject of cultural identities in politics is to be adequately treated.

What such a democratization would have the effect of doing is to exploit an *internal conflict* within the communities between the absolutists and their opponents. It would give the opponents of absolutism the confidence to speak openly against the minority absolutist voices, *when they were ready to do so*. Of course, what it will take to make it possible for them to be ready to do that will be no easy thing to achieve. But no Hegelian process is easy. In any case, an essential step in the "negotiation" of what I called a negotiated secular liberalism is therefore a determined effort by the state to democratize its communities. But part of what makes this a difficult process is that the conflict is not just between the minority of absolutists in the community and those who oppose them, i.e., the majority of ordinary Muslims who have no particular absolutist agenda. There is a further conflict in the hearts of the latter, for they themselves often do have some unarticulated desires and values that are in effect inchoately sympathetic to the absolutists even as they have yet other desires that strongly infirm these desires. Obviously it is the former desires that make them unready to come out and openly oppose the absolutists. But the fact is that those desires *are* infirm. They genuinely are made infirm by the latter desires. It is this internal conflict that the liberal state also has to deal with in the process of what I am misleadingly calling "negotiation." Since it is here that the sources of infirmity in such antiliberal values lie, it is here that the state must find its targets and focal points for internal reasoning with the community.

What will give these ordinary, nonabsolutist Muslims in Europe the confidence to fully embrace one side of their conflicted commitments and combat the absolutists in their community is of course a large and difficult question about which I have written elsewhere, and cannot possibly rehearse at length here. But the general direction of answer was implicit in the historical stage setting I have given. The moral psychology of defensive resentment so bound up with the history of colonial relations, and which continues in local replications within Europe as well as in neocolonial relations between Europe and Muslim countries since decolonization, is precisely the psychology which primarily stands in the way of developing this confidence in the communities. The prospect of openly criticizing the absolutists in the community, or conceding to liberal demands in the face of blasphemy, often seems even to these ordinary and moderate Muslims to be a surrender to a longstanding domineering and pernicious Western culture. And it seems so, even when it is often dictated by some of their own values and their own dislike of fundamentalists. This defensiveness among moderates is what the fundamentalists have consistently exploited, and the liberal state has been unable to create the conditions to allow them to overcome the defensiveness, thereby giving them the confidence to be self-critical enough to resolve these conflicts in their own desires and values. Self-criticism in the face of the historical circumstances I sketched at the beginning of this paper is not a capacity that is easy to come by. It is of course possible and correct to blame Islamic communities in Europe for having failed to cultivate the temperament to be self-critical. But it is obvious that the failure is in part the failure of the state to create conditions whereby that cultivation might be psychologically possible. It is in these terms that we must criticize Europe's inability to address Islamic identity, and not in terms of an uncritical valorization of community over the liberal state.

Deepening Liberal Democracy

Bhikhu Parekh

Liberal democracy represents a remarkably ingenious attempt to reconcile and integrate into a harmonious whole the two different and partially incompatible principles of liberalism and democracy. In this paper, I examine how it does this, what tensions that creates, and how these can be overcome.

I   In the West, both the idea and the practice of democracy were first developed in classical Athens. For the Athenians, democracy was not just a form of government or even a manner of constituting the polity, as many commentators have argued, but a way of organizing individual and collective life. It sprang from and was nurtured by a particular view of man and society, which I shall call a democratic vision of the good life. The vision was articulated in terms of the three closely related ideas of community, equality, and active citizenship.[1]

Briefly, the democratic vision was based on the belief that the individual was embedded in and profoundly shaped by his political community. He derived his values and ideals from it, defined his identity in terms of his membership of the community, and realized his full potential within it. The community was not a transcendental entity enjoying an independent existence but a body of men united in terms of a common structure of public authority, common interests, affections, self-understanding, beliefs about the nature of the good life, and the corresponding moral and social practices and public rituals – in short, a shared way of life. The community existed and flourished as a particular kind of community only when and insofar as its members lived by their shared beliefs and practices. It was basically what they said and did, and had no reality save

---

1 For good accounts, see Lionel Pearson, *Popular Ethics in Ancient Greece* (Stanford: Stanford University Press, 1962), ch. 5 and 7, and Victor Ehrenberg, *The Greek State* (Oxford: Blackwell, 1960), ch. 2; Mogens Herman Hansen, *The Athenian Democracy in the Age of Demosthenes* (Oxford: Blackwell, 1991), provides a rich and detailed account of the workings of Athenian democracy.

through their way of life. The individual and the community were inseparable, and neither made sense in isolation from the other.

Members of the community were all equal. They enjoyed legal and political status and made equal claims on each other and on the wider community. They were also equally important to the survival of the community as a particular kind of community, for if any of them failed to live up to its norms and ideals, the community was diminished to that degree. It mattered to each member how the others lived, for that vitally affected both their collective and individual lives. Since all members of the community were of equal value and had equal status, the community had a duty to ensure that they enjoyed the basic material and cultural conditions necessary to become its equally effective members. If some of them were poor, neglected, or marginalized, they lacked the disposition, the independence, the capacity, the resources, and the leisure to play their full part in the life of the community and to discharge their share of communal obligations. What was more, if the community had no regard for its members' well-being, it could not expect them to care for it either. Although the relations between the two did not rest on an explicit contract, they were informed by a spirit of reciprocity and interdependence that generated certain legitimate expectations on the part of each.

In the democratic vision of the classical Athenians, the equality of citizens did not rule out inequality of wealth and income. Inequality often had beneficial social consequences and, since individuals differed in their abilities and efforts, it was also just. However, there were clear limits to its extent and depth. It should not be so great as to place some at the mercy of others and undermine their independence and equality of status, value, and well-being. Nor should it be so deep as to undermine the community by fragmenting it into neatly separated groups leading different kinds of life and sharing no common experiences, interests, loyalties, and affections.

In the democratic vision, members of the political community conducted their collective affairs themselves. They actively participated in public deliberations on common matters and held public offices. They did so for several inter-related reasons. Since they were equal, they demanded an equal share in taking decisions that would be binding on them. Not to participate in public life was to allow others to decide things for them, and thus to be ruled by them and lose one's freedom. Citizenship, again, was a highly prized public status, a source of one's sense of dignity, and it was a matter of honor that one should assert that status by actively participating in public affairs. Political participation was also a way of affirming membership in the community and showing solidarity with fellow citizens. And it was a way of nurturing the community and promoting its well-being by contributing ideas and experiences to collective deliberation. For the classical Athenians, democracy represented the perfection of the highest realization of the constitutive principle, or inner nature, of the *polis*. Unlike other forms of social organization, the *polis* was unique in being governed by its citizens, and democracy realized its full potential by extending citizenship to all adults.[2]

Citizens strove to deserve their community and competed with each other in being its good members. They were guided by such sentiments as *chresimos* (the desire to be of some value to the community) and *philotima* (zealous ambition on behalf of the community). Citizenship was not confined to the narrowly political arena. The political community was a partnership in the good life and covered all areas of life. Public deliberation about its collective affairs was obviously crucial, for it represented an activity in which the community attained its highest level of self-consciousness and took collectively binding decisions. Citizenship, however, was at work in other areas of life as well. It informed the citizen's roles as father, husband, son, farmer, neighbor, artist, or philosopher, to all of which he brought to bear his responsibilities and obligations as a citizen and whose narrow demands he viewed in a wider communal context. A good citizen sought to excel in his various roles and to enjoy the *kleos* (respect and recognition) of his fellow-citizens for *arete* (skills and virtues) in being a good man.[3]

The democratic vision of life as sketched above was novel and audacious. It cherished the community but ensured that the latter did not become collectivist and oppressive, and it cherished the individual but defined him in communal terms and avoided becoming narrowly individualist. It valued privacy but insisted that it should be informed by public spirit and social responsibility and not regarded as an arena in which one did what one liked. The democratic vision had great faith in the political capacity of ordinary men to deliberate about and govern their affairs and encouraged them to aspire for and occupy high public offices. It viewed economic life from a political perspective and judged economic interests, practices, and inequality in terms of their ability to promote active citizenship, a vigorous public life, and collective well-being.

From the moment of its first appearance, the democratic vision of classical Athens had its fervent champions and fierce critics. Despite disagreements, both were agreed on what democracy stood for, namely a strong sense of community, equality, active citizenship, and the primacy of public life. For the defenders of

---

2 Ehrenberg, *The Greek State*, pp. 43, 51.

3 A good citizen was supposed to love his parents and care for their graves, honor his guests and gods, pay his taxes, put his wealth at the disposal of the *polis*, and so on, and in general, aim to be a "good man." Resolutions passed by the Athenian assembly in honor of public-spirited citizens declared them "good men" who deserved to be emulated. See Ehrenberg, *The Greek State*, p. 68, and Pearson, *Popular Ethics in Ancient Greece*, p. 181.

the democratic vision, these and other related ideas were fundamentally sound and worth fighting for. For its critics, democracy was at odds with human nature, subversive of social solidarity, and politically dangerous. Democracy, they argued, ignored the obvious and ineradicable inequality of talents and discouraged excellence. It placed no limits on the volatile and unregulated will of the masses, encouraged them to develop false notions of their ability and political possibilities, and provoked adventurist policies whose chaotic consequences paved the way for tyrants and dictators. Democracy threatened private property, passed legislation against the rich, and provoked civil wars. It lacked stability, predictability, and historical continuity, for what the people willed today they could just as easily reject tomorrow. In such a climate of permanent uncertainty in which nothing could be planned, any form of civilized life was impossible.[4]

II   Modernity saw the rise of liberalism, which is not just an economic doctrine nor a form of government but, like democracy, a vision of the good life at both individual and collective levels. Although it has undergone important changes during the three centuries of its existence, liberalism's core ideas of the individual, liberty, equality, and civility have remained constant.

In the liberal vision, human beings are, above all, individuals, that is, independent and unitary centers of self-consciousness occupying physically self-contained and demarcated bodies. Every human body represents an individual, and is naturally endowed with the distinctively human powers of rationality, choice, will, and others associated with these. Individuals are the ultimate and irreducible units of moral and political life. Institutions, communities, nations, and states have no intrinsic value or existence independent of the individual, and matter only insofar as they subserve individual well-being. Individuals have certain fundamental interests without which they cannot lead the good life. These interests are derived from human nature, which all liberal writers presuppose in one form or another, and include such things as life, liberty, control over their lives or self-determination, and property or ownership of the fruits of their labor. Individuals are their own masters in the sense that they own and are at liberty to dispose of their physical and mental powers as they please. Some such notion of self-ownership (Locke), sovereignty in oneself (J. S. Mill), or self-mastery (Kant) is a recurrent feature of the liberal understanding of the individual's relation to himself, and is the basis of the liberal view of liberty. The freedom to

---

4 For these and other criticisms, see Cynthia Farrar, "Ancient Greek Political Theory as a Response to Democracy," in *Democracy: The Unfinished Journey, 508 BC to AD 1993*, ed. John Dunn (Oxford: Oxford University Press, 1993).

make one's choices is an expression of and a way of asserting mastery of oneself. The individual should be free to choose and run his life because his life, body, capacities, and so on are all his own, and what happens to them is his business in which others can at best have only an instrumental and indirect interest. Since all individuals are "by nature" masters of themselves and share certain basic needs, interests, and capacities in common, they are all equal. Equality is not a status conferred by society but inherent in and a universally shared feature of what it is to be human. And similarly, liberty is not derived from society but inherent in humanity. Liberty, equality, and the pursuit of fundamental human interests are therefore claims that all human beings *qua* human beings make on each other.

In the liberal vision, the political community is a voluntary association of individuals and is derivative in nature. It is therefore not the community that explains or helps us make sense of the individual as the democratic vision insisted, rather it is the individual who explains and provides a coherent account of the community. This does not mean that the political community is consciously created by individuals at a definable point in time, but rather that its nature and structure are constituted by their consensual acts. The principal task and *raison d'être* of the state is to maintain the system of basic rights by either enshrining them in a constitution or finding other ways of giving them a privileged status, and thereby placing them above both volatile public opinion and the state's own arbitrary exercise of power. The state is only concerned with those interests and rights that all its citizens share in common. Since religion, ethnicity, culture, and so on vary from individual to individual, they are private matters of no public significance and of which the state takes no cognizance. Individuals do, of course, have rights to their religion, culture, and so on, but these generate no claims on the state's protection and support. For liberalism, the state is essentially a coercive institution. Since the role of coercion in human life should be minimized and since political power is always liable to misuse, liberalism insists on the constitutional regulation and separation of powers, the limited state, and leaving as many areas of life as possible to the voluntary cooperation between individuals.

In the liberal vision, individuals are unique in their nature and find their fulfillment in different activities and forms of life. They should therefore be left free to lead their self-chosen lives so long as these do not affect others adversely. Their relations with each other are governed by mutual respect, noninterference in each other's private lives, due regard for each other's rights, respect for the law and rules in general, tolerance, and so on – in short, by the culture of civility. Politics, the conduct of the common affairs of the community, is an activity of limited value and importance. Since the state is largely concerned with maintaining a system of rights and a climate of civility, and since a constitutionally limited state can be relied upon to do so, there is little need for active citizen involvement in the conduct of its affairs. Furthermore, individuals have other legitimate priorities and find such involvement an unnecessary distraction. It is, of course, essential that the government be based on their consent and be held popularly accountable, both of which are ensured by the mechanism of election. Citizens therefore have no political duty other than to vote, and are even exempt from this obligation if they are satisfied with the general conduct of the government.

III　　The liberal and democratic visions of life sketched above share several features in common.[5] Both value equality, cherish human dignity, stress social interdependence, are alike opposed to the collectivist glorification of the community and the subordination of the individual to it, and so on. However, they arrive at and define these common ideas differently, and diverge in several other respects. Liberalism takes the individual as its starting point, whereas democracy begins with the political community. Liberalism takes an instrumental view of the value of the political community, whereas democracy sees it as an important value in its own right. For liberalism, the political community is largely voluntary and based on common subscription to a shared structure of authority. For democracy, it is based on a shared vision of the good life. For these and other reasons, liberalism is uncomfortable with the premodern language of community and prefers instead to talk of society and civil society with their voluntarist and consensual associations.

　　The liberal vision is fearful of the masses and all forms of collective action. The democratic vision has faith in the people and their capacity for moderation and self-correction. The liberal vision values equality of civil and political rights, has little if any interest in reducing economic inequality, and until recently did not see the value of social and economic rights either. By contrast, the democratic vision insists on ensuring full political equality, minimizing economic inequality, and giving all citizens equal access to the conditions of the good life. The liberal vision judges the state on the basis of its ability to maintain civility, protect rights, and ensure prosperity. The democratic vision makes a vibrant political community and active citizenship its primary standards of judgment and evaluates nonpolitical institutions in terms of these. The liberal vision privileges the personal and associational areas of life over the political, sees little

5 For a fuller discussion, see my "The Cultural Particularity of Liberal Democracy," *Political Studies* 40 (1992), pp. 160–175.

intrinsic value in political participation, and aims to foster such civil virtues as mutual respect, self-restraint, respect for the law, and tolerance. The democratic vision sees political participation as intrinsically valuable, a way of affirming solidarity with fellow citizens, sustaining the spirit of community, and contributing to its well-being, and regards nonparticipating citizens as morally deficient. It prizes and seeks to cultivate such political virtues as love of the community, public spirit, mutual concern, public service, a sense of honor, and the spirit of equality. The liberal vision fears the state, minimizes its social role, and concentrates on protecting the individual against it. The democratic vision stresses the emancipatory potential of collective action and seeks to control the state by imposing the community's will on it.

The liberal and democratic visions of the good life, then, share certain features and differ in others. In principle, either can exist without the other. Classical Athens was democratic but not liberal, and a liberal society can exist under monarchy and, indeed, developed in modern Europe by supporting the monarch in his struggle with the feudal aristocracy. In practice, however, the two visions could not ignore each other. Championed by the middle classes and their theorists, liberalism began to consolidate itself from the 17th century onward. From around the last three decades of the 18th century onward, the organized working classes began to appear and make political demands, using the moral vocabulary of the democratic vision to justify these. Liberalism could no longer ignore the moral and political challenge of its rival, democracy, and had to find ways of coming to terms with it. For their part, the democratic critics of liberalism could not ignore its reality and moral appeal either. It was in this context that the "project" or the idea and practice of liberal democracy first made its historical appearance toward the end of the 18th century.

The liberal and democratic visions could be combined in one of three ways. First, one could privilege the former and incorporate as much of the latter as was consistent with it or was historically unavoidable. Second, one could do the opposite and privilege the democratic vision, absorbing as many liberal ideas as were attractive or too deeply rooted in contemporary consciousness to be ignored. Third, one could undertake a dialectical critique of each in the light of the other and develop a genuinely synthetic vision based on a harmonious integration of what one thought to be the best in both. Liberals opted for the first, and democrats for the second. Since the third approach was theoretically most demanding, it was least explored and limited to such writers as Hegel and the British idealists. Since all three approaches seek to combine liberal and democratic visions in different forms, they could all be called liberal democratic, and their preferred society liberal democracy. However, since only the first approach privileges liberalism and upholds its basic principles, the term *liberal democracy* in its narrow sense has come to refer to it alone, and that is how I shall use it in the rest of this paper. The second approach which privileges democracy could by contrast be called democratic liberalism, and the kind of society it advocates social democracy.

IV   Liberal democracy is liberalized democracy. Liberalism is the dominant partner and, as such, sets the terms of their cooperation and determines the limits of democracy. Liberal democracy is committed to such fundamental liberal ideas as individualism, individual liberty, the constitutional protection of basic rights, the limited state, separation of powers, and so on, and incorporates only those democratic ideas and practices that either support the liberal vision or are too deeply ingrained in modern consciousness to be dropped. It is primarily committed to civil and political rights but, unlike the classical liberals, it accepts the democratic idea of social and economic rights either to give meaning to the former or to ensure social stability. Unlike the democrats, however, it sees nothing inherently wrong in great social and economic inequalities and makes no attempt to redress these.

Since it fears the state, liberal democracy incorporates such democratic devices as elections, plural political parties, pressure groups, and peaceful public protest, which check the misuse of power, articulate individual consent, increase the range of citizens' political choices, and hold the government popularly accountable and responsive. However, since it fears the masses and doubts their commitment to individual liberty, it limits their power by placing certain rights above their reach and giving the judiciary pride of place in its constitutional arrangement. Liberal democracy sees little value in participatory democracy and replaces it with representative or what John Stuart Mill called "rational" and "well-regulated" democracy. In a representative democracy, people elect and alienate their sovereignty to representatives who, as distinct from delegates, are left free to follow their own judgment and take whatever decisions they consider proper. Representative democracy is not the same as representative government. The former is government *by* elected representatives, the latter is government by the people themselves *through* their representatives.[6] Unable to meet and exercise political power directly in large modern states, people in a representative government do so through their representatives, who are given clear mandates, may be recalled, are subject to popular referenda, and expected to stay in con-

---

6 Mill observed that the "substitution of delegation for representation" was a great danger in democracy. See John Stuart Mill, *Essays on Politics and Culture* (Garden City, N.Y.: Doubleday, 1962), p. 197.

stant touch with their political masters. By contrast, representative democracy reduces people to a largely passive and subordinate role and transfers effective power to their representatives. Since it does not value active political participation, representative democracy does not provide a system of interlocked and institutionalized public spaces for it.

Liberal democracy represents a remarkably novel form of organizing the political community. It is not a degenerated form of classical democracy as some Helenophiles maintain, but a historically distinct form of democracy that needs to be understood in its own terms. It is what the premodern writers called a mixed form of government, and which they preferred over those resting on a single principle. As its very name indicates, it enshrines at its very heart two distinct principles, which between them represent different human aspirations and visions of the good life and are capable of regulating each other's excesses. Thanks to the creative tension between the two, liberal democracy has the conceptual and institutional resources to open up new spaces of thought, create new political possibilities, and expand society's moral and political imagination.

In practice, however, liberal democracy is unable to exploit these theoretical and political advantages because it assigns a hegemonic position to liberalism and emasculates the radical potential of its democratic component. Its virtues are derived from its liberalism and its consequent capacity to control the excesses of democracy. Liberal democracy has the great merit of cherishing the individual, protecting his or her basic human dignity, safeguarding the individual's fundamental rights, guarding against the pathology of political power, respecting diversity of views, nurturing dissent, and fostering criticism of established ideas and institutions. It is, as a result, better able than any other form of government to guard against crude populism, intolerant majoritarianism, the imposition of social conformity, and moral dogmatism.

The limitations of liberal democracy are derived from the fact that it marginalizes the democratic vision and consequently is unable to regulate the excesses of liberalism. Thanks to its commitment to individualism, private property, the market economy, and so on, liberal democracy generates great economic, social, and political inequalities and lacks the moral resources to provide a critique of them. The inequalities are both interlocked and intergenerationally transmitted and congeal into an oppressive structure or system of inequality that makes it all but impossible for most individuals to break out of its vicious circle. The equality of opportunity and the cultivation of the culture of merit and excellence that the liberal cherishes have therefore little practical meaning. Society gets fragmented into classes and groups that lead vastly different lives and share little self-understanding in common. As a result, the genuinely deliberative democracy that the liberal advocates remains an unfulfilled dream. Political life in liberal democracy is disfigured by clashes of organized interests and the powerful passions aroused by them, and the calm play of reason and the spirit of sympathetic dialogue cherished by the liberal are the obvious casualty. Dominant groups set the general tone of society, and their values and ways of life become the dominant norms. Other values and ideals are devalued and marginalized, creating the very culture of conformity and consumerism the liberal is anxious to avoid. Liberty is reduced to a choice of lifestyle and different forms of consumption, and there is little interest in critical reflection on the prevailing form of life and its values. Large corporate interests with the power to paralyze the economy and destabilize society severely restrict the state's scope for independent action. In the absence of a vigorous participatory culture and an organized countervailing power of active citizens, the state has no capacity to restrict corporate domination. Since it does not pursue, or is at least widely perceived as not pursuing, general interest, its legitimacy declines, its authority is subjected to constant formal and informal challenges, and citizens feel free to circumvent its laws, pressure and blackmail it to serve their national interests, and in general to get their way by whatever means they can. Liberal ideals of the neutral state, culture of civility, respect for the law, pursuit of common interest, and so on have little meaning in such a society.

Great inequalities, corporate domination, atomized individuals, a volatile underclass, apathetic citizens, a remote government, corruption of the very process of the formation of public will by manipulative media characterize all liberal democracies. The coincidence is too striking to be attributed to the contingent failings of this or that liberal democratic state. These evils have deep structural causes, one of the most important being liberal democracy's failure to give adequate weight to the democratic vision and mobilize its egalitarian, community-building, power-generating, and socially transformative potentialities. The democratic vision has its obvious dangers, and liberal democracy is right to hold it in check. However, it also has great strengths which the liberal vision lacks and without which it remains unstable. In its own interest, liberal democracy needs to find ways of giving greater voice to its hitherto marginalized democratic component.

There is also another respect in which liberal democracy needs critical reconsideration. Liberal democracy is committed to a particular vision of the good life. At the individual level, it cherishes choice, enterprise, self-determination, competitive pursuit of interests, autonomy, and so on. At the collective level, it advocates a political community in which individuals abstract away their ethnic, cultural, religious, and other differences, enjoy an identical basket of rights and obligations, and deliberate and act as citizens. The state is expected to be concerned only with what is common to them as citizens, and to take no account of their cultural and other differences. Since this vision of the good life lies at the basis of liberal democracy, the latter requires all its members to share it and uses its considerable moral and institutional resources to ensure that they do.

This creates problems in multicultural societies, which all liberal democracies have increasingly become. Liberal democracy privileges the liberal vision of the good life, embodying it in its public and other institutions and giving it state support and encouragement. Nonliberal ways of life, though not suppressed, lead a shadowy existence, are subjected to different degrees of ridicule or marginalization, denied public recognition and support, and either disappear or become dogmatic and inward-looking. Liberal democracy's assimilationist thrust is unjust because it denies nonliberals the freedom to lead their self-chosen ways of life that the liberal himself enjoys, unwise because it denies the liberal access to the riches of other ways of life or at least the opportunity to engage in a dialogue with them, and also dangerous because, feeling besieged, nonliberal ways of life become insular and resistant to the normal process of change.

Liberal democracy therefore needs to show greater respect for cultural diversity. While insisting that all its constituent communities should respect certain basic principles in their internal affairs and mutual relations, it should allow them secure spaces for growth, respect their differences, apply its general laws to them with due sensitivity to their cultural differences, appreciate that equal treatment does not mean identical treatment, and in general should institutionalize intercultural dialogue in all major areas of life. This calls for concepts of equality, common citizenship, the public realm, the state's relation to culture, the basis of national unity, and so on different from those found in the current conceptions of liberal democracy.

When the conceptual and institutional architecture of liberal democracy is revised in light of all this, we move toward a highly complex society that both is and is not a liberal democracy. It subscribes to liberal and democratic visions, and is therefore a liberal democracy. However, it also introduces the third multicultural vision. As a historical project that began two centuries ago, liberal democracy aimed to reconcile liberalism and democracy. It now has to reconcile three visions, a most challenging task. Like the different ways of reconciling liberalism and democracy discussed earlier, the reconciliation of the three visions can take many different forms. One might privilege any one of them and judiciously incorporate some aspects of the others, or one might see them as equal conversational partners. Different liberal democracies such as Canada, Australia, the US, the UK, and France are currently trying out different forms, each representing a different way of defining and reconciling the demands of liberalism, democracy, and multiculturalism, and each with its characteristic strengths and weaknesses.

Just as classical democracy was replaced by liberal democracy to take account of new circumstances, self-understandings, and moral dispositions, liberal democracy now seems to be giving way to a new form that is multiculturally oriented. This new form lacks a widely accepted name, and its contours are not yet clear. But we catch glimpses of it in the emergence of new beliefs and practices such as regionalism, subnational autonomy, asymmetrical federations, differential citizenship, multiple nationality, group rights, hyphenated identities, state-society partnership, and public role for faith-based communities. Some of these beliefs and practices are suspect and represent hasty responses to misconceived demands; others deepen and enrich liberal democracy. In any case, a wholly new and somewhat untidy three-dimensional form of political community is being gestated in the womb of liberal democracy. It is too early to say whether its birth will be natural, caesarean, or more likely a mixture of both. While the world of politics is full of new challenges and possibilities, much of contemporary political theory remains indifferent or blind to them. Unless it catches up with reality and develops concepts and questions appropriate to its complexity, it is unlikely to have the capacity to guide it.

The Prospects of Radical Politics Today

Slavoj Žižek

Today, in the time of continuous swift changes, from the "digital revolution" to the retreat of old social forms, thought is more than ever exposed to the temptation of "losing its nerve," of precociously abandoning the old conceptual coordinates. The media bombard us with the need to abandon the "old paradigms": if we are to survive, we have to change our most fundamental notions of personal identity, society, environment, etc. New Age wisdom claims that we are entering a new "posthuman" era; psychoanalysts hasten to concede that the Oedipal matrix of socialization is no longer operative, that we live in times of universalized perversion, that the concept of "repression" is of no use in our permissive times; postmodern political thought tells us that we are entering a postindustrial society, in which the old categories of labor, collectivity, class, etc., are theoretical zombies, no longer applicable to the dynamics of modernization ... Third Way ideology and political practice is effectively *the* model of this defeat, of this inability to recognize how the New is here to enable the Old to survive. Against this temptation, one should rather follow the unsurpassed example of Pascal and ask the difficult question: How are we to remain faithful to the Old in the new conditions? *Only* in this way can we generate something effectively New.

Habermas designated the present era as that of the *neue Unübersichtlichkeit* – the new opacity.[1] More than ever, our daily experience is mystifying: modernization generates new obscurantisms, the reduction of freedom is presented to us as the arrival of new freedoms.

Today, in the era of "risk society," the ruling ideology endeavors to sell us the very insecurity caused by the dismantling of the Welfare State as the opportunity for new freedoms. Do you have to change jobs every year, relying on short-term contracts instead of a long-term stable appointment? Why not see it as a liberation from the constraints of a fixed job, as the chance to reinvent yourself

---

1 See Jürgen Habermas, *Die neue Unübersichtlichkeit* (Frankfurt am Main: Suhrkamp, 1985).

again and again, to become aware of and realize the hidden potentials of your personality? You can no longer rely on the standard health insurance and retirement plan, so that you have to opt for additional coverage for which you must pay? Why not perceive it as an additional opportunity to choose: either better life now or long-term security? And if this predicament causes you anxiety, the postmodern or "second modernity" ideologist will immediately accuse you of being unable to assume full freedom, of the "escape from freedom," of the immature sticking to old stable forms ... Even better, when this is inscribed into the ideology of the subject as the psychological individual pregnant with natural abilities and tendencies, then I as it were automatically interpret all these changes as the result of my personality, not as the result of me being tossed around by market forces.

In these circumstances, one should be especially careful not to confuse the ruling ideology with ideology which *seems* to dominate. More than ever, one should bear in mind Walter Benjamin's reminder that it is not enough to ask how a certain theory (or art) declares itself with regard to social struggles – one should also ask how it effectively functions *in* these very struggles. In sex, the effectively hegemonic attitude is not patriarchal repression, but promiscuity; in art, provocations in the style of the notorious *Sensation* exhibitions *are* the norm, an example of the art fully integrated into the establishment. I am therefore tempted to reverse Marx's thesis 11: the first task today is precisely *not* to succumb to the temptation to act, to directly intervene and change things (which then inevitably ends in a cul-de-sac of debilitating impossibility: "What can one do against global capital?"), but to question the hegemonic ideological coordinates. If, today, one follows a direct call to act, this act will not be performed in an empty space – it will be an act *within* the hegemonic ideological coordinates: those who "really want to do something to help people" get involved in (undoubtedly honorable) exploits like Médecins sans Frontières, Greenpeace, feminist and antiracist campaigns, which are all not only tolerated, but even supported by the media, even if they seemingly enter the economic territory (say, denouncing and boycotting companies which do not respect ecological conditions or which use child labor) – they are tolerated and supported as long as they do not get too close to a certain limit.

Let us take two predominant topics of today's American radical academia: postcolonial and queer (gay) studies. The problem of postcolonialism is undoubtedly crucial; however, "postcolonial studies" tend to translate it into the multiculturalist problematic of the colonized minorities' "right to narrate" their victimizing experience, of the power mechanisms which repress "otherness," so that, at the end of the day, we learn that the root of postcolonial exploitation is our intolerance toward the Other, and, furthermore, that this intolerance itself is rooted in our intolerance toward the "Stranger in Ourselves," in our inability to confront what we repressed in and of ourselves. The politico-economic struggle is thus imperceptibly transformed into a pseudo-psychoanalytic drama of the subject unable to confront its inner traumas ... The true corruption of American academia is not primarily financial, it is not only that they are able to buy many European critical intellectuals (myself included – up to a point), but conceptual: notions of "European" critical theory are imperceptibly translated into the benign universe of Cultural Studies chic.

My personal experience is that practically all of the "radical" academics silently count on the long-term stability of the American capitalist model, with the secure tenured position as their ultimate professional goal (a surprising number of them even play on the stock market). If there is a thing they are genuinely horrified of, it is a radical shattering of the (relatively) safe life environment of the "symbolic classes" in the developed Western societies. Their excessive Politically Correct zeal when dealing with sexism, racism, Third World sweatshops, etc., is thus ultimately a defense against their own innermost identification, a kind of compulsive ritual whose hidden logic is: "Let's talk as much as possible about the necessity of a radical change to make sure that nothing will really change!" Symptomatic here is the journal *October*: when you ask one of the editors to what the title refers, they will half-confidentially signal that it is, of course, *that* October – in this way, one can indulge in the jargonistic analyses of modern art, with the hidden assurance that one is somehow retaining the link with the radical revolutionary past ... With regard to this radical chic, the first gesture toward Third Way ideologists and practitioners should be that of praise: they at least play their game straight and are honest in their acceptance of global capitalist coordinates, in contrast to the pseudo-radical academic Leftists who adopt toward the Third Way the attitude of utter disdain, while their own radicality ultimately amounts to an empty gesture which obligates no one to anything determinate.

From Human to Animal Rights   We live in the "postmodern" era in which truth-claims as such are dismissed as an expression of hidden power mechanisms – as the reborn pseudo-Nietzscheans like to emphasize, truth is a lie which is most efficient in asserting our will to power. The very question "Is it true?" apropos of some statement is supplanted by another question: "Under what power conditions can this statement be uttered?" What we get instead of the universal truth is a multitude of perspectives, or, as it is fashionable to put it today, of "narratives" – not only of literature, but also of politics, religion, science, they are all different narratives, stories we tell ourselves about ourselves, and the ultimate goal of ethics is to guarantee the neutral space in which this multitude of narratives can peacefully coexist, in which everyone, from ethnic to sexual minorities, will have the right and possibility to tell his/her story. *The* two philosophers of today's global capitalism are the two great Left-liberal "progressives," Richard Rorty and Peter Singer – honest in their respective stances. Rorty defines the basic coordinates: the fundamental dimension of a human being is the ability to suffer, to experience pain and humiliation – consequently, since humans are symbolic animals, the fundamental right is the right to narrate one's experience of suffering and humiliation.[2] Singer then provides the Darwinian background.[3]

Singer – usually designated as a "social Darwinist with a collectivist socialist face" – starts innocently enough, trying to argue that people will be happier if they lead lives committed to ethics: a life spent trying to help others and reduce suffering is really the most moral and fulfilling one. He radicalizes and actualizes Jeremy Bentham, the father of utilitarianism: the ultimate ethical criterion is not the dignity (rationality, soul) of man, but the ability to *suffer*, to experience pain, which man shares with animals. With inexorable radicality, Singer levels the animal/human divide: better to kill an old suffering woman than healthy animals ... Look an orangutan straight in the eye and what do you see? A none-too-distant cousin – a creature worthy of all the legal rights and privileges that humans enjoy. One should thus extend aspects of equality – the right to life, the protection of individual liberties, the prohibition of torture – at least to the nonhuman great apes (chimpanzees, orangutans, gorillas).

Singer argues that "speciesism" (privileging the human species) is no different from racism: our perception of a difference between humans and (other) animals is no less illogical and unethical than our one-time perception of an ethical difference between, say, men and women, or blacks and whites. Intelligence is no basis for determining ethical stature: the lives of humans are not worth more than the lives of animals simply because they display more intelligence (if intelligence were a standard of judgment, Singer points out, we could perform medical experiments on the mentally retarded with moral impunity). Ultimately, all things being equal, an animal has as much interest in living as a human. Therefore, all things being equal, medical experimentation on animals is immoral: those who advocate such experiments claim that sacrificing the lives of twenty animals will save millions of human lives – however, what about sacrificing twenty humans to save millions of animals? As Singer's critics like to point out, the horrifying extension of this principle is that the interests of

2 See Richard Rorty, *Contingency, Irony, Solidarity* (Cambridge: Cambridge University Press, 1989).
3 See Peter Singer, *The Essential Singer: Writings on an Ethical Life* (New York: Ecco Press, 2000).

twenty people outweighs the interests of one, which gives the green light to all sorts of human rights abuses.

Consequently, Singer argues that we can no longer rely on traditional ethics for answers to the dilemmas which our universe imposes on us; he proposes a new ethics meant to protect the quality, not the sanctity, of human life. As sharp boundaries disappear between life and death, between humans and animals, this new ethics casts doubt on the morality of animal research, while offering a sympathetic assessment of infanticide. When a baby is born with severe defects of the sort that always used to kill babies, are doctors and parents now morally obligated to use the latest technologies, regardless of cost? *No.* When a pregnant woman loses all brain function, should doctors use new procedures to keep her body living until the baby can be born? *No.* Can a doctor ethically help terminally ill patients to kill themselves? *Yes.*

The first thing to discern here is the hidden utopian dimension of such a survivalist stance. The easiest way to detect ideological surplus-enjoyment in an ideological formation is to read it as a dream and analyze the displacement at work in it. Freud reports a dream of one of his patients which consists of a simple scene: the patient is at the funeral of a relative. The key to the dream (which repeats a real-life event from the previous day) is that, at this funeral, the patient unexpectedly encounters a woman, his old love toward whom he still feels very deeply – far from being a masochistic dream, this dream thus simply articulates the patient's joy at meeting again his old love. Is the mechanism of displacement at work in this dream not strictly homologous to the one elaborated by Fredric Jameson apropos of a science-fiction film which takes place in California in the near future, after a mysterious virus has very quickly killed a great majority of the population? When the film's heroes wander in the empty shopping malls, with all the merchandise intact at their disposal, is this libidinal gain of having access to material goods without the alienating market machinery not the true point of the film occluded by the displacement of the official focus of the narrative on the catastrophe caused by the virus? At an even more elementary level, is not one of the commonplaces of sci-fi theory that the true point of novels or movies about a global catastrophe resides in the sudden reassertion of social solidarity and the spirit of collaboration among the survivors? It is as if, in our society, global catastrophe is the price one has to pay for gaining access to solidary collaboration ...

When my son was a small boy, his most cherished personal possession was a special large "survival knife" whose handle contained a compass, a sack of powder to disinfect water, a fishing hook and line, and other similar items – totally useless in our social reality, but perfectly fitting the survivalist fantasy of finding oneself alone in wild nature. It is this same fantasy which, perhaps, provides the clue to the success of Joshua Piven's and David Borgenicht's surprise best-seller *The Worst-Case Scenario Survival Handbook*.[4] Suffice it to mention two supreme examples from it: What to do if an alligator has its jaws closed on your limb? (Answer: you should tap or punch it on the snout, because alligators automatically react to it by opening their mouths.) What to do if you confront a lion which threatens to attack you? (Answer: try to make yourself appear bigger than you are by opening your coat wide.) The joke of the book thus consists in the discord between its enunciated content and its position of enunciation: the situations it describes are effectively serious and the solutions correct – the only problem is *Why is the author telling us all this? Who needs this advice?*

The underlying irony is that, in our individualistic competitive society, the most useless advice is that concerning survival in extreme physical situations – what one effectively needs is the very opposite, the Dale Carnegie type of books which tell us how to win over (manipulate) other people: the situations rendered in *The Worst-Case Scenario* lack any symbolic dimension, they reduce us to pure survival machines. In short, *The Worst-Case Scenario* became a best-seller for the very same reason Sebastian Junger's *The Perfect Storm*, the story (and the movie) about the struggle for survival of a fishing vessel caught in the "storm of the century" east of the Canadian coast in 1991, became one: they both stage the fantasy of the pure encounter with a natural threat in which the socio-symbolic dimension is suspended. In a way, *The Perfect Storm* even provides the secret utopian background of *The Worst-Case Scenario*: it is only in such extreme situations that an authentic intersubjective community, held together by solidarity, can emerge. Let us not forget that *The Perfect Storm* is ultimately the book about the solidarity of a small working-class collective! The humorous appeal of *The Worst-Case Scenario* can thus be read as bearing witness to our utter alienation from nature, exemplified by the shortage of contact with "real-life" dangers.

On account of its utter "realism," *The Worst-Case Scenario* is a Western book par excellence; its Oriental counterpart is *chindogu*, arguably the finest spiritual achievement of Japan in the last decades, the art of inventing objects which are sublime in the strictest Kantian sense of the term – practically useless on account of their very excessive usefulness (say, glasses with electrically run mini-windshields, so that your view will remain clear even if you have to walk in the rain without an umbrella; butter contained in a lipstick tube, so that you can carry it with you and spread it on the bread without a knife). That is to say, in order to be recognized, the *chindogu* objects have to meet two basic criteria: it

---

4 See Joshua Piven and David Borgenicht, *The Worst-Case Scenario Survival Handbook* (New York: Chronicle Books, 1999).

should be possible to really construct them and they should work; simultaneously, they should not be "practical," that is, it should not be feasible to market them.

The comparison between *The Worst-Case Scenario Survival Handbook* and *chindogu* offers us a unique insight into the difference between the Eastern and Western sublime, an insight far superior to New Age pseudo-philosophical treatises. In both cases, the effect of the Sublime resides in the way the uselessness of the product is the outcome of the extreme "realistic" and pragmatic approach itself. However, in the case of the West, we get simple, realistic advice for problems (situations) most of us will never encounter (who of us will really have to face a hungry lion?), while in the case of the East, we get impractically complicated solutions for the problems all of us effectively encounter (who of us has not been caught in the rain?). The Western sublime offers a practical solution for a problem which does not arise, while the Eastern sublime offers a useless solution for a real common problem.

So, back to Singer, one cannot dismiss him as a monstrous exaggeration – what Adorno said about psychoanalysis (its truth resides in its very exaggerations)[5] fully holds for Singer: he is so traumatic and intolerable because his scandalous "exaggerations" directly render visible the truth of the so-called postmodern ethic. Is not the ultimate horizon of postmodern "identity politics" effectively Darwinian – defending the right of some particular species of the human kind within the panoply of their proliferating multitude (gays with AIDS, black single mothers ...)? The very opposition between "conservative" and "progressive" politics can be conceived of in Darwinian terms: ultimately, conservatives defend the right of those with might (their very success proves that they won in the struggle for survival), while progressives advocate the protection of endangered human species, i.e., of those losing the struggle for survival.

In an incident in US academia a couple of years ago, a lesbian feminist claimed that gays are today the privileged victims, so that the analysis of how gays are underprivileged provides the key to understanding all other exclusions, repressions, violences, etc. (religious, ethnic, class). What is problematic with this thesis is precisely its implicit (or, in this case, even explicit) *universal* claim: it is making exemplary victims of those who are *not* that, of those who can be much more easily than religious or ethnic Others fully integrated into public space, enjoying full rights. There is a long tradition of Leftist gay bashing, whose traces are discernible up to Adorno – suffice it to mention Maxim Gorky's infamous remark from his essay "Proletarian Humanism" (1934): "Exterminate

5 Theodor W. Adorno, *Minima Moralia* (London: Verso, 1996).

[sic!] homosexuals, and Fascism will disappear."[6] All of this cannot be reduced to opportunistically flirting with the traditional patriarchal sexual morality of the working classes, or with the Stalinist reaction against the liberating aspects of the first years after the October Revolution; one should remember that the above-quoted Gorky's inciting statement, as well as Adorno's reservations about homosexuality (his conviction about the libidinal link between homosexuality and the spirit of military male bonding), are all based on the same historical experience: that of the SA, the "revolutionary" paramilitary Nazi organization of street-fighting thugs, in which homosexuality abounded up to its head (Ernst Röhm). The first thing to note here is that it was already Hitler himself who purged the SA in order to make the Nazi regime publicly acceptable by way of cleansing it of its obscene-violent excess/excesses, and that he justified the slaughter of the SA leadership precisely by evoking their "sexual depravity." In order to function as the support of a "totalitarian" community, homosexuality has to remain a publicly disavowed "dirty secret," shared by those who are "in." Does this mean that, when gays are persecuted, they deserve only a qualified support, a kind of "Yes, we know we should support you, but nonetheless ... (you are partially responsible for the Nazi violence)"? No, but one *should* insist that the political overdetermination of homosexuality is far from simple, that the homosexual libidinal economy can be coopted by different political orientations, and that it is *here* that one should avoid the "essentialist" mistake of dismissing the rightist "militaristic" homosexuality as the secondary distortion of the "authentic" subversive homosexuality.

One of the divisions in the chapter on Reason in Hegel's *Phenomenology of Spirit* speaks about *das geistige Tierreich* (the spiritual animal kingdom): the social world which lacks any spiritual substance, so that, in it, individuals effectively interact as "intelligent animals." They use reason, but only in order to assert their individual interests, to manipulate others into serving their own pleasures.[7] Is not a world in which the highest rights are human rights precisely such a "spiritual animal kingdom," a universe? There is, however, a price to be paid for such liberation – in such a universe, human rights ultimately function as *animal* rights. This, then, is the ultimate truth of Singer: our universe of human rights is the universe of animal rights.

This, then, is what gets lost in Singer's *geistige Tierreich*: the Thing, something to which we are unconditionally attached irrespective of its positive qualities. In Singer's universe, there is a place for mad cows, but no place for

---

6 Quoted from Siegfried Tornow, "Männliche Homosexualität und Politik in Sowjet-Russland," in *Homosexualität und Wissenschaft II* (Berlin: Rosa Winkel, 1992), p. 281.

7 See G.W.F. Hegel, *Phenomenology of Spirit* (Oxford: Oxford University Press, 1977), p. 178.

an Indian sacred cow. In other words, what gets lost here is simply the dimension of truth – *not* "objective truth" as the notion of reality from a point of view which somehow floats above the multitude of particular narratives, but truth as the Singular Universal. When Lenin says "The theory of Marx is all-powerful, because it is true," everything depends on how we understand "truth" here: is it a neutral "objective knowledge," or the truth of an engaged subject? Lenin's wager – today, in our era of postmodern relativism, more actual than ever – is that universal truth and partisanship, the gesture of taking sides, are not only not mutually exclusive, but condition each other: in a concrete situation, its *universal* truth can only be articulated from a thoroughly *partisan* position – truth is by definition one-sided. This, of course, goes against the predominant doxa of compromise, of finding a middle path among the multitude of conflicting interests. If one does not specify the *criteria* of the different, alternate narrativization, then this endeavor courts the danger of endorsing, in the Politically Correct mood, ridiculous "narratives" like those about the supremacy of some aboriginal holistic wisdom, of dismissing science as just another narrative on a par with premodern superstitions.

In a closer analysis, one could expose how the cultural relativism of the "right-to-narrate" orientation contains its own apparent opposite, the fixation on the Real of some trauma which resists its narrativization. This properly dialectical tension sustains today's academic "holocaust industry." My own ultimate experience of the holocaust-industry police occurred in 1997 at a roundtable in the Centre Pompidou in Paris: I was viciously attacked for an intervention in which (among other things) I claimed, against the neoconservatives deploring the decline of faith today, that the basic need of a normal human being is not to be a believer himself, but to have another subject who will believe for him, in his place. The reaction of one of the distinguished participants was that, by claiming this, I am ultimately endorsing holocaust revisionism, justifying the claim that, since everything is a discursive construct, this includes also the holocaust, so it is meaningless to search for what really happened there ... Apart from displaying a hypocritical paranoia, my critic was doubly wrong. First, the holocaust revisionists (to my knowledge) *never* argue in the terms of postmodern discursive constructionism, but in the terms of very empirical factual analysis: their claims range from the "fact" that there is no written document in which Hitler ordered the holocaust, to the weird mathematics of "taking into account the number of gas ovens in Auschwitz, it was not possible to burn so many corpses." Furthermore, not only is the postmodern logic of "everything is a discursive construction, there are no direct firm facts" *never* used to deflate the holocaust; in a paradox worth noting, it is precisely the postmodern discursive constructionists (like Lyotard) who tend to elevate the holocaust into the supreme ineffable metaphysical Evil – the holocaust serves them as the untouchable-sacred Real, as the negative of contingent language games.

The Möbius Strip of Politics and Economy   What all the new French (or French-oriented) theories of the Political, from Étienne Balibar through Jacques Ran-cière to Alain Badiou, aim at is – to put it in traditional philosophical terms – the reduction of the sphere of economy (of material production) to an "ontic" sphere deprived of "ontological" dignity. Within this horizon, there is simply no place for the Marxian "critique of political economy": the structure of the universe of commodities and capital in Marx's *Capital* is *not* just that of a limited empirical sphere, but a kind of socio-transcendental *a priori*, the matrix which generates the totality of social and political relations. The relationship between economy and politics is ultimately that of the well-known visual paradox of the "two faces or a vase": one sees either two faces or a vase, never both of them – in other words, one has to make a choice.[8] In the same way, one either focuses on the political, and the domain of economy is reduced to the empirical "servicing of goods," or one focuses on economy, and politics is reduced to a theater of appearances, to a passing phenomenon which will disappear with the arrival of the developed communist (or technocratic) society, in which, as Engels put it, the "administration of people" will vanish in the "administration of things." (Does not the same "vase/two faces" paradox occur in the case of the holocaust and gulag? We either elevate the holocaust into the ultimate crime, and the Stalinist terror is thereby half-redeemed, reduced to a minor role of an "ordinary" crime; or we focus on the gulag as the ultimate result of the logic of modern revolutionary terror, and the holocaust is thereby at best reduced to another example of the same logic. Somehow, it does not seem possible to deploy a truly "neutral" theory of totalitarianism, without giving a hidden preference to either the holocaust or the gulag.)

What we are dealing with here is another version of the Lacanian *il n'y a pas de rapport...*: if, for Lacan, there is no sexual relationship, then, for Marxism proper, there is no relationship between economy and politics, no "meta-language" enabling us to grasp from the same neutral standpoint the two levels, although – or, rather, *because* – these two levels are inextricably intertwined. The "political" class struggle takes place in the very midst of economy (recall that the

---

8 See Fredric Jameson, "The Concept of Revisionism," intervention at the symposium *The Retrieval of Lenin*, organized by Kulturwissenschaftliches Institut, Essen, February 2–4, 2001.

very last paragraph of *Capital III,* where the text abruptly stops, tackles the class struggle), while, at the same time, the domain of economy serves as the key enabling us to decode political struggles. No wonder that the structure of this impossible relationship is that of the Möbius strip: first, we have to progress from the political spectacle to its economic infrastructure; then, in the second step, we have to confront the irreducible dimension of the political struggle in the very heart of the economy.

In this context, the first myth to be debunked is that of the diminishing role of the state. What we are witnessing today is a shift in its functions: while partially withdrawing from its welfare obligations, the state is strengthening its apparatuses in other domains of social regulation. In order to start a business now, one has to rely on the state to guarantee not only law and order, but the entire infrastructure (access to water and energy, means of transportation, ecological criteria, international regulations, etc.), to an incomparably larger extent than a hundred years ago. The recent electricity debacle in California makes this point palpable: for a couple of weeks in January and February 2001, the privatization ("deregulation") of the electricity supply changed Southern California, one of the most highly developed "postindustrial" landscapes in the entire world, into a Third World country with regular black-outs. Of course, the defenders of deregulation claimed that it was not thorough enough, thereby engaging in the old false syllogism of "my fiancée is never late for an appointment, because the moment she is late, she is no longer my fiancée": deregulation by definition works, so if it does not work, it was not truly a deregulation ... Does the recent Mad Cow Disease panic (which probably presages dozens of similar phenomena which await us in the near future) also not point toward the need for strict state and global institutionalized control of agriculture?

The key antagonism of the so-called new (digital) industries is thus: how to maintain the form of (private) property, within which only the logic of profit can be maintained (see also the Napster problem, the free circulation of music). And do the legal complications in biogenetics not point in the same direction? The key element of the new international trade agreements is the "protection of intellectual property": whenever, in a merger, a big First World company takes over a Third World company, the first thing they do is close down the research department. Phenomena emerge here which bring the notion of property to extraordinary dialectical paradoxes: in India, local communities suddenly discover that medical practices and materials they have been using for centuries are now owned by American companies, so they now have to be bought from them; with the biogenetic companies patenting genes, we are all discovering that parts of ourselves, our genetic components, are already copyrighted, owned by others ...

However, the outcome of this crisis of private property of the means of production is by no means guaranteed – it is *here* that one should take into account
the ultimate paradox of the Stalinist society: against the capitalism which is the
class society, but in principle egalitarian, without direct hierarchical divisions, the
"mature" Stalinism was a classless society articulated in precisely defined hierarchical groups (top nomenklatura, technical intelligence, army). What this means
is that, already for Stalinism, the classic Marxist notion of class struggle is no
longer adequate to describe its hierarchy and domination: in the Soviet Union
from the late 1920s onward, the key social division was not defined by property
but by the direct access to power mechanisms and to the privileged material and
cultural conditions of life (food, housing, health care, freedom of travel, education). And, perhaps, the ultimate irony of history will be that, in the same way
Lenin's vision of "central bank Socialism" can be properly read only retroactively,
from today's World Wide Web, the Soviet Union provided the first model of the
developed "post-property" society, of true "late capitalism" in which the ruling
class will be defined by direct access to the (informational, administrative) means
of social power and control and attendant material and social privileges: the
point will no longer be to own companies, but to run them directly, to have the
right to use a private jet, to have access to top health care, etc. – privileges which
will be acquired not by property, but by other (educational, managerial, etc.)
mechanisms. The ultimate answer to the reproach that radical Left proposals are
utopian should thus be that, today, the true utopia is the belief that the present
liberal-democratic capitalist consensus could go on indefinitely, without radical
changes. We are thus back to the old '68 motto "Soyons réalistes, demandons
l'impossible!": in order to be truly a "realist," one must consider breaking out of
the constraints of what appears "possible" (or, as we usually put it, "feasible").

Today, we already can discern the signs of a kind of general unease – recall
the series of events usually listed under the name of "Seattle." The ten-year hon-
eymoon of triumphant global capitalism is over, the long-overdue "seven year
itch" is here – witness the panicky reactions of the big media, which – from
Time magazine to CNN – all of a sudden began to warn about Marxists manip-
ulating the crowd of "honest" protesters. The problem is now a strictly Leninist
one – how to *actualize* the media's accusations, how to invent the organizational
structure which will confer on this unrest the *form* of a universal political
demand. Otherwise, the momentum will be lost, and what will remain is the
marginal disturbance, perhaps organized as a new Greenpeace, with a certain
efficiency, but also strictly limited goals, a marketing strategy, etc. In other
words, the key "Leninist" lesson today is: politics without the organizational
form of the party is politics without politics, so the answer to those who want
just the (quite adequately named) "New *Social* Movements" is the same as the

answer of the Jacobins to the Girondin compromisers: "You want revolution without a revolution!" Today's blockade is that there are two ways open for sociopolitical engagement: either play the game of the system, engage in the "long march through the institutions," or get active in new social movements, from feminism through ecology to antiracism. And, again, the limit of these movements is that they are not *political* in the sense of the Universal Singular: they are "single-issue movements" which lack the dimension of the universal, that is, they do not relate to the social *totality*.

Here, Lenin's reproach to liberals is crucial: they only *exploit* the discontent of the working class to strengthen their position vis-à-vis the conservatives, instead of identifying with it to the end. Is this also not the case with today's Left liberals? They like to evoke racism, ecology, workers' grievances, etc., to score points over the conservatives *without endangering the system*. Recall how, in Seattle, Bill Clinton himself deftly referred to the protesters on the streets outside, reminding the gathered leaders inside the guarded palaces that they should listen to the message of the demonstrators (the message which, of course, Clinton interpreted, depriving it of its subversive sting attributed to the dangerous extremists introducing chaos and violence into the majority of peaceful protesters). It is the same with all New Social Movements, up to the Zapatistas in Chiapas: the systemic politics is always ready to "listen to their demands," depriving them of their proper political sting. The system is by definition ecumenical, open, tolerant, ready to "listen" to all – even if one insists on one's demands, they are deprived of their universal political sting by the very form of negotiation. The true Third Way we have to look for is this third way between institionalized parliamentary politics and the new social movements.

Gilles Deleuze's and Félix Guattari's *Anti-Oedipus* was the last great attempt to combine in a subversive synthesis the Marxist and the psychoanalytic traditions. They fully recognize the revolutionary, deterritorializing impact of capitalism, which, in its inexorable dynamics, undermines all stable traditional forms of human interaction; what they approached capitalism with is that its deterritorialization is not thorough enough, that it generates new reterritorializations – a verbatim repetition of Marx's claim that the ultimate obstacle to capitalism is capitalism itself, that capitalism unleashes a dynamic it will not be able to contain. Far from being outdated, this claim seems to gain actuality with today's growing deadlocks of globalization in which the inherently antagonistic nature of capitalism belies its worldwide triumph. However, the problem is: Is it still possible to imagine communism (or another form of postcapitalist society) as a formation which sets free the deterritorializing dynamics of capitalism, liberating it of its inherent constraints? Marx's fundamental vision was that a new, higher social order (communism) is possible, an order that would not only maintain, but even raise to a higher degree and effectively fully release the potential of the self-increasing spiral of productivity which, in capitalism, on account of its inherent obstacle/contradiction, is again and again thwarted by socially destructive economic crises. What Marx overlooked is that, to put it in the standard Derridean terms, this inherent obstacle/antagonism as the "condition of impossibility" of the full deployment of the productive forces is simultaneously its "condition of possibility": if we abolish the obstacle, the inherent contradiction of capitalism, we do not get the fully unleashed drive to productivity finally delivered of its impediment, but we lose precisely this productivity that seemed to be generated and simultaneously thwarted by capitalism – if we take away the obstacle, the very potential thwarted by this obstacle dissipates … Therein would reside a possible Lacanian critique of Marx, focusing on the ambiguous overlapping between surplus-value and surplus-enjoyment. (It is often said that the ultimate products of capitalism are piles of trash – useless computers, cars, TVs, and VCRs …: places like the famous "graveyard" of hundreds of abandoned planes in the Mojave desert confront us with the obverse truth of capitalist dynamics, its inert objectal remainder. And it is against this background that one should read the ecological dream-notion of total recycling – in which every remainder is used again – as the ultimate capitalist dream, even if it is couched in the terms of retaining the natural balance on Planet Earth: the dream of the self-propelling circulation of capital which would succeed in leaving behind no material residue – the proof of how capitalism can appropriate ideologies which seem to oppose it.)

While this constant self-propelling revolutionizing still holds for high Stalinism with its total productive mobilization, the "stagnant" late Real Socialism legitimizes itself (between the lines, at least) as a society in which one can live peacefully, avoiding capitalist competitive stress. This was the last line of defense when, from the late '60s onward, after the fall of Khrushchev (the last enthusiast who, during his visit to the US, prophesied that "your grandchildren will be communists"), it became clear that Real Socialism was losing the competitive edge in its war with capitalism. So the stagnant late Real Socialism in a way already *was* "socialism with a human face": silently abandoning great historical tasks, it provided the security of everyday life enduring in a benevolent boredom. Today's *Ostalgie* for the defunct socialism mostly consists in such conservative nostalgia for the self-satisfied constrained way of life; even nostalgic anticapitalist artists from Peter Handke to Joseph Beuys celebrate this aspect of socialism: the absence of stressful mobilization and frantic commodification. Of course, this unexpected shift tells us something about the deficiency of the original Marxist project itself: it points toward the limitation of its goal of unleashed productive mobilization.

Fetishism Today　　The ultimate postmodern irony is the strange exchange between Europe and Asia: at the very moment when, at the level of the "economic infrastructure," "European" technology and capitalism are triumphing worldwide, at the level of "ideological superstructure," the Judeo-Christian legacy is threatened in the European space itself by the onslaught of New Age "Asiatic" thought, which, in its different guises, from "Western Buddhism" (today's counterpoint to Western Marxism, as opposed to "Asiatic" Marxism-Leninism) to different "Daos," is establishing itself as the hegemonic ideology of global capitalism. Therein resides the highest speculative identity of opposites in today's global civilization: although "Western Buddhism" presents itself as the remedy against the stressful tension of capitalist dynamics, allowing us to uncouple and retain inner peace and *Gelassenheit* (placidity), it actually functions as its perfect ideological supplement. One should mention here the well-known topic of "future shock," that is, of how, today, people are no longer psychologically able to cope with the dazzling rhythm of technological development and the social changes that accompany it – things simply move too fast, before one can accustom oneself to an invention, this invention is already supplanted by a new one, so that one more and more lacks the most elementary "cognitive mapping." The recourse to Daoism or Buddhism offers a way out of this predicament, which definitely work better than the desperate escape into old traditions: instead of trying to cope with the accelerating rhythm of technological progress and social change, one should rather renounce the very endeavor to retain control over what goes on, rejecting it as the expression of the modern logic of domination – one should, instead, "let oneself go," drift along, while retaining an inner distance and indifference toward the mad dance of the accelerated process, a distance based on the insight that all this social and technological upheaval is ultimately just an insubstantial proliferation of semblances which do not really concern the innermost kernel of our being … One is almost tempted to resuscitate here the old infamous Marxist cliché of religion as the "opiate of the people," as the imaginary supplement of terrestrial misery: the "Western Buddhist" meditative stance is arguably the most efficient way, for us, to fully participate in capitalist dynamics, while retaining the appearance of mental sanity. If Max Weber were to live today, he would definitely write a second, supplementary, volume to his *Protestant Ethic* entitled *The Daoist Ethic and the Spirit of Global Capitalism.*

　　"Western Buddhism" thus perfectly fits the fetishist mode of ideology in our allegedly "postideological" era, as opposed to its traditional symptomal mode, in which the ideological lie that structures our perception of reality is threatened by symptoms *qua* "returns of the repressed," cracks in the fabric of the ideological lie. Fetish is effectively a kind of *envers* of the symptom. That is to say, symptom is the exception which disturbs the surface of the false appearance, the point at which the repressed truth erupts, while fetish is the embodiment of the Lie which enables us to sustain the unbearable truth. Let us take the case of the death of a beloved person: when I "repress" this death, I try not to think about it, but the repressed trauma persists and returns in the symptoms. Say, after my beloved wife dies of breast cancer, I try to repress this fact by throwing myself into hard work or a vivacious social life, but then there is always something which reminds me of her, I cannot escape her ghost. In the case of a fetish, on the contrary, I "rationally" fully accept this death, I am able to talk about her most painful moments in a cold and clear way, because I cling to the fetish, to some feature that embodies for me the disavowal of this death. In this sense, a fetish can play a very constructive role of allowing us to cope with the harsh reality: fetishists are not dreamers lost in their private worlds, they are thorough "realists," able to accept the way things are – since they have their fetish to which they can cling in order to defuse the full impact of reality.

So, when we are bombarded by claims that in our postideological cynical era nobody believes in the proclaimed ideals, when we encounter a person who claims he is cured of any beliefs, accepting social reality the way it really is, one should always counter such claims with the question: OK, but where is the fetish which enables you to (pretend to) accept reality "the way it is"? "Western Buddhism" is such a fetish: it enables you to fully participate in the frantic pace of the capitalist game, while sustaining the perception that you are not really in it, that you are well aware how worthless this spectacle is – what really matters to you is the peace of the inner Self to which you know you can always withdraw …

Perhaps the most succinct definition of ideology was produced by Christopher Hitchens, when he tackled the difficult question of what the North Koreans effectively think about their "Beloved Leader" Kim Yong Il: "mass delusion is the only thing that keeps a people sane."[9] This paradox points toward the fetishistic split at the very heart of an effectively functioning ideology: individuals transpose their beliefs onto the big Other (embodied in the collective), which thus believes in their place – individuals thus remain sane *qua* individuals, maintaining the distance toward the "big Other" of the official discourse. It is not only the direct identification with the ideological "delusion" which would render individuals insane, but also the suspension of their (disavowed, displaced) belief. In other words, if individuals were to be deprived of this belief (projected onto the "big Other"), they would have to jump in and themselves

9 Christopher Hitchens, "Visit to a Small Planet," *Vanity Fair* (January 2001), p. 24.

directly assume the belief. (Perhaps this explains the paradox that many a cynic becomes a sincere believer at the very point of the disintegration of the "official" belief.) This is what Lacan aimed at in his claim that the true formula of materialism is not "God doesn't exist" but "God is unconscious" – suffice it to recall what, in a letter to Max Brod, Milena Jesenska wrote about Kafka: "Above all, things like money, stock-exchange, the foreign currency administration, typewriter, are for him thoroughly mystical (what they effectively are, only not for us, the others)."[10] One should read this statement against the background of Marx's analysis of commodity fetishism: the fetishist illusion resides in our real social life, not in our perception of it – a bourgeois subject knows very well that there is nothing magic about money, that money is just an object which stands for a set of social relations, but he nevertheless *acts* in real life as if he believed that money is a magical thing. This, then, gives us a precise insight into Kafka's universe: Kafka was able to experience directly these phantasmatic beliefs that we "normal" people disavow – Kafka's "magic" is what Marx liked to refer to as the "theological freakishness" of commodities.

This definition of ideology points out the way to answer the tedious standard reproach against the application of psychoanalysis to social-ideological processes: is it "legitimate" to expand the use of the notions which were originally deployed for the treatment of individuals to collective entities and to speak, say, of religion as a "collective compulsive neurosis"? The focus of psychoanalysis is entirely different: the Social, the field of social practices and socially held beliefs, is not simply at a different level from the individual experience, but something to which the individual him/herself has to relate, which the individual him/herself has to experience as an order which is minimally "reified," externalized. The problem is therefore not "how to jump from the individual to the social level"; the problem is: How should the decentered socio-symbolic order of institutionalized practices and beliefs be structured, if the subject is to retain his/her "sanity," his/her "normal" functioning? Which delusions should be deposited there so that individuals can remain sane? Recall the proverbial egotist, cynically dismissing the public system of moral norms: as a rule, such a subject can only function if this system is "out there," publicly recognized, i.e., in order to be a private cynic, he has to presuppose the existence of naive other(s) who "really believe." This is how a true "cultural revolution" should be conducted: not by directly targeting individuals, endeavoring to "reeducate" them, to "change their reactionary attitudes," but by depriving individuals of support in the "big Other," in the institutional symbolic order.

---

10 Quoted in Jana Cerna, *Kafka's Milena* (Evanston, Ill.: Northwestern University Press, 1993), p. 174.

It is easy to be "radical" apropos of gay marriage, incest, etc. – however, what about child sex and torture? On what ground are we justified in opposing them without having recourse to the "legal fiction" of the adult autonomous subject responsible for his/her acts? (And, incidentally, *why* should marriage be constrained to *two* persons, gay or not? Why not three or more? Is this not the last remainder of the "binary logic"?) More generally, if we adopt the standard postmodern mantra of the autonomous responsible subject as a legal fiction, what are the consequences of this denial for our dealing with, say, child rapists? Is it not deeply symptomatic how the very same theorists who denounce the liberal autonomous subject as a Western legal fiction, at the same time fully endorse the discourse of victimization, treating the perpetrators of sexual harassment as guilty (i.e., responsible) for their acts? Furthermore, the attitude toward sex between adults and children is the best indicator of the changes in sexual mores: three or four decades ago, in the heyday of the Sexual Revolution, child sex was *celebrated* as overcoming the last barrier, the ideologically enforced desexualization of children, while the Politically Correct ideology of victimization offers the sexually abused child as the ultimate image of horror.

In a recent pamphlet against the "excesses" of May '68 and, more generally, the "sexual liberation" of the '60s, *The Independent* brought back to memory what the radicals of '68 thought about child sex. A quarter of a century ago, Daniel Cohn-Bendit wrote about his experience as an educator in a kindergarten: "My constant flirt with all the children soon took on erotic characteristics. I could really feel how from the age of five the small girls had already learned to make passes at me. ... Several times a few children opened the flies of my trousers and started to stroke me. ... When they insisted, I then stroked them." Shulamith Firestone went even further, expressing her hopes that, in a world "without the incest taboo ... relations with children would include as much genital sex as they were capable of – probably considerably more than we now believe."[11] Decades later, when confronted with these statements, Cohn-Bendit played them down, claiming that "this did not really happen, I only wanted to provoke people. When one reads it today, it is unacceptable."[12] However, the question still hovers: How, at that time, was it possible to provoke people, presenting sexual games among preschool children as something appealing, while today, the same "provocation" would immediately give rise to an outburst of moral disgust? After all, child sexual harassment is one of *the* notions of Evil today.

---

11 Both quotes from Maureen Freely, "Polymorphous Sexuality in the Sixties," *The Independent*, January 29, 2001, The Monday Review, p. 4.
12 Quoted in *Konkret*, no. 3 (March 2001), p. 9.

Without directly taking sides in this debate, one should read it as a sign of the change in our mores from the utopian energies of the '60s and early '70s to the contemporary stale Political Correctness, in which every authentic encounter with another human being is denounced as a victimizing experience. What we are unable even to conjecture today is the idea of *revolution*, be it sexual or social. Perhaps, in today's stale times of the proliferating pleas for tolerance, one should take the risk of recalling the liberating dimension of such "excesses."

For an Agonistic Public Sphere

Chantal Mouffe

My aim in this presentation is to offer some reflections concerning the kind of public sphere that a vibrant democratic society requires, an issue particularly relevant to the type of questions raised by Documenta11 and this symposium. In particular, I want to scrutinize the dominant discourse which announces the "end of the adversarial model of politics" and insists on the need to go beyond left and right toward a consensual politics of the center. The thesis that I want to put forward is that, contrary to what its defenders argue, this type of discourse has very negative consequences for democratic politics. Indeed, it has contributed to the weakening of the "democratic political public sphere" and has led to the increasing dominance of a juridical and moral discourse, a dominance that I take to be inimical to democracy. I submit that the increasing moralization and juridification of politics, far from being a progressive step in the development of democracy, should be seen as a threat to its future existence.

I   There are many reasons for the weakening of the democratic political public sphere, some having to do with the predominance of a neoliberal regime of globalization, others with the type of individualistic consumer culture that now pervades most advanced industrial societies. From a strictly political perspective, it is clear that the collapse of communism and the disappearance of the political frontiers that structured the political imaginary during most of the 20th century have led to the crumbling of the political markers of society. The blurring of frontiers between right and left that we have witnessed in Western countries constitutes, in my view, one of the main reasons for the growing irrelevance of the democratic political public sphere.

Elsewhere, I have shown how the current celebration of centrism and the lack of effective democratic alternatives to the present order has strengthened the appeal of right-wing populist parties. When passions cannot be mobilized by democratic parties because these parties privilege a "consensus at the center," those passions tend to find other outlets, in diverse fundamentalist movements, around particularistic demands or nonnegotiable moral issues. When a society lacks a dynamic democratic life with genuine confrontation among a diversity of democratic political identities, the groundwork is laid for other forms of identification to take their place, identifications of an ethnic, religious, or nationalist nature that generate antagonisms which cannot be managed by the democratic process.

Here I will focus on the reasons and consequences of the decline of a properly political discourse and its replacement by a moral, and even in many cases, a moralistic one. I see this phenomenon as signaling the triumph of a moralizing liberalism which pretends that antagonisms have been eradicated and that society can now be ruled through rational moral procedures and remaining conflicts resolved through impartial tribunals. Hence the privileged role of the judiciary and the fact that it is the legal system which is seen as being responsible for organizing human coexistence and for regulating social relations. Since the problems of society can no longer be envisioned in political terms, there is a marked tendency to privilege the juridical and to expect the law to provide solutions to all types of conflict.

As a political theorist, I am particularly troubled by the pernicious influence of political theory in this displacement of politics by morality and law. Indeed, in the theoretical approach that, under the name of "deliberative democracy," is rapidly colonizing the discursive terrain, one of the main tenets is that political questions are of a moral nature and therefore susceptible to rational treatment. The objective of a democratic society is, according to such a view, the creation of a rational consensus reached through appropriate deliberative procedures whose aim is to produce decisions that represent an impartial standpoint equally in the interests of all. All those who put into question the very possibility of such a rational consensus and who affirm that the political is a domain in which one should always rationally expect to find discord are accused of undermining the very possibility of democracy. Habermas, for instance, asserts: "If questions of justice cannot transcend the ethical self-understanding of competing forms of life, and existentially relevant value conflicts and oppositions must penetrate all controversial questions, then in the final analysis we will end up with something resembling Carl Schmitt's understanding of politics."[1]

This theoretical tendency to conflate politics with morality, understood in rationalistic and universalistic terms, has very negative consequences for democratic politics because it erases the dimension of antagonism which I take to be ineradicable in politics. It has contributed to the current retreat of the political

---

1 Jürgen Habermas, "Reply to Symposium Participants," *Cardozo Law Review* 17, no. 4–5 (March 1996), p. 1493.

and to its replacement by the juridical and the moral, which are perceived as ideal terrains for reaching impartial decisions. There is therefore a strong link between this kind of political theory and the demise of the political. In fact, the current situation can be viewed as the fulfillment of a tendency which is inscribed at the very core of liberalism, which, because of its constitutive incapacity to think in truly political terms, must always resort to another type of discourse: economic, moral, or juridical.

This perspective is exemplified in the work of John Rawls, who extols the US Supreme Court as a model of what he calls the "free exercise of public reason," in his view the essence of democratic deliberation. Another example can be found in the work of Ronald Dworkin, who gives primacy to the independent judiciary, seen as the interpreter of the political morality of a community. According to Dworkin, all the fundamental questions facing a political community in the arenas of employment, education, censorship, freedom of association, etc., are best resolved by judges, providing that they interpret the Constitution by reference to the principle of political equality. There is very little left for the political arena.

Even pragmatists like Richard Rorty, despite carrying out a far-reaching and important critique of the rationalist approach, fail to provide a forceful alternative. Indeed, the problem with Rorty is that, albeit in a different way, he also ends up privileging consensus and missing the political dimension. To be sure, the consensus that he advocates is to be reached through persuasion and "sentimental education," not rational argumentation, but he nevertheless believes in the possibility of an all-encompassing consensus and therefore in the elimination of antagonism.

But this is to miss a crucial point, not only on the primary reality of strife in social life and the impossibility of finding rational, impartial solutions to political issues, but also about the integrative role that conflict plays in modern democracy. A well-functioning democracy calls for a confrontation of democratic political positions. Absent this, there is always the danger, as I pointed out earlier, that this democratic confrontation will be replaced by a battle between nonnegotiable moral values or essentialist forms of identification. Too much emphasis on consensus, together with an aversion to confrontation, engenders apathy and disaffection with political participation. This is why a democratic society requires debate about possible alternatives. In other words, while consensus is necessary, it must be accompanied by dissent. Consensus is needed on the institutions that are constitutive of democracy and on the ethico-political values that should inform political association, but there will always be disagreement concerning the meaning and methods of implementing those values. In a pluralist democracy, such disagreements should be consid-

ered legitimate and indeed welcome. They provide different forms of citizenship identification and are the stuff of democratic politics.

II   In order to defend and deepen the democratic project, what is urgently
needed is an alternative to the dominant approach in democratic political theory, one that would help revitalize the democratic public sphere by stimulating
awareness of the need for political forms of identification around clearly differentiated democratic positions and the possibility of choosing between real alternatives. This is why, against the two existing models of democratic politics, the
aggregative and the deliberative, I have argued for a model of "agonistic pluralism," which acknowledges the role of power relations in society and the ever
present possibility of antagonism. According to such a view, the aim of democratic institutions is not to establish a rational consensus in the public sphere
but to defuse the potential of hostility that exists in human societies by providing the possibility for antagonism to be transformed into "agonism." By which I
mean that in democratic societies, while conflict cannot and should not be eradicated, neither should it take the form of a struggle between enemies (antagonism), but rather between adversaries (agonism).

This is why, in my view, the central category of democratic politics is the category of the "adversary," the opponent with whom we share a common allegiance to the democratic principles of "liberty and equality for all" while dis-
agreeing about their interpretation. Adversaries fight against each other because
they want their interpretation to become hegemonic, but they do not question
the legitimacy of their opponents' right to fight for their position. This confrontation between adversaries constitutes the "agonistic struggle," which I take
to be the very condition of a vibrant democracy.[2]

The specificity of this approach is that it is a way of envisioning democracy
which – contrary to other conceptions – recognizes the dimension of what I
have proposed to call "the political," that is, the potential antagonism inherent
in social relations, antagonism which can take many forms and which can never
be absolutely eradicated. I have distinguished this notion of "the political" from
that of "politics," which refers to the ensemble of discourses, institutions, and
practices whose objective is to establish an order, to organize human coexistence
in a context which is always conflictual because of the presence of "the political." The aim of democratic politics, as I have already indicated, is to create the
institutions through which this potential antagonism can be transformed into

---

2 For a development of this argument, see Chantal Mouffe, *The Democratic Paradox* (London:
  Verso, 2000).

"agonism," that is, a situation defined by a confrontation between adversaries, not the relation "friend/enemy."

Let me stress that this notion of the adversary needs to be sharply distinguished from the understanding of that term found in liberal discourse. According to my conception of "adversary," and contrary to the liberal view, the presence of antagonism is not eliminated but "tamed," so to speak. What liberals call an "adversary" is actually a "competitor." They envision the field of politics as a neutral terrain in which different groups compete for positions of power, that is, their objective is to dislodge others in order to occupy their place, without challenging the dominant hegemony and attempting to transform the existing relations of power. This is merely a competition among elites. In my case, however, the antagonistic dimension is always present since what is at stake is the struggle between opposing hegemonic projects which can never be reconciled rationally – one of them must be defeated. It is a genuine confrontation but one that is played out under conditions regulated by a set of democratic procedures accepted by the adversaries.

Of course, such a view would be anathema to the advocates of deliberative democracy and promoters of the Third Way, who will no doubt condemn it as "Schmittian." But I submit that this is the condition for revitalizing democratic politics and for reversing the dangerous trend of disaffection with democratic institutions that we are witnessing today. This would indeed provide a way in which passions could be mobilized toward democratic designs.

III   So far, I have concentrated on the shortcomings of current theories of democratic politics in order to show how they contribute to shaping the end-of-politics zeitgeist which prevails today and which prevents us from envisioning a properly democratic public sphere. Now I would like to examine a different but related trend, the fashionable thesis put forward by Ulrich Beck and Anthony Giddens that we have entered a new phase of "reflexive modernity" in which the adversarial model of politics has become obsolete. I intend to highlight the consequences of such a perspective and its strong connection with the current dominance of a moralistic discourse. Those who announce the death of the adversarial model claim that the friend/enemy relation in politics is characteristic of classical industrial modernity, the "first modernity," but that we now live in a different, "second" modernity, a "reflexive" one, in which the emphasis should be placed on "sub-politics," the issues of "life and death." For Beck, these are "All the things that are considered loss, danger, waste and decay in the left-right framework of bourgeois politics, things like concern with the self, the questions: who am I? what do I want? where am I headed?, in short all the original sins of individualism, lead to a different type of identity of the political: life and death politics."[3]

In the same vein, Giddens distinguishes between old-fashioned "emancipative politics" and "life politics," which he defines in the following way: "Life politics concerns political issues which flow from processes of self-actualization in post-traditional contexts, where globalizing tendencies intrude deeply into the reflexive project of the self, and conversely where processes of self-realization influence global strategies."[4]

As in the case of deliberative democracy, at the basis of this conception of reflexive modernity is the possibility of elimination of the political in its antagonistic dimension and the belief that relations of friend/enemy have been eradicated. The claim is that in post-traditional societies, we no longer find collective identities constructed in terms of us/them, which means that political frontiers have evaporated and that politics must therefore be "reinvented," to use Beck's expression. Indeed, Beck assumes that the generalized skepticism and doubt prevalent today preclude the emergence of antagonistic relations, since the latter depend on strong commitments to notions of the truth, impossible in an era of ambivalence. Any attempt to speak in terms of right and left or to organize collective identities on the basis of common objectives and to define an adversary is thereby discredited as being "archaic" or "Old Labour" (to speak like Tony Blair).

Discourses like deliberative democracy or reflexive modernity are usually presented as the truly progressive ones, or, at least, better suited to the present stage of democracy. In fact, the chief consequence of envisioning our societies in such a "postpolitical" manner is an inability to articulate any alternative to the current hegemonic order. These approaches render us incapable of thinking in a political way, of asking political questions and proposing political answers.

We should also be aware of the fact that this incapacity is reinforced by the centrality of human rights discourse, which has displaced all other discourses. Indeed, the discourse of human rights currently serves as a substitute for the sociopolitical discourses which have been discredited. As Marcel Gauchet has argued,[5] it has become the organizing norm of collective consciousness and the standard of public action. The problem, as he indicates, is that such a discourse is not interested in – nor does it allow us to grasp – why things are as they are and

---

3 Ulrich Beck, Anthony Giddens, and Scott Lash, *Reflexive Modernization: Politics, Tradition and Aesthetics in the Modern Social Order* (Cambridge: Polity Press, 1994), p. 45.

4 Anthony Giddens, *Modernity and Self-Identity: Self and Society in the Late Modern Age* (Cambridge: Polity Press, 1991), p. 214.

5 Marcel Gauchet, "Quand les droits de l'homme deviennent une politique," *Le Débat*, no. 110 (May–August 2000), pp. 258–288.

how they could be changed. In fact, the insistence on human rights in many cases tends to disqualify the very idea of searching for explanations, because to try to understand is seen as excusing what is deemed "unacceptable." This is why, very often, the ideology of human rights thrives on denunciation. It commands a politics of intentions that is indifferent to the consequence of its actions, a politics of virtuous sentiment that is therefore not vulnerable to criticism.

IV   Putting together all these different elements, the ideological framework in which the dominant consensus is inscribed becomes visible. Such a consensus has two faces, neoliberalism on one side, human rights on the other. Do not misunderstand my point. I am not saying that the discourse of human rights is simply an ideological cover for neoliberalism. I do believe that human rights represent a constitutive component of modern democracy and that they should be valued and fought for. The problem arises when they become a substitute for a truly political discourse and when democracy is reduced to the defense of human rights at the expense of its other dimension, that of popular sovereignty. Such a move impedes a grasp of the nature of modern democracy, which consists in the articulation of two different traditions: the liberal tradition of rule of law and individual liberty with the democratic tradition of equality and popular sovereignty. The tendency to privilege exclusively the liberal component and to treat the democratic element as obsolete has serious political consequences. It is the source of the growing success of right-wing populist parties, which pretend to reestablish popular sovereignty against elites.

It is also in the context of the current hegemony of liberalism that we can make sense of the now-dominant moralistic discourse which has displaced any real political argumentation. Such a displacement is seen as the proof that democracy has entered into a new, more mature phase in which morality has replaced outmoded confrontational politics. However, if we examine the question closely, it is immediately evident that this is far from being the case. Politics, with its supposedly old-fashioned antagonisms, has not been superseded by a higher stage of moral concerns. Politics, with its antagonisms, is still very much alive, except that it is now played out in the moral register. Indeed, frontiers between us and them, far from having disappeared, are continually reinscribed, but since the "them" can no longer be defined in political terms – given that the adversarial model has supposedly been overcome – these frontiers are drawn in moral categories, between "us the good" and "them the evil ones."

Put another way: the consensus at the center, which ostensibly includes everyone in our so-called post-traditional societies, cannot exist without the establishment of a frontier because no consensus – or common identity, for that matter – can exist without drawing a frontier. There cannot be an "us" without a "them" and the very identity of any group depends on the existence of a "constitutive outside." So the "us of all the good democrats" must be secured by the definition of a "them." However, since the "them" cannot be defined as a political adversary, it can only be defined as a moral enemy, as the "evil them." In most cases, it is, of course, the "extreme right" that provides the "evil them" required by the very existence of the good democrats. This reference to the "extreme right" is not very helpful, however, because it has become a nebulous category in which many different movements – from skinheads to right-wing populist parties – are lumped together indiscriminately. This blurs their differences and specific characteristics, and hinders the development of effective strategies for fighting them politically. But, of course, from the point of view of the "good democrats," such differences are irrelevant. What is at stake for them is not a political analysis but the delimitation of a "them" which will provide the conditions of possibility for the "us."

This type of politics played out in the moral register is not conducive to the creation of the "agonistic public sphere" which I have argued is necessary for a robust democratic life. When the opponent is defined in moral rather than political terms, he cannot be envisioned as an adversary but only as an enemy. With the "evil them," no agonistic debate is possible – they must simply be eradicated. They are usually conceived as the expression of a moral plague, therefore it is not necessary to try to understand the reasons for their existence. This is why moral condemnation often replaces a proper political analysis, and solutions are limited to the building of a "cordon sanitaire" to quarantine the affected sectors.

It is ironic that, in the end, the political theory that claims the friend/enemy model of politics has been superseded contributes to the revitalization of the antagonistic model of politics, but this time in a way not amenable to a transformation of antagonism into agonism. Rather than helping to construct a vibrant agonistic public sphere, thanks to which democracy can be kept alive and deepened, all those who proclaim the end of antagonism and the arrival of a consensual society might in fact be jeopardizing democracy by creating the conditions for the emergence of antagonisms that cannot be contained by democratic institutions.

V   I will end by addressing another issue that also concerns the way we should envision the conditions of a democratic public sphere. It is clear that we are today confronted with a set of problems that cannot be tackled at the level of the nation-state but only in a wider context. If we accept the theoretical perspective that I have been delineating here, however, it is evident that this wider context cannot be coextensive with the whole planet. Democratic governance requires the existence of units, *demoi*, where popular sovereignty can be exercised, and this entails boundaries. It is in my view a dangerous illusion to imagine the possibility of a cosmopolitan citizenship that would be based exclusively on an abstract idea of humanity. To establish the conditions for effective democratic self-governance, citizens need to belong to a *demos* where they can exercise their rights of citizenship and this would not be available to a cosmopolitan citizen. Of course, this does not mean that political units must be identical with the nation-state. There are very good reasons to argue in favor of the coexistence of smaller and larger units, according to diverse forms of belonging and the kinds of issues that need to be decided. So, globalization could be structured in terms of a "double regionalization": on one level, the formation of a number of regional unions of diverse nation-states like the European Union which would themselves be composed of subregions made up of parts of various nation-states. This would create the conditions for a new form of pluralism that would greatly enhance the capacities for popular participation at different levels.

In this respect, I find the diverse attempts to elaborate a new form of federalism particularly interesting. Here I have in mind several proposals made by Massimo Cacciari, the former mayor of Venice, who calls for a Copernican revolution that would radically deconstruct the centralist-authoritarian-bureaucratic apparatus of the traditional nation-state.[6] According to Cacciari, the modern state is being torn apart as a consequence of two movements, one micro-national, the other supranational: on the one hand, from the inside, under the pressure of regionalist or tribalist movements; on the other hand, from the outside, as a consequence of the growth of supranational powers and institutions and of the increasing power of world finance and transnational corporations. Cacciari proposes federalism as the answer to such a situation. But his is a very special type of federalism which he calls federalism "from the bottom," as opposed to federalism "from the top," the type proposed as a model for the European Union. This federalism from the bottom would recognize the specific identity of different regions, of different cities, not to isolate them, to separate them from each other, but, on the contrary, in order to establish the conditions of an autonomy conceived and organized on the basis of multiple relations of exchange between those regions and those cities. Such a federalism would combine solidarity and competition, it would constitute a form of autonomy exercised in systems that are integrated in a conflictual mode.

6 Some of these ideas can be found in an interview with Massimo Cacciari, "The Philosopher Politician of Venice," *Soundings*, no. 17 (Spring 2001).

Such ideas, of course, require further development, but I find them very suggestive. If our project is to contest the imposition of a single, homogenizing model of society and the parallel decline of democratic institutions – both consequences of neoliberal globalization – it is urgent that we imagine new forms of association in which pluralism would flourish and where the capacities for democratic decision making would be enhanced. Against the antipolitical illusions of a cosmopolitan world-governance, and against the sterile and doomed fixation on the nation-state, I believe that the type of federalism advocated by Cacciari provides promising insights. By allowing us to envision new forms of solidarity based on recognized interdependence, it might constitute one of the central ideas around which democratic forces could organize in a plurality of democratic public spheres. This would breathe life into the agonistic struggle which, as I have argued, is the defining characteristic of democratic politics. Moreover, this new federalism should not be seen as being specific to Europe – it could stimulate the development of other regional units with their specific identities, units in which the global and the local could be articulated in many different ways and in which diverse types of links could be established within a context that respects differences. This would allow us, not to finish the democratic process – which by nature must remain open and therefore "unfinished" – but to keep it alive and to envision how it could be deepened in a radical democratic direction.

Democracy, Capitalism, and Transformation

Immanuel Wallerstein

I. Democracy and the World-System Up to Now   Democracy has become everyone's slogan today. Who does not claim that democracy is a good thing, and which politician does not assert that the government of which he is a part practices it and/or the party that he represents wishes to maintain and extend it? It is hard to remember that not so very long ago, in the period from the French Revolution up to 1848 at least, "democracy" was a word used only by dangerous radicals.[1] "Democrat" was the label of multiple extreme left organizations in the 1830s and 1840s.[2] For the powers that were in the period of the Holy Alliance, to accuse someone of being a democrat was a bit like accusing someone in the post-1945 Western world of being a communist.

When, after 1848, Giuseppe Mazzini (who called himself a democrat) fell into a major quarrel with the socialists, the latter added the term *social* to their slogan; they talked of being "for a universal democratic and social republic."[3] This is probably the origin of the later name Social-Democrats, the distinction now being deemed necessary because "democrat" alone no longer denoted radical, having been appropriated by others as well whose politics were more

---

1 See the discussion of "democracy" as a talismanic word to rally the revolutionary Left in James H. Billington, *Fire in the Minds of Men: Origins of the Revolutionary Faith* (New York: Basic Books, 1980), pp. 244–246, which describes the evolution of such revolutionary language from "democracy" to "communism" in the period 1789–1848.

2 Most of these groups were ephemeral and small, but see the names they chose: Democratic Friends of All Nations, Fraternal Democrats, Association Démocratique, Comité Central Démocratique Européen. See also the names of journals: *Demokratisches Taschenbuch für das Deutsche Volk*; *Le Débat social, organe de la démocratie*. When, in England, a group seceded from the Working Men's Association in 1837 because it was too peaceable, they called themselves the Democratic Association. See Arthur Lehning, *The International Association, 1855–1859: A Contribution to the Preliminary History of the First International* (Leiden: E.J. Brill, 1938), pp. 4, 11–18.

As late as 1872, Fustel de Coulanges, whose politics were conservative but republican, was accounting for the origins of the Second Empire in this way: "If the republicans who had just chased Louis-Philippe [from his throne] hadn't naively also been democrats and not instituted universal suffrage, it is extremely likely that the Republic would have continued to exist in France these past 24 years." "Considérations sur la France," in François Hartog, *Le XIXe siècle et l'histoire: Le cas Fustel de Coulanges* (Paris: Presses Universitaires de France, 1988), p. 238.

3 See Lehning, *The International Association*, pp. 24–25 and Appendix X, pp. 90–96.

centrist. It would take another half-century at least before conservatives also appropriated the word.

Of course, as we know, it all depends on the content we put into a word, any word. One possible usage of "democracy," one widespread definition today, is freedom from arbitrary political power. In this definition, democracy is more or less the realization of an individualist liberal political agenda. Its outward measures become whether or not there are free elections in which multiple parties contend, whether or not there exist communications media not under the direct political control of the government, whether or not one can pursue one's religious faith without state interference – in short, the degree to which all those things that are usually summarized as "civil liberties" are in fact practiced within the bounds of a particular state.

Using this definition, the historical development of democracy tends to be described as having followed a linear curve. The usual theoretical model starts implicitly with the moment of an "absolute monarch" or its equivalent. Wresting decision making away from the chief executive, or at least forcing him to share his powers with an elected legislature, is part of the story. Limiting the degree to which the state is permitted to intrude in the so-called private arena is another part of the story. Ensuring that critics are neither silenced nor punished is still another part. Employing these criteria, we find that the picture seems to be brightest today in the pan-European world (Western Europe, North America, Australasia) and less good (to quite varying degrees) elsewhere in the world. One part of the furor raised by the inclusion of Jörg Haider's party in the Austrian government was the fear that Austria would begin to look less good on this kind of scorecard.[4] When today Western politicians talk about how democratic a particular country is, this is usually how they are measuring it. Indeed, the US government annually issues formal scorecards of other governments using precisely such criteria.

To be sure, civil liberties are important. And we know exactly how important whenever they are seriously constricted. Under regimes that constrict civil liberties, which we usually label "dictatorships," there is always a certain amount of resistance, particularly by persons who wish to speak out publicly (intellectuals, journalists, politicians, students), an opposition which may be deeply underground if the repression is sufficiently severe. When for whatever reason the regime becomes weaker, and is somehow overthrown, one of the things that

---

4 This is of course only part of the story concerning Jörg Haider. See my lecture from March 9, 2000, delivered in Vienna, on "The Racist Albatross: Social Science, Jörg Haider, and *Widerstand.*" A slightly abbreviated version of the talk appeared in the *London Review of Books* 22, no. 10 (May 2000), pp. 11–14. The complete version is forthcoming.

people tend to celebrate is the end of such kind of repression. So we know that such civil liberties are valued, appreciated, and utilized when and where they exist.

But we also know that, for the average person, while civil liberties are seen as desirable, they are seldom at the top of his/her political agenda. And in those states in which a regime largely respects civil liberties, these liberties seldom seem to be enough to fulfill the average person's sense of what should define a democratic society. If they were, we would not have so much political indifference and so much political abstention. When we look at the so-called liberal states, those with relatively high levels of civil liberties, we discover a whole series of other issues which are of concern to most people, give rise to their complaints, and inflect their political priorities.

The complaints, it seems to me, can be grouped in three major categories: complaints about corruption; complaints about material inequalities; complaints about the inadequate inclusiveness of citizenship. Let us start with corruption. There is an incredible amount of cynicism on this subject, as well there might be. It would be hard to name a single government in the world in the last hundred years that has not known one, several, many corruption scandals. Of course, here again, it is a bit a matter of definition. If we mean by corruption the private purchase of the services/decisions of a public figure (politician or civil servant), this of course occurs all the time, often in the form of "kickbacks" from government contracts. This is possibly more frequent in poorer countries, or more frequently reported. In the case of the poorer countries, the corrupters are quite often noncitizens, persons from wealthier states, both capitalists and representatives of other governments. However, overt bribery is the least of the story.

A much more fundamental issue is the degree to which money buys access. This kind of corruption is pervasive in the operations of the regimes of the wealthier states (precisely those with the better records on civil liberties). Politics in a multiparty system is an expensive game to conduct, and it is getting more expensive all the time. Most politicians, most political parties have financial needs that go far beyond what can be supplied by the relatively small contributions of the mass of their supporters. We all know what happens as a result. Wealthier contributors (individuals and corporate groups) offer large sums of money, sometimes to multiple competing parties at the same time. And in return, they expect a certain amount of tacit sympathy for their needs and explicit access for their lobbying.

In theory, capitalists operate via the market and wish governments to stay out of market operations. In practice, as every capitalist knows, the governments are crucial to their market success in multiple ways – by making possible or impossible relative monopolies, in being large-scale near-monopsonistic purchasers of expensive items, as manipulators of macroeconomic decisions (including, of course, taxation). No serious capitalist can afford to ignore governments, his own and those of any other country in which he operates. But given that politicians must give priority to getting into power or remaining in power, and have great financial needs, no serious capitalist can afford to ignore this obvious source of pressure on governments, or he will lose out to competitors or to hostile interests. Therefore no serious capitalist does ignore governments, and all serious capitalists have in the forefront of their consciousness the fact that politicians have great financial needs. Consequently, corruption is absolutely normal and unexpungeable from the ongoing political life of the capitalist world-economy.

Still, corruption is not merely illegal; it is against the norms, regularly proclaimed, of honest government and a neutral bureaucracy. When a major norm is violated daily, the only possible result is widespread cynicism. And that is what we have. Of course, cynicism can lead to quite different responses. One response is to get our guys in there. Another is to wage battle to limit the damage of corruption. A third is to withdraw from active participation in politics. Each response has its limitations. The problem with "getting our guys in there" is that it seldom changes the gap between norm and reality. The problem with seeking to limit the damage is that it is so difficult to do, so nearly impossible, that it often seems not worth the trouble to try. And this leads more and more people to opt for the third response, withdrawal, which leaves the corrupt to reign undisturbed.

Another possibility, however, is to redefine what one means by democracy, enlarging on it, and insisting on substantive results in addition to mere electoral process. The electoral process of course has known an important evolution in the last two centuries. We have arrived, in virtually every state, at a norm of universal adult suffrage. Considering where the world was 200 years ago, this is a major structural change. And as we have already noted, this is regularly celebrated as the advent of democracy. If we look at the history of the expansion of suffrage,[5] we see immediately that it was always the result of a political struggle. And we see also that the widening of suffrage tended to be a concession by those in power to movements conducted by those who lacked the suffrage.

The principal debate among those who controlled the political machinery whenever such a widening of the suffrage was discussed was always one between

---

5 See, for example, the work of Stein Rokkan, including the article on suffrage extension, "Electoral Systems," in *Citizens, Elections, Parties: Approaches to the Comparative Study of the Processes of Development* (Oslo: Universitetsforlaget, 1970), pp. 147–168; also published in *International Encyclopedia of the Social Sciences*, ed. David L. Sills (New York: Macmillan, 1968), vol. 5, pp. 6–21.

the fearful (who paraded as the tough-minded) and the sophisticated. The fearful were those who argued that allowing wider access to the suffrage would result in significantly negative changes in the control of the state machinery, putting political power in the hands of persons who would undo the existing social system. This was the theme of the "unwashed masses" threatening to displace persons of social substance. The sophisticated were those who argued that, on the contrary, once they were accorded the suffrage, the "dangerous classes" would become, by the very fact of their nominal inclusion in the political process, less dangerous, and the dreaded political changes would not occur or would turn out to be minor.

The incremental concessions advocated by the sophisticated were eventually widely adopted, and the sophisticates turned out to be correct indeed in their anticipations that a widened suffrage would not lead to overturning the system. On the contrary, the concessions did precisely seem to undo the revolutionary inclinations of the unwashed masses. But of course, this is in part because the concessions went beyond those of the suffrage alone. The second set of concessions are those we call generically the "welfare state." If we define this loosely as all state action that supported and made possible increases in wage levels plus the use of the state for a certain amount of redistribution of the global surplus, then we have had the welfare state to some degree for over a century and virtually across the world (though to very different degrees).

Actually, we can divide the welfare state redistributive benefits into three principal categories, the response to three kinds of fundamental demands that average persons have put upon the states. The categories are health, education, and lifetime income. Virtually all people wish to prolong life and good health to the extent possible, for themselves and their families. Virtually all people wish to arrange education for themselves and their children, primarily in order to improve their life chances. And almost all people worry about the irregularities of real income over their lifetime and wish not merely to increase their current income but to minimize sharp fluctuations. These are all perfectly reasonable aspirations. And they have been regularly reflected in ongoing political programs.

Actually, quite a bit has been done along these lines over the past 200 years. In the field of health, we have had governments active in improving sanitation, in providing preventive medicine (such as, for example, mass vaccinations), subsidizing hospitals and clinics, expanding medical education, providing various kinds of health insurance (as well as certain kinds of free services). In the field of education, whereas 200 years ago virtually no one received a formal education, today primary education is available almost everywhere, secondary education is widespread (albeit unevenly), and even tertiary education is available for a significant number of people (at least in the wealthier states). As for guaranteed lifetime income, we have programs of unemployment insurance, old-age pensions, and various other methods of evening out fluctuations over the life span. To be sure, compared to health and education, programs to guarantee lifetime income are far more unevenly distributed across the world-system.

We should be careful how we evaluate these welfare state benefits. On the one hand, they constitute a remarkable structural difference with the situation of 200 years ago, where almost all such programs and mechanisms were unknown and politically inconceivable. On the other hand, these programs have benefited primarily that part of the world's population we might call the cadres of the system, or the middle strata. Such middle strata are not, it is important to note, evenly distributed across the world-system. In a Third World country, at most 5 percent of the population might fall within such a category, whereas in the wealthiest states, perhaps 40–60 percent would.

Thus, looked at through the lens of national statistics, it is the case that in a minority of states the majority of the population is better off today than their putative ancestors were 200 years ago. At the same time, the polarization of the world-system has continued apace, not only between countries but within countries. Furthermore, this polarization is not merely relative, but for some portion of the world's population (difficult to measure but not too difficult to observe) the polarization is absolute.

And yet, while the redistributive effects of the welfare state have been far less good than we are wont to believe, or that the propagandists of the world-system constantly tell us, it is simultaneously true that the cost of such redistribution as there has been is considerable and is reflected in the relatively high tax rates of the wealthier countries. Those who are taxed perpetually complain that it is too much. But it is true that the tax bill is far higher today than 50, 100, 200 years ago – both for the upper and middle strata of the world's population and for capitalist enterprises.

To be sure, there are advantages to capitalists in this redistribution, since it increases effective demand. But it is not at all certain that the increased effective demand is greater than the tax bite, as measured over the long run. And this is true for one simple reason. Politically, the popular demand for democratization has translated into an unceasingly upward curve in the level of demand for redistribution, spreading not only upward within countries, but also outward to more and more countries and therefore upward within the world-system as a whole.

Now this kind of democratization is less popular with capitalists in general than are civil liberties, and the struggle to limit redistribution, to reverse the pattern and reduce the rate to the degree possible, is the bread and butter of conservative political programs. I have no doubt that, repeatedly, conservative forces win victories that enable them to stem the increase in or even reduce the levels of redistribution. But if one regards the picture over some 200 years, it seems clear to me that taxation has followed an upward ratchet. Each reversal has been small compared to the next advance. The neoliberal offensive of the 1980s (Thatcherism-Reaganism) and the globalization rhetoric of the 1990s have been just such an effort to stem the increase. This effort has achieved something, but far less than its proponents had hoped, and the political reaction has already set in across the globe.

Let me now introduce the third set of complaints, that about the inadequate inclusiveness of citizenship. The term *citizen* we know is one thrust upon the world's political vocabulary by the French Revolution. The concept was intended to symbolize the refusal of a system of orders, in which nobility and commoners had different social rank and different political rights. The intent was one of inclusion. Commoners as well as nobility were to be included in the political process. All persons, that is, all citizens, were to be equal. All citizens had rights.

The problem is posed immediately in what is to be included in the "rights" of citizens. Various attempts to have these rights defined very extensively at one fell swoop were beaten back by "counter-revolutions." But there has been a slow extension over the past 200 years, which has accelerated particularly in the last 50 years. One element was the extension of the suffrage, expanding from the propertied to the nonpropertied, from older to younger persons, from men to women, from the core ethnic group to so-called minorities. A second front was the struggle against slavery and then against other forms of servitude. A third front has been the effort to end formal discriminations, by eliminating them from state practices and forbidding them in private practices. Today, we have a long list of sources of discrimination which have become socially illegitimate: class, race, ethnicity, "indigenicity," gender, age, sexuality, disability. And this list is constantly being augmented.

One should point to one last level of complaint about democracy. It is the complaint that we are theoretically limited to complaining about, and doing something about, the amount of democracy in the countries of which we are citizens. There have always been persons who have been solidary with movements in other countries for social justice or for citizenship rights or for national liberation. There have been cosmopolitan individuals who have gone off to other countries to be active in their struggles, including their revolutions. But states have been constrained and have constrained themselves on the principle of reciprocal recognition of sovereignty.

In the 19th century, the reciprocal recognition of sovereignty was accorded only to states considered part of the interstate system, which were defined as "civilized" states. Other zones of the globe that were not considered "civilized" were subject to the self-proclaimed right of the "civilized" states to engage in a "civilizing mission," which involved conquest, administration, and forcible transformation of certain customs. In the heyday of imperialism, in the late 19th century, the term *imperialism* was a word of honor, at least in the countries in which it formed the basis of their policies.

The attitude toward the legitimacy of imperialism changed after World War II. Suddenly, it became a negative word. And we entered the era of the national liberation movements which proceeded to achieve success more or less everywhere in the post-1945 period in their primary aim – local sovereignty for their states. As soon as this occurred, however, a new movement arose, largely in the Western world, in favor of "human rights," which were defined as the various kinds of democratic rights of which we have been speaking, from civil liberties to citizenship rights.

Organizations outside the accused countries were founded, which tried to create political pressure, directly upon the governments of the states defined as having inadequate human rights and indirectly via the governments of the states in which these human rights organizations were located. Pressure could take many forms – publicity, boycotts, and ultimately "the right to intervene." The recent activities of the NATO states in the Balkans have all been conducted under the rubric of "human rights" and the "right to intervene."

So where are we in this discourse about democracy? Is it a reality, a mirage, something in-between? Is it realizable, but not yet realized, as the organizers of this forum seem to suggest in the way they have formulated the question? The apologists of incremental advance assert that much has been accomplished. The spokespersons for the multiple groups that have come into existence to struggle for greater democracy argue, for the most part, that the goal of equal rights is nowhere near to being realized. I think that, if we are to speak to these dissonant evaluations, and in the light of the historical realities I have summarized, we must go over the ground a second time, a bit more analytically, dividing our assessment into three categories: democracy as rhetoric; democracy as practice; democracy as possibility.

II. Democracy as Rhetoric   Why did the term *democracy* evolve from being the expression of revolutionary aspiration to a universal platitude? Originally, in Western political philosophy, from the Greeks through the 18th century, democracy had always been taken to mean what its Greek roots indicate, the rule of the people – that is, the rule of the people as opposed not only to the rule of one person but even more to the rule of the *best* people, aristocracy. So democracy was first of all a quantitative concept. It implied the call for equality in a basically inegalitarian situation, since if there were "best" people, then there must have been "less good" people – ignorant, unwashed, crude, poor.

Who the best people are does not really matter. They have been defined in terms of blood/descent/formal attributions. They have been defined in terms of wealth/property/economic managerial role. They have been defined in terms of education/intelligence/complex skills. And all of these modes of classifying the best have always been accompanied by assumptions that manners/style of life/being "civilized" is a characteristic of the best people. The crucial element has always been to distinguish between two groups, those defined as having the capacity to participate in the process of collective decisions and those said to be without this capacity. Democracy as an idea, as a movement, was originally intended to refuse such a distinction as the basis of organizing political life.

There was never really any important debate on this issue. Indeed, there could not have been one, until the time that the concept of "citizenship" became current in ordinary political discourse. And this cultural shift is the great rhetorical legacy of the French Revolution. We are all citizens now.

Or are we? The basic discussion about the implications of the concept of citizenship took place at two successive moments in time. In the beginning of the 19th century, it took the form of an internal national debate in Great Britain, France, the United States, and a few other countries, centering on the issue of the suffrage.[6] The basic choice was between propertied suffrage, what the French called *suffrage censitaire*, and universal suffrage. We know that eventually, in these countries and then elsewhere, universal suffrage won out; furthermore, what was included in the term *universal* was steadily expanded.

But once the principle of universal suffrage became accepted (even if not fully implemented), the debate shifted location. As suffrage became wider in Western countries (and other elements of civil liberties became more widespread as well in these same countries), the term *citizen* became more legitimate in these countries and was utilized to fulfill its inclusive intention. However, the concept of citizen always excludes every bit as much as it includes. For citizen necessarily implies noncitizen. If the dangerous classes are no longer dangerous, if the uncivilized working classes are now accepted as citizens, then the rhetori-

---

6 See Stuart Woolf on the distinction between nation and people in Enlightenment thought as it informed the thinking of the Napoleonic era: "The 'nation' was understood in a restrictive manner, as the 'educated' or, slightly more broadly, the ruling elites. ... Enlightenment writers always made a sharp distinction between the educated, to whom their message was directed, and 'the most numerous and useful part of the nation.' The 'people,' by definition not depraved but easily influenced, required a moral, technical (and physical) education appropriate for their status, that best equipped them for the life of a laborer." "French Civilization and Ethnicity in the Napoleonic Empire," *Past and Present*, no. 124 (August 1989), p. 106.

cal line between civilized and uncivilized shifts to being one between civilized countries and uncivilized countries. This would then become the chief rhetorical justification of imperial rule, and the rhetorical basis of demanding and obtaining working-class participation in the glories of the civilizing mission.

At this point, "democracy" was no longer being used as a term to express the demands of the understrata in a national class struggle but rather as a term that was justifying the policies of the dominant forces in a world struggle between the so-called civilized and the noncivilized, between the West and the rest. Thus, because the resonance of the concept of democracy had changed, the very groups which dreaded the word in the first half of the 19th century came to adopt it by the end of the century and were using it as their theme song by the second half of the 20th century. At this point, the concept of democracy became primarily a symbol of, a consequence of, a proof of civilization. The West is democratic; the rest are not. The hegemonic forces in the world-economy proclaim themselves thereby the moral leaders. Their hegemony is the basis of progress throughout the world. They offer democracy as a Holy Grail. They therefore incarnate virtue.

III. Democracy as Realization   The new rhetoric would not have worked if there were not some empirical bases to these claims. What were they? To appreciate this, we have to reflect on the fundamental difference between a capitalist and a precapitalist system in terms of social stratification. In a precapitalist structure, the upper stratum holds power because it controls the means of violence. It thereby lays claim to a disproportionate share of the wealth. Those who acquire wealth otherwise than by military appropriation, say via the market, are not defined as part of the upper stratum and therefore live in the eternal fear of confiscation. They seek to avoid this fate by buying their way into the aristocracy, which took time – sometimes as much as four generations – to complete.

The capitalist world-economy is just as deeply stratified as the precapitalist systems, but the relations of the strata are different. The upper stratum holds its rank not because of its past military prowess but because of its past economic prowess. Those who are not at the top but have skills, those we are calling the cadres or middle strata of the system, are not living in fear of confiscation. On the contrary, they are in effect being constantly solicited and appeased by the upper strata, who need their assistance to maintain the political equilibrium of the overall world-system, that is, to hold in check the dangerous classes.

The extension of the suffrage, the benefits of the welfare state, the recognition of particularist identities, are all part of the program of appeasing these cadres, securing their loyalty to the overall system, and most of all obtaining their assistance in maintaining in their place the majority of the world's population. Let us think of the capitalist world-system as socially a tripartite system divided (symbolically) into 1 percent at the top, 19 percent who are cadres, and 80 percent at the bottom. Then let us add the spatial element to which we have already referred. Within the bounds of the singular system that is the capitalist world-economy, the 19 percent are not spread out evenly among all the political units, but rather concentrated in a few of them.

If we make these two assumptions – a tripartite stratification system, with geographical lumpiness – then it seems obvious that the slogan of "democracy" has had enormous meaning for the 19 percent, since it implies a real improvement in their political, economic, and social situation. But we can also see that it has had very little meaning for the 80 percent, since they have received very little of the presumed benefits, whether political, economic, or social. And the fact that a small group of countries has more wealth, and a more liberal state, and multiparty systems that function more or less – in short, the fact that a few countries are civilized – is not the cause but precisely the consequence of the deep inequalities in the world-system as a whole. And this is why the rhetoric rings true in some parts of the world-system and seems so hollow in other parts, the larger parts.

So, democracy unrealized? Of course. One doesn't even need to demonstrate, which can be done, that democracy, however defined, is constrained and limping even in the so-called liberal states. It is enough to note that it is not functioning to any significant degree at all in most of the world. When a Western leader preaches the virtues of democracy to a Third World state, and they do this quite regularly, he is being either willfully blind to the realities of the world-system or cynical in asserting his country's moral superiority. I am in no way defending or justifying the dictatorships of the world. Repression is not a virtue anywhere, not to speak of mass slaughters. It is simply to note that these phenomena are neither accidental, nor the result of the fact that certain countries have uncivilized cultures, nor certainly the result of the insufficient openness of such countries to the flows of capital. Two-thirds of the world do not have liberal states because of the structure of the capitalist world-economy which makes it impossible for them to have such political regimes.

IV. Democracy as Possibility   If democracy is thus quite unrealized in our contemporary world, is it realizable? There are two possible answers: "yes, by further increments"; and "no." There are no small number of people who say "yes, by further increments." The idea is that the benefits accorded to 19 percent could next be accorded to 21 percent and then to 25 percent and then and then. What is needed, say these people, is further organized pressure – by social movements, by NGOs, by enlightened intellectuals, or by the cultural reformation of the uncivilized peoples.

The major argument that such prognosticators have on their side is that this is how it has worked in the last 200 years, where the concessions we may call democratization have indeed been won by struggle, have indeed been won in increments. What this prognosis leaves out of account is the cumulative impact of the incremental change on the functioning of the system. The basic reason for concessions by persons of privilege to demands for democratization is to defuse the anger, to incorporate the rebellious, but always in order to save the basic framework of the system. This strategy incarnates the di Lampedusa principle that "everything must change in order that nothing change."

The di Lampedusa principle is a very efficacious one, up to a tipping point. Demands for further democratization, for further redistribution of the political, economic, and social pie, far from having exhausted themselves, are endless, even if only in increments. And the democratization of the past 200 years, even if it has benefited only my hypothetical 19 percent of the world population, has been costly to the 1 percent, and has consumed a noticeable portion of the pie. If the 19 percent were to become 29 percent, not to speak of their becoming 89 percent, there would be nothing left for the privileged. To be quite concrete, one could no longer have the ceaseless accumulation of capital, which is after all the *raison d'être* of the capitalist world-economy. So either a halt must be called to the democratization process, and this is politically difficult, or one has to move to some other kind of system in order to maintain the hierarchical, inegalitarian realities.

It is toward this kind of transformation that I believe we are heading today. I shall not repeat here my detailed analysis of all the factors that have led to what I think of as the structural crisis of the capitalist world-system. Democratization as a process is only one of the factors that have brought the system to its current chaotic state, and immanent bifurcation.[7] What I see, as a result, is an intense political struggle over the next 25 to 50 years about the successor structure to a capitalist world-economy. In my view, this is a struggle between those who want it to be a basically democratic system and those who do not want that. I am therefore somewhat unhappy about the suggestion of the organizers that democracy may be "an essentially unfinishable project." Such a formulation evokes the image of the tragic condition of humanity, its imperfections, its eternal improvability. And, of course, who can argue with such an imagery? But the

---

7 I have argued this in detail in various places in recent years. See *Utopistics, or Historical Choices for the Twenty-first Century* (New York: New Press, 1998).

formulation leaves out of account the possibility that there are moments of historic choice that can make an enormous difference. Eras of transition from one
historical social system to another are just such moments of historic choice.[8]

If we can never have a perfectly democratic system, I do believe it is possible
to have a largely democratic system. I do not believe we now have it. But we
could have it. So, it then becomes important to go back to the drawing board
and say what the struggle is about. It is not about civil liberties, although of
course a democratic society would have civil liberties to warm the cockles of
John Stuart Mill's heart. And it should have them. It is not about multiparty
systems, a technique of democratic large-scale choice that is only one of many
possible ones, and one not widely used in any arena today other than in national
and subnational periodic votings.

Democracy, it must be said, is about equality, which is the opposite of
racism, the pervasive sentiment of political life in the capitalist world-economy.
Without equality in all arenas of social life, there is no possible equality in any
arena of social life, only the mirage of it. Liberty does not exist where equality is
absent, since the powerful will always tend to prevail in an inegalitarian system.
This is why there are complaints about corruption, endemic to our system. This
is why there are complaints about the uneven realization of citizenship. This is
why there is cynicism. An egalitarian system might be relatively depoliticized
but it would not be cynical. Cynicism is the psychological defense of weakness
in the face of power.

Of course, the call for a system that combines relative equality with a relatively democratic politics raises the question, is it possible? The main argument
against the possibility is that it is historically unknown. This seems to me a very
weak argument. Human societies have existed for a very brief time when all is
said and done. We cannot begin to rule out the future on the basis of our short
historic past. In any case, the only conclusion one can draw from pessimism is
to give up the ghost. The second major argument against equality is the sorry
showing of the Leninist regimes. But, of course, these regimes were never egalitarian, at any point, although at early stages they pursued an egalitarian rhetoric
and may to some extent have believed in it. But their practice was deeply inegalitarian, a mere variant on other regimes in peripheral and semiperipheral zones
of the capitalist world-economy. Their experience tells us absolutely nothing
about the possibilities of an egalitarian social system.

The fundamental issue is that today, at this point in the evolving history of
the capitalist world-economy, further incrementalism is not a real choice. We

8 The argument is spelled out in Terence K. Hopkins and Immanuel Wallerstein, coords., *The Age of
Transition: Trajectory of the World-System, 1945–2025* (London: Zed Books, 1996).

have, it seems to me, reached its limits within the framework of our present historical social system. The system is in crisis and will inevitably change. But it will not necessarily change for the better. This is the political and moral choice of this era of transition. I do not believe there is any reason to assume the inevitability of progress, of political or moral progress. I believe, however, in the theory of possible progress.

What do we then need to do? First of all, we need to be clear about where we are and about the fact that we have choices, because the system is bifurcating and therefore ending. Secondly, we need debate among ourselves (the "us" being those who wish the successor system to be egalitarian) about what political tactics might offer us the possibility of creating such a system, and how one might construct the alliances that are necessary to achieve this. And thirdly, we need to avoid the siren songs of those who would create a new but still hierarchical and inegalitarian system under the aegis of something progressive. None of this is easy. And there is no assurance we can succeed. What we can be sure of is that those with privilege intend to retain it in one form or another, and will fight both fiercely and intelligently to do so.

So, democracy? I feel about it like Mahatma Gandhi, when asked what he thought of Western civilization. He replied, "I think it would be a good idea."

Dialectics of Sovereignty:
Justice, Minorities, Human Rights, Citizenship

Global Justice and the Failure of Deliberative Democracy

Upendra Baxi

Later in his life, Pablo Picasso would say that he had long tried to convince his public about the truth of his lies.

I read the Documenta11 endeavor as a precious opportunity to begin exploring the multiple truths of the singular lie of "democracy," that is, the lie that democracy constitutes self-governance, governance by, for, and of the people. Even if this may seem partially true of nation-societies, it is unlikely ever to be the case with a society of states. In what ways, then, may we speak of *global* "democracy" and "justice"?

Democracy "unrealized" is perhaps not the same sort of happening as may be described under the rubric democracy "betrayed." Either way, although the differences in these two ways of expressing the situation do matter, I am not sure that it is anything but bad news for the deprived, dispossessed, and disadvantaged peoples of the world. The number and generations of such people, and the intensity of their suffering, provide a rough indicator of the state of the world, regardless of the appellation democracy "unrealized" or "betrayed."

I must confess that I have begun this discourse already rather badly, though not for want of good faith. I have used two terms – *suffering* and *peoples* – that, for a variety of reasons, do not characterize the discourse of democracy or the approaches to global justice.

Notions of social/human suffering are rarely foregrounded in the discourse on deliberative democracy. Perhaps Richard Rorty is not too far wrong in suggesting that literature (in particular, fiction) rather than high democratic theory is more attuned to the reality of suffering.[1] Theological discourse inaugurated by a Gautama Buddha or a Thomas Aquinas, I believe, provides an even more munificent source of meditation on the sufferings of the just because it encourages reflection on the contradiction between piety and justice; the resulting

---

1 Richard Rorty, "Human Rights, Rationality, and Sentimentality," in *On Human Rights: The Oxford Amnesty Lectures*, ed. Stephen Shute and Susan Hurley (New York: Basic Books, 1993), p. 133.

"argument from evil" is empowering for its interlocution of the ways of the Divine, with tremendous spillover effect on the legitimacy claims of mere earthly power. The questioning of the injustice of gods raised in the discourse on theodicy remains an important resource for envisioning better human futures under the conditions, circumstances, and conjunctures of humanly ordained sovereign power and resistance. But this is a theme beyond the bounds of my current agendum.

I do not wish to suggest that contemporary forms of discourse on deliberative democracy altogether ignore the fact of human/social suffering, or its causative structures. I do wish to suggest that the discourse remains, on the whole, sanitized and bloodless. Even when concerned with catastrophic practices of cruelty, representations of terror and violence, in the main, provide adornments for the domain of high political theory. On these registers, human/social suffering features abstractly as a question of justifications for inequalities or for the universality of human rights. The voices of human suffering, the power of lamentation of the violated, their creative critiques of global domination, and ways to transcend these, do not simply emerge in this discursivity.[2] When the figure of human/social suffering emerges, it ultimately does so in discursively instrumental ways. One often feels, with Ulrich in *The Man without Qualities*, that all "that finally remains is formulas. What they mean in human terms is hard to say; that is all there is."[3]

The question always is: whether a fuller advertence to the voices of human suffering enables any different kind of theorizing concerning democracy or justice. Is the Rawlsian difference principle just a formula, devoid of "meaning in human terms"? Would taking suffering seriously produce a new episteme for the production of knowledges concerning "democracy" and justice in ways that generate an ethic of fiduciary thinking oriented toward the transformation of structural causes of global injustice and human violation? Epistemic theories concerning democracy are not conative; they do not carry – unfortunately for the suffering humanity – any obligations for thinkers to intervene, so as to enact their beliefs concerning justice in real-life situations. The theoretic hope, at its very best, lies in the potential for construction of realistic utopias, in spite of the

---

2 The "voices" of suffering, we must recall, remains a thriving genre in official discourse of development assistance. But much of this literature is singularly appropriative. Thomas W. Pogge trenchantly observes: "The Bank recently interviewed sixty thousand poor people in the developing countries and published snippets of their responses, 'Voices of the Poor,' on its Web site ... the same World Bank also keeps the number of poor in check by quietly lowering the international poverty line." See his "Priorities of Global Justice," *Metaphilosophy* 32, no. 1–2 (January 2001), pp. 6–24, reprinted in *Global Justice*, ed. Thomas W. Pogge (Oxford: Blackwell, 2001).

3 Robert Musil, *The Man without Qualities*, trans. Eithne Wilkins and Ernst Kaiser (London: Mandarin Paperbacks, 1995), p. 65.

persistence of "dreadful evils" and the "demonic possibility" of Holocaustian political practices.⁴ This hope is also at the same time a repository of human hazards for peoples living under actually existing theories about "democracy," "rule of law," and "good governance." One has only to revisit the recent histories of the Cold War and of contemporary globalization to grasp the problem of the social costs (in terms of hurt and harm, sorrow and suffering caused to peoples) incurred by some performances of "democratic" theorizing.⁵

The very conception of "people" or "peoples" has become increasingly problematic. In these postmodern times, we now ask: Do "peoples" exist as such? Do they exist as amorphous "multitudes"?⁶ And, if so, when under the contexts of doing high theory do they somehow aggregate into "humankind"? Is the concept "peoples of the world" viable or useful? What then follows? Are there classes/clusters of people, some of whom may be said to owe duties to past and future generations? Do present generations owe duties of reparation, rehabilitation, and restitution to those whom previous generations so severely, and so savagely, colonized? If so, how may one conceptualize the "contemporaneity of the non-contemporaneous"? What ethic may, indeed, justify the imposition of these duties on successor noncomplicit generations? Is the category "peoples" so radically heterogeneous as to forfeit all claims to any sensible acts of global justice theorizing? Does the notion of being "citizens of the world," divided as it is into so many orders of sovereignty, make any sense? These are not idle questions, as anyone, for example, concerned with issues of self-determination or the definitional movement in the Draft Declarations of the Human Rights of Indigenous Peoples surely knows.

What is poignant about our times/spaces of understanding is the fact that at a historic moment when the notion of "peoples" has become at last more inclusive, it has also lost its vibrancy and vitality. Hostile discrimination in state and civil society manifested in violent social exclusion (whether on the basis of race, descent, caste, gender, religion, attributes of physical/psychic impairment or disability, and sexual orientation) stands delegitimated by the endless explosion of

---

4 John Rawls, *The Law of Peoples* (Cambridge, Mass.: Harvard University Press, 1999), p. 21.
5 I translate here Thomas W. Pogge's indictment of international theory and practice of development in terms of these costs. Pogge reminds us that "Severe poverty is by far the greatest source of human misery today ... the few years since the end of the Cold War has seen over 200 million deaths due to poverty related causes." He directs our attention to the ways in which policy and mainstream political theory (barring a handful of exceptions) remains complicit: "our failure to make a serious effort toward poverty reduction may constitute not merely a lack of beneficence, but our active impoverishing, starving, and killing of millions of innocent people by economic means" (Pogge, "Priorities of Global Justice," p. 14).
6 See Michael Hardt and Antonio Negri, *Empire* (Cambridge, Mass.: Harvard University Press, 2000).

normatively human rights[7] and the fecund notion of crimes against humanity.[8] This represents, to be sure, an enormous advance in the global moral sentiment. But does it at the same time mark the advent of even an emerging global ethics of interstate relations and movements of human solidarity across the world, an ethics that marks the rejection of what Emmanuel Levinas called the "traumatism of the Other"?[9]

At the same time, practices of global and national politics – even in Euro-American states and societies, but surely not only there – as well as normative theories about deliberative democracy, result in a deep suspicion of the very notion of "peoples." The discourse on *Volksgeist* becomes catastrophic with the emergence of Holocaustian forms of politics. The replication of these forms in the postcolonial and now postsocialist killing fields makes the notion ethically suspect. No doubt, the practices of catastrophic cruelty in the many phases of the Cold War led to a deepening of this theoretical suspicion. Contemporary economic globalization has rendered obsolete/incomprehensible the languages that described, in complex and contradictory modes, the division of peoples into "classes" and "masses" that so decisively guided political destinies of the "people" just a few decades ago. What we do understand are statistical notions of "population," "persons," "citizens," "migrants," "asylum seekers," and the languages of "interpellation" and the various modes of the constitution of "subject-positions." We also understand the languages of critical race and feminist theories that situate the self very differently from, if I may so name these, the "classical" conceptualizations of "peoples."

The moral universe animating approaches to global justice, whether liberal or cosmopolitan, is "peopled," as it were, by individuals or citizens endowed with ethical visions of social cooperation that provide, as it were, a philosophical insurance cover against predation and underwrite the justice of the basic structures of human societies, national and emergently global. It is in this context that one acclaims John Rawls' recent valiant moral endeavor at the rehabilitation of the notion of the law of peoples.[10] In the standard discourse on global justice, however, "peoples" stand reconfigured along the axis of the ethic of duties of care owed to co-nationals as against, or at least very differentially, the nonnationals. Indeed, much contemporary discourse concerning global justice remains insensible outside the arc of this distinction.

---

7 See Upendra Baxi, *The Future of Human Rights* (New Delhi: Oxford University Press, 2002).
8 See Geoffrey Robertson, *Crimes Against Humanity: The Struggle for Global Justice* (London: Penguin, 2000).
9 See Jacques Derrida, *Adieu to Emmanuel Levinas*, trans. Pascale-Anne Brault and Michael Naas (Stanford: Stanford University Press, 1999), p. 11.
10 See Rawls, *The Law of Peoples*.

Anticipations of Justice in International Law; or, What We Might Mean by Global Justice Having thus begun in the middle, that uneasy space that defies the canons and marks the place between "beginning" and "end," allow me to plunge into perhaps the only space that remains sensible to begin "unpacking" these dense and somewhat polemical observations – namely, that "middle," innocent as yet of the "beginning" and "end," furnished by some contemporary approaches to "global justice."

But this task entails attention to some of the following issues: Is the concern with global justice unique to the moral and political theory of Western liberalism? Or does it have a prehistory? How far back in antiquity may we go in tracing the emergence of approaches to global justice? And how do we periodize the different itineraries of ideas concerning global justice? In what ways does discourse concerning justice within nation-societies shape approaches to global justice? How were the spheres of global justice delineated? These and related questions are important; in what follows, I touch briefly upon a couple of issues.

The evolution of "classical" international law was marked by a concern for justice in relations among European, or "civilized," states. It sought to provide for conditions of peace and justice within the "civilized" community of nations, no matter at what exorbitance of costs to the "barbarians" and "savages." Its doctrines of "just war" provided a framework of justification for recourse to interstate aggression; the Grotian *temperamenta belli* spawned notions about just conduct of just war, forbidding disproportionate violence and constructing sharp lines between combatants and noncombatants. The normative history of international humanitarian law is, indeed, rich in its creation of standards of justice amidst the clash of arms. *Pacta sunt servanda* legislated an inner morality of international law of promissory relations. The doctrine of sovereign equality of states fostered some notions of egalitarian interstate relations. The Grotian doctrine of the freedom of the seas marked the beginning of the enunciation of international commons in ways that limited the arrogance of even imperial orders of sovereignty. The international law of peace concerned itself with the morality of civilized relations between states, especially felicitating conduct of international trade and commerce. The notion of *jus cogens* enacted norms of international law that marked the beginning of an enunciatory enterprise limiting powers of sovereignty; nations, free and equal, may not, even by agreement among themselves, seek to legitimate certain forms of human violation such as slavery. And (without being exhaustive) Vitoria's defense of the rights of indigenous peoples of the New World remains a fecund source of thinking about the rights to self-determination of the First Nations and human rights generally. Vitoria also embodies the power of ethical articulation, a power he deployed against the laws of treason against the Emperor and heresy against the Church.[11]

Contemporary discourse on global justice remains shy of acknowledging these classical enunciations of global justice. There are some good reasons for this, the foremost being the grounding of these enunciations in the tradition of Natural Law. The languages of Natural Law have long since become suspect, almost dying a "natural" death. Yet much that gets said today concerning global justice is indeed not far removed from the discursive tradition of secular natural law. "Classical" approaches to global justice, moreover, are regressively Eurocentric and deny equal human worth and dignity to "uncivilized"/"colonial" peoples. Indeed, they often justify a Divine Right to Empire. These furnish good reasons to handle with care the approaches to global justice developed by the founders of modern international law. I am not quite sure that these reasons are *sufficient* to justify wholesale rejection of the classical anticipations of global justice. I also believe that such a rejection may deprive us of an understanding of the moral architecture of interstate relations envisaged by earlier doctrines of the international law of peace and war and even prevent us, at times, from grasping continuities between classical and contemporary acts of theorizing global justice.

This last theme is, to my mind, of some importance. Were we to ask what distinguishes classical from contemporary approaches to global justice, it may be said fairly that while the former are *regressively* Eurocentric, the latter remain at best *progressively* Eurocentric. This, if the distinction were granted at all, constitutes indeed some considerable advance. But even progressive Eurocentrism does not acknowledge the ethical creativity of the non-Euro-American world.[12] It does not fully acknowledge the *creationist* power of theory and practice of the right to self-determination, the ways in which these exposed the poverty of moral justification for colonialism and imperialism. Nor do progressive Eurocentric approaches cognize the ways in which non-Euro-American peoples modified colonial liberal conceptions of rights in some basic ways.[13] For example, the Indian Constitution innovates, inaugurally for postcolonial constitutionalism, the liberal theory of rights by specifically recognizing that assurances of rights should avail against rights-violative civil society formations; it provides

11 But see Peter Fitzpatrick, *Modernism and the Grounds of Law* (Cambridge: Cambridge University Press, 2001), pp. 152–156.
12 See Baxi, *The Future of Human Rights*, pp. 22–27, and ibid., "Colonial Inheritance," in *Comparative Legal Studies: Traditions and Transitions*, ed. Pierre Legrand and Roderick Munday (Cambridge: Cambridge University Press, forthcoming 2002/2003).
13 See, for example, Satyaranjan P. Sathe, *Judicial Activism in India: Transgressing Borders and Enforcing Limits* (Delhi: Oxford University Press, 2000).

a mandate for amelioration, even elimination of rights-violative aspects of the majority Hindu religion; it innovates affirmative action programs not just in relation to education and public employment but in the composition of its federal and state legislatures. India's great constitution-maker, and thinker, Dr. B. R. Ambedkar, raised the most powerful critique of classical liberal theory of human rights.[14] Mahatma Gandhi's notion of *just* freedom, not just *freedom*, articulated the distinction between the exercise of freedom and predation; he insisted that only those forms of freedom may be just that can be exercised in ways nonthreatening and noninjurious to the Other; he provided a thoroughgoing communitarian critique of Western liberal forms of parliamentary democracy and emerged as a founder and forerunner of realistic utopias for a postindustrial society and world. One of the most lamentable features of current theorizing on deliberative democracy and global justice consists in cultivated ignorance concerning ways in which decolonizing nations enriched and extended human discourse.

Let alone at the level of history of ideas, this creativity in its concrete forms through global diplomacy does not find a mention. Contemporary discourse on global justice does not pause to consider the specific contributions of the Third World such as the notion of "the common heritage of humankind" (first developed in the context of the law of the sea conventions), the United Nations Declaration on Social Progress and on the Right of States and Peoples to Development, the Declaration on the New International Economic Order, and the struggle over a just World Information Order. These articulate alternate conceptions of global justice in ways that raise considerations of a modicum of equity in international economic relations.

I mention all of this to signal legitimate anxieties concerning the inherently inegalitarian ways of articulation of visions of global justice that deny the dignity of discourse to the Other of Euro-American thought. With this caveat, I now address the moral universe of some eminent articulators of visions of global justice.

The Second Original Position in the Construction of the Law of Peoples   An important way of constructing notions about global justice is to extrapolate the conceptual repertoire of doing theories of justice in nation-societies to international contexts. This is no doubt a complex and often daunting task, but one

---

14 See Upendra Baxi, "Justice as Emancipation: The Legacy of Babasaheb Ambedkar," in *Crisis and Change in Contemporary India*, ed. Upendra Baxi and Bhikhu Parekh (New Delhi: Sage, 1995), pp. 122–149.

that minimizes cognitive dissonance, the trauma of moving from singular ethical theory habitats to a pluriverse of conflicting conceptions of the good life and multiple positive and critical moralities. The epistemic economies of scale that such acts of theorizing yield are not to be ignored. At the same time, I suggest that we think of these endeavors as an ineluctable consequence of globalized knowledge production, that is, the universalization of the Euro-American habitus/doxa of doing moral and political philosophy. Let us first approach this transposition on its own terms.

Many attempts have been made to extend John Rawls' maxims of justice and prescriptions for a just basic structure of society to the international arena. Foremost among these are the pioneering works of Charles Beitz and Thomas Pogge.[15] Invoking an extension of the Rawlsian original situation to international society, Beitz proposed two major principles of global justice. The first, called "the resource distribution principle," addressed resource-impoverished societies in ways that suggest/impose distributive obligations on the resource-rich societies such that these provide "assurance to persons in resource-poor societies that their adverse fate will not prevent them from realizing economic conditions sufficient to support just social institutions and to protect human rights."[16] Crucial to this view is the moral insight that the "appropriation of scarce resources by some requires a justification against the competing claims of others."[17]

Beitz's second principle, called the "global distribution principle," extends the famous Rawlsian "difference principle" to the community of nations. A global difference principle ought to exist in a now globalizing society, with its highly complex divisions of labor in an international post-Fordist system of production. On this version, global inequalities are just only insofar as they work to the advantage of the worst-off peoples. For reasons of space, I do not address here Pogge's broadly similar conclusion animating a proposal for a Global Resource Tax;[18] nor do I address Martha Nussbaum's "capability thesis,"[19] which entails an important notion that all citizens of the world are entitled to the free and equal exercise of their basic capabilities.

15 Charles R. Beitz, *Political Theory and International Relations* (Princeton, N.J.: Princeton University Press, 1979); Thomas W. Pogge, "An Egalitarian View of Peoples," *Philosophy and Public Affairs* 23, no. 3 (1994), pp. 195–224.

16 Beitz, *Political Theory and International Relations*, p. 141.

17 Ibid., p. 140.

18 For a recent critique, see Hillel Steiner, "Just Taxation and International Redistribution," in *Global Justice*, ed. Ian Shapiro and Lea Brilmayer (New York: New York University Press, 1999), pp. 171–191.

19 Martha C. Nussbaum, "Capabilities, Human Rights, and the Universal Declaration," in *The Future of International Human Rights*, ed. Burns H. Weston and Stephen P. Marks (Ardsley, N.Y.: Transnational Publications, 1999), pp. 65–100; ibid., *Women and Human Development: A Capabilities Approach* (Cambridge: Cambridge University Press, 2000).

I am aware that ethical intuitionalism is never enough and, further, that any elaboration of these moral insights forever remains problematic. I ought however to point out that contemporary international law stances on sustainable human development and human rights do in fact concretize, even validate, these insights. For example: the Law of the Sea Convention (1982) takes special account of the resource-impoverished landlocked states, as does, in a vastly different context, the UNESCO Declaration on the Human Genome and Human Rights (1999), which asserts the immorality of privatizing for profit the results of various human genome projects. So do the working arrangements now in place following the Rio principles of sustainable development, or treaty regimes concerning peaceful uses of outer space and celestial objects. The inner morality of positive international law treaties and related enunciations of newly emergent human rights in the global commons seems to me to respect Beitz's crucial insights.

Beitz's (and Pogge's) principles and proposals are based on an extension of Rawls' original position in which rational individuals, under a veil of ignorance, arrive at a certain rational and reasonable consensus on specifically "fair terms of cooperation for regulating the basic structure of ... society."[20] In *The Law of Peoples*, Rawls constructs a second original position in which free and equal peoples, representing liberal societies, under a veil of ignorance, rationally and reasonably (for the right reasons) choose "ideals, principles, and standards"[21] for the law of peoples. What guides peoples in the second original position are "the fundamental interests of democratic societies, where these interests are expressed by the liberal principles of justice for a democratic society."[22] The actors in the second original position are liberal peoples possessed of a "moral nature," bound by "common sympathies," and living under a "reasonably just constitutional government that serves their fundamental interests."[23] The principles of justice, rights, and social cooperation that peoples form comprise the following assemblage: "1. Peoples are free and independent, and their freedom and independence are to be respected by other peoples. 2. Peoples are to observe treaties and understandings. 3. Peoples are equal and are parties to agreements that bind them. 4. Peoples are to observe a duty of non-intervention. 5. Peoples have a right to self-defense but no right to instigate war for reasons other than self-defense. 6. Peoples are to honor human rights. 7. Peoples are to observe certain specified restrictions in the conduct of war. 8. Peoples have a duty to assist other

20 Rawls, *The Law of Peoples*, p. 30.
21 Ibid., p. 40.
22 Ibid., pp. 32–33.
23 Ibid., pp. 23–24.

people living under unfavorable conditions that prevent their having a just or decent political regime."[24]

There is not a great deal to distinguish these principles from the standards already obtaining in positive international law. Indeed, the latter seem to be more liberal than Rawls' law of peoples would seem to allow; for example, he narrows the range of human rights to basic rights: the right to life (viewed as the right to the means of subsistence and security); to liberty (freedom from "slavery, serfdom, … forced occupation" and liberty of conscience "to ensure freedom of religion and thought"); to property ("personal property"); and to "formal equality as expressed by the minimal rules of natural justice."[25] His law of peoples thus reinvents human rights, at least from the perspectives of international human rights law and jurisprudence, or the "living law" of human rights.

On the other hand, the principles of the law of peoples reinvent human rights far beyond the international law norms summated in Principles 1, 4, and 5. Rawls suggests that peoples in the second original position would not "tolerate outlaw states" and would be justified in using force, if necessary, against these, for such states are "aggressive and dangerous; all peoples are safer and more secure if such states change, or are forced to change, their ways."[26] It must be noted that Rawls is here guided by a rather complex understanding of toleration, and the law of peoples prescribes active intoleration for the category "outlaw" state. Apparently, the law of peoples differs from positive international law in classifying the "political and social world" within which tasks of global justice have to be performed. There are

> five types of domestic societies: the first of these is *liberal peoples* and the second, *decent peoples*. The basic structure of one kind of decent people has … a "decent consultative hierarchy" and these people I call "decent hierarchical peoples"; the other kind of decent people is simply a category I leave in reserve. … In addition, there are, third, *outlaw states* and, fourth, *societies burdened by unfavorable conditions*. Finally, fifth, we have societies that are *benevolent absolutisms;* they honor most human rights, but because they deny their members a meaningful role in the making of political decisions, they are not well-ordered.[27]

Global justice, then, may not be conceived by the law of peoples on the horizontal formal principle of the sovereign equality of all states. The law of peo-

24 Ibid., p. 37.
25 Ibid., p. 65.
26 Ibid., p. 81.
27 Ibid., p. 63.

ples is the law of the society of peoples, well ordered and not so well ordered; liberal and not so liberal, well endowed and burdened by unfavorable circumstances.

I must say, though here only in passing, that I find worrisome and perplexing the constant shift from *people* to *states* and to *societies*. Clearly not equivalent, the relation among the three categories remains undifferentiated. The phenomenon of so-called puppet or vassal states, especially during the Cold War (but not only then), for example, raises intractable ethical questions concerning the rights of states as "political communities" and the rights of political communities within, and against, the "state"[28] that remain undifferentiated in the Rawlsian typology. It now adds to the burdens of ethical theory the problematic of the "outlaw" states/societies/peoples. *Are outlaw states also exemplars of outlaw peoples?* The moral difficulty thus posed is immense, as such equivalence will end up justifying the ethnocide of outlaw peoples! That difficulty scarcely vanishes when prescriptions of global justice are construed as to covertly endorse tyrannicide (recall the justificatory statements concerning attempts and designs of assassination directed against President Gadafi or Saddam Hussein). The difficulty with tyrannicide is that if states, or groups of states, are allowed this privilege, so must peoples. For that to happen in real life, the laws against treason and sedition would have to be characterized as inherently unjust and the acts themselves worthy of justifications available to forms of civil disobedience. Understandably, the Rawlsian presuppositions concerning global justice do not go this far!

Nor do I address here Rawlsian prescriptions concerning intolerance of "outlaw" states, especially his explication concerning the "well-ordered peoples' right to war,"[29] except to say that the ideal criteria constructed by Rawls to define outlawry – whether in terms of human rights or "meaningful participation" in governance – are scarcely an all-or-nothing type of attribute; outlaw configurations characterize all states and societies, even when they may be said to be, and in fact are, writ large on some pathologies of political power. This does not diminish the gravity of the situation everywhere, including especially the "well-ordered societies," in which the rule of law and reign of terror (or as Karl Marx put it, the "force with phrases" and "force without phrases"[30]) permeate, at least from the perspective of the violated, the rule of law with aspects of the gulag

28 Michael Walzer, "The Rights of Political Communities" and "The Moral Standing of States: A Response to Four Critics," in *International Ethics*, ed. Charles R. Beitz, Marshall Cohen, Thomas Scanlon, and A. John Simmons (Princeton, N.J.: Princeton University Press, 1985), pp. 165–194, 217–237.

29 Rawls, *The Law of Peoples*, p. 93.

30 See Upendra Baxi, *Marx, Law, and Justice* (Bombay: N. M. Tripathi, 1993), pp. 85–94.

state. I also remain unconvinced concerning the imagination of global justice that measures people's struggles and aspirations within the prison house of conceptions of liberally well-ordered societies, constituted by a terminal view of human history, a worldview bereft of any suggestion concerning alternatives to global capitalism, a worldview that undergrids the privileged discourse on democracy and justice. These are issues that require careful elaboration, a task surely for another day.

Of What Remains in Global Justice: Duties of Assistance   What I must address here is the severity of Rawls' conceptualization of duties of assistance arising out of his preferred conception of global justice. On his conception, with which it may be reasonable to agree, the law of peoples "holds that inequalities are not always unjust"[31] and that it does "not matter how great the gap between rich and poor may be" so long as "the least advantaged ... have sufficient all-purpose means to make intelligent and effective use of their freedoms and to lead reasonable and worthwhile lives."[32]

> Similarly, in the basic structure of the Society of Peoples, once the duty of assistance is satisfied and all peoples have a working liberal or decent government, there is again no reason to narrow the gap between the average wealth of decent peoples.[33]

This view then leads to a rejection of the strong versions of global distributive justice. Rawls insists that for peoples in the second original position, the Beitz-type formulations will lead to "unacceptable results."[34] The duties of global justice should be minimal and extend transitionally ("not continuously without end"[35]). The duties in any case are owed "until all societies have achieved just liberal or decent basic institutions."[36] They cease thereafter, for to extend them would amount to an interminable and paternalistic denial of, and affront to, the dignity of the law of peoples. The duties, such as they are, extend only to peoples of "burdened societies" to enable, even empower them to "become full members of the Society of Peoples and to be able to determine their own future for themselves."[37] Thus, duties of assistance have as their *target* the "raising of

---

31 Rawls, *The Law of Peoples*, p. 113.
32 Ibid., p. 114.
33 Ibid.
34 Ibid., p. 117.
35 Ibid.
36 Ibid., p. 118.
37 Ibid.

the world's poor until they are either free and equal citizens of a reasonably liberal society or members of a decent hierarchical society." Duties of assistance also have a cut-off point "since for each burdened society the principle ceases to apply once the target is reached."[38]

Given all this, I find it difficult to understand Rawls' rather summary dismissal of Beitz's "global distribution principle." He acknowledges that if "a global principle of distributive justice for the Law of Peoples is meant to apply to our world as it is with extreme injustices, crippling poverty, and inequalities, its appeal is understandable."[39] His concern, rightly, relates to the persistence of such a principle, when "applied continuously and without end – without a target ... – in the hypothetical world arrived at after the duty of assistance is fully satisfied."[40] That theoretical assumption here marshals the might of a counter-factual, the assumption that the "well-ordered societies," in the first place, would have followed the duty of assistance with an unwavering fidelity. It is this that then enables him to distinguish his conception of global justice from the one advanced by the "cosmopolitan view," which remains concerned with the "well-being of the individuals, and hence with whether the well-being of the globally worst off person can be improved."[41]

The law of peoples, however, remains concerned not so much, or at any rate directly, with the "well-being of the globally worst off person," but rather with the concern to elaborate "the foreign policy of liberal peoples" in ways that "act gradually to shape all not yet liberal societies in a liberal direction, until eventually (in the ideal case) all societies are liberal."[42] Relating foreign policies of Euro-American societies to tasks of justice in this way is an inherently unenviable enterprise. Rawls writes in the aftermath of Operation Desert Storm, and we read him now in the midst of Operation Infinite Justice/Enduring Freedom. These horrors, now "promising" a second round of performances of military prowess by the so-called Global Coalition against Terror aimed at the "outlaw" societies, describe our "international political world."[43] At the end of the day, then, if according to Rawls the cosmopolitan view of global justice stands faulted in terms of its purported failures in limiting the scope of intervention by "well-ordered societies" in the pursuit of global egalitarianism, his own perspective now seems to encourage, contrary of course to his original intention, limit-

38 Ibid., p. 119.
39 Ibid., p. 117.
40 Ibid.
41 Ibid., p. 120.
42 Ibid., p. 82.
43 Ibid., p. 83. See Upendra Baxi, "Operation Enduring Freedom: Towards a New International Law and Order?" *Third World and International Law* 1, no. 1 (2002, forthcoming).

less use of force against "outlaw" societies, in ways that render the globally worst-off even more destitute, disadvantaged, and deprived.

From their perspective, the discursive careers and futures concerning global justice remain rather exotically fungible in very much the same proportions as their lives and human rights remain altogether defeasible/sequestered at the altar of the Great March to Progress of the "as yet not liberal societies" toward the eventual global cloning of all human societies into the liberal mold. The ethical agonizing of would-be theorists of global justice remains, then, impervious to their extraordinary here-and-now immiseration, which is relevant only as "raw" material ready at hand for conversion, by feats of sanitized thought, into designer goods of ethical theorizing in globalized epistemic markets. This is, undoubtedly, a harsh thing to say. But then the authentically subaltern utterance has no other language that would enable the violated to express this violence. It summons, with Karl Marx, that order of combinatory "theoretical" praxis which makes possible the emergence of the capability of *suffering humanity to reflect* and *thinking humanity to suffer.*

"Burdened" Societies and Tasks of Global Justice   In the abstract, this endeavor concerned to avoid global moral paternalism appears morally sensible, at any rate until one seeks to unravel the question of how societies came to be "burdened." Rawls is too astute a thinker to overlook the ambiguity of the notion of "burdens"; he simply constructs it with much ethical theory severity. He is concerned with "targets" and "cut-off points" for the amelioration of burdens, however defined or described. On this register, Rawlsian global justice stands conceived in, and universalizes, the paradigm of the American understanding of constitutional affirmative action. Despite this, we still need to acknowledge the point that affirmative action programs, indicted often at the national level as constituting forms of reproduction of ethnic feudalism, may also replicate subordination and subjugation in interstate relations. John Rawls is concerned to avoid this happening.

The "burdens" arising out of "arbitrariness" of natural resources do not daunt Rawls "because ... the crucial element in how a country fares is its political culture – its members' political and civic virtues – and not the level of its resources."[44] This is an important Gandhian insight. But the notion of "burdens" creates, in turn, a whole lot of special burden of explanation! Duties of assistance will vary fundamentally, even radically, depending on the ways in

---

44 Rawls, *The Law of Peoples*, p. 117.

which the notion of burdens is constructed. The narrative constructions of how societies of the global South come to be burdened carry profound implications for any integral enunciation of visions of global justice.

Societies are not only burdened by asymmetrical natural resource or social talent distribution. Burdens also arise from "histories" of colonial/imperial domination, as well as from many catastrophic histories of the various phases of the Cold War/post–Cold War formations; these, even when short of genocide of whole peoples, distort forms of associational and communal life, corrupt the very bases of cooperation and social trust, arrest social and economic development, and destroy major natural resources. Wasting whole nation-societies and peoples in ways that, often obscenely, benefit the metropolis was the motto of colonial administration. To be sure, colonial predation followed different paths, but the ultimate burdens on the colonized peoples were colossal. What kind of duties of assistance would a Rawlsian perspective on the law of peoples prescribe? It does not help to speak of "targets" and "cut-off points" when we stand confronted with issues of restitution, rehabilitation, and reparation arising from centuries-long colonial occupation and subjugation of "decent peoples." Much the same must be said concerning the horrors of the Cold War, during which you were either an "enemy of the people" or a "defender of the Free World," and, regardless of your perception, were always liable to be labeled thus according to the needs of the regime or world "leadership."

When we marshal the organized impunity and irresponsibility of transnational corporations (to evoke Ulrich Beck's phrase regime),[45] and assorted regional and global financial institutions as well as governmental aid agencies, the burdens – despite Rawlsian enunciation of the duties of assistance arising from global justice values – remain immense.

I for one am unable to share Rawls' faith in "political cultures," especially of the well-ordered societies, when confronted with the interminable suffering inflicted on more than 200,000 human beings in Bhopal, who still suffer, seventeen years later, from the aftermath of 46 tons of methyl icosynate released by acts of willful mismanagement by the Union Carbide Corporation. The creation of hazards, converting human lives and futures into global wastelands, is evident in the processes of globalized economic development and many Green revolutions. "Political culture," now more than ever before, remains complicit with the contemporary forces of economic globalization, which insist that trade-related, market-friendly human rights take precedence over the universal human rights of individual human beings.[46]

45 Ulrich Beck, *Risk Society: Towards a New Modernity*, trans. Mark Ritter (London: Sage, 1992).
46 See Baxi, *The Future of Human Rights*.

Without, and outside, a sense – really *senses* – of the histories of catastrophic practices of politics of cruelty, the genocidal practices that "facilitated" colonization and the neo-imperialism of the Cold War, the law of peoples that defines ahistorical "targets" and "cut-off points" remains ethically insensible. Why is the language of reparations and reconstruction sensible for postwar Europe but not for postcolonial Asia or Africa? How are we to measure for the future the burdens of the Palestinian peoples? What duties of reparation stand owed for the enormous cruelty of colonization and neocolonization? What do the French and American "well-ordered liberal" peoples owe to the peoples still recovering from incredible human violations in the former "Indochina"? Do the structurally adjusted peoples of the Third World have any title to redistribution justifiable on the Rawlsian elaboration of global justice? Are the apartheid-violated masses of South African people owed any duties of global justice? Is the archaic United States Helms-Burton legislation against trading with Cuba still justified under the law of peoples?

It is on this kind of contested terrain that current conceptions of global justice founder, at least at the level of "nonideal" theory. The law of peoples, as it were, lets globally dominant states off the ethical hook. They owe *no intergenerational moral duties of reparation* to peoples whom their acts of foreign policy have destroyed through performances of neocolonialism/imperialism. The United States does not even acknowledge any duties of resourcing the United Nations and its specialized agencies except on the unilateral terms dictated by Jesse Helms! One would have thought, assuming the United Nations is a sort of example for social cooperation sustaining the law of peoples, that such duties uncontroversially ensue! Is it *unethical*, by the standards of the law of peoples, to postulate even a very minimal duty of assistance prescribing that the overdeveloped societies/peoples owe a dedication of at least one percent of their GNP, as a matter of nonnegotiable international law obligation, to the "developing" and "least developed" societies?

Patriotism and Global Justice   But the law of peoples shifts (to borrow the evocative title of Salman Rushdie's recent book) the ground beneath their feet. Liberal and decent peoples have everywhere special responsibilities to family, friends, and disadvantaged groups in their own society, and arguably to the "nation" as a whole. These special responsibilities may be said, for some eminently good reasons, to conflict with the demands of global justice, which establishes general responsibility for respecting/affirming the equal worth of all human persons everywhere, especially those "whom the movement for global integration has left behind."[47] But as Samuel Scheffler[48] demonstrates, the conflict between justice and responsibility is acute but not irreconcilable. Nor, as has been argued, does an increase in one's "special responsibilities result in a weakening of one's general responsibilities";[49] and surely we ought not to allow "unlimited claims on people for the sake of global justice."[50]

It has also been argued that special responsibilities created by patriotism may not be ignored by any notion of cosmopolitan, international, or global justice. It is not sufficient to say that patriotism is morally indefensible because it privileges duties toward compatriots over those owed to nonnationals. As especially Charles Jones has recently shown, certain forms of patriotism remain ethically sensible.[51] Let us follow his analysis somewhat closely before we revisit the notion of "patriotism" in relation to global justice.

"Patriotism" defines the moral universe by a "them" and "us" divide. The "us" are citizens of a "nation-state" bound by obligations of fidelity to the "nation" as a whole and to one's fellow nationals. The justice/rights claims of the Other (noncompatriots) remain of lesser relevance, if relevant at all, to similar claims within the "nation" society. Certainly, during times of conflict, patriotism offers a complete moral code that privileges the claims of co-nationals over nonnationals.

Jones distinguishes between two kinds of patriotism: the crude "blanket" kind and a more refined version of what he calls "compatriot favoritism," both of which he finds ethically untenable against the claims of global justice. "Blanket" or "exclusionary patriotism" claims that "non-patriots fall outside the sphere of ethical concern altogether."[52] All of us may agree that this form is simply not "ethically defensible" for the reasons Jones offers and related grounds that one may further furnish. A "better conception" is that of "compatriot favoritism," which, in effect, says, "compatriots take priority."[53] This is a better conception at least in the sense that it implies noncompatriots "must also be subjects of moral consideration."[54] But as Jones so abundantly indicates, the problem of "compatriot priority" remains difficult of sustained ethical resolution. Contemporary Euro-American justice theory does not, at the end of the day, furnish any "good" grounds "for setting up a distributive scheme in such a

47 Samuel Scheffler, "The Conflict Between Justice and Responsibility," in *Global Justice*, pp. 86–106 at p. 106.
48 Ibid.
49 John Kane, "Who Is My Neighbor? A Response to Scheffler," in *Global Justice*, pp. 107–113 at p 113.
50 Ibid., p. 112.
51 Charles Jones, "Patriotism, Morality and Global Justice," in *Global Justice*, pp. 125–170.
52 Ibid., p. 128.
53 Ibid., p. 130.
54 Ibid., p. 140.

way that the strength of a person's legitimate claims depends on that person's citizenship."[55]

I accept Jones' conclusion and applaud the careful reasoning informing it. The difficulty I have with all this is twofold. First, this sort of analysis ignores altogether the fact of *amoral* entities, national and transnational corporations, to whom the very notion of "patriotism" does not quite apply, if at all, as it does to "citizens." If by "patriotism" one means (in any event, a deeply ethically problematic) "love for one's country," by definition, transnational corporations remain incapable of meaningful forms of patriotic affection or fidelity. Second, the enterprise of their subjection to a minimal code of morality entails a very different order of ethical reasoning than available in forms of ethical individualism; it is doubtful whether a naive disaggregating of corporate collectivities into individual citizens imbued with attributes of "patriotism" will help us toward this goal.

Even Rawls permits himself a footnote acknowledgment of the power of corporations to subvert the notions of deliberative democracy:

> When politicians are beholden to their constituents for essential campaign funds, and a very unequal distribution of income and wealth obtains in the background culture, with the great wealth being in the control of corporate economic power, is it any wonder that congressional legislation, is, in effect, written by lobbyists and Congress becomes a bargaining chamber in which laws are bought and sold?[56]

This insight concerning "background culture" seems relevant to Rawls' conversation about "political culture," referred to earlier. It is equally applicable to the making of international ideals, standards, and values. Like the laws and policies of well-ordered societies, many international regimes are increasingly sculpted by multinational corporate lobbyists in near total disregard of the logics and paralogics of expansive human rights. The WTO agreement on Trade Related Intellectual Property Rights (TRIPS) testifies to the power of culture industries as well as of emergent global strategic biotech industries.[57] The temporarily shelved OECD draft of the Multilateral Agreement on Investment (MAI) is so obscenely solicitous of the rights of the foreign investor as to require state parties to openly suspend the application of human rights and environmental standards! We all know that BENGOs (business environmental nongovernmental

55 Ibid., p. 165.
56 Rawls, *The Law of Peoples*, p. 24, note 19.
57 See, for example, *The Life Industry: Biodiversity, People and Profit*, ed. Miges Baumann et al. (London: Intermediate Technology Publications, 1996); Jose Van Dijck, *ImagEnation: Popular Images of Genetics* (London: Macmillan, 1998).

organizations) exceeded in number and influence the ENGOs (environmental nongovernmental organizations) at the Kyoto Conference on Climate Change.[58] (This entire discourse constitutes a requiem for the emergent global "civil society"!) And now with the UN-corporate Global Compact firmly in place, the commanding heights of human rights development seem already to have been captured by the very transnational corporations known to be egregious offenders against those rights. Even the privatization of the United Nations system now seems an acceptable goal.

Transnational corporations, with all their mass disaster–constituting proclivities and potential, constitute the gravest danger to conceptions of global justice and human rights. The arguments of special responsibility and patriotism have prevailed among American national adjudicators confronted with claims for relief and rehabilitation against mass disasters caused by American transnational corporations domiciled in the United States and denying any jurisdiction at the site of disasters. American courts have almost consistently held that foreign plaintiffs do not have standing to sue, as this will confiscate precious adjudicatory time and talent and ill-serve the special responsibilities courts have toward co-nationals for the administration of justice.[59] This represents a state-managerial type of exclusionary compatriot patriotism, ethically suspect, even outrageous, in that it promotes (in Ulrich Beck's felicitous terms) "organised immunity" and "organised irresponsibility" for global capital.[60] Global justice discourse has yet to tackle this most formidable challenge of constructing the justice-responsibilities of global corporations, foreign investors, and international financial institutions.[61]

Norms and standards of global justice are undermined when these forces are able to constantly redraw the boundary between *injustice* and *misfortune*, to which Judith Shklar sought to draw our attention.[62] To convert, for example, Ogoniland and Bhopal into "misfortunes" (side effects of progress, development, and whatever!) is to deny these critical events the languages of "justice." The global corporate switch in the phrase-regimes articulates a new globalizing

58 See Baxi, *The Future of Human Rights*, pp. 42–66.
59 See Upendra Baxi, "Mass Torts, Multinational Enterprise Liability, and Private International Law," *Recueil des cours* 276 (2000), pp. 305–423; ibid., "Geographies of Injustice: Human Rights at the Altar of Convenience," in *Torture as Tort: Comparative Perspectives on the Development of Transnational Human Rights Litigation*, ed. Craig Scott (Oxford: Hart Publishing, 2001), pp. 197–202. See, in a related context, Upendra Baxi, "Bringing Judas Back to the Last Supper? The Tasks of Republican Criminology in Service of Globalisation," in *Punishment and the Prison: Indian and International Perspectives*, ed. Rani Dhavan Shankardass (New Delhi: Sage, 2000), pp. 344–370.
60 Beck, *Risk Society*.
61 See, for a range of insights, *Defying Corporations, Defining Democracy: A Book of History and Strategy*, ed. Dean Ritz (New York: Apex Press, 2001).
62 Judith N. Shklar, *The Faces of Injustice* (New Haven: Yale University Press, 1990).

secular cosmology of the Hindu doctrine of *karma,* which encourages fatalism and disempowers human rights and peoples' activism. For, the languages of misfortune mystify its perpetrators and divest them, singly and in concert, of any and all justice responsibilities.

Approaches to global justice need to shrink to a moral minimum the notion of "misfortune" and thus expand the bounds of responsibility. The challenge reminds us of the great message of Emmanuel Levinas:

> The Torah demands, in opposition to the natural perseverance of each being in his or her own being (a fundamental ontological law) concern for the stranger, the widow and the orphan, *a preoccupation with the other person.*[63]

It is this preoccupation with the misfortune of, and injustice to, the overwhelmingly non Euro-American Other that, in my view, furnishes manifold ethically fecund sites for inaugural labors for discourse on global justice. Like states (or well-ordered liberal peoples), transnational corporations – these enormous concentrations of techno-scientific prowess (the combinatory power of digital capitalism and biotechnology) in these halcyon days of headlong and heedless globalization – ought to be subject to duties arising from conceptions of global justice.[64] The present labors toward the construction of realistic Utopias for a more just, and even a deeply *caring,* world surely remain incomplete without an articulation of the ethical responsibilities of transnational actors, institutions, and globalizing mentalities.

63 Emmanuel Levinas, *In the Time of the Nations,* trans. Michael B. Smith (London: Athlone Press, 1994), p. 97.
64 See Baxi, *The Future of Human Rights,* pp. 132–166.

The Roma and Democracy:
A Nation without a State

Sean Nazerali

Although I have been invited to comment on the theme of the Roma and edu-cation, I shall actually take this opportunity to introduce the interpretation of the state as presented by the International Romani Union, as I believe that it is not only more relevant to the debate at hand, but also a more interesting con-cept for the public as a whole. The idea was presented publicly for the first time in July of 2000 at the Fifth World Romani Congress, the highest international political body of the Romani people. Embodied in the Roma demand to be rec-ognized as a nation, what at first glance appears to be a simple idea in fact has more profound implications, as it also calls for recognition by the international community as a *nation without a state*. This is the crux of a truly revolutionary concept, one that could have a tremendous impact on the very idea of the state in the modern world.

Before launching into the main discussion, however, I would like to offer a few thoughts on the concept of the nation-state. The international system as presently constituted is based on the nation-state as its fundamental building block, its elemental indivisible unit, upon whose absolute sovereignty the rest of the system is founded. Yet this term "nation-state" is in fact a misnomer of sorts, as it combines two quite different elements. The state, as an administrative unit, is rarely contiguous with a nation or people. The very idea of a unified nation in most cases was forged by the bureaucratic and institutional might of states. Recall the words of statesman Massimo d'Azeglio on the eve of Italian unifica-tion: "We have made Italy: all that remains is to make Italians."[1] Indeed, even linguistic unity remained a vision to be realized: only 2 to 3 percent of the citi-zens of the newly emergent Italy spoke Italian.

Although these initial efforts to create Germans, Italians, and so on were quite successful, the idea of the state as a nation-state was never representative of the majority of states and, despite attempts at the end of World War I to grant

---

1 Massimo d'Azeglio, quoted in Eric J. Hobsbawm, *Nations and Nationalism since 1780* (Cambridge: Cambridge University Press, 1990), p. 44.

independent state status to many nations, it continued to be more a prescriptive than descriptive expression. Developments in the last half of the 20th century only confirm this – the idea of a nation-state was and continues to be entirely inappropriate and inapplicable to the newly independent states of Africa, for example, with their borders carved out, as they were, along lines of colonial convenience.

And yet this is not merely a problem of and for the developing world. Increasingly the idea of a nation and a state forged into a single unit is a myth even in the very cradle of the nation-state, in France and Britain, along with the rest of "developed" Western Europe. With mobility increasing on a global scale, the numbers of citizens and residents of the established nation-states has significantly altered their demographic makeup, reconstituting them as states of many nations. With few exceptions, the nation-state as an integrated whole is dead.

Neither the state, however, nor the nation has died. Both continue to be very influential. What I will argue, though, is that it is the nation which is the more powerful – and more useful – concept, and that its harnessing can guide us to a new arrangement of the international system, one more suited to the demands of the modern world.

This is so chiefly for the reason that when we separate the two concepts, we find that it is the state as a construct which has outlived its usefulness as the cornerstone of international relations. Pressured from above and below, the state is increasingly incapable of managing a wide variety of issues, from the economic monitoring and control of transnational corporations to ecological concerns far surpassing one nation's geographic boundaries to the resolution of local relations across both sides of an invented border.

Looking at the pressures emanating from above, it must first be noted that the supranational political level is burgeoning. There is an increasing tendency of states to arrange themselves in a dizzying array of international associations and binding agreements, voluntarily restricting their sovereignty at every turn, a tendency perhaps best exemplified in the evolution of the European Union. Equally important is the growing body of internationally agreed restrictions embodied in the covenants and conventions of the United Nations, and the increasing willingness on the part of states to approve of intervention in the business of other states to enforce certain principles, notably those pertaining to the protection of human rights.

Perhaps a more critical factor in the weakening of state sovereignty, the international economy has overwhelmed the boundaries of the state. Approximately half the world's hundred largest economies are multinational corporations.[2] The forces compelling harmonization of economic policy are increasingly strong and at the same time increasingly rigid. Nowhere is this more evident than with regard to monetary policy, where international currency markets, responding almost instantly to each and every change, have left governments with a minuscule amount of room to maneuver. In essence, the power to set interest and exchange rates – to formulate an independent monetary policy – has been removed from the hands of national governments and entrusted into the care of Adam Smith's invisible one. Yet it is not simply monetary but fiscal policy as well that is being constrained by the forces of the supranational economy. The EU's Maastricht criteria regulating inflation, budget deficits, and national debt were simply a recognition of this fact and an attempt to codify it.

What we are witnessing, therefore, is not simply an upward distribution of power in the economic sphere toward the supranational, but the corresponding decline of the state as the most important actor in the control of that economic sphere. One of the key pillars upon which governmental legitimacy is based, the regulation of the economic levers of power, is being steadily eroded.

From below, on the other hand, we have seen the attack on the state in the flowering of subnational, disintegrative movements, in the most extreme cases culminating in the dissolution of existing state structures (e.g., the Soviet Union, Yugoslavia). Even in more "successful" nation-states, we are witness to a stunning array of subnational interests gaining in strength and influence. As societies become more complex, the number of possible cleavages multiplies as well. Divisions on the basis of gender, race, socioeconomic status, age, sexual orientation, or educational background become more pronounced. A most disturbing trend is the thesis that only members of a group can properly understand and even discuss that group. The particularism in this is readily apparent, with the inevitable logical conclusion that none of these groups will be able to reach a mutual understanding or even hold a meaningful dialogue. The atomization of the nation-state is very pronounced in those states professing a liberal-democratic outlook, and is thus of special relevance to the discussion at hand.

In essence, then, the state is losing its position as *the* fundamental building block, and is instead being replaced by a number of different levels of interaction, each with varying degrees of importance and relevance. This is a frightening prospect for those with vested interests in the contemporary order, and indeed for most serious students of history, as the breakdown of one system of international order is generally accompanied by great violence and much upheaval. Conflicts in the Balkans, Somalia, and elsewhere may well be the tip of the proverbial iceberg, foreshadowing the spread of such conflict across the

---

2 See Mathew Horsman and Andrew Marshall, *After the Nation-State: Citizens, Tribalism and the New World Disorder* (London: Harper Collins, 1994), p. 201.

globe, as states dissolve into their constituent parts. For this reason, the break-down of the nation-state paradigm is heavily resisted by current international structures, which continue to cite the principle of sovereignty as the highest value in world politics.

The image of the world descending into chaos and war once the rampart of sovereignty has been breached is, however, too gloomy a perspective on the challenges that lie ahead. Though the realignment of societies will be long, drawn out, and troublesome, we do have guides to a positive solution.

As is evident from the foregoing, it would be extremely useful to develop a new filter through which to view the world. Several filters of greater or lesser importance have been outlined by theorists over the past decade. The contemporary world has been hailed as the pinnacle of human development – the End of History as outlined by Francis Fukuyama, ruled unchallenged by the philosophy of the Western world.[3] Alternately, we have the idea of a Clash of Civilizations as presented by Samuel Huntington, with the world divided into seven or eight major civilizations, each destined to struggle against the others for survival.[4] We continue to be inundated with positive declarations on the health of the nation-state, and also with various specters of chaos and anarchy, a world so completely atomized that nothing remains but the individual, stripped of any allegiances whatsoever.

It is important to recognize that each of these would-be paradigms is of relevance, though none is sufficient in and of itself. Although integrating supranational forces seem to be in direct opposition to the disintegrating tendencies just outlined, these should not be seen as disparate phenomena, but rather as two faces of the same trend. As the economic pillar of governance erodes, a corresponding erosion occurs in the claim of that system to legitimacy. The economic realm, managed by forces beyond state control, exists almost entirely outside the democratic mandate we demand from our leaders. Yet, "citizens continue to hold their national governments accountable on issues over which states have no autonomous control."[5] Small wonder, then, that we find ourselves wrestling with a crisis within the state. The democratic ideal, that those who live under a system have the right to determine how that system is run, is under serious threat. And as democratic accountability for economic decisions leaks away from the national political sphere, so too does economic policy lose its ability to be a differentiating factor among political parties and interest groups, which

---

3 Francis Fukuyama, *The End of History and the Last Man* (New York: Free Press, 1992).
4 Samuel P. Huntington, *The Clash of Civilizations and the Remaking of the World Order* (New York: Simon & Schuster, 1996).
5 Horsman and Marshall, *After the Nation-State.*

must then define other sources of legitimacy. As a result, social and cultural issues take on greater urgency in national debates, and at election time have often been the key deciding factors. With regard to economic policy, the major parties are often almost indistinguishable. The New Left is new simply because it is no longer left. Faced with an international financial system that is incompatible with traditional leftist economic policy, the Left has had to abandon its economics in order to be allowed to play politics.

Indeed, such has been the impact of this shifting locus of economic control that in the new democracies of Central and Eastern Europe, the entire Left-Right distinction is almost nonsensical, as by the time the parties had begun to form, this distinction had already lost its relevance. Thus we see a "leftist" government in the Czech Republic pursuing privatization and deregulatory policies which are far more "rightist" than those promoted during the years of so-called rightist government.

The search for alternate sources of legitimacy is less problematic in the established democracies. Here, not only do political parties already have well-established social and cultural platforms, but they also have institutions of governance, such as the British Parliament, which have developed their own strengths as cultural institutions apart from their role in actual democratic representation. In newer democracies or proto-democracies, however, the search for forms of legitimacy outside the economic realm has led increasingly to appeals to nationalism and ethnic identity. Historically, the use of national identity as a unifying principle has been subjected to much abuse. It has been utilized as a tool to acquire territory and evict others, but this is actually due in great part to its unfortunate coupling with the idea of a state. Yet national identity need not be tied to territorial ambition, and it is this uncoupling of the two that could lead to renewed interest in national sentiment as an essentially positive phenomenon. Which brings us to the contribution put forward by the Romani nation: the idea of a nation without a state, also referred to as a territory-less state.

In actual fact, I believe it is important to differentiate between the two terms "nation without a state" and "territory-less state," although the declaration made at the last Romani Congress does not make this distinction. The idea of a nation without a state is one that fits well with longer term goals or proposals regarding an entirely new manner of arranging the international system, whereas the concept of a territory-less state is perhaps a very useful short-term transitional phase along the way.

The Roma are often referred to as Gypsies, an inaccurate and, for some, offensive moniker derived from the misconception that they originate from Egypt. In fact, they are an Indian people who left India approximately a thousand years ago, then migrated through Persia into Europe. They entered Europe through the Balkans and via North Africa and up into Spain, and by the 15th century were dispersed throughout Europe. Roma were thus settled in Europe before the beginning of the formation of national identities – long before, for example, the arrival of Europeans in North America – and yet are still regarded by many as foreigners and strangers. They have faced almost continual discrimination across time and place. For example, in the 17th century, on the territory of present-day Austria, Roma were declared outcasts and could be shot on sight. They were regularly banned from certain areas, with strict sanctions on their movement. In 18th-century Bohemia, those caught by the authorities would have their left ear cut off; in Moravia, it was the right ear. Roma were enslaved until 1861 in Romania.

The darkest period of Romani history was World War II. As the only group other than the Jews to be classified as unacceptable solely on the basis of race, they were rounded up and transported to concentration camps. Half a million Roma died in the camps; in areas under direct Nazi control, the number executed reached as high as 95 percent of the total Romani population.

Today, dispersed across the world, though the majority lives in Central and Eastern Europe, the Roma number about 15 million – many more than quite a few other peoples who have claimed statehood, such as the Slovaks, Dutch, or Austrians.

Yet the Roma differ most strikingly in one respect: they neither have, nor wish to have, a territory of their own. This is tremendously important in our discussion of their place in the international system and the makeup of that system itself. By not desiring a territory, not only is their call for recognition as a people with a right to self-determination less threatening (at least initially), but the proposals formulated to achieve this must be qualitatively different than those expressed by many other ethnic groups demanding a voice at the international table. This sets them radically apart from the Kurds, Basques, or Palestinians, all of whom frame their nationalism in the territorial terms of the 19th century. The Roma thus have an ideal opportunity to become the first nation of a new era.

The importance of this should not be underestimated. With the decline of the state, there has been a rise of the nation, and the consequences could be dire indeed. Let us be straight – it is not the rise of nations that is problematic, but the rise of territorial claims that most nations see as an integral aspect of their being. National sentiment *per se* is often beneficial, territorial exclusivity is not. To preempt this, we need another means to deal with rising national sentiment, one that is not centered on the idea of territory. (The appearance in Brussels of Welsh, Basque, Catalan, and Breton offices may be a disquieting reminder of the forces gathering at the gates.)

But before there can be any talk of the future arrangements of a new era, we must look at how the Roma's claims to recognition can be situated within the presently existing system. Obviously, although the state should sooner or later cease to be the foundation stone of the international system, this is more likely to come later rather than sooner. It is necessary, therefore, if this proposal of a nation without a state is to be more than a theoretical contribution, to bring its first steps into line with what currently exists, and to seek a place within that structure. It is in this context that we must begin to explore the possibility of a territory-less state.

What is a territory-less state? How might it emerge, and what functions would it serve? A territory-less state has an institution of government, a population, but no specific territory; it would be sovereign and autonomous, but would share that sovereignty with a wide variety of other levels of institutions – national, regional, and international. To situate this notion of the territory-less state in the context of contemporary international law and norms, we should regard it as the realization of the Romani people's right to self-determination. As a concept, self-determination is well established in international law as a fundamental right of all peoples. The principle was set out in the United Nations General Assembly in 1960,[6] and reiterated at the beginning of both the International Covenant on Civil and Political Rights and the International Covenant on Economic, Social and Cultural Rights, binding treaties that entered into force in 1976:

> Article 1: "All peoples have the right to self-determination; by virtue of that right they freely determine their political status and freely pursue their economic, social and cultural development."[7]

Though this was initially formulated as a principle only with regard to colonial peoples, that definition has broadened to include noncolonial peoples, and the majority of academics now recognize a customary-law value to the right to self-determination.[8]

---

6 Declaration on the Granting of Independence to Colonial Countries and Peoples, Adopted by General Assembly Resolution 1514 (XV) of 14 December 1960.

7 Article 1: International Covenant on Civil and Political Rights: Adopted and opened for signature, ratification and accession by General Assembly Resolution 2200A (XXI) of 16 December 1966, entry into force 23 March 1976, in accordance with Article 49, and Article 1: International Covenant on Economic, Social and Cultural Rights: Adopted and opened for signature, ratification and accession by General Assembly Resolution 2200A (XXI) of 16 December 1966, entry into force 3 January 1976, in accordance with Article 27.

8 See Kristin Henrard, *Devising an Adequate System of Minority Protection: Individual Human Rights, Minority Rights, and the Right to Self-Determination* (London: Martinus Nijhoff, 2000), p. 284.

The principle of self-determination has often been the victim of a poor reputation in international relations, primarily because it is presumed to legitimize secessionist and independence movements. This is not a strictly accurate interpretation, however. General Assembly Resolution 1541, from 1960, sets out three strategies for achieving full "self-government":[9]

1. become a sovereign, independent state
2. conclude a free association with an independent state
3. integrating with an independent state

These clarifications were meant to demonstrate that the principle of self-determination was broader, therefore less threatening, than simply conferring the right to secede, and intended to open up opportunities for a variety of possible arrangements between a state and a minority group. This space was further enlarged in 1970 with Resolution 2625, the Declaration on Principles of International Law Concerning Friendly Nations and Cooperation among States, which adds a fourth strategy:

4. emergence into any other political status freely determined by a people

We can thus distinguish two dimensions to the issue of self-determination, an internal and an external one. The external dimension refers to "the international status of a people in a specific territory, and that entity's relations with surrounding states," whereas the internal dimension is "concerned with the state's structure and other national legal regulations designed to accommodate in a (more) optimal way the separate identities of the various population groups present in a state."[10] It is thus only the external dimension that poses a threat to the integrity of the state, an important distinction to keep in mind.

The right to self-determination in its internal dimension, then, is the right of a people to participate in governance in a manner that respects and protects their culture and traditions. This is generally recognized as a right to democracy, to participate in both the choosing and the running of a government, and the right to some degree of autonomy within the state. What is also clear, however, is that if a people's right to self-determination is abrogated by a state, then that people has a right to secede and seek self-determination in the external sense. General Assembly Resolution 2625 states outright that

---

9 As laid out in ibid., pp. 287–288.
10 Ibid., p. 281.

Nothing in the foregoing paragraphs shall be construed as authorising or encouraging any actions which would dismember or impair, totally or in part, the territorial integrity or political unity of sovereign and independent States *conducting themselves in compliance with the principle of equal rights and self-determination of peoples as described above and thus possessed of a government representing the whole people belonging to the territory without distinction as to race, creed, or colour.* (emphasis added)[11]

Where this condition is not met, therefore, a people is granted the right to secede.

Claims to self-determination are often called into question, usually by denying that a group constitutes a "people," thus excluding that group from the international documents on self-determination, all of which employ this term. Thus, for the Roma, it is important that in future, the term *people* be used in declarations and statements made by Romani political leaders. Although not explicitly articulated in the declaration of nationhood issued at the Fifth World Romani Congress, a declaration of peoplehood should be seen as implicit within it. This is particularly true as the Romani language does not differentiate between a "nation" and a "people." The Declaration of Nation should therefore in fact be interpreted as being simultaneously a Declaration of Peoplehood.

Obviously, simply declaring oneself to be a "people" does not guarantee that one will be accepted as such. Recognizing that, a few comments about the Romani people's current situation are in order. The vast majority of Roma live in Central and Eastern Europe, where they are subject to horrendous discrimination by governments and the population. In Romania, for example, Romani villages have been burnt to the ground with the open support of government policy; in Kosovo, Roma are murdered on a regular basis by both Serbs and Albanians as scapegoats caught in the middle of a conflict not of their making; and in the Czech Republic, they have been denied their basic right to citizenship. Across the region, the "special schools" phenomenon is virtually the norm, whereby dead-end schools initially set up for the mentally handicapped have been turned into dumping grounds for Romani children. In the Czech Republic, it is estimated that some 80 percent of Romani children have been inappropriately classified into these schools. Many Romani villages, neglected for decades, still lack rudimentary infrastructure such as sewage, running water, or electricity. These conditions are in no way the result of a nomadic lifestyle – in many areas of Eastern Europe, the Roma have been a settled people for hundreds of years.

11 Declaration on Principles of International Law Concerning Friendly Relations and Cooperation Among States in Accordance with the Charter of the United Nations, General Assembly Resolution 2625 (XXV) of October 24, 1970.

What emerges from this very brief account is a picture of a people who are routinely denied elemental rights and freedoms. The states in which they live have proved manifestly unable or unwilling to protect and respect their Romani citizens. They have been granted no role in the choosing and running of government, and no autonomy (with the exception of Hungary, where there is at least the appearance of self-governing councils). In such a case, it is obvious that the conditions of internal self-determination have been violated. Although Resolution 2625 would seem to suggest that the Roma have a right to secede, in reality they have no desire to do so. Throughout much of their history, the Roma were emancipated from the land, as nomads. The very idea of territorial exclusivity is an alien one. This unique perspective, although a significant handicap at times, could be a great advantage in the long run, not merely for the Roma themselves, but for the global system.

Let us be clear, though, that the present territorial fixation originates in the idea of the *state* and *not* the nation. The state is unique in that it claims both sovereignty and exclusive authority over a fixed territorial space.[12] Historically, there have existed many other systems of rule that have not been based on the mutual exclusivity of fixed territories. Feudalism, nomadism, the Holy Roman Empire and the church are just a few examples. In the modern era, though, with its state-centered bias, it is necessary to have the form of a recognized state in order to gain access to the highest levels of decision-making power. The Vatican has certainly recognized this, and conforms with institutional expectations by maintaining the fiction of a territory, though it considers its "citizenry" to be composed of all Catholics worldwide. Another contemporary example of a non-territorial unit with many aspects of state status is the Knights of Malta.

Based on the right to self-determination, I therefore believe that the concept of a territory-less state is not only a very effective means through which to assist the formation of a Romani nation, but one that is grounded in international law and custom. The question then immediately arises as to how self-determination can be realized in practice. As stated above, under the terms of General Assembly Resolution 2625, the Roma have a right to "freely determine" their "political status." By calling for a nonterritorial state, they have clearly set this out as their choice. As a state without a territory, the Romani people would be able to achieve full self-determination on a global scale, and would also be able to work out particular autonomous competencies with other states. Autonomy too, as a principle, is not territorially defined. It refers to the "self-government of a specific part of the population ... established on either a territorial or a personal

---

12 See Hendrik Spruyt, *The Sovereign State and Its Competitors: An Analysis of Systems Change* (Princeton, N.J.: Princeton University Press, 1994).

basis."[13] This idea of personal autonomy, sometimes referred to as personal federalism, is that "certain competencies are attributed to communities that are then able to regulate these matters for all its members, wherever they live."[14] These competencies would have to be defined in a manner slightly different in character than standard bilateral treaties, but this too is not unheard of. The Vatican concludes concordats with states, which are focused on the behavior of that state toward its own people within its own boundaries. This is analogous to the way in which a nonterritorial Romani state would interact with others.

What would this achieve concretely for the Roma and for the global system?

First, the Romani people would finally gain a voice at the international level. This is important in two ways: not only would it allow the Romani nation to participate in international negotiations and discussions at the United Nations and elsewhere, but there would also be a government capable and authorized to negotiate as a formal equal with existing state governments and to agitate on behalf of the Roma wherever they live. A mother state can raise issues of its citizens' treatment at international forums and initiate proceedings if abuses have occurred. States, and only states, can bring petitions before the International Court of Justice, the European Court of Justice, and many other forums. In the present state-centered system, it is certainly easier to promote one's interests if one is also a state.

Consider, for example, the International Convention for the Elimination of All Forms of Racial Discrimination (ICERD), one of the most important international documents for the protection of minority rights. Ratified to date by 157 states, the ICERD requires states to provide a wide range of human rights guarantees for all people living within their borders, as well as mandating that each state adopt effective measures to combat prejudices that lead to racial discrimination.[15] The ICERD is a powerful instrument in the struggle to create a global system for the protection of human rights. However, as with all resolutions and treaties in our state-centered system, it is severely hampered by the prerogatives of state sovereignty. Of particular relevance to a potential Romani state, the ICERD contains a provision that state parties to the Convention can refer the behavior of other states to the expert committee for review. It should be noted that this mechanism has never been used in the thirty years the Convention has been in force. State parties have shied away from "infringing" on another state's "sovereignty." A Romani state would have no qualms about using

---

13 See Thomas D. Musgrave, *Self-Determination and National Minorities* (Oxford: Clarendon Press, 1997).

14 Henrard, *Devising an Adequate System of Minority Protection*, p. 313, note 180.

15 Article 7: International Convention for the Elimination of All Forms of Racial Discrimination, General Assembly Resolution 2106 (XX) of 21 December 1965.

the provisions contained in the ICERD and elsewhere to ensure that human rights are being respected and that other states are living up to their obligations. In so doing, a Romani state would breathe life into what have been to date merely paper tigers.

This brings us to the second potential contribution of a Romani state: the strengthening of international mechanisms from the inside. As a state without a territory, the Romani state would be free to concentrate on ensuring that existing international agreements and conventions are implemented and honored. The focus, of course, would be on the way these agreements affect the Romani people, but the increased scrutiny would lead to an overall improvement for all minorities and ethnic groups.

Third, the existence of a Romani state would allow for the creation of Romani transnational structures to strengthen and develop Roma identity. Among other things, these would involve the promotion of the Romani language in television and radio, the advancement of education through the founding of an international university, and the development of research crucial to the needs of the Romani people.

Fourth, the existence of a Romani state without any territorial claims or base would bring into sharp focus how limiting and indeed unnecessary the present international state-centered system is.

At every turn, a Romani state would be reliant on transnational instruments to exert and implement its policies. It would issue no currency of its own, and would in fact have no monetary policy at all, leaving this entirely to the international financial system not only *de facto*, as do other states, but *de jure*. It would have no army, as indeed it would have no territory to defend. In the event of a physical threat to the rights of its people, it would do as all states have agreed to do and refer the matter to the international mechanism at its disposal – the United Nations. Were there to exist or come into being a full international standing army to maintain peace, however, there is no reason why Roma would not accept their obligations to serve in it. Roma are actually well placed to play a vanguard role in this. The Roma have never as a group gone to war against anyone else, but rather have tried to avoid violent conflict. When faced with oppression, their historical response has been to move on. Even under the contemporary attacks by neo-Nazi groups, with no chance to escape the source of the violence by moving away, I do not know of any cases in which the reaction of the Romani community has been to respond in kind.

On the matter of justice, the Romani legal system would begin with the standards of behavior set out in the contemporary system of international law, in time developing its own system of transnational criminal law as well. This could be set up along the lines of the self-governing courts established by many indigenous people, or perhaps like the military courts that operate independently of the justice system of the country in which the military personnel actually serve. Initially, its jurisdiction would have to be negotiated separately with every other state as part of bilateral agreements. In time, however, this could develop into the world's first truly transnational system of justice.

Education, too, would be an amalgamation of local, regional, and transnational approaches. Primary education would be part of the national systems of the countries in which Roma live. At secondary and tertiary levels, there could be opportunities for transnational education, at lower levels through the utilization of new technologies (distance learning via the Internet, etc.), at higher levels through the founding of a World Romani University, the beginnings of which have already been set in motion.

All of these aspects would demonstrate the feasibility of practical transnational administration. The Roma would have a state structure that for all intents and purposes is openly concerned only with social and cultural affairs. In areas outside of its scope, the Romani state would pass responsibility and powers to an international body. Where such an entity does not exist, the Romani state would agitate and lobby for its creation. In effect, the Romani people are proposing a state that frankly admits to what it is: a structure for granting a particular segment of the world's population a sense of identity and belonging. In so doing, we will often be forced to create entirely new blueprints for transnational institutions, gaining valuable experience for the day when the present system of international relations with its state-centered approach is finally abandoned.

A crucial question is how a Romani state would be financed. There appear to be a number of options. One method suitable to the existing system is the VAT or sales tax. Most countries exempt citizens of other countries from paying the VAT when they purchase goods. It is therefore not an insurmountable administrative problem for those countries where the VAT exists to be remitted to a transnational Romani state government. Romani-owned businesses could be registered with the Romani state so that their income tax is remitted there rather than to the tax authorities of the country in which they reside (a method used in jurisdictions such as the Bahamas and Andorra, where large numbers of offshore companies are registered). A more difficult arrangement to work out, but ultimately of more use as a step toward a complete global system, would be the remittance by local tax authorities of a certain percentage of revenues collected. This is already done in many tax jurisdictions – in Canada, for example, where income tax is collected at one time, divided by the tax collecting agency into federal and provincial amounts, and distributed to the appropriate level of authority. Were this method to be introduced on a small scale for the Romani state, it would then provide an excellent blueprint for the financing of any future world or regional government, or, for that matter, for the financing of an institution such as the United Nations itself.

I should now like to turn to the issue of the democratic credentials of this proposed Romani state. How can we ensure that it will operate in a democratic manner? Will it bring more or less democracy to the Romani people? And what lessons for the international community can be gleaned from the workings of the Romani state? None of these questions can be definitively answered at the present time, as the Romani state does not yet exist. But I will attempt to shed some light on the main aspects of the problem.

Obviously, a working democracy requires an institutional structure. For the Roma at the present time, this structure is the International Romani Union (IRU). Founded more than thirty years ago, the IRU has representation in forty countries around the globe, thirty-eight of which sent delegates to the most recent World Congress. It has set up institutional structures for a parliament, a presidium, a president, and an international court. Although representatives to these bodies are not at the present time fully democratically elected, they are chosen by the World Congresses, which are held every five years.

Regarding democratic legitimacy, the holding of elections is the first requirement, though the nature of the Romani state is such that this will not be an easy task. Scattered as the Roma are throughout the world, the very holding of an election is bound to cause enormous logistical problems. However, the main issue is that of who votes. If we are to have a government that represents the Romani people as a whole, it is imperative that as many Roma as possible do vote, and yet at the same time that non-Roma do not. A system of self-governance in which the balance of power is held by others would be a denial of the very term *self-government*. At the same time, it is also unacceptable to require anyone, by force or other means of coercion, to identify him- or herself as a member of any particular group.

Yet the difficulty should not be overstated. Under the present system of territorially based electoral franchise, problems of voting rights arise as well. I myself am registered to vote in a country where I have not lived for nearly eight years, at an address that has not been mine for nearly twenty. In the country where I actually live, I have no registered residency whatsoever. The vast majority of my adult life I have lived in a country where I have no voting rights, while at the same time continue to have the right to vote in a country where I was not born and where I have lived a grand total of one month. With the acceleration in global mobility, cases like my own are increasingly common.

I believe that the most effective manner in which to deal with this issue is through simple self-identification. If an individual wishes to identify as a Roma and register as such, then he or she should be allowed to do so. That person would thereby be entitled to all the rights and obligations of the Romani state. Indeed, this element of choice would give the Romani state *more* legitimacy than a standard state, as each and every one of its citizens will have actively chosen to become part of its polis. A key indicator of the acceptance of the Romani state by the Romani people themselves will be reflected in the number of individuals who voluntarily sign up. But it is important to ensure that by registering as a member of the Romani state, the Roma are not at the same time disenfranchised in their states of residence. I believe this can be avoided with the introduction of dual citizenship. Indeed, perhaps as we expand the concept of identity-citizenship further, it should not be impractical to assume that we will all gradually become members of various constituencies.

I will conclude this discussion with a few remarks on the benefits the international community may be expected to realize from the emergence of a Romani territory-less state. These benefits are of two types, the first concrete, the second more theoretical. Several examples of the first type were outlined above. To reiterate, the existence of a Romani state would:

- Strengthen existing international documents and conventions like the ICERD by fully utilizing the provisions in ways only state parties are permitted to do.
- Press the international community to create a standing army for the UN, along with other international arrangements for the security of the individual.
- Develop a transnational system of justice.
- Develop and implement ways to cooperate with existing states to acquire tax revenues for transnational institutions.
- Develop transnational electoral processes.

The second, more theoretical type of benefit is grounded in the nature of the Romani state. By its very existence, the Romani state will stand as an example to the world that the nation-state is not feasible, and the territory-based state itself unnecessary. It will openly declare itself for what it is, a body focused on social and cultural affairs, existing so as to grant a particular segment of the world's population a sense of identity and belonging. In so doing, we shall strip away the myths surrounding the modern state, and hopefully in the process galvanize a serious discussion about the future of the international system and the place of the state within it.

Philippe Schmitter has identified what he calls the Law of Conservation of Political Energy, that is, "that nothing ever disappears in political life until its replacement has already been discovered and is functioning effectively."[16] In other words, it is necessary to first propose and test alternative institutional arrangements on a small scale. A Romani state could well be that test case.

Ultimately, we would like to see an international system that is no longer based on the fiction of sovereign states interacting on a level playing field and in control of all processes within their borders. In its place, we can envisage a system that acknowledges the actual range of decision-making levels and seeks to accommodate them by means of a different set of authorities. Local issues could be dealt with locally, global issues at a global level, each through distinct institutional structures. Multinational corporations and transnational bodies acting on a global scale would be accountable to a global authority. This would not, and should not, mean that we are all joined in a type of supra-state world federation. Rather, each arena of social interaction would be addressed at the most appropriate level. Economic and ecological issues could perhaps have a common set of ground rules, with an entity given the effective authority to implement them. Cultural and social issues would be dealt with via nations.

For representation to be successful, people must feel that they are being represented. On this ground, the nation is a more powerful and thus more useful concept than the state. By harnessing the nation, and freeing it from the territorial, state-centered trappings that presently encumber it, we can give individuals a sense of belonging to the system as a whole, whereby they can say, "I am Roma, a European, a citizen of the world." In such a system, *all* peoples would become nations without states.

To return to the realm of the present, were we to view the Romani goal of self-determination in the limited context of the European Union, one might say that the Romani state here described is the quintessential European state. Indeed, many of the elements we have proposed on a global scale have begun to take effect in the EU. Perhaps, then, it is in Europe that we can begin to realize the aims and ambitions of the Romani people. As the Union grows stronger, we see not only the accretion of powers by the center, but also the devolution of certain decision making to the lowest possible level – the principle of subsidiarity. We are also seeing the free movement of people throughout the EU. Yet a Frenchman does not become less French because he lives in Greece, nor a Spanish woman less Spanish when she resides in the UK, and it is up to governments to represent members of their nations who no longer have a territorial tie to that state. In a way, then, we can see the European project as bringing on precisely the type of relations I am proposing on a global scale. Issues are handled locally if possible, but matters requiring a higher authority because they transcend several regions are dealt with on an EU-wide basis. I merely take the evolution two

16 Philippe C. Schmitter, "If the Nation-State Were to Wither Away in Europe, What Might Replace It?," in *The Future of the Nation-State: Essays on Cultural Pluralism and Political Integration*, ed. Sverker Gustavsson and Leif Lewin (London: Routledge, 1996), pp. 212–213.

steps further in advocating the complete demise of the individual state within Europe, and then by proposing that this be a global rather than a European phenomenon.

Perhaps we should see this as the Romani contribution to the world.

Inequality, Democracy, and Parliamentary Discourses

Ruth Wodak

In April 1997, Vaclav Havel gave an important and widely reported speech in the Deutscher Bundestag (German National Assembly). Marking a new phase in the process of European integration, his speech began thus:

> After some initial agonizing I decided not to think about what is expected of me, to set aside all lists of politically appropriate remarks, and not to experience this responsibility as a trauma but to make the most of this opportunity to concentrate on a single theme, one which to my mind is exceptionally significant and topical. This theme is nothing more nor less than our perception of one's homeland. I have made this choice for two reasons: the first is that the Czech Republic and the Federal Republic of Germany have one important thing in common. In their present form they are very young states that in many ways are still looking for their identity and are consequently redefining what makes them the homeland of their citizens. And yet, paradoxically enough, both our countries have a long tradition of investigating the nature of their national identity and of cultivating or criticizing different forms of their patriotism. The second reason is the ongoing, unprecedented process of European integration, which compels not only you and us but all Europeans to reflect again on what, in this new age, their homeland means or will mean to them, how their patriotism will coexist with the phenomenon of a united Europe and, principally, with the phenomenon of Europeanism. To what extent is it still true that our native land means simply the nation-state in the classic sense of the term and patriotism merely love for our nation?

In this speech, Havel alludes to the past, present, and future of the two countries and also of Europe. The tensions between the traditional nation-state and new supranational entities like the EU are mentioned as relevant for the discursive construction of identities. Havel also notes the most important strategy and component of identity construction: the question of being same, equal, or different than others. Third, the past is discussed, a most difficult past for the joint and individual histories of these two countries, implicating the Nazi past, the communist past, and the attempt of both states to face and confront these memories.

Fourth, Havel discusses the tension between "homeland" and "global entities," which we find expressed today in globalization rhetoric on the one hand, homeland rhetoric on the other. All these topoi to which Havel refers are important in the attempt to construct a new European identity along the frontiers of a New Europe – which, of course, means Western Europe plus perhaps some of the former Eastern Bloc countries. New borders have been drawn, mainly on an economic level, and we hear the slogan "Fortress Europe" again and again.

Havel captured many of the themes that have since preoccupied leading European politicians such as Joschka Fischer, Jacques Delors, Jacques Chirac, and Romano Prodi, all of whom attempt to sketch a new model for the organization of Europe and for European values. This project is fueled, in part, by the debates on EU Enlargement; however, migration, racism, anti-Semitism, and the inclusion/exclusion of minorities and immigrants also play a significant role. In addition, as Prodi emphasized in his speeches throughout 2000, there is much concern about how to preserve traditional European values and Europe's distinctiveness vis-à-vis the United States and Japan. Prodi also stressed the distrust and discontent among "European citizens," who suspect that EU organizations are undemocratic and that decisions are made "behind closed doors." Moreover, with their individual economies, histories, citizenship laws, and attitudes toward EU Enlargement and the EU organizations, considerable tension exists between the European nation-states on all of these questions. Attempts to resolve some of these tensions were seen most recently at meetings of the European Council in Nizza 2000 and Stockholm 2001.

A discourse analysis and study of various genres – speeches, meetings in the EU organizations, national parliamentary debates, and interviews with EU officials – provide insight into the processes of constructing European identities, citizenship, and democracy in the European Union nation-states. Drawing on studies of this type conducted in the Discourse, Politics, Identity unit of the Austrian Academy of Sciences,[1] I will link research on national and European identities to research on immigration debates in six European Union countries.[2] Of particular importance here is the extent to which globalization trends and the associated coming together of nation-states have exposed new discourses of inclusion/exclusion, and, on the basis of these changes, the extent to which traditional values and institutions/organizations still have a role. Specifically, I will expand upon a large interdisciplinary study, *European Union Discourses on*

---

1 See http://www.oeaw.ac.at/wittgenstein.
2 All of this research, which brought together teams of researchers from different disciplines and academic cultures, is theoretically and empirically based, employing quantitative and qualitative methods wherever applicable.

Un/Employment,[3] and consider new developments in the EU organizations and in European nation-states that we have found striking in our ethnographic field-work and empirical research. In this study, we analyzed the recontextualization of certain arguments about employment policies evident in interviews, committee meetings, debates in the European Parliament, and also in written genres like policy papers, resolutions, and presidential decisions of the EU. Among many other significant results, we found the above-mentioned tensions to be very relevant and dominant. Secondly, we were able to track the development of various EU organizations from economic interest groups to value-oriented entities. The tension between globalization rhetoric and homeland rhetoric was a third major finding, manifested, *inter alia*, in debates about legal measures on immigration. Thus, I will also draw on another recent study, *Racism at the Top*.[4]

After some preliminary theoretical observations on supranational organizations and the discursive construction of identities in the EU, I will draw upon a sample of interviews with members of the EU Commission and the European Parliament, who were asked to define and discuss "European" and "European employment policies." Then, using the models and analysis that Peter Muntigl, Gilbert Weiss, and myself developed as an ethnographic approach in Critical Discourse Analysis,[5] I will explore the search for a new European identity in a typical EU network, the Competitiveness Advisory Group, and consider the functions of such new knowledge elites and networks.

Finally, to illustrate the tension between homeland rhetoric and globalization rhetoric, I will turn to parliamentary debates in six EU member states – the UK, France, Austria, the Netherlands, Italy, and Spain – discussing the conflict management implemented by the EU after the installment of Austria's right-wing government in February 2000, the first official intervention into the governmental politics of a nation-state by the EU. This case exemplifies both the EU's attempt to craft "European" democratic values and the role of expert committees in such a process.[6] Like the attempts to cope with immigration, the confrontation with right-wing populist parties represents a test case for European democracies.

3 Peter Muntigl, Gilbert Weiss, and Ruth Wodak, *European Union Discourses on Un/Employment: An Interdisciplinary Approach to Employment, Policy-Making and Organizational Change* (Amsterdam: Benjamins, 2000).
4 Teun van Dijk and Ruth Wodak, eds., *Racism at the Top: Parliamentary Discourses on Ethnic Issues in Six European States* (Klagenfurt: Drava Verlag, 2000).
5 See Muntigl, Weiss, and Wodak, *European Union Discourses on Un/Employment*, and Martin Reisigl and Ruth Wodak, *Discourse and Discrimination: Rhetorics of Racism and Antisemitism* (London: Routledge, 2001), for the theoretical framework and most important methodological assumptions in Critical Discourse Analysis.
6 See Ruth Wodak, "Diskurs, Politik, Identität," in *Der Mensch und seine Sprache(n)*, ed. Oswald Panagl et al. (Vienna: Böhlau, 2001).

Networks, Globalization, and Homeland Rhetoric   The first thesis is that discourses of inclusion and exclusion have remained a constitutive element of political communication, of a politics of identity and difference. At the same time, dynamic borders have been and are being created, in both time and space, a process described by Anthony Giddens as "time and space/time-space distanciation."[7] David Harvey has also demonstrated these tensions empirically in a number of areas of politics and culture.[8] The sense of unsettlement generated by different types of globalization gives rise to a yearning for simple answers, and these in turn lead to ever more fragmentation and insecurity, contradictions and dichotomies (well described by Stuart Hall some years ago). Concepts such as time, space, border, dichotomies such as "us" and "them" need to be thoroughly reviewed in light of new public spaces and the loss of traditional political values.

Over the past four decades, a complex set of institutions has evolved at the European level. These often were designed to manage growing interdependencies and to coordinate cross-national policy making. Political sovereignty may still rest with states, but in important areas, policy making is also the responsibility of European institutions. How the proliferation and deepening of European institutions have affected the political identities of people living in Europe is unclear. Certainly, the history of some nations begins with the state and its cultivation of national sentiment. Are European institutions having a similar effect on political conceptions in Europe? Are they producing a perception of common fate and unified political identity? The process of institutionalizing Europe might also heighten state and national fears and produce backlash movements to defend state sovereignty and cultural autonomy. Moreover, the debate about a European constitution and restructuring the EU is dominant nowadays. Thus, it is important to study the role of suborganizational systems, the development of new public spaces and networks, and the debate about the aims and goals of the EU, which began life as an economic entity (and, of course, still is) but is now also discussing values and ideals.

The second thesis is that experts, using knowledge management and networking strategies, have replaced older decision-making structures in organizations, governments, and nation-states. This is an immediate consequence of globalization: supranational dynamic and flexible commissions and committees are supplanting cumbersome national institutions to an ever greater extent. In this way, in many areas of life, rapid decisions and judgments that in static bureaucratic systems took too long and were beset with too many obstacles have become both

---

7 Anthony Giddens, *The Constitution of Society: Outline of the Theory of Structuration* (Cambridge: Polity Press, 1984), p. 34.
8 David Harvey, *The Condition of Postmodernity* (Cambridge, Mass.: Blackwell, 1989), passim.

vital and possible. Time has accelerated, and now transcends borders. Problems have become more complex, and so knowledge and expertise are more relevant than ever before. Old-style bureaucrats cannot maintain an overview of this complexity. We therefore speak of new elites, of elites of knowledge.

Let me briefly tie these comments to research on organizations. The study of organizational discourses and practices has always centered around the parameters of time and space. In this work, organizational meanings have been considered both diachronic or logo-genetic, and synchronic or intertextual.[9] More recently, as mentioned above, the notions time-space distanciation and time-space compression have been used to describe both organizations in general and organizational interactions specifically. Time-space distanciation enables the extension of social, organizational, and spatial relations over time, mainly through the storage of both meanings and resources (in, for example, databanks, expert practices and procedures, but also interior spaces and buildings). Time-space compression is mainly that which results from the newly emerging communications technologies, and concerns the effects of these technologies on situated interaction.[10]

The Politics of Identity and Difference   Let us now turn to our main subject, the discursive construction of identities in the EU organizations. The politics of identity and difference has become decisive in our globalized world: globalization rhetoric and homeland rhetoric are in a state of dialectical opposition that is manifest in the conflicts between supranational identities (such as the EU) and national (nationalist) and populist movements. Seyla Benhabib has the following to say on this matter:

> Since every search for identity includes differentiating oneself from what one is not, identity politics is always and necessarily a politics of the creation of difference. One is a Bosnian Serb to the degree to which one is not a Bosnian Moslem or a Croat … What is shocking about these developments, is not the inevitable dialectic of identity/difference that they display but rather the atavistic belief that identities can be maintained and secured only by eliminating difference and otherness. The negotiation of identity/difference is the political problem facing democracies on a global scale.[11]

---

9 See Rick Iedema and Ruth Wodak, "Organizational Discourses and Practices," *Discourse & Society* 10, no. 1 (1999), pp. 1–19.

10 See Rick Iedema, "The Formalization of Meaning," *Discourse & Society* 10, no. 1 (1999), pp. 49–66.

11 Seyla Benhabib, "The Democratic Movement and the Problem of Difference," in *Democracy and Difference: Contesting the Boundaries of the Political,* ed. Seyla Benhabib (Princeton, N.J.: Princeton University Press, 1996), pp. 5ff.

The dichotomization of this complex world into such simple categories is truly the constitutive feature of political linguistic usage, persuasive communication, and political action, but in particular of populist rhetoric, even when viewed from a historical perspective. I should like to turn to this feature by exploring this kind of rhetoric as a response to globalization phenomena.

One of the uses of the division between "us" and "them," between globalization rhetoric and homeland rhetoric, is to present one's own actions positively and, conversely, the actions of others negatively. This is a phenomenon that may be given a clear social-psychological explanation, and which researchers like Gordon Allport and Henri Tajfel spoke of many years ago.[12] "We-and-the-other" discourses have several functions, and in particular that of constituting identity but thereby also that of delimiting and excluding.

The work of constituting, delimiting, and excluding is evident in all the examples taken from our study of EU organizations and presented here. In the first example, European Commission employees and members of the European Parliament (MEPs)[13] were asked "Do you consider yourself to be European and, if so, what are the characteristics of being European?" This question required rather direct self-labeling. The characteristics of "European" most frequently mentioned by all interviewees, grouped according to EU organizational affiliation, are summarized in Table 1.

	Way of thinking; Exchanging ideas; Being concerned with own and others' problems	Different but shared cultures, traditions, history, languages	Way of dealing with social, environmental problems; social model; not US, Japan	Part of geographic map, more than EU	Globally competive, especially against US and Japan	Whole is bigger than its parts: being under one roof; added value of EU; strength in diversity	Vision, way, direction for the future	Model for peace
MEPs	4/13	5/13	4/13	4/13	2/13	3/13	4/13	1/13
EC	1/10	3/10	4/10	2/10	3/10	6/10	1/10	1/10
CM	0/4	2/4	1/4	0/4	0/4	1/4	2/4	1/4
	5/27	9/27	9/27	6/27	5/27	10/27	7/27	3/27

Table 1. Characteristics of "European"

Although no definitive comparison among groups is possible, it appears that MEPs and EC officials, while overlapping in the mention of several characteristics, place different emphasis on certain features. Note, for example, that more than half of the Commission officials (6 of 10) stress the "added value" of the member states being united in the European Union. In the words of one official (EC8), it is necessary to "capture Europe's diversity in an economic way," that "Europe's strength is its diversity." In other words, this economic characteristic underscores the legitimacy of the EU. Working together under "one roof," member states can prosper more than if they were to act independently. Among MEPs, on the other hand, no single cluster of characteristics stands out.

When we combine the responses of all three groups, however, we see that certain characteristics of "European" are somewhat more prominent than others: (1) the "added value" of a united Europe; (2) generally shared cultural, historical, and linguistic traditions, differences notwithstanding; (3) the European social model, one that is emphatically not the same as that of the US or many Asian countries; and (4) Europe as a direction or model for the future. Examining these attributes more closely, we could reasonably argue that they resemble the "matrix of contents" that captures themes relevant to the discursive construction of a nation in the linguistic construction of the *homo Austriacus*: a common culture, a common political present and future, a national body, and the "narration and confabulation of a common political past."[14] Among the characteristics of "European" highlighted by the interviewees, there are repeated references to a common culture and past (i.e., shared cultural, historical, linguistic traditions; similar social models) and a common present and future (i.e., European social model; "added value" of being united; a way for the future). Moreover, if identity is to some extent "based on the formation of sameness and difference," we see this in the frequent assertion that Europe is different from the US and Asia (most prominently, Japan), especially in terms of its social model(s).

12 Gordon W. Allport, *The Nature of Prejudice* (Garden City, N.Y.: Doubleday, 1958); Henri Tajfel, *Human Groups and Social Categories: Studies in Social Psychology* (Cambridge: Cambridge University Press, 1981).

13 We conducted 28 interviews with 14 MEPs, all members of the Committee on Employment and Social Affairs; 10 Commission officials, including 8 from DGV (one of 24 directorates-general, DGV is responsible for employment policy), one from DGXV (financial institutions/company law), and the commissioner in charge of employment and social issues; and 4 Austrian delegates to the Council of Ministers, one to Coreper II (ambassador level, permanent representative), one to Coreper I (deputy level), and one a member of the Council's working group on employment and social affairs.

14 Ruth Wodak, Rudolf de Cillia, Martin Reisigl, and Karin Liebhart, *The Discursive Construction of National Identity* (Edinburgh: Edinburgh University Press, 1999), pp. 57–60.

Let us now turn to my second example, the Competitiveness Advisory Group (CAG) and its discourse of identity and difference, as well as its functions. The CAG, was set up by Jacques Santer, former president of the European Commission, in order to prepare specific drafts and proposals for the Council of Ministers. The group consists of twelve members, two women and ten men, who represent industry, politics, and the trade unions; the European Commission itself is also represented by one member. These representatives discuss highly sensitive issues and draft semi-annual reports. The CAG is chaired by Jean-Claude Paye, former secretary-general of the OECD, whom I interviewed in Paris in September 1998. CAG meetings are audiotaped, and there are handwritten minutes as well as resolution papers.

The CAG is an example of an "epistemic community" or "transnational knowledge community" which "proposes problem definitions, argumentations, and policies."[15] In November 1997, the CAG was asked to draw up an employment policy paper for the Council of Ministers. The final paper manifests clearly the conflicts between employers and trade unions on many levels. It is an attempt to outline a European employment policy, a policy that would change the social welfare states but nevertheless retain European values.

In the interview with Paye, I asked about the decision-making process and his impressions about it as well as about the impact of the CAG's policy papers. The CAG must serve some important function, otherwise such busy and influential people would not take the trouble to meet and spend time together. As already mentioned, networking is one of the main characteristics of such transnational bodies. The second important function is most certainly legitimation: the policy paper serves as a legitimation tool for politicians should they need it. The chairperson himself is well aware of these functions:

I: What happens with these reports. Who *reads* them?

P: *This* is this is uh this is a problem I um spoke a*bout* with uh with President Santer, because – my impression is that uh uh the agenda of uh of uh the [European] Council – according to what I read in – in the *[laughs]* press communiqué is so: – *heavy,* so het-*erogeneous* so di*verse,* that they *can*not – devote uh uh much *time* to to every *sub*ject. – I don't know how it is going *now,* um – let me take the example of this uh report in November *[coughs]* – there were – two reports to the European Council, coming from a wide va*riety* of uh of institutions and I've been *told* that the European *Parl*iament made a report, the [Hungarian Social Council] made a re*port,* uh the – there were – two or three other reports in addition to *ours.* – of *course* – the the heads of [state and govern-

15 Ulrich Beck, "Wie wird Demokratie im Zeitalter der Globalisierung möglich?," in *Politik der Globalisierung,* ed. Ulrich Beck (Frankfurt am Main: Suhrkamp, 1998), p. 39.

ment] haven't been able to to read all all that *stuff*, and not even their *aides*. I have been able – *there*fore I don't know. – I don't know what the the real *im*pact uh uh *is*, – which uh of course is a bit uh – well discouraging.

As is evident, Paye himself is pessimistic about the influence of a group such as the CAG. Nevertheless, he is committed to the work and believes that the debates are important. The papers are circulated widely and – as Paye argues – might have an impact somewhere at some time.

So, we are left with the question of what functions such a group serves and why so much work is invested in a policy paper that may or may not be read by its intended audience. I believe that the main function lies in the establishing of solidarity and networks, of having discussion fora in which European citizens can meet. Only in such a way, at many different places and times, is the construction of a new European identity possible. And at the same time, only through extended debates between the social partners are new economic policies developed. The CAG provides a stage for such ideological debates, a public space where different ideologies and opinions can be aired and negotiated. This, in my view, is the most important function of such advisory groups.

Before turning to the perspective of the nation-states, I would like to illustrate the ideological debates on the new European identity from inside this small group of experts:

M3: ...And my last point is, which you have already mentioned, the high level of education and the professionalism in the European countries. These all are positive. [Et mon dernier point c'était, mais vous l'avez déjà mentionné, le niveau élevé de l'éducation et de la formation professionnel dans la plupart des pays Européens. Ca sont des atouts.]

M9: I think, another strong point which we're just beginning to see is in the context of a global marketplace. Europe's historical positioning around the world. And the fact that uniquely in terms of the main blocks of economic activity – the United States, Europe, and Japan – we in Europe are best positioned to cover the world with cultural and commercial links. And if I can turn to my left, you take Spain, I mean, Spain has rediscovered an Hispanic market which extends not just throughout most of Latin America but also of course in[to] the United States. And we're beginning to find in other parts of the world that we have links, which are old links, which have been dormant and which can come forth, and in terms of, you know, Europe in a global marketplace, that inheritance is very very strong. But we got to capitalize it, and use it.

Paye: Just, a, a sentence adding to that point. European is more international than, than other ones, and ...

M9: Exactly, and it's very much easier as a European to develop commercial partnerships outside your domestic country than it is for Americans, or Japanese. And that's partly because of our inheritance and history.

M4: … maybe, our diversity …

M9: … that too …

M3: Diversity is a richness, not a weakness, to a large extent.

M9: There are two layers to it: I mean, the, the, there is the diversity and that in one sense or another we cover the globe, but there is also the, the history and the way in which we have operated. We do have a more global view of the world than the Americans, far more so.

M3: Exactly, it is the long-term favor of fallout of our colonial past. Yeah, after thirty years of independence of all our former colonies we can say that now, today. Without being accused of neo-, neocolonialism. Yeah.

F1: In a more friendly way, in our entrepreneurship. Our ancestors went out sailing, to do business.

M6: Well, American multinationals have done well but, I mean you, I mean the, the, the, many sectors, I'm not saying your sector, but I mean, one cannot forget that …

M9: I, I, I'm not … the Americans, in that sense, and all I'm saying is that they do have a blind spot. And their blind spot is often their inability to make partnerships outside their domestic base. And they have significant blind spots within Europe, in, Europe is Europe is Europe, except there is an English-speaking bit in the UK, and they have difficulty in sensing the differences between countries, and it, it's much tougher for them. Whereas we have something which we haven't used for a long time, but is, is, is coming forward here, and, I, I, I do take the Hispanic point is very strong as you know and me too well, in all sorts of businesses, telecommunications, financial services, you name it, they've found a new market.

Paye: Alright, do you see any other strong points, or should we move to the next session?

This sequence is one of the few in which spontaneous discussion occurs. It is like a brainstorming session where everyone contributes to the characteristics of a new European identity, one which stands in contrast to the US and Japan. One might have the impression that committee members are trying to convince each other that specific European aspects should be viewed as positive and not negative. This sequence also functions to emphasize group solidarity. Without analyzing it in detail, I would like to point out two main linguistic strategies employed here: legitimation and difference. All the characteristics mentioned in this short dialogue point to Europe's traditions in justice and welfare, education and professional expertise. Specifically, Europe's internationalism is mentioned, its history of "contact" with other parts of the world (colonialism!), in contrast to the US. Other characteristics are added during the session. Unlike racist discourse on immigration,[16] diversity is here defined in a positive way, as richness of cultures and traditions and languages. All the positive characteristics reassure committee members that Europe has a chance in the world market even though taxes are higher and labor laws stricter. Specific Europeanness is constructed interactively. Another strategy, typical in discourses on identity, consists of constructing uniqueness by distinguishing oneself from others, in this case the US and Japan. The entire exchange is very significant in the meeting. It creates optimism and confirms for committee members that there are indeed solutions to European economic problems. A positive self-assessment makes everyone feel stronger. Thus, this passage also constructs the identities of the committee members. Note that a national identity, namely Spain, is held up as an exemplar, *pars pro toto*. The "Hispanic example" provides an illustration of what Europe could achieve.

To summarize: Europe is in search of a new employment policy because of global structural changes, but this new policy should be different from that of the US and Japan. The politics of identity and difference – to return to our topos – becomes very visible as well as the impact of regional, national, and supranational identities. Secondly, it must also be emphasized that such a debate can occur even in a committee dealing with pure economics, with un/employment defined as an economic not a social problem.

Discourse and Politics: Us and Them　　　In the final examples, I would like to turn to homeland rhetoric, illustrating the tensions between the EU and its member states.

First, let me summarize some of the aims of our study *Racism at the Top*, in which we compared six member states on immigration issues, thus illustrating the tensions between the values of tolerance/diversity and racism/exclusion. Our main research questions can be condensed as follows: How do elite politicians from all parties in six EU countries speak about immigration and immigrants? How are immigration laws discussed and which arguments are brought into parliamentary debates by which parties? We chose two years, 1996 and 1997, for our quantitative analysis; however, for the interpretation and context description, the sociopolitical developments of the last three decades were included.

16　See Ruth Wodak and Maria Sedlak, "'We demand that foreigners adapt to our life-style': Political Discourse on Immigration Laws in Austria and the United Kingdom," in *Combating Racial Discrimination: Affirmative Action as a Model for Europe,* ed. Erna Appelt and Monika Jarosch (Oxford: Berg, 2000), pp. 217–237.

Parliamentary debates are a genre of political discourse and of the political arena as such; no specific features distinguish parliamentary debates from other genres of persuasive discourse. The distinction lies in the functions of parliamentary discourse: lawmaking, legitimation, and social control. It is reasonable to ask why we should bother to study parliamentary debates if they are not the "real" arena of decision making and official politics. We believe that in democracies, parliamentary debates are *the* forum of public space in which citizens have access to lawmaking and to political conflicts and controversies. As long as parliaments function, democracies are alive! Moreover, debates are often televised and thus reach millions of viewers who gain insight into policy making.

We could not analyze entire debates, as these were very long and ultimately not significant for our research aims. Thus, we chose case studies for each country and analyzed these qualitatively, focusing on topoi, metaphors, argumentation, fallacies, self-presentation, and actors-description. This selection of linguistic indicators is justified because it is precisely in the argumentation, in the applied strategies and topoi, as well as in the use of referential terms that the distinction between "us" and "them," and the nature of that distinction, becomes most transparent. The quantitative analysis, in which we coded debate topics as well as the parties and persons involved, was done for comparative purposes.

Generally, as our discourse analysis shows, parties of the Left and Right in most of the countries, despite socioeconomic differences, are extremely polarized on immigration issues. The Western European democratic tradition demands tolerance and acceptance of refugees; the extreme Right and some rightist parties openly violate this principle, using the topoi of threat, criminality, and job loss in debates to block liberal immigration policies. The Right uses much more rhetorical devices and metaphors as well as legitimation strategies. They "turn the tables": the victims are not the refugees but the population at "home," which is spending too much money to support immigrants, and meanwhile is exploited and at risk of losing jobs and political rights. However, with the exception of the inflammatory discourse of the extreme Right, these arguments are coded and legitimized via a number of linguistic devices along lexical, semantic, syntactic, and textual dimensions. Parties in most of the countries present themselves as "tolerant and democratic," while simultaneously disparaging immigrants. Thus, groups of actors are constructed discursively, which allows presentation of the in-group as positive and the out-group as negative. Also, in all countries, there is a classification of types of foreigners into "good" and "bad," more threatening and less threatening.

Numbers and statistics play a central role in all countries as well: an economic discourse is employed and functionalized to mask racist attitudes. Secondly, a discourse of "security" evolves: the government must protect voters and the in-group against criminality, unemployment, and various other threats. A very important strategy is the generalization of singular experiences with "bad" foreigners, which thus are used to characterize the entire group. The opposition may counter these claims with a "discourse of solidarity": everyone has a moral duty to assist those who are at risk of poverty. Or it may deploy a discourse of "positive diversity": the European countries need diversity and are multicultural, not monocultural; they are all countries of immigration. When faced with such arguments, the extreme Right sometimes presents foreigners as "nonhumans," thereby dehumanizing people and robbing them of their rights.

In France, the discussion is polarized between the political Right and Left, and implicit and more-or-less explicit racism is restricted to the Right and extreme Right. Antiracist movements in France are very strong, compared to Austria for example. Discussions on immigration and nationality seem to reflect a more general political crisis related to the decline of the nation-state and the perceived need to preserve historically constituted identities. In the Netherlands, which has a very long history of relative tolerance, the taboo against explicit racism is even stronger, thus a coded language is used. Policy making is thus much more consensual, and discursive consciousness seems relatively highly developed. The evolution toward stricter immigration policies is justified with positive self-presentation drawing upon the tradition of tolerance and a self-image of a "civilized country using careful procedures."

The discussion in Great Britain is polarized between left and right parties, and the topoi of "illegal immigrants" and "criminality" is quite prominent. The same holds true for Italy, where, however, these topoi are counterbalanced by a discourse on solidarity and human rights, along with argumentation aimed at legitimizing immigration. The majority center-left coalition has succeeded in maintaining these positive themes – whether symbolically or substantively – as constitutive parts of the debate. The history of immigration is invoked, however, not just to support antiracist positions, but also for positive in-group representation of the "good" immigrants of the past versus the "bad" ones of today.

The fact that immigration in Spain is more recent and has not yet reached a large scale is explained by the history of Spain itself as an emigration country. Thus, parliamentary debates on immigration are rare. The identification with emigrants prohibits explicitly racist statements. Moreover, there are no extreme right-wing parties in parliament which clearly would oppose immigration. Nevertheless, as illustrated in our research, implicit racist utterances are to be found. Spain is seen as the entrance to the "European fortress" and the main focus here is the demand for preemptive policies to control future immigration.

In Austria, we also find the polarization between Left and Right in discussions on asylum and residence of foreigners. In contrast to the other countries, the extreme Right is very strong and seems to lead the discussion. Antiracist movements are rather weak. Explicit racism is not taboo and is openly expressed in parliament. The discourse of the mainstream parties reflects the arguments of the Right, in an attempt to appropriate the Right's popularity and win voters. In the debates, it is presupposed that foreigners are criminal. Foreigners are categorized into three groups: legal residents, asylum seekers, and new immigrants, which are more or less welcome dependent on their home country.

To summarize, anti-immigration parties use the following arguments: (1) Immigrants and asylum seekers abuse the system; they live on taxpayer money. (2) Immigrants are a danger to society (criminality). (3) Lax immigration policies encourage illegal immigration. (4) Significant numbers of immigrants work illegally; they are a threat to employment. (5) Asylum seekers cost too much (topos of numbers). (6) "Firm" but "fair" immigration policies are necessary (topos of positive self-presentation). The opposition argues that: (1) Harsh immigration and asylum laws violate human rights. (2) Tighter asylum and immigration rules encourage illegal immigration. (3) "Civilized" and "tolerant" countries are obliged to assist people in need. (4) People will lose their jobs (the "race card" is functionalized to win voters by the topos of threat). (5) Harsh anti-immigration laws encourage racism and hurt ethnic minorities. (6) Diversity is important for Europe.

Racism is produced and reproduced through discourse. Antiracist discourse the same! The results of our research thus hold practical implications for public discourse about the Other. The detailed analysis in the case studies of each of the six countries reveals the specific quality and dynamic of these discourses when manifested in debate and makes political interests and ideologies transparent. This, ultimately, will allow for the development of alternative strategies of argumentation and conflict.

Conclusions   Summarizing, I would like to conclude this talk with a discussion of the EU's first attempt to "punish" a member state for not acting according to the values of the *dispositif ideal*. I refer to the case of the "Three Wise Men" who judged the behavior of Austria's right-wing coalition government, which assumed power in February 2000. The fourteen other member states immediately implemented "measures against the new government," which were recontexualized as "sanctions against Austria" in official discourse. Offended by the EU's actions, Austrians rallied to support the government. The sanctions had precisely the opposite effect intended by the EU (strengthening the coalition rather than weakening it), prompting member states to come up with an exit strategy. This is when the Three Wise Men were called upon: the former Finnish president, the Spanish chancellor, and a prominent German political scientist, who visited Austria twice, spoke to many delegates, officials, and NGOs, and issued an extensive report in September 2000. Among other things, the report assessed the populist discourse of the FPÖ (Freiheitliche Partei Österreichs – Austrian Freedom Party) and came to the conclusion that the FPÖ is a right-wing populist party with extremist elements.

What functions does such an expert committee fulfill? First, there is the critical question concerning the status of "experts" and "knowledge management." It is common these days for commissions to have a transnational brief: recall the Waldheim Commission and the Historians' Report, or the moratorium on the *Wehrmacht* exhibition. The case of the Three Wise Men does not fit into this schema, because here it was not only a question of scientific experts but of "elder statesmen" who, under considerable time pressure, had to exercise diplomatic and political conflict management and legitimize the "exit strategy" upon which member states had already informally agreed. As Romano Prodi, president of the EU Commission, declared in June 2000 when the Three Wise Men were put to work, they should be "quick, quick, quick." Diplomacy is reflected in the language they used, a language that is not scientific but vague. In their report, this vagueness is particularly evident in statements based on documents and testimony from NGOs, thus on reported speech.[17]

The usurping of political action by such political entrepreneurs, as Paul Krugman has described them, is a characteristic of the globalized society.[18] Both Krugman and Ulrich Beck even speak of a "committee regime," referring to Van Schendelen's research.[19] Static national organizations are, to an ever greater extent, being replaced by such transnational networks. This was already apparent in the decision-making mechanisms of the EU and the CAG.[20] The intervention of such international committees of experts demonstrates, however, that traditional national borders are no longer valid, that is to say, that "abroad" and "home" are becoming blurred, that foreign policy is becoming

---

17 See Margaretha Kopeinig and Christoph Kotanko, *Eine europäische Affäre: Der Weisen-Bericht und die Sanktionen gegen Österreich* (Vienna: Czernin Verlag, 2000).

18 Paul Krugman, *Peddling Prosperity: Economic Sense and Nonsense in the Age of Diminished Expectations* (New York: Norton, 1994).

19 M. P. C. M. Van Schendelen, "EC Committees: Influence Counts More Than Legal Powers," in *Shaping European Law and Policy: The Role of Committees and Commitology Processes in the Political Process,* ed. Robin Pedler and Guenther F. Schaefer (Maastricht: European Institute of Public Administration, 1996), pp. 25–38.

20 See Muntigl, Weiss, and Wodak, *European Union Discourses on Un/Employment,* pp. 73ff.

internal policy, and that the language of experts has assumed a dominant role. Professional roles and definitions are changing: in our EU research, it was quite evident that we are approaching a politicization of the bureaucracy and a depoliticization of politics. An entire register of competencies is expected and used: bureaucrats must be able to negotiate like diplomats, they are often experts in a particular subject, and they develop policies. Politicians administer these policies and attempt to "sell them." And it is at this point that political rhetoric takes over. We are dealing here with an example – even in the case of the Three Wise Men – of those *epistemic communities* or transnational communities of knowledge and expertise that, as Ulrich Beck says, "develop, own, and provide common definitions of problems, causal assumptions, and political recommendations."[21] International organizations increasingly depend on this kind of transnational expert rationale, which, conversely, is invading ever more arenas of social practice. What is characteristic of such communities is that the border between reflective-distanced expertise on the one hand, and political action on the other (or "policy making" as we call it today) is disappearing. In fact, it is no longer possible to determine clearly who is the politician and who the expert.

This case of conflict management also has enormous implications for the formulation of new European values and identities. It was the first time that "measures" were taken against a nation-state and EU member for violating the values of democracy, justice, and equality. The action taken by the fourteen member states clearly shows that the EU organizations, in their search for a European identity, have evolved from purely economic interest groups into something else – purveyors of a system of values. This is what makes the Austrian example so pertinent to the development of Europe, which Tony Judt calls "an idea" not "a region."[22] Of course, many questions remain. What will be the EU's response to other, more powerful member states with populist parties in the government (a question discussed at Nizza and likely to be formalized after the Italian elections)? Is national sovereignty still respected? The political models presented for Austria are not, of course, restricted to that country or to the present day. Globalization and homeland rhetoric, as well as right-wing populism, are on the increase throughout Western Europe, a fact powerfully demonstrated in a number of election campaigns, such as the recent one in Belgium by the Vlaams Blok. Although the specifically Austrian stimulus for the EU's actions was the "sloppy handling of its National Socialist past," the measures taken against the new Austrian government must also be evaluated in this larger context.

---

21 Beck, *Politik der Globalisierung*, p. 21.
22 Tony Judt, *A Grand Illusion? An Essay on Europe* (New York: Hill and Wang, 1996), p. 139.

In Brussels and Strasbourg, home to the EU organizations, one is struck by the semiotics of the buildings: they are like fortresses or churches, big stable structures where entrance is controlled by many passwords, guards, and X-rays. Everyone busily runs around through endless corridors, eleven languages are to be heard, and many intercultural gestures and misunderstandings can be perceived. In these complex organizations, where gender, age, ideologies, political parties, lobbies, national, regional, and European interests clash, consensus is nevertheless achieved. These slow, bureaucratic organizations have created small, flexible, and dynamic networks to enable rapid decision-making and consensus-building, bypassing all the possible hurdles. But it is precisely these networks that are untransparent, inaccessible to European citizens. Members of these networks are occasionally interviewed and their work reported on, such as the case of the Three Wise Men; or prominent elites make decisions without even listening to them, as in the CAG. These transnational networks of experts – the new knowledge society – are supplanting all our well-established forms of institutional action and knowledge.

This takes us back to our beginning, to Vaclav Havel and his observations on the functioning of new globalizing processes and the search for patriotism and supranational identities. Our perceptions of national identities and of political organizations have changed. Parliamentary discourses and their analysis have illustrated aspects of legal decision making in the nation-states and the prevailing prejudices and beliefs related to "immigrants" and "foreigners." How will these problems be resolved on the transnational scale? And in what ways will European citizens have access to decision making and information? What impact will antidiscrimination guidelines have? And how to cope with antidemocratic movements and ideology, with discrimination, racism, xenophobia, and anti-Semitism? The European Union is confronted with the monumental task of constructing European values of tolerance and diversity. The answers to all of these questions lie in the future. And, I believe, these questions lie at the heart of the EU's future.

It is appropriate to end with Tony Judt's succinct statement on the European problem, found in his book *A Grand Illusion? An Essay on Europe*:

> If we look to European Union as a solution for everything, chanting "Europe" like a mantra, waving the banner of "Europe" in the face of recalcitrant "nationalist" heretics and screaming "Abjure, abjure," we shall wake up one day to find that far from solving the problems of our continent, the myth of "Europe" has become an impediment to our recognizing them. We shall discover that it has become little more than the politically correct way to paper over local difficulties, as though the mere invocation of the promise of Europe could substitute for solving problems and crises that really affect the

place. Few would wish to deny the ontological existence of Europe, so to speak. And there IS a certain self-fulfilling advantage in speaking of it as though it existed in some strong collective sense. … "Europe" is more than a geographical notion but less than an answer.[23]

23 Ibid., pp. 140–141.

Unrealized Democracy and a Posthumanist Art

Iain Chambers

The work of art allows us to glimpse, for an instance,
the there in the here, the always in the now.

Octavio Paz[1]

I   How should citizenship and its accompanying political and cultural agency be conceptualized in the present-day context of transnational economies and international global framing? And what has art got to do with it? Out beyond the pleas for solidarity, ecological responsibility, and the recognition of a global multicultural heritage, the world is riven by local wars and planetary poverty. The brutal historical discrepancy between a rich, overdeveloped, minority and a poor, underprivileged and underrepresented, majority persists.

I commence from this cruel benchmark. For neither a profound structural redistribution nor ethical sea change able to challenge a narrowing horizon of expectation seems imminent. No one is giving up what they have. Yet how then does one speak of citizenship, with its associated *individual freedom for* future action and *freedom from* immediate want, in a world where, for the majority, the concept crumbles into rhetorical dust before the implacable insistence of simply surviving? Or, rather, and this would be altogether more disquieting to consider: the demand for civic freedoms and justice from the fields and sweatshops of the rural and urban poor perhaps exceeds the classic sense of citizenship, peculiar to the property and propriety of urban modernity, that we are accustomed to employ.

The world, as the Palestinian intellectual Edward Said notes, is full of "undocumented people," both in the bureaucratic and historical sense.[2] This, he continues, is the noncosmopolitan mass that exists beyond art, subjectivity, and political and cultural representation. This is the reverse side, the dark side, of Benedict Anderson's noted insistence on the anonymous state of nationhood.[3] Such peoples are "exiled" in many ways; not only, and most obviously, in the form of physical and material dislocation, but also economically, politically, and

---

1 Octavio Paz, "Pintado en México," *El Pais*, November 7, 1983.
2 Edward W. Said, "The Mind of Winter: Reflections on Life in Exile," *Harper's* (September 1984).
3 Benedict Anderson, *Imagined Communities: Reflections on the Origin and Spread of Nationalism* (London: Verso, 1991).

culturally excluded from the agenda that dictates global development and "progress." But if the overdeveloped world requires the rest of the planet for economic and material resources, not to speak of the persistent presence of an abjected alterity that cruelly mirrors and measures its own privileged identity, it also manufactures a dramatic counter-space from where such an identity comes necessarily to be critically and dramatically reassessed. A state of powerlessness reveals potential powers. Of course, nothing is encountered or lived in such stark black-and-white terms. Worldly configurations and locations are altogether more complex and hybrid in their formation and articulation. No one simply occupies a single category, destined to respect its premises forever. Yet we surely live in a time, simultaneously characterized by globalization and crises, when it is necessary to return to the sobering structures in which political change and cultural transformation occur. Here it is important to recognize in the increasingly creolized conditions of metropolitan life not only the enrichment of the First World, but also the charged demands of other worlds that continue to exist far beyond the superficial grasp of a beneficial domestication.

II   Here, rendered vulnerable by proximity and the intersection of my world by the worlds of others, my identity is both contested and reconfigured in the reply to such "intrusions." The countervailing excursion of other identities into "my" world, induced by the breaking open and scattering of a previous locality, is invariably explained in terms of the radical configuration of late modernity. This is a historical moment that has been irreversibly invested by the interactive economic, social, cultural, and political procedures of "globalization." Yet my identity formation also invokes deeper historical currents. I am carried back at least to that instance in which the West and the "world" are recognized and institutionalized as stable conceptual frames of reference in a particular period, place, and population.

The instance the West identifies itself and simultaneously establishes the world in its image is clearly the historical moment when a certain intellectual and cultural formation confidently brings all under a single point of view, subject to a unique and unilateral perspective. Fears and desires are objectified, a sense of "home" and "abroad," of the domestic scene and "otherness," firmly established. What today is experienced as a "loss" is surely the taken-for-granted security of such premises. If this "world picture" (Heidegger)[4] is an integral part of the initial disposition of occidental modernity, of its powers and the subse-

---

4 Martin Heidegger, "The Age of the World Picture," in *The Question Concerning Technology and Other Essays*, trans. William Levitt (New York: Harper & Row, 1977).

quent mapping of itself on the rest of the globe, then its contemporary interrogation, displacement, dislocation, perhaps alerts us to a potential epochal shift?

Notwithstanding the sociological understanding of symbolic interactionism and its notion of identity emerging in the relationship between self and society, here we encounter an already more complex historical, cultural, and psychic configuration in which there emerges a historically elaborated self rather than a stable essence who is subsequently stitched or sutured into external political and cultural structures and processes. The "out there" is also "in here," the portal is porous, and whatever is repressed outlines the representation. This is to propose not merely a commonwealth of identification, but also an uncomfortable understanding of identity, including its deepest psychic recesses, being formed, articulated, extended, and explored as a "way in the world."[5] This passage has precise historical, political, and philosophical contours and configurations. Such is the space, and the limits, of modern, occidental identity.

In the opening sequences of Werner Herzog's film *Cobra Verde* (1988), itself based on Bruce Chatwin's *The Viceroy of Ouidah*,[6] there occurs a discussion between a Brazilian plantation owner and Francisco Manoel da Silva, the future slave trader portrayed by Klaus Kinski. It goes like this:

> I've another forty sugar plantations just like this one. I alone produce ... 120,000 tons per year, and all of it goes to England. They've abolished the slave trade. They seize our ships, and yet without us they wouldn't have any sugar. Look at the way they buy the sugar, you'd think our rivers were overflowing with the stuff. It's grotesque.

In the "progress" that the Caribbean poet Derek Walcott justly calls "history's dirty joke,"[7] here in the mid-19th century we encounter an abolitionist Great Britain that since 1833 patrols the high seas, seizing vessels involved in the slave trade, while continuing to enjoy the benefits of slave labor in the cotton that dresses its citizens and the sugar that goes into the tea cups on domestic breakfast tables.

This suggests that the much-quoted process of "globalization" is not simply a contemporary phenomenon, but is rather integral to the making of occidental modernity from the beginning. It was inaugurated with the possibility of reducing the world to a single map or "world picture," to a unique point of view representing the interests and desires of the occidental observer. In this picture, the

---

5 V. S. Naipaul, *A Way in the World* (London: Minerva, 1995).
6 Bruce Chatwin, *The Viceroy of Ouidah* (London: Picador, 1982).
7 Derek Walcott, "The Schooner *Flight*," in *Collected Poems 1948–1984* (London: Faber & Faber, 1992), p. 356.

forced black diaspora out of Africa into slavery, the systematic exploitation and genocide of the Americas, emerge as central, not peripheral, to the global making of the modern Western world. Within this modernity, the specific geopolitical location of the observer assumes a universal relevance: occidental subjectivity and objectivity become one. This, of course, is humanism, and it helps us to understand the political significance of a proposed "posthumanism" as the reinscription of locality and limits into the point of view, the voice, the knowledge, that now finds itself speaking in the interstices of a heterogeneous, rather than homogeneous, world; a world, as Paul Gilroy consistently reminds us, that was historically constructed in terror as well as in reason.

III   It is impossible to free oneself from a past that has brought us to where and how we inhabit today. A citizenship, a democracy, historically formed in and through the structural inequalities that configured modernity, is not an abstract moral category, but a historical process realized in regimes of power. Here, again, lies the centrality, proposed by C. L. R James and recently reiterated by Paul Gilroy, of slavery to the making of Atlantic democracies.[8] The expansion of commerce and civil rights is intertwined and directly inscribed in the stipulation of the American Constitution by a slave-owning plantocracy. Further, it is the exploitation of the New World that contextualizes the political demands of the rising European bourgeoisie and the French Revolution, not to speak of its subsequent and paradoxical inspiration for the slave rebellion of its richest colony: Saint Dominique, later Haiti.

Such an altogether more undecided and heterogeneous understanding of modernity, composed of a series of always incomplete "projects," serves to remind us of paths not taken, of possibilities blocked in blood and repression, of processes and procedures that, even if they have disappeared, recall the irreducible quality of the world and its multiple kind. The "archaic," the repressed, and the unruly lace modernity, forcing the latter to register its transformation, its transit, its accidental quality and potential loss of control, no matter how powerful the appeal to the homogeneous prospect of "progress." In this there lies a freedom, frequently unrealized, but awaiting, in which we, too, are invited to participate.

To insist on the historically contingent is also to insist on the travel and elaboration of identity, subjectivity, and "citizenship" in language, where history

---

8 C. L. R. James, *The Black Jacobins: Toussaint L'Ouverture and the San Domingo Revolution* (London: Allison & Busby, 1980); Paul Gilroy, *The Black Atlantic: Modernity and Double Consciousness* (Cambridge, Mass.: Harvard University Press, 1993).

encounters a reply that exceeds its institutionalized grammar. It is where the prosaic and the poetic exceed and interrogate inherited political identifications. It is where, to repeat Okwui Enwezor's observation, "we are moved to question whether the notion of democracy can still be sustained only within the philosophical grounds of Western epistemology."[9] Here the "I" moves through the translated and translating space of the world, becoming a subject for whom knowledge, sense, and truth are irreducible to a unique point of view. Such a subject exists *besides and beyond* occidental humanism. Opposed to the abstract, patriarchal universalism that humanism once proposed, this is a subject that registers the diversification of centers and yet paradoxically is precisely *more human* in recognizing its own specific limits and location. This sense of one's self proposes a less assured and altogether more unguarded appropriation of where we come from (tradition, memory, nostalgia), as well as of the historical, political, and cultural structures and institutions in which we come to identify our passage through the world.

IV   In the last two decades it has been, above all, the interruption of postcolonial studies that has sought to critically articulate such a situation. Here there emerges the insistent reply of diverse worlds that are no longer separated, out there, at a distance, but which emerge in insistent border crossings that simultaneously register, resist, and reroute the passage of transnational capital. From elsewhere arrive the "them" who refuse to remain "them," but who at the same time refuse simply to become "us"; that is, who refuse to negate either the "roots" or the "routes" that render a "there" also a "here."

The social, cultural, and political import of this reconfiguration of "here" and "there" perennially echoes in the necessary and disquieting alterity of art: the aesthetics (and ethics) of disturbance that reveals a gap, an interval in the world, that signals a limit and establishes a transit, a passage elsewhere. It is in this space – historically nominated with such terms as the sublime, the uncanny, alterity – that the pedagogical languages of institutional identity, busily seeking to legitimate the narration of nation, citizenship, and cultural subjectivity, are interceded and deviated by what refuses to make sense or speak in *that* prescribed way. What this understanding of art holds out is the promise of interrupting such an order, of punctuating the homogeneous, historical time of "progress" that the West considers itself to represent. The art of the interruption, art as interruption, both brings to light our prescribed state – its limits and loca-

9 Okwui Enwezor, "Democracy Unrealized," in *Platform1_Documenta11: Democracy Unrealized* (brochure/conference program) (Kassel: Documenta11, 2001), p. 4.

tion in time and place – while also opening out on to the possibility of revisiting, reciting (in the sense of reworking), and resiting (in the sense of transporting) those languages elsewhere. Here the prescribed is overtaken by the inscription, by the event, both artistic and ontological, that exceeds the syntax of expectancy and the semantics of institutional sense.

Here I would like to offer an example from popular metropolitan culture (although in this perspective the distinction between popular and elite cultures and art is of little significance) to underline how the space of the same city, of urban and youth culture, of music and the languages of identity, are translated and transformed to reveal other histories, cultures, and identities within the same scene. In Gurinder Chadha's short film *I'm British But …* (1990), we see a band of Asian musicians playing Bhangra music on a rooftop in Southall, London. Whether deliberate or not, this image recalls the scene of another group playing on a rooftop in London some twenty years previously: the Beatles performing "Get Back." In the repetition and doubling of the same metropolitan space and its associated languages, there emerges the use of the same languages – musical, metropolitan, and mediafied – to propose two different places. The former is that of Beatlemania, "swinging London," and public white youth culture, the second is that of the diasporic music, culture, and identity of Bhangra. What comes home in this comparison is not merely the articulation of cultural and historical difference taking up residence in the same space. The later Bhangra formation is not so much something imported from the elsewhere of the Punjab but is rather a particular and local urban elaboration, springing out of the same complex historical and cultural locality as the earlier metropolitan Britain represented by the Beatles.

Art revisits and reworks the conceptual language that contains us. It is art, according to the "postmodern primitive," Cherokee artist Jimmie Durham, that is "looking for connections that cannot, may be, should not, be made."[10] In art's insistence on the ontological event of language – as what occurs in the transitory configuration of sound, language, structure, and vision: of our being in language and of our language in being – ideas about ourselves, about our democracy, our citizenship, our identity, are historically radicalized and transmuted into temporal processes. Here they are rendered open-ended and vulnerable to the journey of interpretation, to the interruption of an ongoing, worldly interrogation.

In this altogether more fractured perspective, we meet the broken narratives of an elsewhere that refuse to fit into the unfolding of our lives. Any narrative, any accounting of the world, that is willing to receive and offer hospitality to

---

10 Jimmie Durham, *The East London Coelacanth* (video) (London: Institute of Contemporary Arts, 1993).

the disturbance that uproots the *domus* and invites us *not to feel at home at home* (to quote Adorno)[11] renders the universal story many of us think we are living, more localized, limited, *unsettled.*

In the poetic power of languages to reconfigure space in a diverse understanding of place, location, and identity, "home" is rendered an altogether more open-ended and vulnerable habitat. The latter provides less the comfort and consolation of an eventual homecoming and more the perpetual point of departure for a journey destined to render uninhabitable previous understandings. This is why ideas of institutionalized multiculturalism and "tolerance" are ethically and historically insufficient. As the links between language, land, and identity are inhabited by other histories and subsequently stretched to breaking point, it becomes possible, and urgently necessary, to envisage a diverse worlding of the cultural, historical, and political languages that represent us, and in which we represent ourselves.

Here, if the world is rendered less provincial, it is, above all a West, so used to self-confirmation in every corner of the planet, that is deprovincialized. This propels us to acknowledge Dipesh Chakrabarty's important announcement of "provincializing Europe."[12] Or, more paradoxically, given that it is the habit of provincialism to consider itself always at the center, it brings us to deprovincialize Europe. It is in this context that a certain failure or "weakening" of thought and theory, proposed by the contemporary Italian philosopher Gianni Vattimo,[13] references the conclusion of the universal singularity of the occidental view (*teoria*) of the world, leading to a subsequent opening provoked by the journey of its languages beyond previous borders and orders.

In breaching the confines of the local and the familiar in order to travel in a space authorized by language itself, the ethical and the aesthetic are radically reconfigured. In the shift of language into a posthumanist landscape where no single subject, history, or culture is able to authorize the narration, or the interpretation, there occurs a marked displacement from questions of property, origin, and identity to more transitory differentiations in the heterogeneous becoming of the world. In this shift from the unilateral optics of representation (invariably concentrated in the subject-centered pragmatics of realism and the ideology that truth lies in visual transparency) to the altogether less guaranteed reception of poetic disturbance and interrogation, there emerges the potential of a cultural politics that exceeds both instrumental rationality and institutional arrest.

---

11 Theodor W. Adorno, *Minima Moralia*, trans. E. F. N. Jephcott (London: New Left Books, 1979).
12 Dipesh Chakrabarty, *Provincializing Europe: Postcolonial Thought and Historical Difference* (Princeton, N.J.: Princeton University Press, 2000).
13 Gianni Vattimo, *The End of Modernity: Nihilism and Hermeneutics in Post-modern Culture*, trans. Jon R. Snyder (Oxford: Polity Press, 1988).

Borrowing from the observations and annotations that constitute Walter Benjamin's Arcades project,[14] there here emerges the idea of collecting the refuse of the city, the fragments of the histories and languages of modernity that are found, as it were, casually in the streets, in order to evoke an unexpected critical mix. Like a DJ revisiting and reelaborating existing rhythms and riffs, this operation carries us toward a new horizon of sense. Using the inherited languages and quotidian details in which we are enveloped in order to articulate a reply is to invest the prescribed with the inscribed, the pedagogical with the performative. In this manner, language is carried elsewhere into another, often unsuspected, configuration. In the "scratch," in the "mix," the borrowed, recycled, and spontaneous but necessary practices of translation and bricolage provide a decisive critical metaphor for a more extensive understanding of contemporary cultural forms and forces. As Karen Tranberg Hansen insists in her study of the secondhand West that dresses Zambia, everything acquires a "second life," a further meaning.[15]

In this particular configuration, open to histories, memories, and possibilities that arrive from elsewhere, identities cannot be lived in a state of understanding that is already fully established and realized. Identities become a point of departure, an opening on to the continual elaboration of becoming. This is to dispute a sense of modernity which, as Friedrich Nietzsche noted, attains the peak of nihilism in reducing the multiplicity of life to the metaphysical singularity represented by the presumed sovereignty of individual identity.[16] Rather, it is the case that the rationalist productivity of modernity, striving to harness and homogenize the world, is continually interrupted by its own languages transporting it elsewhere. Here unilateral desires and powers are deviated in a dissemination in which no one place can claim to own the language in which it appears and speaks. This is to insist on a limited sense of a world that is always susceptible to translation but cannot be transcended. The seemingly limitless reach of a unique and homogeneous understanding of technology and economy, of citizenship and political rights, of aesthetics and ethics, today the globe, tomorrow ... comes to be arrested, brought up short, in the excess of language and history custodized by art. From this unsuspected, often unwelcomed, supplement emerges the promise of the questions that continue to question.

14 Walter Benjamin, *The Arcades Project*, trans. Howard Eiland and Kevin McLaughlin (Cambridge, Mass.: Harvard University Press, 1999).
15 Karen Tranberg Hansen, *Salaula: The World of Secondhand Clothing and Zambia* (Chicago: Chicago University Press, 2000).
16 Friedrich Nietzsche, *Beyond Good and Evil*, trans. R. J. Hollingdale (Harmondsworth: Penguin, 1973).

Counter-Politics:
Direct Action, Resistance, Civil Disobedience

New Rules of the New Actonomy 3.0[1]

Florian Schneider/kein mensch ist illegal

A hot Saturday at the end of June 1997: Khaled had just topped the European charts with "Aisha," and in France the *sans papiers*, people without valid immigration documents, had occupied one church after another and called upon filmmakers to shelter illegal aliens. In Germany, a prohibition upon asylum seekers' working had been issued and the criteria for deporting offenders beefed up. What had so recently called itself civic society rolled over and played dead. Early that morning, we arrived at Kassel with a car full of video equipment and were allowed, after much debate, to park in the shade of the Orangerie. Documenta X had opened the week before, and for the next hundred days, on the site of a planetarium and a museum for the history of technology, there would be a temporary media laboratory for Internet activists. No one knew what would happen next or, most importantly, why it should. The first visitors were already lining up at the main entrance. Inside the "Hybrid Workspace," a few dozen artists, media activists, unionists, refugee advocates, and antiracists had assembled. A few hours later, we had decided upon the slogan *kein mensch ist illegal*, or "no one is illegal," set up our equipment, and opened our doors to the public.

Four years later, everything and nothing has changed. For months, the governments of the old European nation-states have been discussing their dramatic shortages of labor, especially in high-tech and IT sectors. The EU Commissioner admitted that Europe had lost its battle against clandestine migration. A debate about immigration was raging in Germany, which seemed likely to end in nothing other than reforms worsening the conditions of immigrants and a new wave of criminalization. The assertion "no one is illegal" was more topical

---

1 This text is based upon the lecture held during the platform in Vienna as version 1.0. The current version was discussed, extended, developed, and reconstituted on many levels and in cooperation with various individuals inside and outside the campaign "kein mensch ist illegal" ("no one is illegal"). The sections in italics have been published as version 2.0 under the co-authorship of Geert Lovink. Continuing versions are planned for the future and will be published under open content license at http://new.actonomy.org.

than ever, but it was now supplemented by a second slogan: *Jeder Mensch ist ein Experte* (Everyone is an Expert) rigorously demanded global freedom of movement, including rights of entry and permanent settlement, for all human beings. This was not just a matter of questioning the prevailing clichés and trivial definitions of expertise of the analogue age. Above all, the slogan attacked the *idée fixe* of dividing immigrants into useful and nonuseful workforces.

Time is running out for Reformism. This is the golden age of irresistible activism. Accelerate your politics. Set a target you can reach within 3 years – and formulate the key ideas within 30 seconds. Then go out and do it. Do not despair. Get the bloody project up and then: hit hit hit. Be instantly seductive in your resistance. The moral firewalls of global capitalism are buggy as never before. Corporations are weakened because of their endemic dirty practices, mad for profits. The faster things change, the more radically we can act. The faster things change, the more radically we must *act.*

"no one is illegal" is a double negation open to various meanings. In the first place it says: don't expect us not to support refugees and immigrants just because they don't have valid residence permits and are thus illegal! Don't expect us not to help with entry and transit, with the procurement of work permits, with access to medical care, education and training, residence and material subsistence issues! At the same time, "no one is illegal" is not a new NGO, not a charity organization, which performs charitable acts out of seeming selflessness. Instead, it aims at building up networks, establishing contacts, exchanging knowledge, linking various strategies, and developing contextual justifications in order to publicize work that in previous years had been carried out secretly, underground. It was not to celebrate the individual things we had been able to achieve, but because these few things suddenly seemed to be endangered and thus had to be supported, indeed augmented.

Radical demands are not by default signs of a dogmatic belief system (they can be, of course). If well formulated, they are strong signs, penetrating deeply into the confused postmodern subjectivity, so susceptible to catchy phrases, logos, and brand names. The green-liberal idea of slowly changing capitalism from within no longer works. Not because the Third Way parties have "betrayed" the cause. No. Simply because their project is running out of time. Global systems are in a state of permanent revolution, and so is subversive politics. Society is changing much faster than any of its institutions, including corporations. No one can keep up. There is no time anymore for "rational" planning. The duration of a plan, the time necessary for its implementation, is simply no longer there. This mechanism turned the baby boomers into such unbearable regressive control freaks. There is no more time to go through the entire trajectory from research to implementation. Policy is reduced to panic response.

Our numbers were few and our endeavors began slowly. We have learned a great deal and have tried from the beginning to use new means of communication for our purposes. In the space of a few days at Documenta X, we were able – thanks above all to emails, mailing lists, and websites – to build an informal network that included local points of contact in almost all of Germany's larger cities. Repeatedly over the past few years, major exhibitions, invitations to museums and galleries, independent events, tent colonies, and conferences have provided temporary headquarters for campaigns with clearly defined short-term goals. "no one is illegal" has no official or permanent structure. There is no one who would be willing or able to represent or be responsible for the network as a whole. Tactical considerations inspired this sort of construction, the aims being to avoid promising what could not be delivered or realized, to avoid political infighting, and to avoid the homogenization of a process that from its inception and at heart was supposed to serve a variety of purposes. Above all, "no one is illegal" is a slogan available for use to all who are attracted to it and want to contribute their specific knowledge and skills to the totality of its activities.

Government policy is reduced to panic response. For the complex society its enemies are the blueprints of five years ago. The future is constantly being redefined and renegotiated. Global systems are in a state of permanent flux between revolution and reaction – and so are subversive politics. Society is changing much faster than any of its institutions can handle. In short: no one can keep up, and here lies the competitive advantage of today's mobile actonomists.

"no one is illegal" is not a plea to government lawmakers for a relaxation of legal restrictions, a bit of humanitarian consideration in scandalous individual cases, nor a concrete proposal for bringing populations under better control by liberalizing or deregulating certain aspects of global migration. "no one is illegal" is something that goes without saying, a platitude, albeit one that can entail dramatic consequences. There is no need to spill much ink about the practical, on-site work. The crux of the matter is heartfelt, immediate, and uncomplicated action. Our approach is goal-oriented – the only thing that matters is the concrete improvement of the situation of people without clearly defined residence status. The campaign commenced at a time when, throughout Europe, the legal punishments for "illegal entry" and "illegal residence" were being drastically increased. "no one is illegal" cites a text by Elie Wiesel, who many years ago posed the question: "How can a person be illegal?" It is only against the backdrop of the official policy of zero immigration and systematic criminalization of foreigners that the slogan acquires its special meaning. Its radicalism, however, is not just a matter of context. It is put into practice not by the many small individual gestures of support and help, but by the mass crossing of borders that people undertake for whatever reasons.

Instead of lamenting the disappearance of politics, the public, the revolution, etc., today's activists are focusing on the weakest link defining the overall performance of the system: the point where the corporate image materializes in the real world and leaves its ubiquitous and abstract omnipresence. Shortcut the common deliberations about the dichotomy between real and virtual. Get into more sophisticated dialectics. It's all linked anyway, with power defining the rules of access to resources (space, information, or capital). Throw your pie, write your code. Visit their annual stockholder meeting, and do your goddamned research first. What counts is the damage done on the symbolic level, either real or virtual.

"Activism" was something of a foreign word in Germany when "no one is illegal" first began. Traditional labels like "human rights supporters" or "politically committed individuals," "antiracist initiatives" or "solidarity movements," had proved to be failures. *Aktivismus*, borrowed from English, suggested itself as an alternative, containing the idea of activity, an approach that was as offensive as it was constructive and that signaled the greatest possible degree of flexibility and self-confidence. The trick was to avoid despair in a seemingly hopeless situation, to explode smug contentment and cynicism, to reject the role of the do-gooder, to go beyond mere technical expertise and simply offering services, and to match radical aspirations with a practice that developed new, if also precarious, forms of subjectivity. What makes activism so irresistible is the acceleration that accompanies its initial phase. All efforts are directed toward a goal, with every movement adding to the whole and leading all the more quickly to real progress. No time for looking back – that is what makes activism so appealing and exciting.

The new actonomy, equipped with pies and laptops, consists of thousands of bigger and smaller activities, which are all by themselves meaningful, manageable, and sustainable. For this we do not need a General Plan, a singular portal website, let alone a Party. It is enough to understand the new dynamics – and to use them. Create and disseminate your message with all available logics, tools, and media. The new actonomy involves a rigorous application of networking methods. Its diversity challenges the development of nonhierarchical, decentralized, and deterritorialized applets and applications.

The border camps are without doubt one of the most successful concepts developed in conjunction with "no one is illegal." Since the summer of 1998, twelve such action camps have taken place along various borders in Europe and North America. Starting with the borderline rave and border-opening action near Görlitz at the German-Polish border, and continuing to the second border-hacking festival staged last August on the beach at Tijuana along the US-Mexico border, the tent colonies are a persuasive example of globally distributed network activism. For several days in the summer of 2001, some 2,000 participants succeeded in disrupting operations at Frankfurt airport as part of a protest against the internment camps on airport grounds and the approximately 40,000 deportations that take place there annually. Whether at the G-8 summit in Genoa or at the Straits of Gibraltar, on the Polish-Byelorussian or the Slovenian-Croatian border – in various contexts, with various goals and from constantly shifting perspectives, activists attempt to disrupt a postmodern border regime that makes the international transfer of money, goods, and capital ever easier, while choking off the global flow of refugees, immigrants, and other migrant populations.

As is the case in most political, social, and cultural areas, network technologies have replaced traditional forms of asserting authority on national borders. Checks now take place practically everywhere in real time. Chip cards, biometric systems, electronic collars regulate access to proprietary, privileged, or otherwise restricted areas and collate images of human movement in gigantic databases. The surveillance of the electronically equipped border by means of heat, infrared, radar, and satellite technology has undergone a dramatic change in significance. Today's borders are not so much about racist permission and refusal of entry as about user profiling. The ultimate aim of postmodern border management is above all the filtering of presumably useful from nonuseful immigrants.

In the spring of 2002, further noborder camps will be staged in front of a refugee camp in the Australian desert, and a planned European-wide camp at Strasbourg the following July should provide another temporary highlight. In front of the European Parliament, the European Court of Human Rights, and the headquarters of the Schengen Information System,[2] activists will engage in a whole spectrum of actions, from distributing information to disruption, pranks, fakes, and border jamming. The communicative and networking levels of the movement will also be further developed within the European context.

Invent and connect as many intentions, motivations, causalities as possible. Nowadays activists use multilayered and multiple voice languages that extend far beyond the immediate purpose of a campaign or a concrete struggle, and in doing so, create a vision much larger than what is accessible right at the moment. This mechanism requires a reassessment of the rhizomatic micro-politics that sprang up in response to the centralized macro-politics of the decaying communist parties in the 1970s.

The political arena has dissolved into thousands of fragments, and yet it is precisely in this chaos that network activism can break new ground with novel forms of political articulation and activity. What the various approaches have in

---

2 The Schengen Information System is a huge database designed to collect information about stolen vehicles and illegal immigrants, and was recently expanded to include political activists as well. See http://europa.eu.int/scadplus/leg/en/lvb/l33020.htm.

common is that they are extremely flexible, operate within a tactical and strategic pluralism, are concerned with formulating a contemporary concept of solidarity and self-determination, and seek to link immediate local conflicts to global issues. The constructive result is a nonorganized movement of movements – a self-determined, networked thinking that explicitly promotes various approaches and connections. As a form of social engagement directly relating to the realm of production, this is constitutive for the collective appropriation of knowledge and power.

Laws of the semiotic guerrilla: hit and run, draw and withdraw, code and delete. Postulate precise and modest demands, which allows your foe to step back without losing face. Social movements from the last century opposed the nation-state and disclaimed its power. In the new actonomy, activists struggle against corporations and new forms of global sovereignty. The goal is obviously not so much to gain institutional political power, but to change the way things are moving – and why. The principle aim is to make power ridiculous, unveil its corrupt nature in the most powerful, beautiful, and aggressive symbolic language, then step back in order to make space for changes to take effect. Let others do that job, if they wish. There is no need for a direct dialogue in this phase. Exchanges on mediated levels will do. Complex societies have plenty of mediators and interfaces. Use them. Indirect contact with power-to-be does not affect your radical agenda as long as you maintain and upgrade your own dignity, both as an acting individual and as a group.

"Deportation.Class" is the name of an autonomous campaign that developed from the network "no one is illegal" in the summer of 1999, after four people, over the space of a few months, were killed by police escorts during deportation proceedings at airports or aboard planes.[3] Everyone who flies knows that the seating policies of commercial airlines follow a cleverly designed system of crass and fine distinctions. At the front of the aircraft are the business nomads who possess not only sufficient frequent-flyer miles but the right sort of passport. Behind them are the masses who may have booked promptly but do not seem truly cut out for earning money. In the last rows are people who may not

---

3 All were asylum-seekers. Nigerian Marcus Omofuma died in May 1999 during a deportation operation on a Balkan Air flight from Vienna to Nigeria; one witness reported that police had "wrapped the entire upper part of his body and arms with adhesive tape like a mummy stuck to the seat." That same month, Sudanese national Aamir Ageeb was killed aboard a Lufthansa flight; his arms and legs had been bound by German federal border police, a motorcycle helmet had been placed on his head, and his head had been forced between his knees. In March 1999, Palestinian Khaled Abu Zarifa died of suffocation at Zurich-Kloten airport after police guards placed adhesive over his mouth and strapped him into a wheelchair. In September 1998, Semira Adamu, a Nigerian seeking asylum in Belgium, died as the result of abuse inflicted by police escorts at Brussels airport. In an earlier incident, in August 1994, Kola Bankole, another Nigerian national, died of heart failure aboard a Lufthansa flight from Frankfurt after being restrained, sedated, and gagged by federal border police.

have booked their own tickets at all – people who aren't flying of their own free will, but who sit there in handcuffs, restrained or sedated, on board to be deported.

The specific tactic of the "Deportation.Class" campaign consisted of finding a weak spot or, to use a different metaphor, the weakest link in the chain. It first set its sights on the Lufthansa corporation, whose worldwide network of routes allows it to transport people to any country on earth. The "Deportation.Class" campaign began with a competition of ideas to create a corpus of parodic slogans whose graphic realization seemed particularly advantageous or felicitous. The collective brainstorming before the official public launch of the campaign at the International Tourism Exchange in March 2000 in Berlin resulted in an explosion of ideas. Online and off, on websites and in print, in film spots and short animation, the campaign progressed in various directions. It was not necessary to develop a single "corporate identity" – the immense costs of this were left to Lufthansa with its highly paid employees and professional resources. The activists merely played the role of communications guerrillas, conserving their strength so as always to appear where the enemy least suspected. The activity, however, was theater, not war. In actions that were more like performances than traditional political demonstrations, the activists took every opportunity to publicize the practice of transporting deportees on commercial flights, which had in the meantime also come under judicial scrutiny. Activists created confusion at travel agencies and ticket counters, at firm-run training centers and flight schools, at trade conventions and the Lufthansa partner day at the World's Fair 2000. At the Hamburg airport, for example, activists disguised themselves as employees of an advertising agency, purportedly conducting a survey among Lufthansa passengers as to their readiness to be reseated from business or tourist into deportation class. Most of those asked did not categorically refuse: "If it's cheaper, why not?"

Information leaflets were often torn angrily from the hands of the activists, who were used to dealing with far greater harassment, and some surprising feedback flooded into Lufthansa call centers. The employees there presumably had to receive some additional advance training in denial, after prank promotional material began appearing in travel agencies advertising the "deportation class." "Book with the Lufthansa deportation class," read the pamphlets, which were produced in German, English, and Spanish. "We are offering a thirty percent price reduction on all flights since a separate zone has been reserved in our aircraft for the transport of deported asylum seekers." "Waiting-list priority" and an "increased baggage allowance" were also promised. The Lufthansa corporation had no choice but to call a hasty press conference on April 11, 2000 and distance itself from the "cynical and inhumane proceedings." Needless to say, they meant the pamphlets, not the deportations. Score one for the activists of "no one is illegal," as the tabloid newspaper *Bild* ran the now legendary head-line: "Poor Lufthansa!"

In the coming months, the managing directors of the formerly state-run air-line decided to play deaf – without much success. Following the lead of the unions, the pilots' organization Cockpit endorsed the idea that flying should be voluntary. Cockpit advised its members, who represent the sole authority on planes while airborne, not to transport anyone who did not actually want to fly. The results that can be achieved with goal-oriented protest and efficient tactics became evident in July 2000, when the Hungarian airline TAROM, which had carried out deportations every Tuesday from Frankfurt airport, did an abrupt about-face after the simultaneous occupation of all its offices in Germany and canceled the weekly chartered flight used for them. As the reason for its change in policy, TAROM cited its desire not to be targeted by the "Deportation.Class" campaign.

These days a well-designed content virus can easily reach millions overnight. Invest all your time to research how to design a robust meme which can travel through time and space, capable of operating within a variety of cultural contexts. The relationship between "small is beautiful" and "subversive economies of scale" is constantly shifting. Low-tech money-free projects are charming, but in most cases lack the precision and creative power to strike at society's weakest link. Be ready to work with money. You will need it for the temporary set-up.

In the weeks leading up to Lufthansa's annual shareholder meeting, media reports were dominated by a promised online demonstration, which had been announced to Cologne police and other authorities and which was to com-mence with a symbolic mouse click on June 15, 2001 at precisely 10 o'clock in the morning, in front of the city's main arena. Simultaneously, from 10 to 12 a.m., the Lufthansa server was to be overloaded – or, at least, its response time significantly slowed down. This was something of a premiere, although it was not the first time that the metaphor "online demonstration" had been used for an electronic gathering. It was a software that supported mass protest in which people across the world could easily participate, akin to a denial-of-service attack, except that the goals, means, and schedule had been openly announced and were both locally and temporally restricted. The point was certainly not to inflict maximum damage but to effect a symbolic condensation: the long-awaited synchronicity of online and offline; the media-savvy dramatization of a just cause, which could not have been publicized and disseminated so broadly with traditional means; the trial run for a controversial, if promising, form of action that both visualized and globalized protest; and, as paradoxical as it might sound, a hybrid of immaterial sabotage and digital demonstration.

In the aftermath, both sides claimed victory. The organizers of the online demonstration emphasized that the Lufthansa homepage was virtually inaccessible for two hours, illustrating this with some nicely drawn diagrams. Lufthansa spokespeople admitted that some jams had occurred but spoke likewise of the effectiveness of their defensive strategy, which focused on alternative telephone line capacities. Whole sub-networks were apparently placed on the Web where critical requests for information were detected. The logical consequence was that those who protested there automatically had success, if only in their own eyes.

On the symbolic level as well, there were two victors. The online demonstration, which had been explicitly and primarily concerned with attracting maximum publicity for the cause, drew enormous international attention to the "Deportation.Class" protest against Lufthansa, far beyond what would have been possible with traditional methods. Articles in the *Wall Street Journal* and the *Washington Post,* wire reports speeding around the globe, massive debates online over a set-up by television stations and print publications – soon every article, whether in magazines or dailies, the Internet or provincial newspapers, was reporting on the Lufthansa shareholder meeting with catchy headlines about the online demonstration. On the other hand, the Web technicians at Lufthansa could proudly point out that they had successfully controlled the damage from an "aggressive attack." The server did not collapse, as many protesters secretly hoped, but remained online – if at the cost of temporary local unavailability. Even the immense costs incurred by the Lufthansa technicians could be justified. The firm was able to demonstrate, albeit grudgingly, a certain competence in dealing with new challenges.

Think in terms of efficiency. Use the staff and infrastructure on the site of your foe. Acting in the new actonomy means cutting the preliminaries and getting to the point straightaway. A campaign does not rely on one's own forces alone, but on those of one's allies and opponents as well. Outsourcing is a weapon. It is a means of giving someone else the problems you cannot solve yourself. Remember that you won't get very far without a proper infrastructure such as offices, servers, legal frameworks to receive and pay money, etc. However, you can also treat these institutional requirements as flexible units. You do not need to own them, the only thing you need is temporary access so that you can set up the equipment necessary for that particular project.

The nice thing about virtual reality is not only that both sides can be right in claiming success, but that the final tabulation of pluses and minuses has little meaning, to say nothing of it driving events. It is a typical win-win situation. According to the concepts of Net activism, however, the matter does not end there. The main challenge of virtual forms of protest has an entirely pragmatic dimension. The materiality of virtual protest resides in the interactivity, the communication between networked activists who are not divided into senders and receivers, but function simultaneously as participants and organizers. What does networking actually mean in this context? Net activism, as rudimentary as the genre might be at present, essentially proceeds on three levels.

For starters there is the immediate networking within a movement. Communication gets translated from the analogue to the digital medium: mailing lists and communication before, during, and after them, as well as static websites, conceived as bulletin boards or archives for the activists themselves. This primary form of networking leads to the creation of virtual communities, which do not differ greatly from offline communities except insofar as the individuals concerned do not necessarily ever meet face to face, even though many do. A further outgrowth of this is the step-by-step discovery of the practical applications of new technologies.

A second level is concerned with splicing together the space between movements. This is a matter of networking between people from different contexts, the inspiring and motivating surroundings in which new forms of activity can be discovered and developed: campaigns, meta-databases, diverse activities settled on the borders between the online and offline world. Insofar as interfaces are concerned, issues of subjectivity and interactivity become decisive: mutual offers of help, technical and intellectual support instead of division of labor, collaboration, open sources, and collective productivity. The goal is to connect the greatest number of possible approaches so that virtuality, with its endless capacity for activity, yields a greater use value than when individuals, groups, or movements are left to their own devices.

The third level consists of the virtual archiving of unanticipated and incalculable movements. The ambition is to use the Web as a platform for purely virtual encounters, ones that no longer or ever more infrequently refer to a romantic offline reality: e-protests such as online demonstrations, electronic civil disobedience, immaterial or digital sabotage as the result of future social conflicts. It is an oxymoron that contains an enormous potential.

Act in a definite space and with a definite force. Dramaturgy is all that matters. Precision campaigns consist of distinct episodes with a beginning and end, an either smooth or harsh escalation and a final showdown. Accept the laws of appearance and disappearance. Don't get stuck in structures that are on the decline. Be ready to move on, taking with you the (access to) infrastructure of the previous round. Action is taking place in a variety of locations and thus refers in a positive way to a new stage of people's globalization from below. One that is not just an empty, endlessly extended market, but full of energy.

At the moment, the great challenge seems to be a redefinition of sabotage, not in the traditional, destructive sense, but as constructive, innovative, and creative practice. The pathological aspect of traditionally understood protest militancy resides to a great extent in its auto-destructiveness: trying to give others a bad conscience, burning down one's own neighborhood, striving for radicalism without reflection and desire for communication, and smugly fetishizing repression. Sabotage is the practical antithesis to this, being derived from the word *sabot*, a wooden shoe secretly placed inside a machine so as to block production. The interruption aims at decreasing human efficiency so that the resultant material losses direct attention to concrete demands or a general dissatisfaction. Classical sabotage, as it evolved toward the end of the 19th century, could take three forms: a reduction in the quantity of either production or services, or the application of specialist knowledge to attack the quality of production.

Refuse to be blackmailed. If attacked, take one step aside or ahead. Don't panic. Take all the options into account. No one needs cyberheroes, you are not a lone hacker anymore. The attack may be done by a single person but, remember, we are many. The corporate response may be harsher than you expect. It may be better to avoid a direct confrontation, but don't trust the media and the mediators. Ignore their advice. In the end you are just another news item for them. If trouble hits you in the face, scale down, retreat, reorganize, get your network up, dig deep into the far corners of the Net – and then launch the counter-campaign.

Like strikes, sabotage in its classical form takes direct aim at the profits of a company in order to ensure the fulfillment of certain demands. Immaterial sabotage, on the other hand, is directed at the *image* of a corporation. In contrast to the boycotts organized by social movements of the 1980s, which kept participants in their status as consumers voting with their wallets, immaterial sabotage taps the creativity and productivity, the collaboration and collectivity unleashed among its wandering, ineffable, mutually networked participants. The goal is not to get the greatest number of people behind you but to achieve directly a change in or amelioration of a certain condition. It is therefore felicitous to concentrate on the weakest link in the chain, the image or global corporate identity of a concern, which can be attacked with a wide variety of tactics and techniques.

Historically, in cases where the right to strike either was rendered ineffective or was denied to workers, sabotage proved to be an appropriate, if illegal, means of firm-internal confrontation. Hardly a bad legacy to take up in a situation where it is clear that what the powers-that-be envision under globalization cannot be effected in the long term by scattered street battles before convention halls. Too many things have changed too quickly in the world for the long-overdue redefinition of political practice and theory not to revive experiences from other historical watersheds. New concepts have to be developed and old ones injected with new content, while struggles need to interact with absolute immediacy, regardless of whether they are old or new, and no matter where they take place and how they end up. How many people participate is just as irrelevant now as it was during the New York barmen's strike at the end of the 19th century. It was through the free, indirect speech about working conditions that patrons became so disgusted and the industry quickly caved in to the demands of a badly organized union. What went down in labor history as "open mouth sabotage" provided the cornerstone a hundred years later for the Net activism of the "McLibel" campaign. The website, on which McDonald's critics worldwide provided material supporting two pamphleteers accused in London of libeling the corporation, was one of the most visited sites of the mid-'90s. The "Deportation.Class" campaign certainly had a more difficult task since the phrase "denial of service" was understood literally: the aim was for Lufthansa to refuse to transport prisoners. What is needed is what during the 1980s was called "imaginative forms of resistance," itself something of a euphemism. Today, the conditions exist to create the material basis for fulfilling this almost forgotten promise.

Program and compile subject-oriented campaigns! These days, a lot of people talk about a global uprising, which is only in the beginning stages and definitely not limited to the so-called battles against the three acronyms: WTO, WB, and IMF. But the urgent question of that movement is: What new types of subjectivity will emerge from the current struggles? Everyone knows what's to be done, but who knows what we are fighting for and why? Maybe it doesn't matter anymore: net.activism has a charming fragility. In the end it means permanently revising and redefining all goals.

The 20th century was not the century of refugees, as has been so often claimed, but the century of borders. Borders establish personality, create or change subjectivity. Illegal crossing of boundaries destroys what previously was and now lies in the past: professors are turned into cleaners, people with countless talents and enormous experience become refugees and migrants, compelled to tell stories to the authorities of flight, torture, persecution, starvation, and misery, and thus pigeonholed – even in the rhetoric of well-intentioned supporters – into the role of the victim.

The slogan "Everyone is an Expert" connects rhetorically with the double negation "no one is illegal," turning the latter's simplicity, redundancy, and necessary understatement into a political tactic of over-affirmation. At the February 2000 computer convention CEBIT, in Hanover, after a quarter century of a full stop on immigration, a loudly trumpeted policy of zero migration, and an increasingly brutal regime of EU borders, German Chancellor Gerhard Schröder declared that an acute shortage in qualified personnel in the IT sector demanded a liberalization of Germany's complicated laws concerning foreigners. The call for "Indian IT experts" made the rounds throughout Europe in a matter of weeks, and soon other sectors of the economy joined the protest against institutionalized hostility toward immigration, which until then had only been whispered behind cupped hands. Politicians and administrators reacted with confusion to the new situation. The results in Germany were a host of new policies that added to the chaos of already existing laws and a number of election campaigns featuring despicable wordplay such as "foreigners we can use instead of foreigners who use us." That slogan in particular sought to exploit the Western-European xenophobia of the 1990s, with its German catchphrase "the boat is full."

"Everyone is an Expert" may seem at first glance to be a tactical exaggeration, one which on top of that plays upon Joseph Beuys's statement that everyone is an artist. In the first instance, the project was to establish a database, allowing people legally excluded from the official labor market in Germany to publicize their knowledge and skills and thus to achieve a social respect systematically denied to them by institutions and the economy. The idea was to link people who possessed or were looking for a wide variety of skills. In the meantime, the intrinsically connected issues of freedom of movement and informational self-determination have emerged at the forefront. Anyone wishing to use the database "Everyone is an Expert" has the opportunity to input multimedia, digital self-portraits into the system without regard to profitability, usefulness, identity, or confirmation. "Everyone is an Expert" is characterized by voluntary, self-determined associations, blurred relations, ornamental variety, and multiplications in various strategic contexts, which all draw attention to the incalculable difference and holism of all productive practices. The plan is to develop various splice areas that are open, mobile, and universally accessible. In the accompanying exhibitions and catalogues, a selection of the content collected thus far will be prepared so as to disseminate as much information as possible about direct and indirect applications and possible uses. As part of the events, self-determined experts will also elucidate the background, conditions, and implications of the project.

The revolution will be open source or not! Self-determination is something you should share. As soon as you feel a certain strength in a certain field, you can make your power productive as positive, creative, and innovative force. That power opens up new capacities, producing again and again unexpected and incalculable effects.

Today, solidarity consists of communicating struggle. Networking has to be based on the uniqueness and diversity of various practices of resistance. The burning questions of this movement of movements are as follows. How can these diverse practices be brought together without being homogenized? How can commonalities be found – not *despite* but precisely *as* diversity – so as to allow for creativity and constructiveness? How can the wide variety of origins,

perspectives, and motivations be not only respected but promoted, simultaneously and universally?

Collaborations like the noborder network, in which activists from more than
twenty European countries have been linked up, have as little to do with mere
exchange of information as with claims to being representative. Cooperation
takes place on the basis of the enormous differences that persist, despite all har-
monizing efforts, within EU policies on migration and asylum. Experiences
must be shared, talents represented, and knowledge exchanged, if we are to keep
up with the situation. Those who work together soon notice how fruitful it can
be to share existing capacities and resources in order to solve problems, carry out
joint action, begin collective processes, coordinate with other networks, and
constantly recoordinate one's own activities.

*Ignore history. Don't refer to any of your favorite predecessors. Hide your admira-
tion for authors, artists, and familiar styles. You do not need to legitimize yourself by
quoting the right theorist or rapper. Be unscrupulously modern (meaning: ignore
organized fashion, you are busy with something else, anyway). Create and disseminate your message with all available logics, tools, and media. The new actonomy
involves a rigorous application of networking methods. Its diversity challenges the
development of nonhierarchical, decentralized, and deterritorialized applets and
applications. In the meanwhile, leave the preaching of the techno religion to others.
Hide your admiration for everything new and cool. Just use it. Take the claim on the
future away from corporations. Remember: they are the dinosaurs.*

What is new about the new actonomy? In the end, what is considered new
today has less to do with something entirely unknown and never seen before
than with the universality of constant change. Even global transformations are
eventually exhausted, both spatially and temporally. And when the end of the
end (for example, the end of history) is reached, everything that can happen or
must be done must go back to the beginning. Happily, such a new beginning
encompasses far more now than ever before. It is high time to scroll, to look
both forward and backward, to step aside and to think ahead.

*Read as much business literature as possible and don't be afraid it may affect you.
It will. Have enough ethics in your guts that you can deal with that bit of ideology.
Remember that activism and entrepreneurial spirit have a lot in common. So what?
Benefit from your unlimited capacity for metamorphosis. With the right spirit, you
can survive any appropriation. Free yourself from the idea that enemy concepts compromise the struggle. You don't have to convince yourself, or your foe. The challenge is
to involve those who have not yet joined the struggle. The challenge is to use resources
which may not belong to you, but which are virtually yours.*

Borders are there to be crossed. Their significance first appears when they are
violated. The types of violations states try to prevent reveals the character of the

society they harbor. The battle against borders is a battle against infrared cameras, plastic handcuffs, and dragnet sweeps, against restricted horizons, resentment, and racism. More than ever, it is also a struggle for the long-overdue redefinition of the public sphere as jointly used space and mutually determined time. To the extent that so-called globalization does nothing more than establish new borders and distinctions between people in order to realize boundless profits, the corruption of the global capitalist regime becomes more and more apparent. Thus the struggle against borders becomes a truly constructive conflict over the principle of open sources and free, equal, global access. Access to the right to have rights. Access to the material goods necessary for survival and the immaterial resources that represent the basis of creativity and creative work. Access to the communicative networks in which knowledge is circulated. Everything else is in the stars, and that is the way it should be. Nothing can predict how and where people will determine their destiny when it lies in their own hands.

Translated from the German by Jefferson Chase

The State of Hate in America:
The Growing Conflict Between Identity Politics and Multiculturalism

Mark Potok

It is an honor and a delight to speak here in the auditorium of Vienna's Academy of Fine Arts, not least because an Austrian who did his best to send my father to Auschwitz some sixty years ago once held sway in this beautiful city. Times certainly do change.

I would like to begin this presentation on the American radical right by saying that ten days from now, there will be a trial in Alabama that has to do with the bombing of a black church in Birmingham about forty years ago, at the height of the American civil rights movement. Two men are scheduled to be tried on that date, men who are now in their sixties and seventies and in rather ill health. At around the same time, Timothy McVeigh, convicted of bombing the Oklahoma City federal building in 1995, will be put to death in a federal execution chamber.

I mention these two cases to point up the fact that there is a significant difference between the old radical right in the United States and the contemporary radical right. The comparison between Bobby Frank Cherry, allegedly one of the bombers of the 16th Street Baptist Church in Birmingham who killed four little black girls in 1963, and Timothy McVeigh, who murdered 168 people in Oklahoma, is instructive. For one thing, of course, there is the difference simply in the body count in the two cases. The fact is that the contemporary radical right is willing to murder people who have absolutely nothing to do with the state, with the FBI, with law enforcement agencies, with any of their perceived enemies. That was not true in the past. In fact, the murder of the four little girls in Birmingham appears to have been an accidental byproduct of a bombing that was supposed to "merely" frighten black people back into submission.

There are other differences as well. Until the fall of the Berlin Wall in 1989, the radical right in the United States was all about opposition to communism and supporting "100% Americanism." It was, in effect, a restorationist movement, aimed at bringing back what was seen as a golden era of the past. What the extremists sought to restore was white supremacy, the Jim Crow laws of the South that held blacks in legal chains, the oppression of black people in the

United States. Today, we are looking at a movement that is completely revolutionary, not restorationist in any sense. It is anticapitalist and anti-idealist. And that is quite the opposite of the past.

The contemporary radical right – in America and in Europe – is also antiglobalization. There is a struggle going on across the Western hemisphere between the forces of globalization and those who favor localism and identity politics. In the words of one writer, Benjamin Barber, this struggle boils down to the battle of "Jihad vs. McWorld." On the one hand, we see forms of tribalism characterized by exclusionary attitudes toward "the other"; on the other hand, multiculturalists who essentially view the world as a single place – who favor integration, interaction among different peoples, multiracialism.

Let me pause here for a moment to say a few words about the Southern Poverty Law Center, where I work. The Center, which is now thirty years old, was set up to seek social and racial justice, work having to do with poverty and with class and race issues. Lawyers at the Center have brought a number of lawsuits that forced the integration of the Alabama state police and increased black representation in legislatures across the South. We have done a lot of prison work and a great deal of anti–death penalty work, much of it focused on the fact that there is a huge racial disparity in the way the death penalty is imposed in the United States – quite apart from the barbarism of the death penalty to begin with. We also monitor, and maintain the largest database on, extremist groups and individuals. In addition, the Center has been involved for years in educational efforts to teach our children the importance of tolerance.

Through the lens of my specialty, the radical right, I will explain some of the reasons for the recent rise of neofascism in the United States, then discuss the Center's response to these problems.

Throughout its history, the American radical right – far more than extremists in most European countries – has been driven by conspiracy theories: extremely far-out ideas like the weather machine that is supposedly hidden away in a basement somewhere in Brussels and used by clandestine global elites to destroy American crops and American farmers. Despite this fondness for the wacky, I want to stress the point that these people – even the craziest among them – are often motivated by real sociopolitical phenomena, and it is a mistake to simply label those who comprise the radical right as lunatics outside the parameters of society and reason. To do this misses the social and political realities undergirding the movement, what is driving it and therefore how to combat it.

That said, let's go back to the 1980s, when the most important group on the radical right was the Posse Comitatus (Latin for "the power of the county"). The Posse was the first fairly broad-based group in the United States to specifically identify Jews as the principal enemy. But more important to our discussion, the

Posse was quite successful for a time, for a period of seven or eight years in the Midwest, operating in the heart of the American farm belt. The Posse Comitatus gained adherents during the 1980s in the context of huge numbers of farm bankruptcies, with literally tens of thousands of farmers losing their land for a variety of historical reasons. One of them was the embargo on grain shipped to the Soviet Union imposed by President Jimmy Carter. In addition, farmers had been very strongly encouraged by federal officials to expand their holdings and turn small family farms into agribusinesses by borrowing. The third important factor was a very sudden and sharp jump in interest rates that made borrowing money extremely expensive. The upshot was that tens of thousands of people lost livelihoods and land that had been in their families in many instances for four, five, six, even seven generations. The fury generated by this situation, a deep-seated and legitimate anger in the heart of the United States, was virtually ignored in the corridors of power. No one in Washington, D.C., made any effort either to help farmers who were losing their land or to provide an explanation as to why this was happening. It was an invisible disaster. The silence emanating from Washington created a breach, and into this breach stepped the organizers of the Posse Comitatus.

Before the Posse arrived, farmers had already begun to build a movement – a movement that was not opposed to the government but, on the contrary, was asking that the government increase price supports. The Posse came in and, like a virus, injected its poison into the situation, suggesting that Jewish cabals, blacks, and others were the culprits attacking American farmers. So what began as an essentially progressive movement – one that asked the government to help its citizens survive – became a wildly anti-Semitic and white supremacist movement that inspired a number of people to murder Jews, homosexuals, police officers, and others.

Ultimately, the Posse died off. It acquired such a bad reputation, was involved in so many murders, that in the end it could not survive. But the important point is that, in the absence of a competing explanation for what was happening to those farmers, ideologues of the radical right were able to twist a fundamentally progressive movement into an anti-Semitic, racist, backward-looking, and very violent one. My argument in general is not that the rise of neofascism or of radical racism is a direct product of economic hardship. But economic instability can create openings for the propagandists of the extreme right.

With the fall of the Soviet Union in 1989, the situation of the radical right all over the Western hemisphere changed dramatically. The bogeyman of Communism, the lifelong enemy of the hard right, was no more. So as the 1980s came to a close and the 1990s began, there was a shift to a focus on the federal government as the chief enemy. It was no longer the aim of the radical right to defend "100% Americanism," to defend the flag. Suddenly, we had the shocking spectacle of radical rightists – rather than leftists – burning that flag.

It was in this context that the American militia movement was born. In a very real sense, it began with a 1992 incident in Idaho. A white supremacist named Randy Weaver, who was being sought by the police on illegal weapons charges, holed up with his family in a cabin on top of a mountain known as Ruby Ridge in an eight-day standoff with the FBI. An FBI sniper shot and killed Weaver's wife as she held a baby in her arms. His fourteen-year-old son was also killed, as was a federal agent. Although Ruby Ridge did not get a lot of press in the United States, it absolutely energized the radical right, which saw the incident as a classic example of what the government does to dissidents, especially those on the right: it murders them in their own homes. Shortly afterward, in late 1992, there was an important meeting, variously called "The Gathering of Christian Men" or "The Rocky Mountain Rendezvous," in which 160 of the leaders of the extreme right came together to formulate a response to the Ruby Ridge incident. Some very specific ideas gained currency at that meeting, including the idea of largely abandoning explicit racism in favor of building a mass movement around opposition to the federal government. The gist of the new strategy was, "Let's not talk about black people, let's not talk about the Jews, let's instead talk about gun rights and the dictatorial power of the federal government." And, of course, the issue of gun rights has a powerful appeal in the United States, with its frontier history, particularly in the rural areas of the country. As people left the meeting armed with a fresh plan and eager to mobilize a mass movement, suddenly in Waco, Texas, there erupted a confrontation between a cultlike religious group known as the Branch Davidians and the government, which was seeking to serve warrants on the group of about a hundred people for amassing all kinds of illegal weapons, including machine guns and other lethal equipment.

The confrontation began with a shootout between federal agents and the Davidians, and was followed by a siege lasting fifty-one days. More than eighty people remained inside the Davidian compound when the FBI tried to flush them out with teargas. The building caught fire and burned, killing all but a few of the Davidians inside. Despite claims of government-sponsored murder, the Davidians in fact set their own building on fire, committing mass suicide. I say this authoritatively because I was there, covering the Waco siege and later the trial of the surviving Davidians as a reporter. There is no question that the government did not burn down the compound, nor did it shoot people fleeing the fire, as the conspiracy fabulists insist. Sadly, many Americans believed, and still believe, that the federal government set that fire. In other words, in their view, the government was perfectly willing to murder eighty men, women, and children in order to crush the gun-toting Davidian dissidents.

Waco set the radical right on fire, so to speak. More than any other event in the last quarter of a century, it brought extremist ideas – in particular, hatred of the federal government – into the mainstream. As a result, over the next few years, the militia movement experienced phenomenal growth. Tens of thousands of Americans – if not hundreds of thousands, or even, by some estimates, millions – joined up, seeing in Waco the hallmark of a government gone mad. It did not matter that much of the popular understanding of Waco was false, and derived directly from right-wing conspiracy theorists. The militia movement largely succeeded in portraying the events in Texas as the acts of a government willing to go to any lengths to suppress dissent – especially if the dissent involved heterodox religion and the amassing of weapons.

The April 19, 1995, bombing of the Alfred P. Murrah Federal Building in Oklahoma City was specifically conceived as revenge for Waco – payback in the horrifying currency of children's ripped and shredded bodies. As I mentioned earlier, it also established a new standard of terrorist attack – a standard that allowed for no innocent bystanders, only those for or against the enemy. The fact that the vast majority of the 168 people murdered in Oklahoma had nothing to do with any conceivable enemy of the radical right was irrelevant. All that mattered was the body count.

And that legacy remains with us to the present day. Since 1995, terror from the radical right eclipses almost all of the attacks predating Oklahoma City – both in number of attacks and in the ambitiousness of their scope. Prior to the bombing, the FBI typically carried about a hundred incidents of suspected domestic terrorism as part of its caseload. Today, the average number of cases is about a thousand at any given time. Certainly, most people in the United States thought that after Oklahoma, terrorism of that sort from domestic forces would surely diminish. Who, after all, would be willing to follow in the bloody footsteps of McVeigh and Terry Nichols? In fact, quite the opposite has occurred. There have been twenty-nine or thirty major domestic terrorist plots in the United States since Oklahoma, none successful, but enormous in scope. The authors of these plots contemplated, among other things, blowing up an elementary school along with 10,000 other people in Texas; bombing Internal Revenue Service buildings as well as various other private and government buildings; and assassinating people, including several on the staff at the Southern Poverty Law Center.

The Oklahoma City bombing changed the landscape in the United States in other ways too. One of these has to do with law enforcement. Over the decades, many law enforcement personnel have been sympathetic to the radical right. In the 1950s and '60s, law enforcement was as often as not involved in the Ku Klux Klan and other white supremacist groups. But two things have happened since then. Policing in general has become more progressive, certainly among chiefs and other high-ranking officers. And secondly, in Oklahoma City, the victims were children, Social Security recipients, working people dropping their children off for day care, men and women with no relation to any perceived enemies of the extreme right. And if any sympathy for the radical right remained among police, it surely dissipated after the 1998 murder of a police officer outside an abortion clinic in Birmingham, Alabama.

For all of these reasons, there has been a major crackdown by law enforcement on radical right groups in the United States. This crackdown has nothing to do with speech, or with members of these groups sieg-heiling or wearing swastikas on their sleeve or saying unkind things about Jews or blacks or others of their enemies. Those things are all considered free speech and, as such, are protected by the Constitution's First Amendment. The crackdown is about crime, as defined in American legal terms – murder and other forms of violence, gun violations, threats against officials including judges. A survey conducted a few years ago found that as a result of threats made by right-wing extremists, one-third of American judges were carrying weapons into their courtrooms. This should give you an idea of the atmosphere prevailing in the United States in the years since the Oklahoma bombing.

Let me briefly describe where I think we stand today. As we enter the new millennium, a number of new trends are shaping contemporary extremism. One of them is that the radical right movement in the United States has been Nazified. Now the enemy is not nearly so much the black man or even the homosexual – the enemy is the Jew. The Southern Poverty Law Center does an annual count of extremist groups, and in the last year we have seen the emergence of fifty new neo-Nazi groups. At the same time, the militia movement – made up of much "softer"-line groups which in general are not explicitly racist – has been declining steadily since its peak in 1996. So while soft antigovernment groups are on the wane, the number of very hard-line, revolutionary, fascist groups is rising. We are also seeing attempts by extremists to take over churches in the American South and to instill in them a profoundly antidemocratic ideology. At the same time, although to date the issue of immigration has not figured strongly in extremist rhetoric, the economic downturn will probably change that situation. In other words, anti-immigrant violence is bound to rise in coming years.

Another trend is the internationalization of the radical right movement. Until recently, the Center focused exclusively on American hate groups. We were not concerned with groups outside of our borders because they did not have an impact on local problems. This is no longer true. It is impossible to monitor and investigate the American radical right without tracking European groups as well. For example, white power music – which is probably the single most important factor in the recruitment of youth to the radical right movement – and the neo-Nazi skinhead phenomenon were exported from Europe to the United States. Now, unfortunately for Europeans, US extremist groups are returning the favor by hosting large numbers of websites in European languages for Europeans. The German government, for instance, says that 80 percent of German-language neo-Nazi sites are now hosted on American computer servers. In addition, there is a great deal of networking among leaders of these groups, so that we quite often see Nick Griffin, head of the British National Party, or American rightists visiting Jean-Marie Le Pen, leader of France's Front National.

Another trend that began in Europe but seems to be making its way across the ocean is a kind of convergence of left and right, of the radical left and the radical right. Of course, the US does not have much of a radical left anymore. But this convergence, which is well established in Europe, does seem to be beginning in America. A recent example: a group called the Earth Liberation Front, a left-wing ecoterrorist organization that has burned down a number of new buildings in the name of environmentalism, announced that it was henceforth targeting federal buildings. The reason I find that so remarkable is that federal buildings are precisely the same target selected by Timothy McVeigh and others on the radical right. My point is that the enemy for both the far left and the far right is in many ways the same. The left may call it "transnational capitalism" while the far right complains of the "New World Order," but they are basically talking about the same thing.

In its latest count, the Southern Poverty Law Center identified 602 hate groups operating in the United States, a number that rose steadily over the latter part of the 1990s. In a healthy economy, we would normally expect to see a decline in hate-group and white supremacist activity, which has been historically true in the United States. But during the 1990s, in the context of extremely low unemployment and almost zero inflation, the opposite occurred. From 1997 to 2001, the number of hate groups jumped from 400 to over 600. Why has this happened?

One key reason is changing demographics. By the year 2050, minorities – blacks, Hispanics, Asians, and others – will outnumber the white population for the first time in America's modern history. In August 2000, the white population of California, the largest state in the country, dropped below 50 percent. In the next thirty or forty years, state after state will lose these white majorities, which have run the country for most of its history. As a result, the politics of state after state are changing significantly. This has generated fear among many whites, a fear exploited by the radical right. "Listen white man," the white supremacist organizer declares, "you are losing your country. This is not the white Christian nation that your forefathers built." That kind of argument resonates for many Americans.

Thirty years of effective organizing has also contributed to the numerical rise of the radical right. The movement learned a lot during the Posse Comitatus days in the Midwest. And most of the organizers are not what one might expect. They are not stupid men. The leader of the principal neo-Nazi group in the US, for instance, a man named William Pierce, is a former university physics professor.

Another important factor is the Internet. It must be said that the role of the Internet has been overblown in many cases, particularly in Europe. I do not think that every time a teenage boy visits a neo-Nazi website, he mutates into a National Socialist. This is a ludicrous claim with no evidence to back it up. However, the Internet has been important in unifying the movement and giving it a sense of momentum. In America, the typical white supremacist twenty years ago was a man who sat alone in his living room shaking his fist at the ceiling, a person afraid to go down to the corner bar and express his ideas because he might very well be punched in the nose. The Internet has changed all of that. Now there is a venue in which people can talk to each other, where new people can be brought into the movement very rapidly, where people leaning toward radical right ideas can explore them without having to attend a Klan rally, where kids can easily become involved in this kind of ideology without their parents' knowledge. It is a very private world.

Another factor is the recasting of Nazism in a religious framework. In the United States, unlike Europe, Nazism has been hooked up with the extremist theology known as Christian Identity – a violently racist, anti-Semitic, and heretical reading of the Bible wherein whites figure as the lost tribes of Israel. The person responsible for this linkage was George Lincoln Rockwell, the founder of the American Nazi Party and a man who made hate holy. Knowing that Americans are far more religious than most people, certainly more than Europeans, Rockwell gave his ideology a theological basis that appealed directly to Americans. Just as important, especially in a nation of immigrants, Rockwell also redefined what it is to be white: one no longer had to be classically Aryan to fit the bill. One could be Greek, Italian, Spanish, even Iranian and be considered white within this new, broader definition. It bequeathed the Aryan ideal to the vast majority of Americans, not merely an elite Germanic subgroup. Finally, the advance of Holocaust denial has helped to make Nazism respectable. After all, twenty years ago, the average Klansman's father had fought the German Nazis and did not take kindly to hearing them described as heroes. Now, the idea that the Holocaust is a myth created by the Jews to fool the rest of the world has become firmly entrenched on the extreme right. And, of course, it helps that this kind of propaganda is not illegal in the United States.

A perceived loss of national sovereignty has spawned its own peculiar set of anxieties. In the US, for instance, the radical right inflamed fears that the United Nations was going to rob America of its power and independence. The typical conspiracy scenario is that one day soon the UN's blue helmets will be marching into Iowa and Ohio to impose martial law and send all good Americans to concentration camps or worse. Similar ideas are circulating around Europe. The radical right in England, for instance, is going crazy over the idea of losing the pound note, of losing that picture of the Queen on every piece of currency.

Ultimately, the most important reason for the rise of hate groups in recent years does go back to the economy. Throughout the 1990s, we were repeatedly told that the economy was doing well, and in some ways that was true. But the deeper reality is that, over the last fifteen or twenty years, the United States has seen the development of a two-tiered economy in which the number of professional, upper-middle-class jobs has shrunk while the pool of low-skill service-sector jobs – in fast food restaurants, hotels, etc. – has expanded. The upper working class and the lower middle class have been under tremendous pressures as jobs move abroad and other structural changes in the economy occur. So there are a great many Americans who, for instance, made $50,000 working in steel mills or auto plants fifteen years ago, and who today are managing a fast food restaurant in western Pennsylvania and making $18,000 a year. My father's generation were pretty much guaranteed a decent job in a factory; their wives would not have to work and their children would be taken care of. That is patently not true anymore, and the sense of betrayal felt by many working people is a breeding ground for the toxic ideology of the radical right.

In many ways, the struggle has shaped up as a kind of battle between competing visions: one of a multicultural, democratic, multiracial world, and the other a kind of ethnic nationalism, an identity politics marked by parochial tribalism. This latter phenomenon is manifested in the United States in a variety of ways. Recently, we have witnessed the emergence of a strong new movement, what I have called the "neo-Confederate movement," made up of "pro-South" groups that want to reconstitute the Confederacy, the old South. Basically, these groups are saying, "Slavery really wasn't so bad, and anyway it was all sanctioned by God in the Bible," that racial segregation was not really such an onerous thing, just a system to protect the integrity of both races, and so on. These kinds of ideas circulate principally among white supremacists but find a parallel in a number of black supremacist groups, in particular the New Black Panther Party. The differences between the new and the original Black Panther Party are revealing. The original Panthers were very much old-style leftists, building coalitions with white leftists, Puerto Rican leftists, and others to oppose police brutality and address other forms of social injustice. The New Black Panther Party is chiefly interested in proclaiming the guilt of the Jews. According to the new Panthers, the Jews ran the slave trade, the Jews are the invisible hand guiding the destruction of blacks in the United States. These kinds of ideas seem to be animating more and more ethnic groups around the Western hemisphere, fueling ethnic hatred and opposition to globalism and multiracialism.

So what is to be done? First, let me address a major conflict in this regard between European governments and the US, not to mention antiracist organizations on both sides of the Atlantic. Certainly the great debate in Europe has to do with the criminalization of speech. At virtually every international conference, the Americans, no matter what their politics, left or right, have defended the First Amendment and argued that censoring speech is not useful. But the Europeans – and apparently most of the rest of the world – seem to agree that the Americans are naive, if not foolish, for making a distinction between speech and conduct. There is little chance that Americans will change their view, or that the US Constitution will be amended. In any case, there is no evidence whatsoever that suppressing this kind of speech undermines the radical right. In fact, it is the very countries that have most criminalized speech which have the most serious problems with extremism. If the Germans ban the NPD, they will instantly create a group of criminals, people who have little to lose by taking up the gun. In Germany, too, there have been a large number of raids in which white power music CDs were snatched up and a few people thrown in jail. The unfortunate but very real side effect has been that the Germans are helping to finance the radical right. These illegal CDs have become hot merchandise, more lucrative to move than selling hashish, according to Interpol. A group like the Hammerskins – a truly frightening neo-Nazi organization operating in both Europe and the United States – can now finance itself for decades to come.

The Southern Poverty Law Center has developed a variety of strategies for combatting the radical right. The Center became known mainly for its legal work, but first I would like to say a few words about my own work there. My background is in journalism. I spent twenty years at large newspapers in the United States, and what I do now at the Center is edit a quarterly magazine called the *Intelligence Report*, which covers the American radical right. The *Intelligence Report* is circulated to Center donors, police officials, and reporters, but is not sold on newsstands. We do not compete with journalists, which means that much of the press has come to rely on the Center and its magazine to inform their own stories. Because many of the more prominent American hate groups are adept at masking their racism and anti-Semitism, passing themselves off as mainstream conservatives, and because information about the radical right is hard to come by, there has turned out to be a genuine need in the United States for a magazine that specializes in investigative journalism exposing these groups. Sometimes, these exposés can be devastating.

Not long ago, for instance, we discovered that the leader of a neo-Nazi group called the Knights of Freedom had in fact changed his name. He was known among his brethren as Davis Wolfgang Hawke, which had a nice Aryan flavor to it. But it seems that until Mr. Hawke went away to university, he had been Andy Greenbaum, son of Hyman Greenbaum, who is Jewish. Although some may consider it a low tactic, we published that fact without hesitation, fully aware of what the outcome would be. And to be sure, the group imploded. What was supposed to have been a mass march on Washington produced a turnout of four pathetic young neo-Nazis.

Another major exposé involved a group called the Council of Conservative Citizens, an outfit that claimed mainstream credentials. Using a variety of sources, we revealed what the group and its leaders were all about when not on television defending themselves. We also exposed the links between Senate Majority Leader Trent Lott, that is, the leader of the Republican party in the Senate. Lott had been playing ball with the leaders of this white supremacist group for several years. We reproduced pictures showing the Majority Leader posing with members of the Council in his Senate offices. The story was picked up by virtually every major newspaper in the United States.

Among the Center's legal cases, probably the best known are civil lawsuits brought against white supremacist groups in the United States. We have done this by using a new legal technique devised by lawyers at the Center that some people have termed "vicarious liability." In essence, the technique relies on the lower standards of proof required under US civil law, and aims to hold groups and their leaders financially accountable for the criminal acts of their members. A high-profile example is the civil suit brought against the Aryan Nations, the most infamous neo-Nazi compound in the United States with a long history of violence. The Center had been waiting for an appropriate case through which to challenge the group. That opportunity finally came a few years ago when a woman named Victoria Keenan and her nineteen-year-old son were driving by the Aryan Nations compound and stopped their car because the boy had dropped something out of the window. After retrieving the item, they restarted the car and it apparently backfired. And the Aryan Nations people, certain they were being attacked by "the Jews," went crazy. Heavily armed Aryan Nations security guards jumped into a pickup truck and chased the woman and her son for about two miles, all the while shooting at them. They forced them into a

ditch, pistol-whipped her, and threatened to kill them. The Keenans escaped
when another car came down this lonely road in the middle of the night. The
Center sued the Aryan Nations on behalf of Victoria Keenan and her son.

Cases such as this are commonly misunderstood as speech cases. In fact, they
are analogous to a civil liability case brought against a department store. In the
Aryan Nations suit, we argued that the leader of the group, Richard Butler,
hired people fresh out of prison and armed them to the teeth with semi-auto-
matic weapons. He provided no training, no supervision, no policies to follow
as to when to use force – the normal kinds of things that an employer is
required to do in supervising armed security guards. And then he set them loose
on the community, telling them the Jews were coming to get them. Had a
department store known that a delivery truck driver in its employ was an alco-
holic and allowed him to drive until the day he mowed down a crowd of school
kids, the liability would be enormous. And that was exactly our argument in the
Aryan Nations case. Richard Butler did not supervise his employees in any kind
of rational way and ought to be held liable. The court obviously agreed, award-
ing the largest judgment in history against a hate group – $6.3 million.

Another legal strategy employed by the Center is to allege a type of civil conspiracy. A few years ago, we brought a case against a group called the Christian
Knights of the Ku Klux Klan. What we showed was that, although the leader of
the group had not specifically instructed his Klansmen to burn down a particular black church, he had talked in general terms about how black churches
ought to be burned down and he had talked in specific terms about how he
hated "those people down the street." He had suggested that should one of his
Klansmen burn the church, he would take care of him, protect him from law
enforcement.

In addition to investigative journalism and legal challenges, the Center also
sponsors a major educational initiative called Teaching Tolerance, which creates
materials for teachers and children aimed at producing a better, more tolerant
world. Among other things, Teaching Tolerance publishes a high-quality magazine in which teachers can find strategies for inculcating democratic values in
kids. Teaching Tolerance also produces videos, for instance, *Starting Small*,
which challenges the concept of "whiteness." One of our videos, in fact,
received an Academy Award.

Overall, the Center's goal has been to do high-impact work. The Center is
financed almost entirely from individual donations, mainly through direct-mail
fundraising, and it has managed to build an endowment, a war chest, of well
over $100 million. That kind of money makes possible the kinds of cases our
lawyers take on, and the publication of high-quality magazines like the *Intelligence Report*. We are not a grassroots organization in the sense that we do not

work on the community level. Hundreds of organizations in the US do that type of work very well, and we try to act as a national resource to these groups. We want to put the *Intelligence Report* into the hands of people who are doing antiracist work. We want to put the *Teaching Tolerance* magazine into the hands of teachers who are instructing kids, because, after all, our children are ultimately the answer to the problems we are facing. To go back to the idea of making it illegal to deny the Holocaust, I would suggest again that the answer is not censorship – it is in dealing with our children, the inheritors of our planet, honestly and forthrightly. Given the choice between criminalizing Holocaust denials or teaching our kids about what really occurred, I think the answer is obvious. The problem with the Holocaust is not that it has been talked about too much. It is that it has been discussed too little.

An Eclectic Atlas of Urban Europe*

Stefano Boeri / Multiplicity

1. USE: Uncertain States of Europe   The European territory is today an extraordinary field of study and experimentation: a palimpsest of heterogeneous environments, where the new urban condition operates as a powerful matrix, meeting less obstacles than elsewhere in spite of the innumerable preexisting structures with which it has to deal. It is a landscape at the mercy of uncontrolled and eccentric forces which have undermined many parts of it, but one that is also the cradle of experiences of urban life offering a glimpse of the future. Alongside the chaotic invasion of single-family residences, the geographic imperialism of the great commercial enterprises, and the standardization of historic cities to meet the demands of tourism, we can find highly advanced forms of ethnic cohabitation in some historic centers. In the diffuse European city, we encounter modes of living that have been freed from functional specialization and we discover panoramas of unconscious beauty in the random points of contact between historic locations and infrastructures.

It is an original model of the city, different from that of the United States as well as that of Asia, which at times can look disheartening, at others fertile, but always incredibly heterogeneous.

Some months ago, arc en rêve, a major French architectural institution, asked us[1] to represent our research on European urban conditions within the larger exhibition *Mutations*.[2] We decided to present our Eclectic Atlases of Euro-

---

* *Ed. note:* The lecture delivered in Vienna by Stefano Boeri with Francisca Insulza and John Palmesino was based on issues developed in the following contribution, parts of which were previously published in Boeri's "Notes for a Research Program," in *Mutations* (see note 2).

1 Multiplicity (Stefano Boeri, Maddalena Bregani, Francisca Insulza, Francesco Jodice, Giovanni La Varra, John Palmesino) is a mobile research group on contemporary urban conditions. Its goal is to constitute new networks in order to address new themes connected with contemporary urban analysis. In the case of USE research, Multiplicity comprises a network of seventy researchers from fifteen different countries.

2 Rem Koolhaas and Harvard Project on the City, Stefano Boeri and Multiplicity, Sanford Kwinter, Nadia Tazi, Hans Ulrich Obrist, *Mutations* (Barcelona: Actar, 2000), published on the occasion of *Mutations: événement culturel sur la ville contemporain,* Bordeaux, Entrepôt, November 24, 2000 – March 25, 2001, organized by arc en rêve centre d'architecture, Bordeaux.

pean urban conditions in the exhibition as works-in-progress (a mise-en-scène of our methodology).

We chose to observe innovation in urban Europe. Or, better said, to focus on processes producing innovative phenomena in the physical urban European environment. When I say "innovation," I do not mean simply change or addition; innovation is something that establishes new relationships between space and society, between the physical environment and social behaviors. This immediately obliged us to carefully select our media of research and abandon magazines, books, and readings produced by the elite academic European architectural world. Working from these kinds of texts, we would have had little understanding of what was really happening in terms of innovation.

We had to disperse our efforts across a huge environment, recognizing that the most interesting innovations are often not to be found in the center. More often they are located at the periphery, in the marginal hidden areas beyond the perimeter of our gaze.

What we have observed is not simply change – at least, not architecturally recognizable change. Rather, we have seen processes of radical spontaneity able to produce genuinely new effects in the physical environment, which at the same time provoke a high degree of uncertainty.

We began collecting case studies. We reduced the earlier seventy case studies to the thirty-six that are in the exhibition catalogue – though we are still working on them. Then we settled on eleven case studies for the exhibition. We worked with photography, video, diagrams, and various other tools. For each of these eleven situations, we had very different types of representation.

2. Eleven Innovative Processes   The first case study (USE 10)[3] is in Tyneside, an old industrial mining district near Newcastle, in northwest England, where old industries have been completely abandoned in recent years. It is interesting to see how these huge abandoned environments are now used as places for leisure, being continuously developed into an incredible series of playgrounds.

The second case study (USE 01)[4] is in Belgrade. Traditional shopping markets that were destroyed during the war or by the embargo that followed have now been replaced by a multitude of small shopping stalls. These molecular shops have invaded the entire public space of the city, not just the squares and streets, but effectively replacing all ground-level shops.

3 John Lonsdale, "USE 10: Tyneside: Shifting Margins," in *Mutations*, p. 393.
4 Ana Džokic, Milica Topalović, Ivan Kucina, Milan Djura, and Marc Neelen, "USE 01: Belgrade: Gray Realm," in *Mutations*, pp. 380–381.

The third case study (USE 05)[5] is Benelux (Belgium, Netherlands, and Luxembourg). These last few years, there has been a marked intensification of movement across political borders. Many middle-class professional people choose to live near a border and work on the other side, availing themselves of the different social and economic conditions on both sides. The physical effect of this intensification of movement is to create a diffuse city that covers a vast area; it is a seemingly never-ending city with the same elements everywhere.

The fourth case study (USE 08)[6] is about Pristina, the principle city in Kosovo that, in a certain sense, has become a new city in the last few months. We have a group of researchers here observing a very paradoxical situation. The first paradox is that a war that was intended to check mono-ethnicity has produced a monocultural situation. Before the war, Pristina was inhabited by 250,000 people, 20 percent of whom were Yugoslavian Serbs; since the war, Pristina has 500,000 inhabitants, of which only 0.2 percent are Serbian; other minorities have also been completely eliminated. The second paradox is that, despite this monocultural dimension, Pristina now has the largest number of foreign people of any city in Europe. Counting all the people from the United Nations and numerous nongovernmental organizations, we calculated that some 60,000 people from forty-five different countries currently live in Pristina. So we really have two cities here: one is a city of permanent citizens – the Kosovars and Albanians – whose public space has been completely destroyed and abandoned over the last ten years; then there is also a new city "floated" over the first city, composed of a number of islands or enclaves, each of which has no direct relation to the others nor to public space. Two parallel cities.

The fifth case study (USE 06)[7] takes us to the former East Germany, where one major project to improve the infrastructure is simply to double the width of the main east-west highway. This is the A4 freeway that crosses Germany from Görlitz to Eisenach, a grand eight-lane highway which, arriving at the Polish border, becomes an eight-meter-wide street.

The sixth case study (USE 02)[8] is in Paris, in the 13th Arrondissement. In 1972, a huge public housing block was built, the parts of the complex rigidly and vertically differentiated by function. All the towers were designated as

5 Carole Schmit, "USE 05: Benelux: Transnational Opportunism," in *Mutations,* pp. 386–387.
6 Giulio Padovani, Alessandro Floris, Andrea Soffientino, Daniela Borroni, and Rosafa Basha, "USE 08: Pristina: Parallel Lives," in *Mutations,* pp. 390–391.
7 Carole Ducoli, Massimiliano Gherzi, Stefano Giussani, Valentina Gugole, Lorenzo Laura, Silvia Lupi, and Pier Paolo Tamburelli, "USE 06: RFA-RDA: Automatic Engineering," in *Mutations,* p. 388.
8 Yves Dubalin, Panos Mantziaras, and Jean-Louis Violeau, "USE 02: Subversions and Diversions: The 'Italie' Slab in the 13th Arrondissement of Paris," in *Mutations,* pp. 382–383.

USE 01
Belgrade: Gray Realm

apartments, with the ground floor for shopping and other public facilities, and several underground levels for parking. In 1974, immigrants from China and northern Asia began to occupy this housing block, not simply adapting what was there, but subverting the use of space. Now, after more than twenty years of reinhabitation, the tower has become a wildly heterogeneous space filled with different activities on different floors – art and craft workshops, religious centers – while on the ground floor different ethnic minorities hold fairs and festivals in shop spaces. And the underground car park has become a multilevel bazaar extending 25 meters underground.

The seventh case study (USE 07)[9] is in Elche, a small city in Spain. Elche exists because of three very large textile companies. These last few years, there has been a sort of "explosion" of these companies, so now the entire urban tissue is occupied, industry even spreading through apartments.

The next case study (USE 04)[10] involves the phenomenon of raves or techno parties, which has spread from northern to central to eastern Europe. Techno parties work like *eruptions*, very slowly building events: they start with a gradual dissemination of information about when and where the techno party will take place; the participants – rave or techno "tribes" coming from all over Europe – learn the location only a few hours before the start of the party. The venues are often abandoned industrial buildings or places not used by the local population. The event itself lasts six or seven hours during the night, then everything suddenly disappears and all the participants disperse back to their homes.

9 Francisca Insulza, "USE 07: Elche: Invisible Factories," in *Mutations,* p. 389.
10 Paolo Vari, "USE 04: Raves: Rave Parties: Nomadic Flames," in *Mutations,* p. 385.

USE 02
Subversions and
Diversions: The "Italie"
Slab in the 13th
Arrondissement of Paris

The ninth case study (USE 11)[11] is in the tiny country of San Marino in central Italy, an old town perched on a rock close to the Adriatic Sea. It is an historic urban center, but nobody lives there. In recent years, it has become something of a theme park: it opens at 8:30 a.m. and closes at 8:30 p.m., inhabited only by vendors and visitors – a shopping mall in the true sense of the term. Visitors enter through enormous gates and must leave their car in a car park. The entire public space is monitored by security television.

The tenth case study is in Switzerland (USE 09).[12] A new urban habitat is emerging around the Alps. A great number of small-sized, high-technology firms (micro mechanics, pharmaceutics, biotechnology, electronics) are increasingly framing portions of "in control" nature. Increasing access to innovative technologies, and the accelerated spread of know-how, accompany an accurate and orderly landscape construction. A Perfect Nature is staged: it is fenced in, all-panoramic, without residual parts, accurate in details, exact in its diversity: the wood, the green meadow, the roadside footpath, the wood-fenced farm, the chrome-fenced hi-tech firm. In the core of Europe, a new transnational zone is arising in which a suitably technicized landscape is an additional value asset for high-income firms and users.

Finally, the last case study (USE 03)[13] is in southern Sicily, in a small city called Mazara with an important fishing industry, where the last fifteen years

11 Guido Musante and Gianandrea Barreca, "USE 11: San Marino: From the Historic Center to the Shopping Mall and Back," in *Mutations,* p. 394.
12 John Palmesino, "USE 09: Alps: Naturality," in *Mutations,* p. 392.
13 Franco La Cecla, Stefano Savona, and Ilaria Sposito, "USE 03: Mazara, La Goulette: A Mirror-Border," in *Mutations,* p. 384.

USE 03
Mazara, La Goulette:
A Mirror-Border

have seen a clandestine invasion of immigrants from North Africa. This has been a place of incredible exchange: part of the Tunisian population began to inhabit Mazara and part of the Sicilian population began to inhabit a district in Tunisia. Now we have these two satellite-cities on different sides of a sea that demarcates not only two political continents, but also two religions, two worlds. It is a "mirror border," because each of these two populations continually reflects the other side through an ongoing exchange of goods, foods, and marriages.

3. The European Spatial Device   Observing these case studies, we decided to develop the idea of Europe as a cultural entity rather than a geographical continent; an entity that has been built up through the inertia of certain "long-term" structures acting on the spatial environment of social relations – structures that only become manifest in the course of the territory's processes of change.[14]

Europe as a local dispositif for the mutation of material space, whose geographic scope appears through its continual shifts (Athens, Jerusalem, Rome, Constantinople, etc.). Europe as the field in which a highly particular and original dispositif for the modification of inhabited spaces operates, reproduces, and splits off from itself.

Indeed, if we turn toward the past, we might observe that the history of Europe is that of a continual invention of complex constructive entities, able to

14 Jacques Levy, *Europe: Une géographie* (Paris: Hachette, 1997).

USE 04
Raves: Rave Parties:
Nomadic Flames

organize a multitude of individual fabrications into a system of clear and repro-
ducible rules.[15] The rural farm and the urban courtyard, but also the 19th-cen-
tury cluster and the publicly planned residential district, are entities capable of
establishing an internal principle of variation "on a theme," while at the same
time guaranteeing themselves a clear physiognomy, distinct from the other parts
of the surrounding territory. The European "sentence" is a fundamental element
of urban syntax, because it articulates and organizes the conjugation of the minimal units of discourse, providing a recognizable code for a given set of individ-
ualities (the minimal elements of inhabitable space). The code – a set of spatial
regulations establishing proportions and criteria of contiguity for the "urban
facts" – offers each individuality the possibility to reinvent a space of its own,
and thus to add something to the sentence itself each time.

On the one hand, each innovation, each individual invention, is absorbed by
the intermediary level of the organization of space; on the other hand, each one
acts as an adhesive, a "link" to the urban system taken as a whole.

It might then be possible to develop a genealogy of European space by
observing this "median" dispositif of organization and change. For example, by
observing its capacity to metabolize ancient and exotic cultures, to absorb and
reinvent "other" forms and spatialities, by reinterpreting certain of their characteristics. The history of European architecture is not the evolutionary history of
one or more constant "styles," but rather a succession of colonizations and external reinterpretations of monuments and cultures of inhabitation within a tolerant and "open" system of rules. Indeed, it is precisely in this repetition of the

---

15 Cf. Krzysztof Pomian, *L'Europe et ses nations* (Paris: Gallimard, 1990).

USE 05
Benelux: Transnational
Opportunism

reinterpretive gesture, more than in its results, that we can recognize a constant, structuring element in European space.[16]

In the same way, one could observe the effects of this dispositif in its cumulative capacity.[17] Fundamentally, European space is transformed by accumulation, addition, and superimposition, but rarely by outright replacement or elimination. The invention of new urban entities, new typologies of habitat, does not depend on a tabula rasa, as it may in other cultures of inhabitation; rather it demands the reuse and reconversion of the existing urban materials.

Metabolization and accumulation also explain a third structural characteristic of the European dispositif: the extraordinary density of the alternating phases of construction and reconstruction of the territory, which also occurs in its most densely urbanized parts. There is a very high density of typically urban relations – exchanges, itineraries, transnational flows of persons, good, and ideas – which go beyond the literally built density. The history of the European city is also that of the continual pursuit of *urbs* by *civitas*.[18]

The contemporary European territory is the product of this spatial dispositif. A palimpsest of works and projects which still today displays a particular balance between the principles of variation and those of difference: between the rules which underlie the constitution of a part of the city, which govern the acceptable variation of its subsystems, and those which, to the contrary, lend it

16 Cf. Joseph Rykwert, "Europe and Its Mongrel Architecture," *Rassegna* (Bologna), no. 76 (1998), and J. L. Cohen, "Intangible Europeism," *Rassegna,* no. 76 (1998).
17 Cf. André Corboz, "Le Territoire comme palimpseste," *Diogène* (Paris), no. 121 (1983), pp. 14–35.
18 Cf. Massimo Cacciari, *Geo-filosofia dell'Europa* (Milan: Adelphi, 1994).

USE 08
Pristina: Parallel Lives

cohesion and identity by fixing the particular, or the different, within the urban context. An equilibrium which does not only produce an articulated system of changes, but tends to organize innovation and thus to create original spaces, often produced by the reinterpretation of exogenous traditions in their encounter with the local syntax of the territory.

The paradigm of European space as a local dispositif of innovation suggests a conception of identity which is not linked to a border project or to the recognition of an available context, but instead to a material phenomenology of the European territory, with all its adaptations, rough edges, idiosyncrasies; with all its heredities and its forms of openness to transformation.[19] This paradigm does not demand an aggregate representation of the continental territory, it does not define its inner and outer limits, nor describe its territorial subsystems. Yet it can help us recognize a mode of spatial change which, although it manifests itself within an historical framework, can potentially act anywhere. In the same way that a discursive form – an exclamation, an exhortation, an imperative – can be adapted to any part of a discourse, so the European urban "sentence" is the characteristic form of an unlimited spatial dimension, extensible through the action of a local dispositif but nonetheless deeply rooted in and consubstantial to the experiences of European culture over time.

European space has extended in the past toward Asia, it has colonized parts of America, and it has more recently contracted with the phenomena of globalization: because the European territory is not a system of national states, nor the

---

19 Cf. Hans-Georg Gadamer, *Das Erbe Europas* (Frankfurt am Main: Suhrkamp, 1995).

USE 09
Alps: Naturality

perimeter in which a tradition is perpetuated.[20] It is a highly particular mode of change and innovation of European space.

4. Variation and Difference   In the contemporary European city, the interaction between global energies and local structural conformations has radically altered the relation between the principles of variation and difference.

Today the principle of difference no longer acts between contiguous and diachronic urban components (i.e., between the 19th-century city and the Renaissance city, between the modern suburb and the 19th-century grid, etc.), but rather between the single molecules of the urban organism's vast territorial sprawl:[21] between the family house and the contiguous shopping mall, between the shopping mall and the adjacent low-rise building, between the car wash and the industrial shed with the built-in house, etc. In the same way, the principle of variation does not have effect within the boundaries of vast or compact urban parts, but rather operates with the declination of a few families of urban forces that regulate the composition of the emerging city. This variation is thus reduced to infinite adaptations, conformations these elementary components can take on through surprising leaps and improvised solutions in varying territorial contexts.

20 Cf. Vittorio Gregotti, *Identità e crisi dell'architettura europea* (Turin: Einaudi, 1999).
21 Cf. Rem Koolhaas, "The Generic City," in Rem Koolhaas and Bruce Mau, *S, M, L, XL* (Rotterdam: 010 Publishers, 1995).

USE 11
San Marino: From the
Historic Center to the
Shopping Mall and Back

The exploration of the new European territories marks the end of the syntactical dispositif of territorial organization and innovation which seemed to allow for a deeper identification of the distinctive features of European cultural identity. The dynamics appear chaotic, unpredictable in their trajectory, and therefore all the more powerfully charged with uncertainty.

The USE Project aims to rediscover, in the new territories of contemporary Europe, the field of action of the "sentence" that structured the older European city as well as its modern counterpart. To do so, it observes the forms of combination that cloak the various urban facts in the course of their evolution. It tries to show how forms of interaction and combinatory regularities persist in European space, organizing the evolution of the territory and reflecting certain levels of the self-organization of established society and its minorities. How, behind the apparent chaos, there is in fact an excess of organization, of regularity, an excess of evolutionary patterns.

5. Self-Organization   The novelty of this with respect to the observations carried out on the historical territory of the classical and modern cities resides precisely in the fact that today these organizational dispositifs no longer tend to be imposed by a desire external to the protagonists of the modification. Instead they are largely controlled and managed by the protagonists themselves, even when they appear beneath the repetitive form of codified decision-making procedures.

Thus it is possible to trace a dividing line between the evolutionary patterns observed from this median viewpoint. On the one hand, they describe highly repetitive processes of modification that interject very little resistance into the great, global energies of the overall mutation. Processes that appear as simple and mechanical transpositions into the European space of forms of interaction and modes of change that find their source in the three major currents at work here, as in other geographic regions: the emergence of a mass individualism in the behaviors relative to consumption, habitat, leisure time, and travel; the local importance of systems of professional rationality, fundamentally closed and impermeable; the spread of transnational flows of persons, goods, and ideas.

On the other hand, a gaze that observes the mutations in real time, that samples portions of time and circumstances of transformation, can also encounter forms of *autopoietic*[22] innovation of inhabited space. Places and territories that seem able to adapt in original terms to the great global energies; limits within which the local dispositif of innovation – and not simply change – begins to fully manifest its staying power and long duration. In the new territories of diffuse urbanization, all these forms of innovation in inhabited space encounter an initial friction that rearticulates them into a limited series of evolutionary assonances; a series of mechanisms that composes these individual acts within the major waves of change.[23] These mechanisms can be described with the help of metaphors:

Linear attractors. First we recognize certain sequences of linear development, especially along major axes (commercial streets and corridors, industrial buildings near the ring roads, entertainment and sporting facilities near the major rivers). The logic that presides over these "urban events" depends on the presence of a linear attractor that establishes the orientation and constitutes the major reference point for a series of heterogeneous buildings: an urban street, a watercourse, or even a less materialized element like a bike path or an open space.

Bowling pins. A second principle of self-organization is the change brought about by the introduction of autonomous elements on the terrain. In recent years we have seen the construction of enormous "containers" at isolated places along the traffic routes that grid the urban areas: integrated shopping centers, sports and leisure complexes. Anonymous and stereotypical in appearance, they offer a variety of spaces and circulation patterns inside. The locations are frequently chosen as a function of ease of access and available parking space.

---

22 Cf. Humberto Maturana and Francisco Varela, *Autopoiesis and Cognition: The Realization of the Living* (Boston: Reidel, 1980).
23 Cf. Stefano Boeri, Arturo Lanzani, and Edoardo Marini, *Il territorio che cambia* (Milan: Abitare/Segesta, 1993).

Islands. Another change is induced by the appearance of introverted "islands" within which similar objects and lifestyles are reproduced: protected residential zones, reception centers for immigrants from outside the EU, production zones, residential suburbs with guarded entryways, housing projects that repeat the same building with minimal variations on the facade, etc. These islands share five characteristic features: the repetition of similar-sized construction elements; the high degree of internal organization; the independence of the spaces; the homogeneity of the inhabitants and their behavior; and the fact that they result from a single design project.

Cloning zones. The spontaneous repetition of the same urban elements generates another transformation. Entire stretches of urban territory have been modified in recent years by the accumulation of separate development projects with similar characteristics. New urban zones have appeared – with the construction of "commercial containers," with the imitation country houses that spring up like mushrooms, with the detached houses built in concentric circles on hills around enlarged city centers or in ribbons along the crests. The repetition is spontaneous, rather than being codified within definite limits.

Grafts. Another mode of the alteration of the territory is "insertions" by the replacement of elements. In certain quarters, radical transformations appear in a very short time, but within a broad spatial context. There is a succession of precise, independent, small-scale alterations, profiting from the availability of spaces that are "empty" in both the physical and symbolic sense: for example, the replacement of one or more parts of an urban complex, but also factories or office buildings resembling isolated hangars in the middle of the countryside.

Zones of metamorphosis. Large parts of the city appear different by comparison to the very recent past, but without us being able to identify the speed or nature of the changes. Houses or apartments are transformed into offices, stores and studios appear in former workshops at the back of courtyards: examples among many others of a process of "internal transformation" rather than a "replacement" of individual components. When many of these restructurings appear in a single area and over a short time, in a repetitive but almost invisible series, the effect on the city can attain critical dimensions, capable of radically altering the symbolic but also the spatial identity of an area.

6. Multitude   Finally, what we see is the repetition, inside and outside the compact city, of a limited number of compositional patterns for this multitude of isolated fragments: the suburban residential quarter, the well-defined industrial or artisanal zone, the tourist center, etc. These patterns reflect a limited number of dynamics of basic interaction at work in the construction of our territory through the self-organization of our society into subsystems, conducted by "minorities" which act as microcosms of autopoiesis (extended families, ethnic and professional clans, cultural communities, leisure or consumer associations). Even when they are superimposed upon each other, these dynamics rarely enter into osmosis: they reproduce without mutual contamination, and are simply laid down on a territory which is already laden with the traces and symbols of the disappearance of ancestral modes of inhabitation. In short, the "syntax" of the new cities consists in a few rules of organization for a multitude of words: it is an impoverished language making a repetitive use of only a few small fractions of a rich vocabulary.

In Europe, the contemporary urban territory brings together a multitude of individual, unsynchronized actions within a few very regular physical movements – distinct from each other by their rhythm, duration, and intensity. Each of these regular movements is reproduced in different, distant spaces, and reveals a specific self-organization of social relations and decision-making processes.

"Self-organization" in this context is not used to mean only spontaneity, informal, or noninstitutional processes of territorial change. Rather, self-organization – which often creates spaces of innovation – means above all that settlement rules (that give order to a certain set of individual tremors) are produced and shared by subjects that participate in the system itself. These are relational rules, designed and eventually readapted throughout time by the forces acting within the system; rules that often take on, together with the linguistic set appropriate to that system, a common and coded meaning.

In a certain sense, Europe is an urban society which continues to produce intermediate entities, where horizontal links prevail over hierarchical structures.[24]

7. European Upheavals   The often random repetition and assemblage of these combinatory regularities generates vast upheavals in the European territory, grand currents that move between physical space and society. These are dynamic energies, similar to the ones that produce the great telluric movements. They reshape large portions of space, but only take on visible configuration when they come into contact with the long-term "structures" of the European territory.

And like telluric movements, they also have a rhythm of change – those thousands of tiny quivers that suddenly culminate in a radical shift of the tec-

---

24 Cf. Giuseppe De Rita, *Accoglienza e poliarchia* (Rome: CNEL, 1994).

tonic plates. Grafts, densifications, condensations, punctuations, these upheavals are radical in terms of physical geography, and often indifferent to political geography. They move across the territory and become visible in a few punctual sites, where they fully manifest their power and, in a certain sense, their ungovernability as well. Only in these places of emergence can they be observed.

The USE research has begun to analyze a few of these punctual places where the upheavals take on a dense, recognizable materiality. Although these are specific cases, they are emblematic of the mutations that traverse great expanses of the European territory.

Inundation. The invasion of public ground in Belgrade by informal, mobile forms of commerce (USE 01)[25] is but an extreme and radical version of another form of mutation that colonizes entire stretches of open urban space in Europe. It is not simply the model of the bazaar. The most innovative aspect lies in the fact that this invasion everywhere generates a form of collective space which is at once hyper-fragmented and dense. A molecular space, parceled out by multiple gestures of appropriation, seems to be the inevitable outcome of every form of collective interaction in the open space of the European city.

Détournement. The case of the Parisian housing complex that lodges a small Chinese city (USE 02)[26] leads us to reflect on the cumulative tendency of European space, on its resistance to replacement and its capacity to develop processes of metamorphosis which are invisible from the outside. There is an accumulation of small internal modifications which, in a critical situation, suddenly produces a catastrophe that modifies the content of the built entity. The signifier then survives the disappearance of the signified. These self-organized processes of symbolic subversion suggest how, in Europe, the most hierarchical and rigid entities are better able to resist the mutations than the generic, hybrid architecture inspired by the false rhetoric of "flexibility."

Osmosis. The case of Mazara in its relation to Tunis (USE 03)[27] confirms the paradox of an openness to symbolic subversion in sectors of the European city which are less physically malleable than others. But above all, this exchange constitutes a play of mirrors between two shores which have much in common (even if they are separated by one of the most significant European frontiers). It represents the constitution of reciprocal spaces along the European borders, places where the continental divides slowly undergo a process of osmosis.

25 See Džokic et al. (note 4).
26 See Dubalin et al. (note 8).
27 See La Cecla et al. (note 13).

Eruptions. The raves, great self-constructed events (USE 04),[28] reveal an extreme version of another mutation of European space. Its principal feature is an apparently irreversible rupture between the characteristics of physical stasis and semantic stability, a rupture emerging in a great many new sites of social interaction. As though, in Europe, a mobile strategy of "fecundation" of the territory by discrete points were the sole resource that could be opposed to the immobile and rigid structure of the great commercial facilities. The new double geography of collective places seems to be born directly of the collapse of the multiple, open, and at the same time rooted nature of the local history that characterized the traditional public spaces. In the void left by this disappearance there are hyper-coded, static spaces on the one hand, and undercoded, itinerant spaces on the other.

Intensification. The intrication of spatio-temporal cycles of urban life in a vast transnational region like Benelux (USE 05)[29] confirms the extension into European space of typically urban habitation behaviors. This extension is gradually transforming Europe into the sum of a small number of large, polycentric urbanized regions (the "Blue Banana," the Randstad, the Île-de-France, the Adriatic corridor, etc.). Thus urban European society and its multiple, erratic minorities trace out a city without edges, but full of internal limits and thresholds of passage that measure and "mark" their movement. From these transitory lifestyles, issuing from a pendular motion, emerge individual projects of an "enlarged" citizenship, where differences of origin and destination fade away. What decides our identity are the itineraries we most frequently follow, the landscape sequences we create, the perceptual strips we memorize.

Expansion. The intermittent doubling of the A4 freeway in Germany (USE 06)[30] leads us to reflect on the role of the great infrastructures as the ultimate visible and explicit form of public intervention on the European territory. A determinist form of mutation, which seeks to act simultaneously on the vast portions of the territory – a veritable counterpoint to the fragmentation and miniaturization of the processes of transformation. But the self-organization of the public bureaucracy often generates forms of autistic decision making. The paradox of the huge infrastructural projects, necessary but interrupted, or thrown into question after their completion – for instance, the exemplary cases of the Schipol and Malpensa airport centers – clearly reflects the risk of public intervention on the densely populated territories of contemporary Europe. Overwhelming yet also weak, these infrastructures are often the sym-

28 See Vari (note 10).
29 See Schmit (note 5).
30 See Ducoli et al. (note 7).

bols of a modernization which is unable to adapt to the mutations currently underway.

Dissemination. The case of Elche (USE 07)[31] leads to a reflection on the reciprocal contamination which is established in Europe between small (often family-run) firms and the private residence. The hybrid typology of the house-factory is conjugated infinitely, becoming the elementary cell of an urbanized and rarefied territory, encompassing in a single building the diverse functions that formerly divided the territory. The explosion of work at home as a self-organized form of participation in the production cycle now plays its role in the gradual shift of the European single-family home to the status of a "networked monad," where a maximum of isolation is materialized along with a maximum of connections. Networked capsules in an extended city: this is an infinitely repeated (more than infinitely varied) spatial model that translates the new genetic code of the European suburban territories.

Transplant. Pristina with its garrison clusters (USE 08)[32] leads, on the contrary, to a reflection on the mutations by self-organized "grafts" that increasingly affect the central areas of many European cities, as the specialized niches develop. The circuits of the European community in Brussels – like the fashion world in Milan, the financial milieus in Frankfurt and London, the contemporary art world in Paris and Berlin, to name just a few other examples – have an even greater tendency to function as "networked enclaves": local nodes grafted onto a context with which they maintain only a limited exchange, while continually remaining in contact with a specialized world network. When it is not transformed into a theme park, the geometric center of many European cities becomes the shell for these globalizing niches, which often have no relation to each other.

Clearing. The huge theme park that is being built up around the Alps (USE 09)[33] expresses the degree to which nature and history, in Europe, are not only simulacra to be recopied in a watered-down image, as in the great North American entertainment parks; they are also real environments that a multitude of parasites undertake to enclose and sell as rare resources. And often these self-organized theme parks represent a pivotal center for zones of active production, rooted in the economy of the territory.

Inertia. Playful incursions into the former mining regions of Tyneside (USE 10)[34] let us glimpse the way the ruins and the voids left by industry could, in the

31 See Insulza (note 9).
32 See Basha et al. (note 6).
33 See Palmesino (note 12).
34 See Lonsdale (note 3).

absence of any unifying project, become a new "nature" able to host temporary practices. In Europe, the occupation of these areas still awaiting heavier investments represents the extreme version of a tendency to constitute intermittent collective places that use the discontinuous morphology and the inertia of the industrial terrain as a natural ground. Places as generous and "expansive" in their functional identity as these are unable to inscribe any durable traces on the European territory.

Pulsation. The case of San Marino (USE 11)[35] is ultimately just a radically exaggerated version of a form of mutation that is common to many centers in Europe, which deliberately choose to make the urban environment into a museum and to exploit it as a tourist machine fed by the cyclical pulsations of the floods of visitors. These theme parks based on the counterfeiting of the authentic, and on a process of reciprocal imitation between historical centers and shopping malls, conform the tendency of European space to turn systematically back on itself and on the tokens of its past. History as a guaranteed income, nostalgia as a form of surplus value.

8. Toward a Nondeterministic Urbanism   These upheavals, among many others researched in the USE project, are often born of a network of horizontal, non-hierarchical relations, micro-powers that condense the multitude of individual vibrations into one stable configuration.[36] Yet despite their power and widespread diffusion, most of these configurations have no relation with the world of architecture, which only participates on the scale of the micro-transformations, the tiny quivers that compose each upheaval.

The fact is that these upheavals, often innovative but sometimes also at the origin of perverse and regressive phenomena, are never carried out by a deterministic and readily identifiable project, located within a single institutional matrix. There are no authors, no great strategies to be celebrated. Their power actually confirms the marginality of architectural practices and urban planning in Europe. A marginality which is paradoxically repeated each time someone tries to "govern" these processes, with the illusion of being able to control them from inside (a belated version of the principles of participation in architecture) or from the heights of an exterior authority principle. Escaping this condition of powerlessness simply implies accepting the ungovernability of a great deal of the contemporary territory, at least in the sense of an irreducibility to any intentional and univocal predetermination. This means learning to act in a context

---

35 See Barreca and Musante (note 11).
36 Cf. Aldo Bonomi, *Il Trionfo della moltitudine* (Turin: Bollati Boringhieri, 1996).

directed by different, highly variable subjects. European space, which is a palimpsest of projects sedimented in time, is also today the field of action for an indeterminate and changing number of subjects, many of whom maintain a temporary relationship with the territory. A battle of codes and interpretations ceaselessly unfolds upon this field, which is continually being rewritten, where almost nothing is ever erased, where the long-term structures are often temporarily hidden by others which are less powerful and enduring, but currently more visible.

I believe that the new themes for architectural practice are all there: the capacity to intervene in mechanisms of individual variation, the care of new and temporary community spaces, the attempt to use the economic power of certain building processes to produce a symbolic added value that redeems them from their egotism.

But a new paradigm for interpretation of the emerging city is needed, one that can take the place of the model we inherited from the sixties.

9. Eclectic Atlases   The diffuse city and its scattered dynamics are not simply a new "part" of the European city. They represent the visible and emergent form of a new urban condition that transforms the nature and the very concept of the city, exerting its effects on the classical city as well. An urban condition which is born of a substantial transformation of the relation between individuals and urban space, and which, to be represented and appropriated, requires a different strategy of observation than the one that has formerly been employed for the classical European city.

It is an urban condition nourished by long-distance associations, new spatialities, but also new forms of citizenship. A condition impossible to decipher with the vocabulary and the interpretive categories constructed in the 1960s to analyze the old European city. That now-useless vocabulary continues to make the distinctions between "center" and "periphery," between "public space" and "private space," between "emergent areas" and "parts of the city." In the new European territories, these categories simply do not work, and merely slip over the surface of things.

But we need more than a new vocabulary. Symptoms of a more profound disease are apparent in our visual culture, in the ways we usually represent and think the urban dimension. If we take heed of these visual symptoms, usually overlooked, we will likely hear a more radical call: the call for a new paradigm in the conceptualization of urban phenomenon.

In certain parts of Europe, "eclectic atlases" are being created to propose new ways of studying the correlations between space and society.[37] The documents are heterogeneous, but similar in their visual approach. They take the form of an "atlas" insofar as they seek new correlations between spatial elements, the words we use to name them, and the mental images we project upon them. And they are eclectic because the basic criteria of these correlations are often multidimensional, new, and experimental. For this kaleidoscopic family of studies and investigations, chaos is not the reflection of external phenomena, but only a way of conceiving the territory that has worn threadbare and must be replaced. The eclectic atlases offer various entries to the representations they construct. They observe the European territory in search of the individual, local, and multiple codes that link the observer to the phenomena observed: the physical city, its inhabitants, and the "inner city" of the observing person. They produce provisional maps in which the territory is not represented as a continuous mineral substrate, nor as a stable "state of things," but instead as an interlace of sinuous configurations which are reversible and never share the same temporal frame. These atlases most often observe the territory from several viewpoints at once: from above but also through the eyes of those who live in the space, or on the basis of new, impartial and experimental perspectives. By adroitly interlacing the viewpoints, the eclectic atlases propose a multiple visual thinking that abandons the utopia of a synoptic vision from an optimal angle of observation. Their most interesting characteristic is the way they seem to mesh with their field of observation: an eclectic gaze on an eclectic territory. They experiment unsystematically with "lateral" ways of seeing and representing the territory of the European city. The viewpoint used by this approach, which proposes an "abductive" logic for the conceptualization of space, is the one best able to grasp the characteristics of the new European urban condition.

This research paradigm offers a new "strategy" of vision, and suggests four major revisions of the techniques for the representation of the territory.

First, the new paradigm seeks to account for the mutations in real time, introducing a temporal element which is generally absent from the disciplines that study inhabited space.

Second, it proposes observations limited to certain samples of the territory, with an attitude of hunting for clues, testimony, and indicators that are often temporary and have been left behind in the space by new, as yet unstandardized behaviors.

Third, this logic of sampling supplements the zenith view through a system of coordinates and criteria which are used for the choice of the punctual places of research, and for the comparison of the results.

37 Cf. Stefano Boeri, "Eclectic Atlases," *Daidalos,* no. 69/70 (1999), pp. 102–113.

And fourth, the new paradigm inquires into the identity of those who inhabit the space and construct its representations. In other words, it seeks to enrich the notion of the "landscape" by research into the complex identity of its users, and into the forms of dynamic perception and memorization of inhabited territories.

The eclectic atlas is an attempt to introduce a new dimension into the research on European space. In sum, it can be said that the maps produced by interweaving these four "lateral" gazes are attempts to observe the territory *while* it changes. This means abandoning one's confidence in two-dimensional, aggregate cartography, which often includes a hypocritical effect of "distancing" that absolves the observer of any personal responsibility. It also means renouncing a naive form of representation of the landscape, reduced to a montage of statistical frames.

Convinced that the city is not only a stratification of "levels of realities" but also a collective mode of reflection on space, persuaded that each stage of the city's evolution implies and also requires a "leap" in the forms of its representation, this project can help us cast new light on the intermediary dimension of the evolution of inhabited European space.

While satellites incessantly send us two-dimensional images of the aesthetic chaos which reflects the cities of the 20th century, from some points of inhabited space we are receiving images that are less presumptuous but much richer in information. Registering what happens between space and society, they reveal a territory where a few recurring rules organize a multitude of bulky buildings, and these almost never constitute figures visible "from above." The kaleidoscope has become the best metaphor to represent a space shaped by a society organized through introverted, uncommunicating microcosms.

Though it may be true that the arrogant viewing angle of the impersonal zenithal paradigm has fixed the coordinates for the conception of 20th-century urban space, the contemporary city seems to demand that we learn to see it anew – and that we begin by learning to see *ourselves* in it, as individuals and as groups.

The USE project is born of a sampling of the places and processes of mutation, whereby European space and its intense, unlimited activity finally comes to light. And uncertainty transforms into innovation.

Arquitectos Sin Fronteras–España (ASF-E)

Marta Calsina and Elsa López

Arquitectos Sin Fronteras–España (ASF-E) is a nongovernmental development organization operating on a nonprofit basis. It was founded in 1992 by a group of architects and technicians who had previously collaborated with other NGOs.

ASF-E is an association of people who participate as volunteers in cooperative projects in the fields of architecture, infrastructure development, and town planning. Its main activities are "Third and Fourth World" projects, along with raising public awareness and making public criticisms related to both these "worlds." We support the most underprivileged populations in developing countries, that is, those who suffer from a situation of extreme poverty or exclusion. We also work with the most vulnerable populations of the so-called Fourth World in our own country, without discriminating on racial, gender, sexual, religious, philosophical, or political grounds. ASF-E reports on, and informs the Spanish public about, the needs of the populations with which we work.

As a nongovernmental development organization, ASF-E collaborates on projects in which the main goal is the economic and social development of the area concerned. We focus on cooperation for development rather than emergency aid. We work, normally on technical aspects, *together* with those organizations in the Third and Fourth Worlds who request our assistance and who have knowledge of the problem to be addressed. We listen to their requests and analyze, together with them, the needs of the beneficiary population in order to provide comprehensive solutions. The aim is to promote self-dependent and self-managed local development that will improve the population's quality of life and satisfy basic needs, always with a respectful attitude toward the environment.

ASF-E is active in developing countries in Africa, Central and South America, Asia, and Europe. It also has small offices in several Autonomous Communities in Spain. Each group runs its own projects, although there is overall coordination. Some 50 percent of ASF-E's projects are related to education, such as schools, materials manufacturing workshops, and technical training. A further

25 percent are health projects, such as centers for primary, nutritional, and child health care. The rest are basic infrastructure and housing projects: water supply, wastewater treatment, community centers, housing construction and rehabilitation. We follow a similar process in each of our projects. Once the needs and functions of the building or infrastructure have been defined, we map out a construction plan, taking into account available building materials, local customs, and local technologies, making improvements where necessary. We also try to ensure that project financing benefits the largest possible number of people.

ASF-E's activities are based on two different kinds of economic resources: its own income and institutional funds. It is quite hard to obtain either of them.

The organization's own income derives from membership fees and contributions by architectural associations, firms, and individuals. These account for 10 percent of all its resources. ASF-E currently has more than a thousand members all over Spain. The aim is to increase this figure to a number large enough to guarantee the organization's financial independence and to encourage people who are not architects to become members and to collaborate on projects.

Here we will discuss a few projects carried out in Catalonia involving the Fourth World, as we think the issues raised in these projects are most relevant to this conference.

The Fourth World Committee of ASF-E   We work on Fourth World projects because we cannot remain indifferent to the growth of poverty and social exclusion in our towns: poverty alongside wealth.

The Third and Fourth Worlds are not independent realities. We need to link them and make sure we do not forget either of them. Both are the consequence of a dominant economic system that favors a minority and plunges the majority into poverty. The issue of poverty is so serious that the European Economic Community thought it necessary to define it in relation to the per capita income of each country.

In Spain, the poverty line is officially set at below a monthly income of 42,800 pesetas (around US$238) per person, which is well below the official minimum wage. According to a report by FOESA (Foundation for the Promotion of Social Research and Applied Sociology), in 1996, 8.5 million people lived below the poverty threshold. In the province of Barcelona, 618,760 people out of a total population of 4.2 million, or 14.8 percent, were poor. The poor are becoming younger: 52 percent are under forty, while four out of ten are under twenty-five. Poverty is also becoming more urban. In cities like Barcelona it is still worse, because everything is more expensive. It is surprising and contradictory that when society experiences growth, which is normally measured by economic indices, more poverty is generated among a large part of the population. Wealth and poverty often go together, and we have almost accepted this as an inevitable or "natural" condition.

Marginalization springs from society's rejection of certain groups of people, which prevents them from integrating into it. This rejection is not a consequence of economic factors alone. There are groups who have been marginalized for other reasons, such as undocumented immigrants, the long-term unemployed, the homeless, AIDS sufferers, the mentally ill, the disabled, women, young people with casual jobs, old people. These groups are becoming larger, but the problem is very difficult to quantify for many different reasons.

The current economic and political system is the main reason why these groups exist. It is the direct cause of emigration, forcing families to leave their countries in order to escape from misery or war. When they reach wealthy countries, they usually encounter social rejection because of their different customs, and the illogical fear that they might take the few existing jobs.

Of all issues that can generate social problems, certainly one of the most pressing is housing. Many people are faced with the impossibility of renting a flat due to economic hardship or rejection by owners, neighbors, and public officials. Their situation is made worse by speculation in the housing market and rising land prices. In Barcelona, since 1999 the price of housing has risen 15 percent. Now rents are around 50 percent of average income and available rental units make up less than 30 percent of the housing stock. At the same time, there are 40,000 unoccupied flats in the city.

The substandard housing in our towns, the sink housing estates and the inner-city slums, concern us as architects and as citizens. Fourth World problems must be approached from multiple perspectives, as the different causes of marginalization are related. That is why well-coordinated, interdisciplinary collaboration between specialists in different fields is required.

The steps taken by governments are completely insufficient and fail to alleviate the problem, since they never tackle it structurally. Many volunteer civil and religious groups have been working on this issue for a long time, but have been unable to solve the problem because of its very magnitude. Fourth World issues should be dealt with comprehensively *by governments*, with all the necessary means and resources. Civil society organizations should only help and collaborate, as their means are limited. Nowadays the situation is just the reverse.

Project 1: Demolitions   Over the past few years, many blocks of flats, squares, and people have disappeared from the old part of Barcelona. In their place are new buildings and shops or vacant spaces.

Demolitions

This is the result of the large-scale town planning operations defined in the PERI (Special Inner-City Refurbishment Plan), whose objective is to equip the district with open spaces, improve infrastructure, and put up new housing. All these operations have been carried out at great social cost. Older neighborhood populations, traditionally low income, have been negatively affected by the expropriations and the subsequent gentrification of the area. For instance, in the neighborhood known as La Ribera, 525 dwellings were demolished and 353 families relocated, but it seems that the expropriation negotiations were not entirely aboveboard; in some cases the owners were even threatened. Meanwhile, the price of land has increased and higher-income people have moved into the area.

In contrast to the flashy "makeover operations" carried out under PERI, much of the old housing in the area remains substandard. This demonstrates that the local government has no intention of providing support for maintaining and rehabilitating the existing houses, which are often owned by people with few economic resources. The people in this situation want a home in the same neighborhood, fair compensation for expropriation of their property, and contracts that benefit the deedholder's spouse or children. In addition, they are asking that every legal occupant of a flat be entitled to the same benefits, not just those who have been living in the neighborhood for more than five years.

ASF-E collaborated on a project for a building located on Carrer de Sant Rafael, twenty meters from the Rambla del Raval and right beside one of the new facades in the old part of the city. The tenants of this building were concerned about its condition (cracks, damp, etc.) and fearful of the owners. When the local authority did not respond to their requests for assistance, the tenants

Demolitions

contacted the housing program of SODEPAU (Solidaritat per al Desenvolupament i la Pai), an NGO that helps immigrants obtain housing, among other activities. Since ASF-E and SODEPAU have a collaboration agreement, they asked us to provide a technical diagnosis of the building. We organized a team of volunteers comprised of architects and students to conduct the diagnosis and prepare a report. The aim of the report was to put pressure on the local authority to repair the building. Site visits verified structural defects and substandard conditions such as the lack of showers and proper ventilation. In short, the building was unfit for habitation.

Our report, together with the partial collapse of the building, accelerated a resolution. First, all the tenants were removed from the building. Negotiations began between tenants, the owner, SODEPAU, and the local authority. It was eventually agreed that the flats would be sold to the tenants at an affordable price. The tenants then set up an owners' association, a necessary first step in applying for a grant from the Ciutat Vella refurbishment program, a scheme run by the local authority for the old part of the city. This launched a different process, because now the affected families were the owners, which meant they were responsible for the state of the building and repairs to it.

Together with the families and SODEPAU, ASF-E drew up a renovation plan and submitted it to the Ciutat Vella. Approval by this office entitled the owners to a grant equal to 20 percent of the cost of the work. All of this took quite a long time and, meanwhile, the families had to live with relatives or rent another flat. When the project was finally approved, we asked the local authority to grant the relevant planning permissions cost-free and to help in contracting a building company.

Demolitions

The construction work was divided into two phases. The first, more urgent, phase involved shoring up the structure, changing the water, gas, and electrical installations, improving sanitation, refurbishing the common spaces, and replacing the bathrooms. This was done by a building company at a cost of 19 million pesetas (around US$105,555). The second phase, renovation of the interior of the flats, was done by the families with their own resources. Since they have limited means, the families worked together, sharing skills and investigating alternative sources for materials and labor.

In this case, it was possible to put people before economic interests. The eviction of a group of tenants was prevented and, in the process of defending their rights and rebuilding their homes, the families developed methods of solidarity and self-management. They were able to remain in their homes, where they have ties to neighbors and schools, and their quality of life improved dramatically. Moreover, working together, we prevented the demolition of a building that is part of the city's history and forced a recalcitrant local authority to become involved in the process.

We believe that our experience on this project provides a model for tenants and organizations facing similar circumstances.

Project 2: Espacio Vihtal   The exhibition *SIDA: Paisaje interior (AIDS: Interior Landscape)*, organized by Cristina Molina and staged, together with other ASF-E projects, at the premises of the Architects Association in Barcelona, is a far cry from the kinds of exhibitions normally seen in such venues.

The text below is by Judith Cobeña of the Citizens' Anti-AIDS Association of

Espacio Vihtal
Photographs by
Cristina Molina

Catalonia, coordinator of the Espacio Vihtal program, which among other things is a daycare center, training space, transit flat, individual care service, and open space for art. The name, suggesting a vital space or a space for life, is also a pun on VIH, which, in Catalan and Spanish, is the equivalent of HIV in English.

In Barcelona, despite it being a European city at the forefront of design and culture, there still exist many difficulties ... when it comes to exercising one of the basic human rights enshrined in the European Charter, signed, among others, by the city of Barcelona: the right to decent housing.

The organizations that support people infected by HIV are daily forced to help many of them find a place to live, but the owners of the housing available on the market are not inclined to accept as a tenant somebody with the HIV label. Even government entities, which ought to ensure that every citizen enjoys the right to housing, present obstacles when it comes to offering sufficient and adequate spaces in public buildings designed to provide shelter or when it comes to granting organizations such as ours the chance to use or rent premises to compensate for the poor public-sector response to this issue. HIV/AIDS still stigmatizes the individuals concerned and the organizations that support them. We regard the generation of a discourse in favor of free access to the latest retrovirus treatments that does not take into account the satisfaction of basic needs as akin – since we are talking about a space that can be lived in – to attempting to build a house starting with the roof. Everybody, whether or not infected with HIV/AIDS, should have their medical care, food, and housing needs satisfied, at least in the European cities that boast of their high standard of welfare ...

The photographs of *AIDS: Interior Landscape* also seek to convey the idea that the interior spaces in which people affected by HIV/AIDS live, or manage to survive,

Espacio Vihtal

reflect the dignity of their inhabitants, in spite of the precarious situation to which they are subjected. We hope that looking at these photographs will serve to make us all more decent.

The collaboration between ASF-E and the Citizens' Anti-AIDS Association of Catalonia (Associació Ciutadana Anti-SIDA de Catalunya – ACASC) began as a result of the need for improvements in the building where the organization's offices are located. The building was in an extremely precarious state and the organization operated with no official support.

ACASC requested our support and collaboration and this opened a relationship and participation process different from the typical one. ASF-E undertook the technical analysis of the building's condition through a volunteer team that involved both ACASC staff and its client population. Once the project was drawn up, together we began the process of obtaining funds from private and public entities. We negotiated with the local authorities, and struck deals with construction companies to reuse materials left over from other jobs. We hired workers through NGOs that assist immigrants. The construction process was monitored on a weekly basis by all the parties concerned. Finally, we publicized the organization's work by arranging for *AIDS: Interior Landscape* to be shown at the Architects Association in conjunction with a series of roundtable discussions.

As a result of this alternative way of working, more groups and individuals were involved in the project: the beneficiary population, architects, students, members of other participating NGOs. It was possible to obtain funds from private foundations and material donations from building companies. The AIDS

Youth

issue was publicized in an unusual venue. The construction work was done by other vulnerable people, helping to train them for the job market. And the original architecture of the building, hidden under many layers, has been recovered, providing a quality space for people who are fighting for their lives.

Project 3: Youth   The number of poor youth in Catalonia has been growing. They suffer from casual employment, relying on temporary employment agencies for jobs, and must continue living with their parents because of the lack of cheap flats for rent and the vicious circle of consumption.

In 1996, a group of squatters occupying a former cinema in Barcelona asked us for a study of the building's condition. Shortly afterward, the squatters were evicted. They had turned the building into a social center and this was favorably regarded by the local residents, who demonstrated against the heavy-handed eviction initiated by the local authorities. The excessive police repression and residents' support for the alternative recovered space swayed public opinion in favor of the squatter movement, which denounced speculation by owners, estate agents, and construction companies through direct action, occupying abandoned buildings in the city. They demanded that the right to a home take priority over property rights. They created their own information media through which they publicized and criticized police repression of the movement. And they created self-managed alternative spaces in which they organized community activities.

ASF-E could not remain indifferent to such a process, so we arranged a public forum at the Architects Association where squatters could explain the situa-

Youth

tion. Following this, on May 29, 2000, in the same venue, we organized a debate entitled "Are Youth Citizens with Full Rights? Housing, Space, and Emancipation." The invited speakers included:

- The chairpersons of the civil rights, housing, and youth committees of the Barcelona City Council
- The general director of the architecture and housing department of the Catalan government
- A representative of the Federation of Neighborhood Associations of Barcelona
- A squatter (who chose to speak from the floor rather than the platform)
- A member of the Barcelona Youth Council
- The chairperson of Arquitectos Sin Fronteras
- A member of MAPAFS (a group of parents alarmed at the police repression of an antifascist demonstration in the city)
- A lawyer
- A member of the Federation of Immigrant Associations in Catalonia
- A member of Avalot, the youth wing of the UGT trade union in Catalonia

Transcripts of the proceedings were sent to all the speakers as well as the Local Government Federation of Catalonia, and posted on ASF-E's website. The discussants proposed a variety of actions and made a number of policy recommendations, among them, to pressure the different levels of government to:

- Decriminalize squatting.
- Establish equitable land policies that are responsive to community needs.
- Develop new policies for reclaiming abandoned buildings, whether public or private.
- Encourage imaginative solutions and alternatives to the housing problem.
- Grant immigrants full citizenship rights.
- Provide young people with opportunities to set up new projects without erecting barriers beforehand.
- Tax those who profit from town planning (builders, transport companies, etc.) to fund affordable housing for young people.
- End discrimination against immigrants in access to rental housing.
- Promote spaces in the city that reflect and reinforce the mixing of different cultures.
- Respect and remove restrictions on alternative models of management characteristic of young people, such as Centres Socials Okupats (Squatted Social Centers).
- Encourage and respect young people's autonomy, and end the criminalization of youth.

The speakers identified a number of other significant issues. First, *the city should be a cultural and educational space for the young* but, unfortunately, politicians view it as an electoral market. It is therefore necessary to actively search for sites and resources and to be open to self-administration and new possibilities. Second, all citizens have *the right to be informed* about what is happening in their neighborhoods, which implies an overall approach to government that is neither restrictive nor bureaucratic. Third, different levels of government have the option and the opportunity to provide resources for *creating a city that is beneficial and hospitable to its young and elderly*. The gulf between the city and its young and old citizens, evident in the paltry resources directed toward these groups, is a danger that could throw the democratic system into crisis. Finally, noting the inflexibility of various levels of local government, speakers insisted that *the city must learn to be receptive to new models of participation arising from changes in society*.

As a consequence of these discussions, a civic platform was established to investigate the conclusions and recommendations, which will also be published in a forthcoming volume.

Meanwhile, the emblematic building that had sparked the mobilization – the old cinema in Barcelona – was demolished by the city in 1999. As of March 2001, a new building is being constructed in its place with no visible sign of who is behind the project and what the structure will be used for.

Migrating Objects

Project 4: Migrating Objects   According to data from a survey conducted by CIS (Social Research Center), immigration occupies third place in the list of problems of most concern to Spanish people, after unemployment and terrorism.

Compared to other European nations, the proportion of immigrants in Spain (2.5 percent of the population) is low, but immigration has been increasing considerably in a process that now seems irreversible. The recently enacted Foreigners Act, more restrictive than its predecessors in some respects such as basic rights, came in for heavy criticism from NGOs, trade unions, and political parties, and inspired civil disobedience.

On January 20, 2001, several hundred people, mainly from Southeast Asia and Africa, began a sit-in at a church in the center of Barcelona. It lasted forty-seven days, the last fifteen of which the participants were on hunger strike. Their demand was "Papers for Everyone." This action was joined by numerous other immigrant groups who organized sit-ins in nine other churches around the city. These struggles had a major impact on life in the city and garnered widespread support, culminating in a demonstration of 50,000 people.

Meanwhile, we should point out that certain segments of the population, either through ignorance or influenced by the opinions and statements of government officials and sensationalist media headlines such as "huge waves of immigrants" or "an avalanche of foreigners," consider immigration a disaster for the city and the country. Such groups couch their racism in appeals to preserve "our" culture and "our" identity against intrusions by foreign elements.

It is within this context that ASF-E proposed the project *Migrating Objects*, in collaboration with the artist Eulàlia Valldosera. Her works have focused on

Migrating Objects

new definitions of the subject and its inescapable separateness from its environment, starting from body issues and their projection upon the immediate surroundings: the home, what she calls "the house of the self." More recently, she began a series entitled "interviewing objects," which consists of interviews with people about the objects in their private spaces, which she redefines as the turning point of our identities.

Immigration poses challenges to conventional understandings of the relationship between citizens, and underscores the urgent need to foster and encourage cooperative relations between different groups of people within communities. *Migrating Objects* is an educational initiative designed to assist the interventions of individuals and associations concerned with social integration. The project consists of a video and other visual materials about immigration and the home, with the aim of spreading knowledge about the diverse ways in which immigrants settle into and interpret a new place, in a language combining poetry and anthropology. We intend to contact immigrant associations in Barcelona and interview a selection of people about the objects in their homes which create an emotional map of the territory they have occupied. The coincidences and divergences in the statements about the objects reveal much about the lives of their owners, their social status, psychological experience, and biography. Working with Valldosera, we created a typology of objects consisting of:

- Objects that hold memories of the place left behind.
- Objects that the immigrant has found in his/her new city and that have been given a new interpretation and function.

- Objects that substitute for others that the immigrant cannot afford for economic or other reasons.
- Objects whose value or function we do not know because they belong to a domestic ritual which is unknown to us.
- Objects common to every culture onto which are projected identity, social status, the division between private and public spaces, gender, family relationships, and so on.
- Objects that demonstrate the immigrant's need to appropriate his or her new space.

Migrating Objects is a reflection on humans' territorial instincts. It is also an indirect investigation into housing conditions in Barcelona revealed through the micro-stories of objects that reside within the homes of immigrants. It attempts to understand and communicate to others the customs of newly settled communities. With this project, we have tried to create a space in which people can reflect on the transformation leading to a multicultural society.

Conclusions   The interventions by Arquitectos Sin Fronteras in the city of Barcelona and its metropolitan area are painstaking and fraught with difficulties. They reveal the pockets of poverty and exclusion, and the extreme governmental neglect of a population that is increasing locally and internationally as a consequence of the advance of capitalism.

While economic and political elites construct the "Barcelona of the Future" with the symbolic buildings of multinational corporations, emerging throughout the city are groups weaving a network of resistance in the face of this society of capital by creating alternative spaces and voices.

ASF-E's small contributions are part of this network of resistance.

Demokratische Offensive

Isolde Charim, Gerald Eibegger, Robert Misik, and Rudolf Scholten

I. What is the Demokratische Offensive (Demokcratic Action Group/DO) reacting to?
The activities of the DO are not aimed at perfecting a democracy not yet fully
realized. Nor do we attempt to envision any sort of normative ideal. Our purpose is to oppose an actual concrete phenomenon: the political situation in Austria in the last two years, which has placed democracy itself in jeopardy.

The problem we have in Austria is not one of lack of electoral participation,
or anything similar, but a challenge to democracy as such posed by the presence
of a far right party in the government: the Freiheitliche Partei Österreichs (Austrian Freedom Party; FPÖ). This has not led to the abolition of democracy – as
in the case of a putsch – but, through various strategies, has turned democracy
into lipservice, has emptied out its content.

Democracy must be understood historically. In Austria, this means that it
must be understood in relation to the history of National Socialism. This is the
boundary against which Austrian democracy is constituted and defined. It is
precisely this boundary, this agreement, that the far right seeks to reshape,
exploiting this shift for political profit. The legitimacy of the present Republic –
and its capacity to elicit the support of its citizens – is doubly challenged. The
tactics of the Right consist, on the one hand, in calling upon the letter of the
law. Simultaneously, they exploit juridical gray areas – for example, the prohibition on Nazi political activity – in an attempt to undermine the very idea of
legal legitimacy.

In short, this amounts to an attempt to redefine democracy in radical right-
wing terms, to manufacture a new form of legitimacy.

Accordingly, the DO fights to preserve democracy as it has existed until
now, and by doing so, inject new energies into what has become a hollow institution. The battle for the preservation of democracy in its previous incarnation
is therefore also a struggle for its revitalization.

How does the Demokratische Offensive react?   The DO is a civil-society movement. The first thing to be made clear, however, is that we entertain no illusions
about civil society. It is untrue, as has been claimed, that civil society was nonexistent in Austria until now. But it was merely invisible because its function was
almost exclusively restricted to building consensus. What is new in the current
situation is that this "passive" situation finds itself confronted with a kind of
counter civil society that is active in two ways.

First, that it does not participate in consensus-building (the new legitimacy)
but, rather, opposes it. Second, these activities are realized in new forms and
new formations that go beyond the traditional boundaries of political activity,
creating new actors and practices.

We are well aware that civil society does not offer a remedy for all of democracy's ills, and that it does not function as an autonomous realm outside institutionalized areas of politics. On the contrary, the new political players aim to insert
themselves into and transform the established political apparatus.

It follows, then, that one is not concerned with raising consciousness or conviction or enlightenment, but with creating and articulating a – maximally heterogeneous – political milieu, with the production of a counter-appeal. Accordingly, all of our actions have both a ritual and a performative dimension, like
political demonstrations: the activities themselves produce the subjectivities
toward which, in turn, they are directed.

It also follows that this is not a question of morality versus politics. We are
dealing with political phenomena, such as racism, against which we pose a political position. And this position defines itself according to the struggle about the
signifier: democracy.

Isolde Charim

II.   One question is: What happens under what conditions? For example:
What are the "platforms" in the context of Documenta, which over the years has
developed into an established major art event that no longer comes in for any
serious critical scrutiny? What is the significance of the "platforms" in this context for art, and what is the significance of this context for the "platforms"?
Especially in conjunction with the topic of democracy, it is important to ask:
Who is allowed to participate in this discourse and who is excluded from it?

What is true for art is equally and obviously true for discourse, since neither
can exist outside the conditions of their production. To call democracy into
question therefore also requires consideration of the threat to democracy. The
current political situation in Austria compels such a consideration. In a recent

public diatribe, Jörg Haider, de facto leader of the FPÖ, drew a comparison between a brand of detergent and the president of the Israelische Kultusgemeinde (Jewish Religious Community) in Vienna, Ariel Muzikant.[1] This statement must be read as an allusion to the production of soap from the bodies of the exterminated during the Nationalist Socialist era.

The DO, a constitutive part of the civil protest in Austria, operates within this specific situation. Our strategic concerns thus demand maximum efficacy. The activities of the DO might be described as mediatory. Central aspects of our work consist of building possibilities for collaboration between NGOs, loosely organized and/or nonorganized sectors of civil society, and traditional political institutions that have recently become part of the opposition. We also strive to mediate between the subculture and the establishment (including the latter's presence in the mass media). The perviousness thereby produced can be seen as an opportunity for social development.

One cannot underestimate the role to be played by the noninstitutionalized opposition in resisting the dismantling of fundamental democratic structures in Austria. The consciousness and self-confidence engendered by collective action, coupled with the reappropriation of spheres of influence from political parties, should lead – after what is hopefully the imminent demise of the FPÖ within the government coalition – to a social constellation that will promote the further development of democracy.

Gerald Eibegger

III. Established dissidence: on the specifics of the Demokratische Offensive Austria is both a typical example of its time and a special case all its own. In this country a right-wing government is in office, a government which includes the far right FPÖ. In its attacks upon the institutions of the welfare state, the government is guided by leitmotifs of budget cuts at the expense of social programs and, more generally, of the primacy of economics over politics. Such an orientation has become "common currency" nearly everywhere in Europe. But the current Austrian government is unique insofar as the tone is set by a racist party whose politics fall outside the European mainstream, and which views its critics not as rivals but enemies, whose "ruling mentality" is guided by a mood of revenge for thirty years of social democratic chancellorship. All who oppose this government are forced into a dissident position.

---

1 *Ed. note:* "Ariel" is the name of a popular detergent in Austria and Germany.

It is crucial to understand this, if one wants to understand the specifics of the "democratic awakening" that occurred a few weeks after the 1999 election. This awakening brought 70,000 Viennese to the city center in a demonstration against a "coalition with racism." The formation of the ruling cabinet in the winter of 2000 was accompanied by daily demonstrations, largely spontaneous, attended by up to 20,000 people. This led to the largest political demonstration in the history of the Republic – some 300,000 protesters gathered in Vienna's Heldenplatz. Since then, a relatively stable protest milieu has evolved, a well-coordinated network of activists, initiatives, and NGOs.

The DO is a "pressure group" encompassing many of these initiatives and NGOs, as well as individuals who have become politically active since the October 1999 election, and thanks especially to the mass demonstrations staged under its name, the DO has gained international prominence. But it is important to say that not all the protest actions in Austria during the past two years have occurred under its aegis. Far from that. But the DO strives to enlist as many cooperative partners as possible. Two leitmotifs inform our activity: the goal of maximum publicity and for collaboration that goes beyond the limits of the "normal" protest milieu. The result is a flexible structure for which the term "organization" is something of a misnomer.

Our activities have spawned an oppositional network that includes independent leftists, unorthodox NGOs, critical economists, sectors of the Austrian Social Democratic Party, selected trade unions, prominent academics, the Green Party, and newly politicized groups representing immigrants (chiefly from Turkey) and refugees from Africa. Disparate elements have joined forces: initiatives of the leftist "subculture" and the politically marginalized cooperate with establishment figures from art, culture, journalism, academia, the media, i.e., those spurred to action by the virulence of the far right's racist campaigns and its assault on democracy.

This specific character of the movement has created another one: oppositional networks have begun to penetrate the middle strata, traditionally known as the "bourgeois center." The unique feature of this process is that protest and oppositional agitation are no longer solely the province of "outsiders," NGOs, and groups from the left margins of the political spectrum. All of these entities now cooperate with established figures and political apparatuses. The process is difficult: people are forced to work together whose political background, social status, and daily habits do not make them logical candidates for cooperation.

The DO is not a party. Our territory is beyond the established parties, but within the arena dominated by party politics. It was precisely within this arena that the far right party first monopolized political opposition in Austria, then seized power, simultaneously pushing politics and policies further to the right. This fact inspired the conviction that only the appearance of a new player within this arena could change the dynamics of the "game."

The DO's success in acting within this arena as a factor that must be taken seriously is an expression of the heightened political crisis in Austria. It is also an indication that new political formations can gain a foothold in areas that have thus far been occupied exclusively by "establishment politics."

Robert Misik

IV. A comparison of traditional parties and civil-society platforms reveals quite divergent loyalties, responsibilities, and obligations. Parties are beholden to close-knit networks of regional and/or interest-driven groups, and must constantly adjust their policies in response to internal pressures. Civil-society organizations, on the other hand, are guided solely by the content of their aims. Whereas parties proceed via compromise between substructures with differing programs, civil-society initiatives pursue their aims single-mindedly. The constraint of compromise is foreign to them.

Political parties derive their legitimacy from member votes and, especially, from the share of the vote they achieve within the general electorate. Civil-society organizations derive their legitimation from no other source than the democratic idea that all people have the right to make their voices heard and to participate in public discussion. Responsible only to its own goals, these kinds of organizations are the "booming" branch of democratic society.

The unique situation in Austria is that civil society has created a political space for itself as a democratic player, a space in which the parties – even the oppositional ones – cannot move with the same freedom. With increasing frequency, the ruling coalition in Austria is transgressing boundaries that, over the fifty-five-year democratic history of the Second Republic, seemed inviolable. Anti-Semitism and racism have become successful campaign slogans, even if in Vienna voters gave a slap in the face to all those who so blithely mouthed them. It is true that during the previous government, the lack of political openness with respect to foreigners occasioned much critique. Nonetheless, the attitudes represented above all by the Austrian Freedom Party should not be seen as the worsening of a previous situation but, rather, as the violent displacement of

---

2 *Ed. note:* The ruling coalition tried to fast-track a program of privatization, deregulation, and welfare "reform" which was inaugurated under the slogan "Speed Kills," meaning that anyone opposed to the policies would be mowed down.

democracy by authoritarianism. The government's motto "Speed Kills" is more than a faux pas in formulation.[2] It is an object lesson in their approach to democratic liberties.

A frequently heard objection to civil vigilance is that it is hysterical and exaggerates the significance of the political shift in Austria, the implication being that people should not get so easily excited. The fact that the author of this "diagnosis" is one of the people who wrote the Right into power demonstrates that conservative opportunists are intensely afraid of persistent civil vigilance. The government desires a return to normality, that is, an acceptance of the unacceptable. But since the entry of the FPÖ into the government, civil society has set new standards for political vigilance and accuracy in Austria. Its victory is that, after the present unfortunate intermezzo, a new government – however constituted – cannot simply take over from where the current one began.

Rudolf Scholten

Translated from the German by Jefferson Chase

Chronicle of DO Activities

November 12, 1999
Demonstration
"No Coalition with Racism"
Stephansplatz, Vienna
ca. 70,000 participants

December 1999
Collection of signatures supporting
migrants' right to vote at bodies
representing interests (like unions)
and supporting a law against
discrimination

January 31, 2000
Public announcement of the
Demokratische Offensive

February 2, 2000
Demonstration against the formation
of a ruling coalition between FPÖ and
ÖVP
Ballhausplatz, Vienna
ca. 20,000 participants

February 19, 2000
Demonstration
"Say 'No' to a Coalition with Racism"
Heldenplatz, Vienna
ca. 300,000 participants

March–June 2000
Collection of signatures demanding the
dissolution of the government and new
elections

March 2000
Meeting of a delegation from the DO
with the European Council in Lisbon
Talks with Council President Jaime
Gama (the Portugese Secretary of
State), Gerhard Schröder, Robin Cook,
an emissary of Jacques Chirac, etc.

May 27, 2000
"New Election Day – Night of Protest"
Open-air symposium and concert
staged in front of the Federal Chancellor's office
Ballhausplatz, Vienna
ca. 12,000 participants

November 10–12, 2000
Conference "Forming Opposition"
Together with party strategists from
the Social Democrats and the Greens,
the Educational Trade Union Committee, the School for Fine Arts, the
Rail Union, and NGOs. Guest lecturer: Pierre Bourdieu, "Raisons d'agir"
Künstlerhaus, Depot, Kunsthalle, and
Secession, Vienna
ca. 2,000 participants

March 16, 2001
Rally "Show Your Face! Raise Your
Voice! – Equal Rights for All"
Together with the Wiener Wahl Partie
and SOS Mitmensch
Stephansplatz, Vienna
ca. 15,000 participants

(www.demokratische-offensive.at)

Enacting the Unrealized:
Political Theory and the Role of "Radical Democratic Activism"

Oliver Marchart

The notion of Democracy Unrealized is open to a double interpretation. Most obviously it refers to empirical shortcomings in our political reality. From a historical understanding, democracy does not empirically live up to the glorious ways in which it is presented as "realized" (or on its way to final realization) by liberal Western "actually existing" democracies – we only have to think, as recent examples show, of the ongoing infringement of human rights, the economic deprivation of large sectors of the population, the effective denial of citizens' participation in the actual processes of decision making, etc. As Okwui Enwezor put it in the outline for this symposium, Western democracies perceive themselves "at best as 'incomplete implementations' of equality and justice on which modern democracy is based, rather than limits, flaws, dead-ends, and problematics inscribed in the principles themselves." In reaction to this presumption, though, one should start "bringing to light what liberal democracy promises but fails to deliver." Yet in contradistinction to *empirically* "unrealized democracies," there is something which exceeds even this form of political failure: and this excess is what I would call – thus sticking to the conference title – *Democracy Unrealized*. In doing so, I will propose to differentiate between empirically or factually "unrealized democracies" and "democracy unrealized," whereby a more philosophical interpretation can be given to the latter notion.

During the last few years, a figure of thought has evolved within political theory from which the notion of "Democracy Unrealized" is given a more radical twist (compared to the idea of an empirically unrealized democracy). The basic idea behind that twist is that there is something to democracy which *necessarily* remains *unrealizable* – to which we aspire but which does not necessarily have to be attained or achieved – that it is the *promise* of democracy rather than the latter's realization which gives all its force to it. Within the poststructuralist trajectory, we can think of Derrida's quasi-concept of a *democracy-to-come*, of Laclau and Mouffe's idea of a radical democracy which must remain unachievable if it is to be effective, or of different Lacanian versions of an ethics of democracy where the latter is defined as an "impossible good." Yet this figure of thought is not to be found in the poststructuralist trajectory alone; there are postfoundationalist versions of civic republicanism and neopragmatism – Arendt, Skinner, Barber, and others – in which the common good remains necessarily empty and, thus, open to an endless process of contestation. In those cases, the *res publica* of the republic is defined, again, as a necessarily impossible, rather than substantive, good – and, thus, as *unrealizable*. So the idea of the necessarily unrealizable or the radically unrealizable can be found in postfoundationalist political thought at large – even where it is not manifested or formulated in an explicit way.

Based on these considerations, my presentation sets itself a double task. First, and after some considerations as to the role of democracy as political slogan, I shall seek to establish the theoretical framework in which figures of "democracy unrealized" have been conceptualized in recent political thought and philosophy. But while such critique or deconstruction of actually existing democracies is obviously located at a theoretical level, there is another level on which a similar critique is launched *in practice*. This is the field of what I would call Radical Democratic Activism and whose logic I will analyze in a second step. Again, it is at the moment of the factual shortcomings of actually existing democracies where most current forms of social and political activism set in. They set in, this will be the main thesis, with the experience of unrealized democracy, but what they encounter is the promise of democracy unrealized.

Let me start with the most basic or the most trivial form in which we encounter "democracy" on an everyday level. Where do we encounter democracy? First and foremost, of course, in political discourse, and there democracy is nothing else but a signifier. As a political signifier, it is closer to the nature of a slogan than it is to the nature of a highly sophisticated concept of political philosophy or constitutional thought. So I am well aware of the fact that we should not make the mistake of approaching the political signifier in the same way as we would approach a philosophical concept. It would be ludicrous to judge the political slogan "democracy" along scientific or philosophical standards of, for instance, internal coherence or descriptive adequacy. It is not the role of a political signifier to figure in a nicely or coherently structured theoretical argument. A political signifier, rather, is a weapon. It can kill, at least potentially, as we all know from propaganda discourse. And it can do so because it is related to a field of forces and hegemonic struggle in which relations of power, domination, subordination, and suppression are constantly negotiated, but also, on the other hand, attitudes of agreement, allegiance, or silent consent and consensus, of blind as well as ironic or cynical belief are constantly produced. This is the field of what Antonio Gramsci called hegemony.

Before moving to political thought proper, it is necessary to analyze the political role of democracy as a signifier and then think about how to articulate – that is, to *link* – whatever concept of democracy we would like to propose on a theoretical level with the political signifier. If we now analyze the latter's function in political discourse, we will immediately be confronted with the phenomenon of its very ubiquity. Democracy is everywhere and apparently means everything. It has become what Stuart Hall, with reference to Ernesto Laclau, very cogently called a "horizon." Let us therefore come back to Laclau's original definition of horizon: "We call *horizon* that which establishes, at one and the same time, the limits and the terrain of constitution of any possible object – and that, as a result, makes impossible any 'beyond.' Reason for the Enlightenment, progress for positivism, communist society for Marxism – these are not the names of objects within a certain horizon but of the horizon itself."[1]

Nowadays, democracy seems to have assumed the status of such a horizon. Put simply: in the politico-discursive struggle I have described, democracy seems to be the winner, at least for the time being. But what does it mean to win a hegemonic struggle? Even as it is certain that no hegemonic struggle is won once and for all, that there will always be moments of crisis or counterattacks, counter-projects which might weaken the attained hegemony at some point, what *can* be said is that a certain particular project, a certain signifier (like democracy) can reach a point of hegemonic expansion at which it turns into a horizon. This horizon then establishes what Laclau calls both the limits and the terrain of construction of political objects. That is to say, firstly, it defines the very limits of what is thinkable politically at a certain point in time: it defines what might still be thought as an alternative *within* that horizon and it relegates into the unthinkable any alternative *to the horizon* as such. And secondly, this implies that any alternative – as soon as the horizon is established – must be formulated on the very terrain of the horizon. That is to say, it must take over the terms imposed on it by the latter's regime of what is thinkable or imaginable politically at a certain point in time.

If we take these general characteristics of a horizon and apply them to the question of democracy, assuming that the signifier of democracy indeed plays the role of the political horizon of our times, then it follows that the constitution of political objects – objects in the sense of both political objectives (demands) and political identities (actors) – is governed to a large extent by the horizon or the imaginary of democracy. This means that democracy constitutes

---

1 Ernesto Laclau, *Emancipation(s)* (London: Verso, 1994), p. 102.

both the terrain on which political demands and projects have to be constituted *and* sets certain limits to that constitution.

This is not to claim that it could not happen that some people still formulate their political goals in nondemocratic terms, let's say, the dictatorship of the proletariat or on the basis of supremacy. Such nondemocratic political goals indeed happen everyday, and on both the left and the right (an example would be American survivalists). My point, however, is that those objects, demands, or identities constituted *beyond* democracy can link up neither with the hegemonic horizon of political discourse, nor with the basic regime of what is imaginable politically in our times. Thus they are segregationist or sectarian by nature – and therefore relatively ineffective as far the realization of their literal demands is concerned. Even though there might be some long-term trickle-down effect of their ideology into mainstream discourse, this would only be possible if their ideology is accepted by mainstream "democratic" discourse itself. It is important to note at this point that a horizon is not only an "intellectual" or cognitive construct; it is a *real* thing with real effects (I have already mentioned that signifiers can indeed kill). This is the reason why, I assume, for Laclau it is possible to speak about the constitution of *objects*, not only the constitution of mere "ideas," namely, because they are intrinsically connected with real material practices and contexts – so intrinsically that it is impossible to separate them, that is, to separate the material from the semantic, even for analytic purposes.[2]

Let us now switch from the level of the signifier to the level of the signified. Or to put it somewhat reductively: Where does the specific *meaning* of that horizon of democracy come from? From the mere ubiquity of the signifier of democracy it does not follow that democracy is bare of a certain specific meaning, a particular inflection. There are dominant ideas about the meaning of democracy and there are marginal ideas about the meaning of democracy. And since we obviously cannot refer to an eternal Platonic idea of what democracy substantially is, because the meaning of the latter cannot be based on any ground or foundation of knowledge as to the substantial qualities of such "really real democracy": since this is not feasible anymore, the question becomes *which* hegemonic project or attempt succeeds in defining and arresting the meaning of democracy. Which project succeeds in filling up the empty signifier or the horizon of democracy with its own content, its own demands, its own goals? The main struggle going on today, I would hold, is the struggle over the answer to this question. It is not a struggle between democracy and its other (that is, whatever lies beyond that horizon), but a struggle within that horizon and on the ter-

---

2 In other words, it makes no sense to look for a "real material base" behind the horizon, for instance, in terms of a determining relation between base and superstructure.

rain of that horizon over the particular meaning and inflection of that very horizon. In other words: everybody is playing with the same signifier – the question is: which signified will be temporarily attached to it.

The answer to the question of who seems to have managed to hegemonize that empty horizon by now is blatantly clear and has been given time and again in the course of this symposium – it is that particular Western liberal model of democracy which presents itself as the only game in town. This Western liberal model is happy to provide a minimal formal framework of democratic institutions which, nevertheless, are very closely articulated with the promotion of a free market and the forms of subjectivation of free-market individuals. A model which is promoted – with a little help from the World Bank and the IMF – on a global scale. Where it is not yet realized it surely is "on the right track." In the case of the former socialist countries, it can be observed most clearly which particular version of democracy is or was at the end of the horizon: after the breakup of the former model of a so-called People's Democracy, the empty signifier of democracy has been filled up again with the idea of a free market so that the horizon of democracy, at some point, became by and large synonymous with capitalism (something which, by the way, attests to the fact that a horizon does have a phantasmatic dimension, a motivating force, so that it can turn into an object of desire).

Now, one can and must of course critique the fact that the Western liberal model of democracy has become such an all-encompassing horizon. This was one of the points repeatedly made by Slavoj Žižek: that it has become impossible to think of any alternative to the current ideology of democracy, the reason being that democracy has attained worldwide hegemony and has cancelled out any possible or imaginable alternative. But the problem Žižek encounters by trying to step out of the horizon – and I take his recent attempt at reviving Leninism as part of that project of transgressing the horizon of democracy as such – is that he cannot provide any answer as to what he wants to find behind the horizon. So, when critiquing the latter, he himself seems to conflate democracy too much with the particular Western liberal-capitalist version of it, and then seeks to step outside that horizon. But the fact that there is no wholesale alternative available to the democratic horizon does not, at any rate, imply that it is impossible to *redefine* the horizon from within. It is possible to redefine the horizon because its currently hegemonic meaning – the Western liberal one – is the contingent outcome of a whole set of struggles which by definition is open-ended even as it seems to have "won" for the time being. So there is no reason why it should be impossible to fight for a, let's say, more radical, egalitarian, and participatory version of democracy. A fight which definitely would take place within the horizon of democracy but against that particular impostor – Western liberal democracy – which presents itself as the latter's final and total incarnation.

Perhaps it might be feasible to fight for an even more fundamental or radical version like "democracy unrealized," to which I will now turn. The more fundamental or philosophical topos of a "democracy unrealized" – something which stands in contradistinction to the many ways in which "unrealized democracy" presents itself today with all its empirical shortcomings – is not so much about and in favor of a *specific* content than it is about the *structure and very nature of the horizon itself.* The question then is not so much: How is the empty signifier of democracy going to be filled with what content and who is going to succeed with what version of democracy? but rather: How should the horizon itself be structured in order to function democratically?[3]

In order to answer this question, it is advisable to have recourse to those philosophical attempts at thinking the nature of a horizon which functions democratically. As I mentioned before, what those deconstructivist, Lacanian, or, generally speaking, poststructuralist versions of "democracy unrealized" (a democracy which is unrealized not because of some factual shortcomings or problems which could be solved in the future, but because it must remain necessarily unrealizable, it must remain an impossible good) share with certain versions of civic republicanism (with Arendt, Skinner, or Barber) is the fact that they are postfoundationalist. This means that they do not anymore assume the existence of a solid ground, a fixed foundation or an Archimedean point from which one could revolutionize society as a whole. So, for instance, they do not live in the actually existing socialist illusion that – given that economy is the base or the foundation which determines the political superstructure – we only have to socialize the means of production and then everything will follow and the way is free for a socialist and eventually communist society. For postfoundationalist theories, the economy (or any other social instance for that matter) is not the ground of the social, not because they are anti-Marxist but because from

---

3 Even as I am very well aware of the fact that if we find an answer to the latter question we will again have to make a content out of that answer – that is, we have to formulate it as a political demand and fight for it politically – so that the question of the nature of the horizon is of course linked to the question of political contents proposed. And yet, to look at it from this angle still is a completely different way of approaching the problem. I am not saying the philosophical figure of thought is a solution, or *the* solution: but it keeps open the problem *as problem* (without prematurely claiming to have found the final real or ideal meaning of democracy), and this is its advantage. But of course, all the following philosophical solutions run into the problem of dirty hands, which you cannot escape if you want to put a program or an idea or even a promise (like in Derrida) into effect politically. For the problematic logic of a merely "futural" democracy without any realism, see Oliver Marchart, "Gibt es eine Politik des Politischen. Démocratie à venir betrachtet von Clausewitz aus dem Kopfstand," in *Das Undarstellbare der Politik. Zur Hegemonietheorie Ernesto Laclaus*, ed. Oliver Marchart (Vienna: Turia + Kant, 1998), pp. 90–119.

their point of view there can be no such a thing as a ground in the first place. And – this is one of the conclusions to be drawn by political theory – if there is no firm and eternal ground of community, there can be no substantial or traditionally pregiven *common good* either. Yet this absence of a *substantial* single communitarian common good must not necessarily lead into the liberal myth that there is no common good at all.

Rather, what follows from the postfoundationalist premise of the groundlessness of the social is that the common good has to be defined again and again in a conflictual way, and each good has to be enforced as a particular one against competing goods, that is, it has to universalize itself without, though, ever attaining the position of a complete or final universal good. As is the case with the dimension of ground, the dimension of the common good does not simply disappear either, but remains there as an empty horizon of public action which has to be defined again and again. It is present in its very absence, it is, as it were, present only "virtually," but still present. As Chantal Mouffe puts it: "The common good can never be actualized, it has to remain a *foyer virtuel* to which we must constantly refer but which cannot have a real existence. It is the very characteristic of modern democracy to impede such a final fixation of the social order and to preclude the possibility of a discourse establishing a definite suture."[4]

Not only the common good but also the *res publica* itself – understood both as republic and as the public thing or matters of the public interest – becomes an impossible object. In its most prominent form, an idea similar to this has been advocated with respect to democracy by Jacques Derrida with his concept of a *démocratie à venir*. According to Derrida, democracy is nothing which is already realized but it is a good which would disappear as soon as it is realized. Thus, democracy for Derrida has the structure of a promise. This is not a democracy which will be present and can be attained in reality at some point in the future, nor is it the *utopian* dream of a beautiful soul which would not have to be realized at all. It is neither a future reality nor is it a Utopia without any reality. And this is because, paradoxically, that future has to take place here and now, which means we cannot simply delegate the realization of democracy, its "coming," to a more distant point in linear time or to future generations.

It is the insistence on the actualization of the "to come" in the "now" which characterizes democratic struggle. In subaltern struggles, that "now," as Dipesh Chakrabarty argues, was countered, opposed, and put off with a "not yet" by the colonizers (the latter claiming, for instance, that the democratic consciousness

4 Chantal Mouffe, *The Return of the Political* (London: Verso, 1993), p. 114.

of the population is *not* sufficiently developed *yet*). Against their oppressive discourse of the "not yet" – which inscribes the postponed event into the historicist narrative of linear time – it is the "global insistence on the 'now' that marks all popular movements toward democracy."[5] Chakrabarty gives the example of India opting for universal suffrage for a still predominantly illiterate people. There, in the Constituent Assembly, the idea was defeated that "Indians as a people were not yet ready to rule themselves." What else was this position, Chakrabarty asks, "if not a national gesture of abolishing the imaginary waiting room in which Indians had been placed by European historicist thought?" And while in the day-to-day practice of governing the Indian state, historicist thought might still be prevalent, "every time there is a populist/political mobilization of the people on the streets of the country and a version of 'mass democracy' becomes visible in India, historicist time is put in temporary suspension."[6] So the promise of a democracy "to come" must by no means be confused with the "not yet" of the colonizers and oppressors as the latter is constructed in terms of linear historicist time, as a historical event which is just to be postponed because of circumstantial reasons.

Contrariwise, the promise of democracy – and this is the main point which is interesting for us – does not have a concrete positive or ideal content. The promise which is inherent in that futural structure of a democracy-to-come shows itself only in the suspension of historicist time, in the moment of the *failure* of democracy to realize itself. It is shown only in what we have called "unrealized democracies," that is to say, in the actual democracy's "failure, inadequation, disjunction, disadjustment, being 'out of joint.'"[7] So it is not only in seemingly atavistic rollbacks into military dictatorships, or nationalist or so-called fundamentalist uprisings, that a gap is revealed between the *ideal* of democracy (or at least what liberal democracy presents as an ideal of democracy which cannot be improved upon anymore) and factual political reality. No, it would be easy to show, Derrida holds, "that, measured by the failure to establish liberal democracy, the gap between fact and ideal essence does not show up only in these so-called primitive forms of government, theocracy, and military dictatorship. … But this failure and this gap also characterized, *a priori* and by definition, *all democracies*, including the oldest and most stable of so-called Western democracies."[8] All democracies, then, are and always have been *unrealized*

5 Dipesh Chakrabarty, *Provincializing Europe: Postcolonial Thought and Historical Difference* (Princeton, N.J.: Princeton University Press, 2000), p. 8.
6 Ibid., p. 10
7 Jacques Derrida, *Specters of Marx: The State of the Debt, the Work of Mourning, and the New International*, trans. Peggy Kamuf (New York: Routledge, 1994), p. 64.
8 Ibid.

democracies by definition. This is not only a historical account. Derrida's claim is much more radical. For him, the promise of democracy only arises in that very gap between the supposedly realized and the unrealized, between fact and ideal, between, as we have put it, unrealized democracy and democracy unrealized. Derrida: "That is why we always propose to speak of a democracy *to come*, not of a future democracy in the future present, not even of a regulating idea, in the Kantian sense, or of a utopia – at least to the extent that their inaccessibility would still retain the temporal form of a *future present*, of a future modality of the *living present*."[9] But, as we have shown, while Derrida is talking about a future which cannot be presented in the *present*, it still has to be actualized always *in* the here and now. It is at this point that we encounter the necessity, and I will return to it later, of "radical democratic activism," defined as the performative putting into effect that which nevertheless remains unrealizable.

So why does this postfoundational argument play itself out on the level of the nature of the horizon rather than on the level of its content? The point here simply is that democracy, envisaged as "democracy unrealized," does have practical political consequences in that one has to accept that a horizon by nature is something very different from a ground. A horizon is shifting, by definition it can never be arrested, it does not constitute a fixed reference point or substantial ideal. And these "negative" qualities have to be accepted so that Laclau can define a truly democratic society in the following way: "A society is democratic, not insofar as it postulates the validity of a certain type of social organization and of certain values vis-à-vis others, but insofar as it refuses to give its own organization and its own values the status of a *fundamentum inconcussum*. There is democracy as long as there exists the possibility of an unlimited questioning; but this amounts to saying that democracy is not a *system* of values and a *system* of social organization, but a certain inflection, a certain 'weakening' of the type of validity attributed to any organization and any value."[10]

It is in the sense of the above quote that Michael Cholewa-Madsen has recapitulated what can be said about the figure of "democracy unrealized" in all its different postfoundational philosophical topoi or figures: "Radical democracy is something *tensional* (Laclau and Mouffe); it is something to be *attempted*; something which has a *futural* (Derrida) or *différantial* (Critchley) character – it is always democracy *to come*, it is a *vanishing point* (Žižek), i.e. something to which we must constantly *refer*, but which can *never be reached* (Mouffe); its value is *indeterminate* (Laclau); and it does not have any particular objec-

9 Ibid., pp. 64–65.
10 Ernesto Laclau, *New Reflections on the Revolution of Our Time*, trans. Jon Barnes (London: Verso, 1990), p. 187.

tives (Laclau), in short *an 'impossible' task which makes radical democratic relations possible.*"[11]

Before eventually returning to the question of radical democratic activism, I would like to briefly touch upon some historical and institutional conditions under which the impossible task of "democracy unrealized" could in fact be "integrated" into our framework of "unrealized democracies." To do this, I would like to turn to another political philosopher: Claude Lefort.

Like the other theorists mentioned, Lefort is a *post*foundationalist rather than a radical *anti*foundationalist, that is to say, even as there is no single or fixed particular foundation of society which could take up that role, *the dimension* of a "ground" (in the form of a horizon) cannot completely disappear if society is still to have *some* identity. Lefort makes it very clear that a point of reference is still required, though democratically it has to be established in a different, purely nonsubstantive way. What characterizes the democratic dispositive then is that it keeps the place of power empty and refrains from positing any particular positive ground. Yet the multiple forms of *ideology* have taught us that the groundlessness of the social and the emptiness of power *can* be denied and occluded. Hence, something more is required for the democratic dispositive to be "realized" to some extent: the emptiness of the place of power has to be *institutionally* recognized (as much as the groundlessness of society is theoretically accepted by postfoundational political thought) and *discursively actualized*. What has to occur is the institutional recognition that the place of power has always been – and will always be – empty. The democratic dispositive, hence, provides an *institutional framework* which guarantees the *acceptance* of the groundlessness of the social.

The paradoxical goal of the institutionalization of groundlessness is achieved within the democratic dispositive by the following set of "arrangements" – which of course should not be understood as mere mechanical applications. The first has been mentioned already: the disincorporation of the place of power. This is accompanied by the "disentangling" in democracy of the sphere of power, the sphere of law, and the sphere of knowledge. Power is in constant search for its own base of legitimation because the principles of justice and of knowledge are no longer incorporated in the person of the ruler.[12]

---

11 Michael Cholewa-Madsen, "Enacting the Political," *Angelaki: Journal of Theoretical Humanities* 1, no. 3 (1994), p. 40.

12 For a more extensive summary of Lefort's position, see Oliver Marchart, "Division and Democracy: On Claude Lefort's Post-foundational Political Philosophy," *Filozofski Vestnik/Acta Philosophica* 221, no. 2 (2000), pp. 51–82; and "Zivilgesellschaftlicher Republikanismus: Lefort und Gauchet," in *Politische Theorien der Gegenwart. Eine Einführung*, ed. André Brodocz and Gary S. Schaal (Opladen: Leske & Budrich, 1999), pp. 119–142.

The fact that such a single ground disappears, though, does not imply the disappearance of the *questions* of social institution. Since they cannot rely on any external source of "founding," they turn into questions of autonomous *self-institution* of society. And it is now *within* society where all questions of autonomous self-institution are negotiated. This is made possible by the separation of civil society from the state. Furthermore, a *public space*[13] is carved out of civil society in which no monarch, no majority, and no supreme judge can decide which particular debate is legitimate and which one is not. Democracy is "founded upon *the legitimacy of a debate as to what is legitimate and what is illegitimate* – a debate which is necessarily without any guarantor and without any end."[14]

That never-ending debate (the ongoing process of questioning, as Laclau would have it) – which forms public space – was historically secured by the Declaration of Human Rights. The notion of human rights points to a territory which – as a consequence of the disentanglement of power, law, and knowledge – is located *beyond* the reach of power. Human rights are declared within and by civil society itself and are part of the auto-institution of the latter. It goes without saying that nothing could be more alien to Lefort than grounding human rights within the *nature* of man. This would again posit a further positive ground behind society's *absent* ground. Lefort prefers inquiring into the paradoxes of the declaration of rights. Once declared, however, human rights produce an ultimate frame wherein positive law can be questioned: "From the moment when the rights of man are posited as the ultimate reference [as a horizon, O.M.], established right is open to question."[15] Human rights do *not* constitute a new positive ground, they do not consist of certain sets of preestablished eternal principles: they are characteristically open with respect to their content. Although human rights, *in principle*, expose all particular established rights to questioning, they guarantee however that one right cannot be questioned: *the right to have rights*, as Lefort formulates with reference to Hannah Arendt. Once acknowledged, human rights enable more and more social groups to claim their right to have rights (historically: workers, slaves, women, immi-

---

13 In more concrete terms defined by Lefort in an Arendtian way as "a space which is so constituted that everyone is encouraged to speak and to listen without being subject to the authority of another, that everyone is urged to *will* the power he has been given. This space, which is always indeterminate, has the virtue of belonging to no one, of being large enough to accommodate only those who recognize one another within it and who give it a meaning, and of allowing the questioning of right to spread." Claude Lefort, *Democracy and Political Theory* (Minneapolis: University of Minnesota Press, 1988), p. 41.

14 Ibid., p. 39.

15 Claude Lefort, *The Political Forms of Modern Society: Bureaucracy, Democracy, Totalitarianism* (Cambridge, Mass.: MIT Press, 1986), p. 258.

grants, gays and lesbians, etc.). Lefort's point – and this is where what I call radical democratic activism comes in again – is that the *extension* of human rights
to more and more groups – and, since they have to openly *struggle* for their
inclusion, the extension of public space – is not an arbitrary addition to the
democratic dispositive but is *absolutely necessary* for democracy. The constant
call for inclusion of more and more groups (today, for instance, for the rights of
homosexuals, jobless people, or immigrants) – the call for their inclusion in the
category of those who have the right to have rights – is what generates democracy again and again. This is the meaning of Lefort's notion of human rights as
the *generative principle* of democracy.[16]

It should be clear by now how this relates to the question of democratic
activism: a generative principle (a principle generating a *democracy in process*)
does not only exist in the heaven of ideas, rather, it has to be actualized by way
of inclusion of the previously excluded, and this always has to happen in practice, it has to happen here and now, and it has to happen against very powerful
forces which resist their inclusion. Therefore, that principle of human rights –
and democracy for that reason – cannot be denounced in good old leftist fashion as a bourgeois plot, as an insidious deception on the level of the ideological
superstructure which seeks to hide what "really" happens on the level of the
economy. It is from this traditional position of leftist ideology critique that one
could be tempted to renounce the very notion of human rights. But that is not
the only alternative. There are basically two paths open: either we denounce
democracy or human rights, etc., as bourgeois, that is, as intrinsically illusionary
and deceptive, or we can recognize that they function as a horizon which indeed
is open to redefinition and can be enlarged. And this is the tradition not of
those revolutionary movements which tried to transgress the horizon of
allegedly "formal bourgeois democracy" but of the civil rights movements which
instead sought to expand that very horizon.

That is why all the classic left defamations of democracy as a bourgeois
plot are really missing the point. To give but one example: There is, on the radical left, a widespread apprehension of the Zapatista movement that it constitutes a revolutionary movement in the traditional sense – albeit with
(post)modern means and rhetorics. A closer look, however, will reveal that the

---

16 It should be mentioned that, for Lefort, the "institutionalization" of rights is an ambiguous enterprise since it is both a necessary condition for an awareness of rights to evolve and constant threat
to rights in as far as it tends toward bureaucratization and concealment: "On the one hand, the
institutionalization involves, with the development of a body of law and a caste of specialists, the
possibility of concealment of the mechanisms indispensable to the effective exercise of rights by the
interested parties; on the other hand, it provides the necessary support for an awareness of rights"
(*The Political Forms of Modern Society*, p. 260). This shows that Lefort is conscious of the paradoxical nature of any *ontic* institutionalization of *ontological* conditions.

EZLN (Zapatista National Liberation Army) is not seeking the overthrow of the political system as a whole, thereby instituting something of a people's republic. Rather, their fight – which is centered around a notion of indigenous rights – is about the democratization of Mexico as a whole. For this reason, the EZLN is best portrayed as a democratization movement – and not as a revolutionary one. I am giving this example in order to make the difference more concrete and graspable between the classical revolutionary form of activism (for example, Maoist Third World liberation movements that tried to overturn democracy as such and to institute some sort of people's republic) on the one hand and current forms of radical democratic activism on the other. Radical democratic activism does start with the experience of unrealized democracy (and it is quite obvious that the Mexican democracy is utterly unrealized in many respects), a democracy which does not deliver what it promises. But that point or experience is precisely the point of emergence of democracy unrealized, of, to put it in the words of Derrida, a promise which arises in the very gaps and fissures and failures and shortcomings of actually existing democracies.

And if we now think about the relation between factually unrealized democracy and the promise of democracy unrealized, between the empirical "ontic" democracies and the "ontological" dimension of democracy as a promise, then it seems to be the case that nowadays it is democratic activism which performs the intertwining or *chiasm* – to use a term from rhetorics which became important in philosophy – of these two levels. In other words: it is democratic activism which stands at the point of this crossing between unrealized democracies and democracy unrealized – simply because what presents itself as promise at the horizon has to be enacted here and now even if its complete fulfillment is impossible.

One of the many names of such enactment is "radical democracy": the radicalization of demands for equality and the pluralization of the areas in which such demands are being articulated. While "radical democracy" is the name advocated by Laclau and Mouffe in particular, this project which the title of this platform "democracy unrealized" refers to – the project of a participatory, non-dogmatic, and open-ended process of democratization – can and does have many names ("strong democracy" is what Benjamin Barber would call it, for instance). There is no need for a single name, since it is instantiated through a multiplicity of democratic practices which nevertheless share one thing: they locate themselves within the horizon of democracy while simultaneously fighting against the liberal ideology of a supposedly realized democracy so that they insist on the unrealized nature of democracy. And this precisely is the crossing point where these activist *practices* tie in with the theoretical notion or structure of democracy unrealized (unrealizable) or a democracy-to-come. Since from a philosophical point of view it is not "democracy" which is realized by those forms of radical democratic activism but, paradoxically, "democracy unrealized": it is the contingent and always only temporary enactment of something which, as such, must remain unrealizable. This paradoxical task of realizing something which in principle must remain unrealizable is taken up by radical democratic activists (not literally but structurally) who are no longer seeking to achieve some sort of ideological closure of the whole of society in the way traditional ideologists did (they do not, in other words, present a fully fledged picture of a perfectly democratic society).

Therefore, these new activist practices – for instance, the antiglobalization movement – cannot be reduced anymore to a single ideological core or homogeneous worldview. Rather, they are structured as a contingent linking of a plurality of demands. What unites them, then, is not so much a positive content – and definitely not a substantial ideology of the "good society" – than the conviction and insistence with respect to actually existing democracy that *this is not it*. They are radically democratic in the sense that they are driven by the conviction that democracy is far from being realized under conditions of corporate power and the worldwide hegemony of some sections of the West. Therefore, the main antagonism today is not the one between democracy and its totalitarian other but it runs right through the core of democracy: it is the antagonism between actually existing liberal capitalist regimes which claim to have realized democracy, on the one hand, and ongoing processes of and demands for radical democratization, on the other. This antagonism – an antagonism *internal* to democracy – is what is enacted by forms of democratic activism that carry the demands for equality into more and more social spheres.

Hence, their aim (or practice) is not to "realize" democracy and, thus, turn it into one more ideology of closure. Rather, it is through their concrete actions that – *ex negativo* – they demonstrate the ideological nature of *all* claims supposing the actual realization of democracy. What they expose through their practice is the fact that a particular regime – liberal Western democracies – has captured and hegemonized the notion of democracy and now presents itself as the latter's unrivaled and unsurpassable realization. Therefore, to sum up, radical democratic activism is structured as the *practical proof* of the fact that democracy is not and cannot be fully realized but nevertheless has to be actualized here and now as a promise whose eventual fulfillment would not be the "realization" of democracy but its final dissolution.

Democracy in the "Center" and Global Democratic Critique[1]

Enrique Dussel

In general, any reflection on democracy is situated on the horizon of thought of the "center" (Western Europe and the United States). Here I shall include post-colonial subject matter. In addition, reflections on democracy frequently deal with the possibility of democracy's normativity, the normativity of the rational and fraternal consensus.[2] Here I shall make room for the question of the norma-tivity of struggles for the recognition of new actors, who appear on the horizon of the system like previously invisible ghosts. This invisibility is the most subtle repression that is inevitably fulfilled from the perspective of the legitimacy of a valid, positive, democratic order in power. Today Alterity,[3] Difference, Exterior-ity – unintentional in the majority of cases; at other times conscious; though the most important is the first type – become the central theme in the future, popu-lar, world democracy in the process of globalization, supposedly structured around a nonexistent "global citizen,"[4] an apolitical world market of winners of competition, exclusive of the "losers."

---

1 This exposition will be brief, like the thesis statement of the symposium discussion; a longer ver-sion may be considered in a book on which I am currently working. The title is *Política de libera-ción*, intended as a continuation of my previous book *Ética de la liberación en la edad de la global-ización y de la exclusión* (Madrid: Trotta, 1998). There is a Portuguese translation (Petrópolis: Vozes, 2000), and the book is forthcoming in English at Duke University Press; there is a shorter version translated into German, and also forthcoming in French. For democracy, see the articles in Robert E. Goodin and Philip Pettit, eds., *A Companion to Contemporary Political Philosophy* (Oxford: Blackwell, 1999), pp. 411ff, and *Contemporary Political Philosophy* (Oxford: Blackwell, 1997), pp. 78ff.

2 In *Politics of Friendship* (London: Verso, 1997), Derrida tries, I believe, to show a dimension of the drive of politics left behind by the discursive formal rationalism in politics. It is still possible to effect a Derridean deconstruction of brotherhood (of us) from the exteriority of the excluded: we would thus have a *politique de la solidarité* in the technical sense.

3 A philosophical category devised by Emmanuel Levinas, *Totality and Infinity* (Pittsburgh: Duquesne University Press, 1990).

4 See Michael Hardt and Antonio Negri, *Empire* (Cambridge, Mass.: Harvard University Press, 2000). I believe that the "global citizen" is still empirically nonexistent.

I. Rethinking the Concept of the Political   A first level of discussion, although merely contextual and introductory for the proposal of this paper, would be on the "concept" of the political itself. In this sense, there are too many reductionist positions, since the part is taken for the whole, thereby reducing the political to one of its dimensions – certainly existent, but within a much greater architectonic complexity.

I shall use the word "principialism" to refer to those who only concern themselves with the "principles" of politics, but who neglect all the other levels, or at least they consider them secondary.

Foundationalists are those who believe that the task of political philosophy always begins with the "foundation" of principles, which are otherwise explicit. Political life may exist without an explicit awareness of the principles, which nevertheless always operate concretely, and without which there can be no political action.

Formalist proceduralists are those who believe that all politics is a question of "equitable," "reasonable," and practical procedures, free of normativity.

Extreme materialists are those who diminish the possibility of political action itself,[5] defending the position that, given the existence of economic laws, history may well pass over politics since its inevitable course is by definition unavoidable.

Anti-institutionalists are those who, assuming the citizen to be an ethically perfect subject, always consider institutions to be repressive, unjust, or unnecessary. Certain anarchist positions affirm this thesis. There are left-wing anarchists, like Bakunin, who operate from the perspective of the utopia of an ethically perfect subject. There are also liberal anarchists, who greatly distrust and challenge the public institutions of the State (hence the "minimal State"[6]) on behalf of the subjective rights of individuals (in the first place, the right of private property).

There are also formalists of discursive reason who, in formulating a politics of legitimacy, forget the material, social, and economic aspects of political life.

The most influential theoreticians of the political in our day are those who believe that politics is played out exclusively on the strategic level. Some believe that the strategic reason of means-end is the practical political reason proper (Max Weber)[7] – a position criticized by the first Frankfurt School under the name of "critique of instrumental reason." Whether because it delimits politics

---

5 See Ernesto Laclau, *New Reflections on the Revolution of Our Time*, trans. Jon Barnes (London: Verso, 1990).

6 See Robert Nozick, *Anarchy, State, and Utopia* (New York: Basic Books, 1974).

7 Max Weber, *Economy and Society: An Outline of Interpretive Sociology* (Berkeley: University of California Press, 1986).

to an opposition between enemies and friends as that which ultimately defines the political field (Carl Schmitt);[8] or whether because the struggle for hegemony is the determining note of the political (Ernesto Laclau).[9] All of these aspects are certainly moments of the political, but in no way are they either the only ones or the most important.

I believe that the concept of the political is complex and its architectonics is up for debate. Nearly everything indicated by the traditions is "necessary" but not "sufficient." "Sufficiency" is more all-embracing. Following the three levels proposed by John Rawls (principles, institutions, ends),[10] or developing the two "parts" of Karl-Otto Apel[11] (*Teil* A and *Teil* B, although he would need a *Teil* C),[12] which could also be those of Hegel[13] or Aristotle,[14] we would have the following strata: (A) the implicit political principles (the universal); (B) the political institutions (the specific); and (C) the strategic political action on the concrete level (the singular).

(A) Synchronically, the political field (and time, diachronically) is "delimited," defined," "in-framed" by *implicit* "principles" that intrinsically exist in political action itself (whether or not they are discovered later in an explicit fashion through theoretical reflection). Obviously, this is questioned by those who believe, each in his own way – like Richard Rorty[15] and Ernesto Laclau – that politics cannot have principles; a position that I would accept if the principles were defined in an explicit, dogmatic, or metaphysical way. The entire discussion centers, then, on "how" these principles are understood. If they are an explicit *a priori* of reason that must be understood in order to "apply" them, it would be a matter of something like an impossible universalist conscientialism,

8 Carl Schmitt, *The Concept of the Political* (Chicago: University of Chicago Press, 1996). See Enrique Serrano, *Legitimación y racionalización. Weber y Habermas: la dimensión normativa de un orden secularizado* (Barcelona: Anthropos, 1994).

9 See Laclau, *New Reflections on the Revolution of Our Time*, and *Emancipation(s)* (London: Verso, 1996).

10 John Rawls, *Theory of Justice* (Cambridge, Mass.: Harvard University Press, 1971).

11 Someone could find that the coincidence is practicable since both, in very different ways, are renovators of the Kantian tradition.

12 Karl-Otto Apel, "Diskursethik als Verantwortungsethik," in *Ethik und Befreiung*, ed. Raúl Forneto-Betancourt (Aachen: Augustinus Buchhandlung, 1993), pp. 10–58.

13 Hegel is a necessary reference for this entire question. In the first place, his "civil society" (or "bourgeois [*buergerliche*] society") is distinguished from the "State." But in the "civil society" he deals with three levels: the moment that I call "material," "the system of needs" (§§ 189–208), the formal level of the "application of justice" (§§ 209–229), and the instrumental or strategic level of political practicability proper (§§ 230–256). See G. W. F. Hegel, *Werke*, ed. Eva Moldenhauer and Karl Markus Michel (Frankfurt am Main: Suhrkamp, 1971), vol. 7, pp. 339–397.

14 Aristotle distinguished between "principle" (*arkhé*), "deliberation," and "practical choice" (*prodíresis*).

15 See some of Richard Rorty's theses in "The Priority of Democracy to Philosophy," in *The Virginia Statute for Religious Freedom: Its Evolution and Consequences in American History*, ed. Merrill D. Peterson and Robert C. Vaughan (Cambridge: Cambridge University Press, 1988).

because no politician has ever acted in that fashion. On the other hand, if the principle is understood as that which allows us to fix the horizon that concretely delimits the political field *as political*,[16] in this case the principle is constitutive of the field and of the political action itself *as political*. The principle determines the limit; it is the "frame" within which the political continues to be possible as political. It thus marks a limit of possibility (of the political) and its impossibility (as political). Among the diverse political principles we must speak of a "democratic principle."

(B) In the second place, political action also remains – on another level – delimited or "in-framed" by political "institutions." The strategic struggle does not act within an "empty" field, but rather within a field that is *already occupied* by a network of relations where the nodes are citizens (of "flesh and bone") and their relationships are functional. "Functional" not only within the political community (or society), but also within many other practical systems that are ever present (in some cases as "the social") in the political functionality. The politician, the citizen, the representative, the leader, the political parties, the movements, etc., walk in a "mine field" – since the political field has limitations, delimitations, frames that comprise part of the exercise of power, a structure of forces that mutually support one another, as Foucault would say.[17] Whoever does not take these institutional delimitations into account loses legitimacy, a loss that may produce unexpected political consequences. When Julius Caesar crossed the Rubicon, or when Miguel Hidalgo rang the bell to convoke an army, the institutionality in force was broken. That is why the legitimacy in force is no longer considered and the political sense of this anti-institutionalist action must be evaluated (in the case of Caesar, it would be through assuming the dictatorship or the "empire"; in the case of Hidalgo, through confronting even death, but being later recognized as the founder of a new political order). In these cases, action is no longer justified by the foundation of legitimacy that makes up the institution.

(C) Finally, on the concrete level of action, political praxis is found in the construction of community life, of the common good, but also in the struggle for hegemony which, abstracting from the limitations and the "fullness" of the principles and institutions, may abstractly consider the political field as "empty" (metaphorically), in order to be "filled" by the strategic action that will define in

---

16 The "political field" is not the "military field" or the "sports field," to use just two examples. The rules (or principles) of the political force me (ethically, but in an intrinsic way, politically) not to eliminate the *political* enemy. In the "military field," on the other hand, it is legitimate to eliminate the opponent.

17 See Michel Foucault, *Discipline and Punish: The Birth of the Prison*, trans. Alan Sheridan (New York: Vintage Books, 1979).

each case the objectives of action in light of the concrete position of the "end" (Weber), of the enemy (Schmitt), or of the antagonist (Laclau). The fact that the enemy/antagonist may be different on each occasion and that in each case he may emerge from another position, and therefore variously redefine the political field, does not mean that the *implicit* political principles are not in force. For example, the principles "You must not kill the antagonist" or "You must honestly allow the antagonist to have reasonable democratic freedom" are necessary, since their unfulfillment would annihilate the struggle for "hegemony" *as hegemony*, making it something else: an act of war, of totalitarianism, or of authoritarianism, which as such is not political and, furthermore, in the long run would self-destruct.

II. Democratic Normativity (Principles, Institutions, and Democratic Praxis)   If we distinguish equivocally between ethics and politics, we observe the loss of political normativity – this is, to a certain degree, Kant's position, which distinguishes between morality and legality, the latter being properly political.[18] This leads either to an empty proceduralism that cannot motivate the political will or, even worse, to immorality in politics, which is what is most common today: "Politics has nothing to do with morals!"

If ethics and politics are united as political ethics, this is filled with normativity, but it loses as politics. Politics no longer possesses the specificity characteristic of politics, which is not nor should be merely a collective part of ethics.[19] If we propose that the political principle (which for Habermas is only the democratic principle) is a principle different from the moral principle, but that both are dependent on the discursive principle, some questions necessarily arise: Would this latter principle also be normative? And if it were normative, how would it be different from the moral principle? And if it were not normative, the Ethics of Discourse would have ceased to exist. This is why Apel proposes that the discursive principle is already the moral principle, but then the difference between the moral and the political (*Teil* A) principles should be thoroughly clarified, as should their differential application (*Teil* B), and above all the difference between moral and political action on the strategic concrete level (which is not clearly defined in Apel's architectonics).

---

18 See this theme in Immanuel Kant's *Metaphysics of Morals*, in *Werke*, vol. 7 (Darmstadt: Wissenschaftliche Buchgesellschaft, 1968), pp. 336ff.

19 Vittorio Hoesle has written a *Moral und Politik*, but I am precisely trying to overcome this position with the proposal that follows. See Vittorio Hoesle, *Moral und Politik: Grundlagen einer politischen Ethik für das 21. Jahrhundert* (Munich: Beck, 1997).

If we recognize the fact that the realm of the ethical (and also the moral)[20] never has a concrete specific field as such, since the abstract ethical subject is always somehow a concrete "actor" of a role or "function" within some "system" (and even the daily *Lebenswelt* does not cease to be an existential system in which the "role" of mother or father, son or daughter, etc., is played out), we conclude that the ethical performs in the actions that are fulfilled in these concrete practical fields, of which politics is one (others could be the family field, the field of gender or the erotic, the sports field, the military field, the economic field, the educational or pedagogical field, etc.). Each one of these fields "subsumes" the ethical principles and transforms them into the specific principle. Thus the political (or family, gender, sports, economic, etc.) principles are strictly political: they subsume the ethical principles *as political*. For example, if producing and reproducing human life is a material ethical principle, the ethical enunciation "You shall not kill another human being!" becomes political: "You shall not kill the political antagonist in the struggle for hegemony in which you are involved!" This political imperative is not equal to the one that commands: "You shall not kill your market competitor!" – which would be economic.[21]

Among the principles of politics we find the formal principle of legitimacy of politics as such, which we could call the "Democratic Principle," and which could be enunciated approximately as follows: There is legitimacy in every political institution or action that has been resolved based on the recognition of all members of the political community as equal, free, autonomous, with brotherly will,[22] and whose practical resolutions have been the fruit of consensus (and of common will) as a conclusion of rational arguments and honest tolerance, and not through domination or violence; that is, having carried out all procedures and keeping in mind the criterion of symmetric participation of those affected. The political subject, the citizen in the final analysis, by having taken part in all of the decisions, is obliged by them (normativity characteristic of sovereignty as the origin of the dictate and as the consignee of the obligation), not only toward the performance of what was reconciled, but also to assume the responsibility of the consequences of such decisions (as institutions or actions).

This Democratic Principle, briefly indicated thus, generates "legitimate" institutions, since "legitimacy" is nothing more than the fulfillment of said prin-

---

20 In my book *Ética de la Liberación*, I have distinguished between "the ethical" in a material sense (ch. 1) and "the moral" in a formal sense (ch. 2). There is still a third level, that of the "principle of practicability" that becomes essential in politics, as we shall see.

21 I explain this question in the aforementioned *Política de Liberación* (ch. 1), on which I am currently working (this holds for all of the statements in this paper).

22 I am thinking about the "material" or "emotional" moment of the democracy of "brotherhood," a concept elaborated, as indicated above, by Derrida in *Politics of Friendship*.

ciple or, in other words, the institutions or actions generated within the political field that respect the very sense of the political *as political*, that attain legitimacy by having allowed (or oriented) those affected toward a symmetrical rational (and voluntary) participation. This principle that subsumes the ethical moment, though it is not abstractly ethical but strictly political, is found in the origin of all legitimate institutions and political actions whose goal is justice.

Since direct democracy had to be implemented as "representative" democracy, the Democratic Principle is the necessary mediation between the individual will of each elector and the elected as representative. This principle makes possible and legitimizes "representation" without leaving the members of the political community unarmed before the elected representatives, but rather always as the last sovereign instance exerted in the new elections, or in corrective actions throughout the process of representation (plebiscites, lawsuits, public demonstrations, critical consensus of public opinion, acts of passive disobedience, and even justified rebellion, etc.).

In effect, political institutions are considered legitimate or democratic if in their constitution or reforms they have carried out this Democratic Principle. The democracy of a constituent assembly consists of having observed this Democratic Principle in its convocation and election of members, and in having allowed and developed the symmetrical participation of those affected in the very dictation of the constitution. This principle must also figure in the constitution itself of the State as the universal procedure on all institutional and procedural levels of the State, as a first definition of the political order that is being established by the political constitution. The entire system of institutions based on the constitution, and the human rights dictated in its preamble, must have as a condition of possibility the fulfillment of this Democratic Principle. The separation of powers, their mutual fiscalization, the federative structure of the State, the organization of political parties, the free and secret elections, the type of representation, etc., must be procedures that allow for the fulfillment of the Democratic Principle. The institutions are democratic because they perform, structure, and functionally define the actions with a claim to political legitimacy. These institutions are not purely procedural structures; they are likewise normative instances (they force their fulfillment practically and intersubjectively).

In the same way, the political order is completed in the permanent actualization of all its relations of power, of force (Foucault), within the political field, through the political actions that are like the nodes of the networks (Castells) that pass through that field of tensions – in principle, of brotherhood, of service, of shared life – but also as a field that is mined by always possible enemies. In the field of the struggle for hegemony (Gramsci) of the historical block in power, the Democratic Principle remains overdetermined by the Principle of

Political Practicability, which reveals "the possible" and distinguishes it from "the impossible." It was rightly said that politics is "the art of the possible" – it is in this intersection between the Democratic Principle and the Principle of Political Practicability.

Therefore, a valid political order is the totality of the institutions and strategic actions that the members of a political community perform in a territory, in a given time.

III. The Crisis of Democratic Legitimacy from the Exteriority of the Victims   For me, as a Latin American philosopher at the beginning of the 21st century, the most urgent theme of political philosophy is not simply to study how to give stability to a legitimate political order, consensually resolving possible conflicts, at least in appearance. For me, the most urgent theme is not the stability of the Totality (as Emmanuel Levinas would say) of the political order, but rather the Exteriority of this order, the invisibility of its victims, of the majorities.

Indeed, using Karl Popper's argument against perfect planning,[23] it is categorical that no valid political order could be perfect. For that, it would need an infinite intelligence, at an infinite speed, and, I might add, a general, pure, and infinite will in the functional generosity of its motivations. Since this is impossible, we may categorically express that, as every political order is imperfect, it is inevitable that it will produce negative effects, even though these may be unintended (unintentional). Those who suffer the negative effects of the political order with pretensions to justice we shall call "victims."[24] The victims of every political order suffer some type of exclusion, unless they are considered political subjects, and therefore they are not actors taken into account in political institutions (or they are repressed to the extent that they cannot overcome a merely "passive," perfectly manipulable, citizenship).

It is interesting to note that the intellectuals who suffered European fascism (Antonio Gramsci[25] in Mussolini's Italy and Hannah Arendt in Nazi Ger-

---

23 Karl Popper, *The Poverty of Historicism* (London: Routledge, 1997).
24 See this theme in my *Ética de la Liberación*, ch. 4.
25 Gramsci was the inventor of the current concept of "civil society." See Antonio Gramsci, *Prison Notebooks* (New York: Columbia University Press, 1992). Cohen and Arato partially recognize this; see Jean Cohen and Andrew Arato, *Civil Society and Political Theory* (Cambridge, Mass.: MIT Press, 1995), ch. 3, pp. 142ff. Gramsci thus distinguishes the "civil society" of both the State and the strictly economic level (which appears as the physiognomy of the "social"), giving special importance to the level of political, social, and cultural practices. In addition, Gramsci, long before Habermas, made of the consensus an essential moment of the process of hegemony of the "historical block of power," but he showed (against Habermas and Laclau) that the social factor (and, indirectly, the economic factor) requires that the political society (the State) begin to use coercion (losing the legitimacy of hegemony as consensus) when the "social block of the oppressed" (the

many[26]) were the first to distinguish, in the current sense, between state (political society) and civil society.[27] And intellectuals experienced the total invasion of the political and civil field by the (totalitarian) State. The Exteriority of political society (of the State) thus struggled for the recognition of its rights within a nascent "civil society" which, although "public," nevertheless does not have the use of the legitimate coercive apparatus of the State (it does not exert state "politicity"). Along with "public opinion," these are realms that carry out critical functions of the State, broadening the space of civic subjectivation, a democratic complement of political consensus and of the formation of the democratic will.

In this civil society, differential forces are thus born that are organized in the Exteriority of the established order, effecting struggles for the recognition of new political (and, obviously, social, economic, cultural, etc.) rights. These collective actors of the most diverse appearances have been called the "New Social Movements."[28] These movements, from a political point of view, turn many excluded or "passive" members, who inhabited the territory controlled by the European states at the end of the 18th century, into political subjects of an "active" citizenship. Indeed, at the very heart of the French Revolution, the "revolution of equals" (let us recall Babeuf in 1794) had already confronted the triumphant bourgeoisie. The social, workers', and peasants' movements (the labor and trade unions of the 19th and 20th centuries) extended citizenship to the wage laborers of the capital, who were neither property owners nor sufficiently literate at the beginning. The women's suffrage movement subjectivized a second immense sector of the population who, when excluded, became "semi-active" citizens (because they were nevertheless far from being able to enjoy the full use of the psychological, cultural, and material conditions from which they were excluded by patriarchalism). In recent times, senior citizens have begun to make themselves present.

    people) begins its "movements" in a political struggle, which many current theoreticians forget. See Jürgen Habermas, *Between Facts and Norms: Contributions to a Discourse Theory of Law and Democracy* (Cambridge, Mass.: MIT Press, 1996). Paradoxically, it is more complex and interesting for us than for Cohen and Arato, Habermas, and Laclau.

26 Hannah Arendt doubts that the social can be considered political. Her particular blindness before the material aspect of politics explains the use of Arendt's work against the contentious social movements within the central societies or those dependent on capitalism during the "Cold War." Her partial comprehension of Marx's thought led her to misunderstandings. See the following: Maurizio Passerin d'Entrèves, *The Political Philosophy of Hannah Arendt* (London: Routledge, 1994); Margaret Canovan, *Hannah Arendt: A Reinterpretation of Her Political Thought* (Cambridge: Cambridge University Press, 1992); Seyla Benhabib, *The Reluctant Modernism of Hannah Arendt* (Thousand Oaks, Calif.: Sage, 1996); Enrique Serrano, *Consenso y conflicto* (Mexico City: Interlínea, 1996).

27 A distinction that previously had another meaning; for example, in Hegel.

28 See, among others, Alain Touraine, *Critique of Modernity*, trans. David Macey (Cambridge, Mass.: Blackwell, 1995), and Anthony Giddens, *Sociology* (New York: Harcourt Brace, 1982).

But, in a more decisive fashion – and one that will certainly become even more important in the short and long terms – the ecological movements (which simultaneously struggle for the survival of humanity in the long run and, for this very reason, for future generations) increasingly gain not only a social sense, but also a strictly political one. It is the clamor, and challenge, of the material aspect (the reproduction of human life, in the final analysis) par excellence which moves those organizations that are being called "green" in different parts of the world (between the "red" of the left and the "black" of fascism and death). The Meadows Report in 1972[29] opened awareness to this previously invisible aspect of politics.[30]

The same could be said of the movements against racial discrimination in both the US and South Africa, as well as other countries of the contemporary world.

All of the New Social Movements transversely penetrate political and civil society and overdetermine one another. Thus feminism determines the movements that struggle against racial discrimination and environmental degradation, showing that, in the final analysis, exclusion is "feminized" in a preponderant way, racism is exerted firstly against women of color, who also suffer the worst ecological and urban conditions.

The democratizing process, upon transforming and broadening the horizon of "active" citizenship to new political subjects previously excluded (political subjectivation), signifies a radicalization, universalization, and greater symmetrical participation of the formerly affected (the formerly affected who we discover today as "new" victims). Critico-democratic awareness can never claim to have finished the task of broadening that qualitative horizon of the active, participatory, symmetrical citizenship in exercising political power. It is an always open task, historical par excellence, and novel because each new civilizing or human advance inevitably creates new exclusions due to its own systematicity (as we would say with Niklas Luhmann[31]).

IV. Democracy in the Postcolonial World (Global Victims)   In the postcolonial world, there is technically no liberalism, republicanism, Bonapartism, fascism, etc., in the sense that these sorts of regimes acquired in Europe or the United

---

29 See Donella H. Meadows, *The Limits to Growth: A Report for the Club of Rome's Project on the Predicament of Mankind*, 2d ed. (New York: Universe Books, 1974).

30 Hans Jonas shows this convincingly. See *The Imperative of Responsibility: In Search of an Ethics for the Technological Age* (Chicago: University of Chicago Press, 1984).

31 See Niklas Luhmann, *Social Systems* (Stanford: Stanford University Press, 1995).

States. All of these political and ideological expressions are configured in another way on the postcolonial periphery.

Modern Europe's process of globalization, when it had yet to become the "center" of the world system,[32] began with the invasion of Latin America in 1492, thereby giving birth to the colonial world, a constitutive component of Modernity.

Paradoxically, and considering Latin America as part of the world periphery, dependent liberalism, which emerged in the struggles of anticolonial emancipation (from 1810 in Mexico and the Southern Cone; 1804 in the case of Haiti), does not face a powerful monarchical or republican State, but rather an *external* metropolitan State (the Spanish, French, English, etc., State), and *internally* will have the responsibility, precisely contrary to classical liberalism, of founding the State. Therefore, 19th-century Latin American liberalism had many of the traits of republicanism (affirming the denied colonial identity, remembering traditions, defining itself in the face of the old metropolises). At the same time, it had to affirm the public rights of the State in order to extend the institution of private property, which had no prior tradition among the poor (until very recently peasants, and even the indigenous in certain countries, held community ownership of the land), with the goal of creating the conditions of a preindustrial capitalism dependent on exports in the face of the only institution that had survived since colonialism: the Catholic Church (before which French anticlerical Jacobinism and the secularism of Littré would be of great use for the new State, and therefore the institutions would take certain forms, unknown in the Anglo-Saxon and Germanic world). Since it is the landowning oligarchy (politically, a federal oligarchy that is economically linked to the internal market) or the liberal minorities (unitarian minorities linked to the external market) who found the State, they will be more concerned with preserving their own privileges (subjective rights, such as property in the hands of the oligarchy) before those of indigenous Afro-Latin Americans, impoverished peasants, or postcolonial marginals, whose customary community rights (which the colonizers had respected) would be diminished, thus reducing them to misery in a regime of exclusive property (exercised only by landowners of the inner areas with the goal of autonomy, or merchants and liberals in relation to capitalist powers, which formerly were the metropolises located in port cities).

The process of creating the conditions that make a formal democracy possible in the Latin American postcolonial world, as one may imagine, travels a long

---

32 See Immanuel Wallerstein, *The Modern World-System*, vol. 1 (New York: Academic Press, 1974), and Andre Gunder Frank, *ReOrient: Global Economy in the Asian Age* (Berkeley: University of California Press, 1998).

temporal road: the entire 19th century and the first part of the 20th. Against the backdrop of what could be assumed will be the phenomenon of so-called populism – which is not exactly French Bonapartism nor German or Italian fascism – emerges the first manifestation of a democratic regime.

Between the two World Wars, between 1914 and 1945, conditions were ripe for the effective extension of citizenship and voting rights to the great popular majorities. The populist project of capitalist industrialization, headed by a particular national bourgeoisie, allowed the nascent bourgeoisie to lose its fear of the political participation of the masses, which were thus constituted as the support for a national project of industrial development based on import substitution, competitive with the "central" capitalism called "imperialist." Irigoyen (1918) and Perón (1946) in Argentina, Vargas (1930) in Brazil, Cárdenas (1934) in Mexico, and gradually throughout the Latin American subcontinent, popular governments were elected thanks to nonfraudulent elections by the large majorities. This is the most important democratic process of the 20th century. The charismatic leaders of these democratic movements must be distinguished from the European fascist leaders, and even from the Stalinist type. The latter attempted world, or at least European, domination. The former, on the other hand, sought national emancipation from the neocolonialism into which they had fallen. However, around 1954–55, beginning with the coups d'état against the democratic governments of Arbenz in Guatemala organized by the CIA,[33] Nasser in Egypt, and Sukarno in Indonesia, events that coincide with the end of "European" colonialism in Africa and Asia, the United States launched its project of expansion and control of the postcolonial periphery in the years of the Cold War. We must inquire into the conditions of democracy in this global situation.

To be sure, in Latin America it is the United States that, from this moment onward (1954), would have total hegemony in the implantation of diverse political models (at least, none were imposed without the explicit complicity of the US embassies, the State Department, and the leadership of all the armies of the area under the command of the Pentagon, which had provided an excellent

33 The fruit (plantain or banana) that the United Fruit Company extracted from Guatemala was called "bitter fruit" by the journalist Stephen Schlesinger (*Bitter Fruit: The Untold Story of the American Coup in Guatemala* [Garden City, N.Y.: Doubleday, 1982]). Jacobo Arbenz had an industrial development plan, but the conservative groups of the US (with their bourgeois representatives in Congress) aborted that autonomous capitalist development and turned it into a guerrilla war that the State Department organized for thirty years. Resulting in thousands of deaths, these acts should be judged by future International Tribunals as genocidal violence against humanity. All of the Central American wars of the 1960s, '70s, and '80s have no other origin. What is certain is that today, at the beginning of the 21st century, Central America cries out in its misery, in its exploitation, in its illiteracy, in a situation that is worse now than in the 1950s.

education in its military schools to the best of the Latin American army). The period of developmentalism (1954–68, from the fall of Vargas and Perón to the worsening of the Brazilian dictatorship under the intellectual leadership of General Golbery) proposed a model of democracy that, in a way, imitates the one applied in Europe. Thus, some Christian democracies (in Chile, Venezuela, and other countries) were able to win elections. But formal democracy (Frondizi in Argentina, Kubitschek in Brazil, Frei in Chile, etc.) concealed Latin America's deepening state of dependence after the failure (helped along by the penetration of the continent by those entities called "transnational corporations") of populism (the most recent peripheral capitalist project aimed at national autonomy).

In the face of developmentalism's failure, due in part to social pressure from below and in part to the unscrupulousness of the United States in its application of the exploitation model (the US never planned to organize a symmetrical "common market" like the Europeans, but simply to extract wealth from its so-called backyard), the bitter pill of military totalitarianism was dispensed (in order to make viable a capitalism dependent on exports).[34] When the "National Security" dictatorships failed, they left the Latin American people with substantial debt at exorbitant interest rates. It was necessary to restore the legitimacy of the State in order to pay off the debts that had been invented, inflated, contracted by antidemocratic (and therefore illegitimate) governments behind the back of the people, and deposited by corrupt elites (who were also perverted by the double standard of the US) into the banking houses of the "center."

When the recent phase of "democratization" began – since 1984, first in Argentina and Brazil – all the Latin American governments, now legitimate, were so burdened by debt that it was economically impossible to lead their respective countries in an honest fashion. Moreover, the neoliberal monetary policies of the World Bank and International Monetary Fund demanded that measures be undertaken that further impoverished all the countries in the region. As I write these lines, Argentina, which in the early 20th century competed with the United States and had a currency stronger than those of Canada and Australia, has reached a crisis that is leading the majority of its population

---

34 The responsibilities of the United States in that entire project have yet to be judged. The massiveness, universality, and similarity of all the Latin American military governments from the late 1960s to the mid-1980s does not indicate a plan that any Latin American national army had within its capabilities. The State Department was definitely the origin and point of control of the entire model, justified, obviously, by the ideology of the Cold War. As US Secretary of State who encouraged the decisions taken by Augusto Pinochet, Henry Kissinger was directly responsible for the coup d'état in Chile, and therefore indirectly responsible for the death of Salvador Allende. Pinochet has now been justly tried for these crimes.

into total immiseration, while funds for the education system, the universities, and even the state-run bureaucracy have evaporated. In Mexico, 40 percent of the population lives below Amartya Sen's poverty line; in Brazil, the situation is worse – and these are the three major countries that in the 1930s successfully drove the populist project, until they were targeted as opponents in the process of competition in the world market, and destroyed.

In this context, we can see that political philosophy must take into account the material aspect of the reproduction of the life of the citizen (food, clothing, housing, education, etc.), levels that for the United States and Europe may be considered "the social," which for Hannah Arendt does not comprise a determining aspect of the political field. Even for Ernesto Laclau, on account of his partial critique of Marxism – which is sound in other ways – it has fallen into an anti-economicist reductionism, which makes the discovery of the political within the economic aspect impossible. And if this is valid for Latin America, how much more so for postcolonial Asia (if we think about the misery of Bangladesh, of India, or of Afghanistan), and in an even more acute way, for Africa (which Europe irresponsibly destroyed in its colonial period, abandoning it at the moment of organizing its respective postcolonial states, where the political life of ethnic groups still had great significance).[35]

All of this is exacerbated by the so-called globalization of financial and transnational capital. Competing for the opening of markets in postcolonial states, with no reasonable stipulations for mutual benefit, what is being produced is simply a genocide of the poor part of humanity located in the Global South. The democracy of so-called rich countries is sustained by the transfer of value, of wealth, from poor countries – a fact proven by the "dependence theory," which was never refuted,[36] and it is therefore explicable that political philosophers (Bobbio, Habermas, Rawls, Laclau, etc.) exclude its material

---

35 I would like to emphasize that the savage colonialism of Belgium, England, France, etc., played out its politics of dominance by pitting one ethnic group against another. With postwar emancipation, the populations whose African territories were assigned to them by the metropolises (a result of the Congress of Berlin in 1885, and of later modifications) should have organized their new states. In the postcolonial context, the homogeneity of the European-modern citizen was impossible. The cultural heterogeneity of the ethnic groups demanded a new political system. But not only did Europe not help to consolidate it in the colonial period, but it also destroyed any such possibility (using interethnic confrontation instead of constituting interethnic parliaments that could have educated the different ethnic groups on tolerance and governability). Indeed, each African state today should comprise something like a Chamber with representation of the ethnic groups (with veto power in essential questions: a Senate), and another with proportional representation (of national parties that would slowly organize: a House of Congress). African democracy demands new solutions since the European-US models (and their respective political philosophies) are not very useful. Theoretical Eurocentrism is harmful, but universally extended.

36 See my book *Towards an Unknown Marx: A Commentary on the Manuscripts of 1861–63* (London: Routledge, 2001), ch. 14.

aspect (the economic, the globalized capitalism, which shows itself in the political field of postcolonial states, like the *social* "discomfort" of the popular masses, which will continue to grow in the near future, and which need a new and more critical political philosophy).

V. Democratic Struggles of the New Political Actors in the Periphery of the Current Globalization Process   The "passive" citizenship of Latin America (more integrated into the world system), southern and eastern Asia, and especially Africa (nearly excluded from this system), which makes up 85 percent of today's humanity,[37] is quite diverse. The symmetrical participation of those institutionally affected in the political field will take on very different dimensions in each cultural, economic region, in each country, in each area, in each social sector, in each distinguishing type of excluded person, of victims of the colonial, capitalist, sexist-patriarchal, racist, etc., system. In each sector, a New Social Movement undertakes the necessary organization of the struggle for democracy, for differential symmetrical political participation, initially legitimate and against the old legitimacy that slowly becomes illegitimate, thanks to the fight for recognition of the Movement. These new actors, previously "passive" citizens, subjectivate their position and become active in a renewed, broadened, and qualitatively deepened democratic political field.

Moreover, on these cultural, economic, and political continents (Africa, Asia, Latin America), the New Social Movements of civil society, though also the critical political parties in the political society or the State, are *overdetermined* by differentiated histories that are completely different from those of Europe or the United States. North American feminism cannot propose the same objectives as Latin American or African feminism. Spivak describes feminist actions in India that must begin from another point of affirmation than feminism of the "center." The same could be said of the countries within the horizon of cultures oriented by the Muslim religion. What in one case (for example in a Muslim country) is a *transformation* in the arena of women's liberation, does not mean that it is so in the United States or Europe (where it might be interpreted as an action overcome long ago on that cultural horizon). But the difference does not lie in the fact that the countries of the center of the process of female democratization are increasingly more advanced, and that we must wait for postcolonial countries to catch up to that point, but rather that each one in its own horizon has positive qualities from which the others can learn.

---

37 See the *Human Development Report 1999* (New York: Oxford University Press, 1999).

Postcolonial feminism certainly has a more critical economic (anticapitalist) and political (in terms of the critical participation of women) awareness – let us recall the women commanders of the EZLN (Zapatista Army of National Liberation) – than the often purely antisexist or antipatriarchal feminism of the "center." Both movements can learn from others, and frequently the new social movements of the "center" learn more than those of the postcolonial world on account of the complexity and overdetermination into which the latter has been plunged. The feminism of the center, inevitably, has the usufruct of the economic exploitation of women at the periphery. The latter are indirectly the victims of the former. It is not extraordinary that they are more critical with respect to the economic and political aspects of the process of democratization.

Finally, I should like to call attention to the fact that in the struggle for global democracy, there is a macro-structure that is being questioned. Indeed, many agree with the notion that the State[38] is no longer important:[39] for instance, economists who advocate the opening of national markets and neoliberals who distrust the State, because the market is global; and much of what remains of the Left, because the State has served precisely to become the instrument of a globalization that has been so destructive to the great majorities of the South. Therefore, the argument goes, the democratic struggle is in the hands of NGOs (nongovernmental organizations), solidarity groups (as in Seattle), and other intermediate organizations pitted against the private transnational structure controlled by global bureaucracies (financial, transnational corporations) and backed by NATO (and, in the final analysis, by the US military, as seen in the Gulf War and Kosovo). In sum, the *Empire* (Hardt-Negri) before the anonymous "global citizen," ultimately defined as a "consumer" in a total global market. This economicist understanding of subjectivity must be opposed by a *repoliticization as democratic participation* of actors in the intersubjectivity of the political community on its different levels of participation and representation: direct participation in the base political communities (local meetings; consumption, production, self-defense groups, etc.), and indirect participation through democratic representation on all levels (the municipality or county, the state or province, etc.).

---

38 I never write "national" state because there have almost never been "national" states. Spain, France, Germany, the United Kingdom, Italy have not organized states of "one" nation, but rather states controlled by a nation (Castille, Île-de-France, the Prussians, England, the industrial North, etc.) dominating other nations (Basques, Galicians, Midi, Scotland, Mezzogiorno, etc.). Perhaps only the United States is a state with one nation, but actually this nation of many cultural origins has been slowly establishing itself since 1620 in a process as yet incomplete. In reality, the modern European states were plurinational, but did not recognize themselves as such (hence today's attempts to construct a Europe of "nations" and not of "states").
39 See, for example, Hardt and Negri, *Empire*.

But the *repoliticization of citizens' intersubjectivity as community actors* is impossible without the existence of the State, which is not only an instrument of globalization (and this is possible through citizens' demobilization that becomes "passive"), but also the only site for regulating those financial, industrial, and military structures that are in a pure "state of nature." And the United States, the *home state* of the large corporations and the final reference of world financial capital, is the state that opposes moving from the "state of nature" to a true "civil state" or cosmopolitan political state.[40]

Paradoxically, George Soros[41] speaks of the need for an "Alliance of democratic States," showing that the State is, in the final analysis, currently necessary in order to establish certain rules for the governance of global financial capital, just as the Lisbon Group had asserted. The concept of a "global citizen" is a dangerous mirage. There is no citizen of the world without real mediations from a political society (the State). Democracy cannot be exercised on a world level, at least today, and for some time to come (perhaps centuries). It requires a political community that has organized a political society (the State), and which is energized by the perspectives of civil society, within one territory with its own culture, language, traditions, identity. Globalization must help to deepen this identity rather than erase it, or the supposed global democracy will be one more mechanism of cultural and political (and, in the final analysis, economic) annihilation and alignment of the identity of the concrete community subject, of the intersubjectivity that has taken millennia to construct. The post-traditional situation is not postcultural. It is still not possible to think about a global culture (which perversely must speak one language, would impose one hierarchy of values, one religion, one traditional ethic, one literature...). It would simply be a totalitarian culture. It is necessary to fight for a healthy polyphonic development of the great human experiences expressed in the rich linguistic, cultural, religious diversity of different worldviews that, much more than the vegetable and animal species, speak to us of the splendor of Life, since its supreme realization is a fully developed human life. And just as the vegetable and animal

---

40 See Peter Spiro, "The New Sovereigntists," *Foreign Affairs* 79, no. 6 (November–December 2000), pp. 9–15. This article deals with US opposition to participation in the United Nations (e.g., not paying its dues), an International Tribunal, ecological protocols, and an international monetary and banking policy. The United States prefers to sabotage all the institutions that in the long run could organize a legitimate cosmopolitan structure in order to privilege a unilateral policy (of the United States with each potential negotiator), which allows that country not to depend on any "outside" judge. The Empire does not wish to be judged by anyone. Only it can judge all. The *Pax Americana* is grounded in the strongest army on the global level. The insignificant *Mare nostrum* of the Romans seems like a military political pygmy compared to this structure, which is the result of the end of the Cold War in 1989. This is the dark horizon of democracy in the postcolonial world.

41 See George Soros, *Open Society: Reforming Global Capitalism* (New York: Public Affairs, 2000).

species are becoming extinct, so too are the languages, cultures, and ethnic groups being genocidally exterminated in Asia, Africa, and Latin America.

Finally, and from a point of view of the political, which subsumes implicit ethical principles as constitutive of political principles themselves, a political philosophy must be developed that justifies the legitimacy, normativity, of the movements of *transformation* of the institutions and the rules of political hegemony from the perspective of the victims (intra-statal or global). In the first place, there are critico-political principles[42] that authorize the *transformation* of all political instances based on the victims of said instances. In the second place, it is not a question of *including* (many people talk about "inclusion," but it is necessary to indicate that "to include" without *transforming* the entire structure is like "pouring new wine into old wineskins," and therefore to relapse into the old in which Difference is retrapped by Identity). It is a matter of *transforming* the given order with creativity, novelty. That is, a second level of critical politics is to study the criteria of legitimacy of the transformation of the institutions themselves. Finally, a third level is the justification of the legitimacy of the praxis of liberation that transforms the given order, with partial reforms, but also, on very few occasions of human history, with revolutionary change (a revolution that today would be practically impossible, but which could not be declared categorically, *a priori*, impossible in the future). The democratization process of the postcolonial world demands theoretical and practical novelties to which we philosophers of politics are frequently unfaithful.

In Mexico, after a political order that was certainly democratic from 1934 to 1940 with Lázaro Cárdenas, but which later fell into bureaucratism and antidemocratic corporative corruption, the EZLN is not asking for indigenous autonomy to be "included" in the same constitution that excluded it, but rather it is asking for a *transformation*[43] of the very "spirit" of the constitution. It is not a question of a process of "inclusion," but rather of a novel, analogical, and transforming "creation." It is not simply a matter of creating a new room for those excluded from the old house. It is necessary to build a new house, with a new layout. Otherwise, the indigenous, the women, and the Afro-Americans will be assigned to the "servants" quarters … as before, as always.

Translated from the Spanish by Vincent Martin

---

42 There are political principles that make up all "political order" in force. But there are also critical political principles that justify the critique and transformation of all political order. This is the theme of the second part of my *Política de Liberación*, in preparation.

43 See my *Ética de la Liberación*, § 6.3, dedicated to showing what *transformation* (*Veraenderung*) means in Karl Marx's *Theses on Feuerbach*: "Philosophers have only interpreted the world in different ways; what we need to do is to *transform* [*veraendern*] it." See Karl Marx and Friedrich Engels, *Werke*, vol. 3 (Berlin: Dietz, 1956), p. 7.

The Subject of Politics – The Politics of the Subject

Cornelia Klinger

My point of departure is the by now well-founded assessment that the ongoing processes of globalization threaten to topple established forms and norms of politics, the sovereignty of nation-states, as well as welfare agendas or legal systems – in short, globalization unsettles the subject of politics. I will take up these issues from a related but slightly different angle. My guiding question will be: What happens under the conditions of globalization to individual and collective subjects, to issues of self and identity? In short: When the subject of politics is in jeopardy, what follows for the politics of the subject?

This question is motivated by two general premises which concern the past; the first one is well known, the second one adds a particular focus to my initial question:

First, there is a conjunction between the rise of the modern nation-state and the equally modern concept of the subject. The field of the political is desocialized in the process of modernity insofar as immediate personal and social relations are replaced by anonymous structures and institutions. The individual subject is set free and is encouraged to free him- or herself from the bonds of his or her immediate social environment. At the same time, matters of personal identity, positioning, and alignment do not vanish but, on the contrary, acquire new significance and enhanced importance.

Second, the subject and issues of subjectivity have played a prominent role in specific areas of the political, namely in the make-up and outlook of so-called social movements and new social movements (some have also been dubbed cultural movements) which focus on questions of identity and on the recognition and representation of identities. So my guiding question includes the following: What will be the fate of movement politics, of identity politics, under the sway of globalization? The evolution of democracy has not been promoted by parties and parliaments alone. Social movements of various stripes have also contributed in often controversial, less acknowledged (and sometimes even suspect) but nevertheless important ways to this project. Due to their more flexible and spontaneous character, social movements have provided crucial impulses to broadening the scope of democratic consciousness and action. The recently accelerated and intensified process of globalization affects the conditions and options of social movements as much as those of other established institutions of traditional democracy.

From its onset, the process of modernity headed into two divergent directions. It was divided between a process of rationalization and an equally important process of subjectivization: "Modernity is not based upon one single principle. … It is the result of a dialogue between Reason and Subjectivity."[1] This cleavage between reason, rationality, or objectivity on the one hand, and the subject, the collective and individual self, selfhood or subjectivity on the other, occurs in the aftermath of the decline of a concept of transcendence that shaped the meta-physical worldview of Christianity.

It is important to emphasize that *both* sides share the initial positive experience of liberation from the constraints of an all-encompassing holistic order (catholic in the original sense of *kat-holon*):

Autonomy in the perspective of rationalization is defined along the lines of function, efficiency, expediency, economy, and material utility without regard for any "higher" point of view, for religious or moral prescriptions of any kind. It involves a continual differentiation and pluralization of subsystems, a frag-mentation of reality, an opening of ever new horizons launching an immense increase in the range of human knowledge and agency.

Autonomy on the part of the subject implies that human beings are no longer assigned a position, rank, and place in a hierarchically structured eternal order, but are set free to find for themselves the meaning and essence of exis-tence and determine its aims. As a consequence, the quest for identity and the pursuit of happiness become the two most important obsessions of the modern subject striving for self-assertion and self-determination, self-expression and self-fulfillment: "discourse about identity seems in some important sense dis-tinctively modern – seems, indeed, intrinsic to and partially defining of the modern era."[2]

Despite this common ground, as far as the point of departure in the process of secularization and their shared participation in the rising principle of auton-omy is concerned, it is at the same time obvious that rationalization and subjec-tivization steer into different directions. Rationalization, following the princi-

---

1 Alain Touraine, *Critique of Modernity*, trans. David Macey (Cambridge, Mass.: Blackwell, 1995), p. 6.
2 Craig Calhoun, *Critical Social Theory: Culture, History, and the Challenge of Difference* (Cambridge, Mass.: Blackwell, 1996), p. 193.

ples of function and efficiency, is exclusively focused on instrumental aspects. Rationalization is concerned with means (the standard definition of rational action is "to choose the optimum means of reaching a given end"). Subjectivization is about meaning, the significance of existence, the aims and ends of action. Or, put a different way: rationalization refers to the spheres of economy, technology, science, law, administration, the state; it pertains to the level of institutions, or, in short, to the system. Subjectivization, instead, refers to the life-world of individuals and communities, to belief systems/religion, personal aesthetic expression/art, and the private sphere of intimate relationships. Rationalization results in a differentiation of spheres; but subjectivization, albeit ensuing from the same process of decentering, must perform a contrary movement of closure, centering the subject. Ideally, of course, the opposite characteristics of rationalization and subjectivization may be understood as complementary, as belonging together. Like means and end, function and meaning are supposed to mutually involve each other, as two halves of a whole and hence as achieving or at least aspiring to an ultimate harmony. And it is obvious that both processes not only go back to the same historical roots but move in close correspondence with each other. Georg Simmel, an early and one of the most brilliant analysts of modernity, observed: "Individualität des Seins und Tuns erwächst ... in dem Maße, wie der das Individuum sozial umgebende Kreis sich ausdehnt"[3] – Individuality of being and doing unfolds in the same measure as the social context of the individual is expanding. I will return to this point later, referring to it as "Simmel's law."

First we have to take a closer look at the ways in which subjectivization works. What comes into immediate focus is the strong tension not only between the two opposed complementary processes, but the considerable strains within the concept of subjectivity itself.

The centering and unifying task to which the subject has been assigned, in the aftermath of the demise of traditional concepts of order, is extremely difficult to fulfill and becomes more precarious further in the course of the irreversible and ever increasing process of differentiation and pluralization unleashed by the process of rationalization. The subject is forced to take up the godlike position of a transcendental nodal point in order to ensure the unity and totality of being and experience. "But the principle of subjectivity is not powerful enough to regenerate the unifying power of religion in the medium of

---

3 Georg Simmel, *Soziologie. Untersuchungen über die Formen der Vergesellschaftung*, vol. 2 of *Gesammelte Werke* (Berlin: Duncker und Humblot, 1983), ch. 10: "Die Erweiterung der Gruppe und die Ausbildung der Individualität," p. 527.

reason. ... The demotion of religion leads to a split ... which the Enlightenment cannot overcome by its own power."[4] Within the philosophical discourse of modernity, this problematic ontological position of the subject entails the hypothesis of a break between an intelligible and an empirical subject ("a problematic doubling of the self-relating subject"[5]); in the context of other discourses and in social reality, the subject sets out on a search for safe foundations of identity. This search leads more or less directly to the categories of nature and culture. This is the moment when identity politics is born in Western thought.

It goes without saying that in some sense nature and culture have always existed. Their conceptualization, however, begins only in the late 18th century. The concepts of nature and culture substitute notions of origin and tradition, which played comparable roles in religious, mythological, and metaphysical narratives of premodern times. The idea of origin in an act of creation refers to a transcendent anchorage mediated to the present through the chain of tradition. Nature and culture, however, are completely modern ideas, since they lack a foundation in transcendence; rather, they are designed to make up for this very loss. Yet the modernity of these two concepts is partly concealed, as it is their mission to balance the effects of modernity and cover at least some of its costs. Thus a powerful tension exists between background and intent. Therefore, culture and nature belong to a class of concepts that I would name "concepts of nostalgia" because they attempt to recapture what is about to vanish or is already lost. In this effort to keep alive something that is gone, such concepts do not exactly *recover* but rather *dis*cover or even "invent" what they are supposed to conserve. Zygmunt Bauman describes this paradox very lucidly: "Aspects of experience come into focus and begin to be debated in earnest when they can no longer be taken for granted; when they cease to be self-evident ... The more feeble they seem, the stronger is the urge ... to demonstrate the solidity of ... their foundations. 'Identity' is no exception; it had become a matter of acute reflection once the likelihood of its survival without reflection began to dwindle."[6] And further: "... at no time did identity 'become' a problem; it was a 'problem' from its birth – was born as a problem (that is, as something one needs to do something about – as a task), could exist only as a problem ... 'Identity' is a name given to the escape sought from uncertainty. ... Though all too often hypostasized as an attribute of a material entity, identity has the ontological sta-

4 Jürgen Habermas, *The Philosophical Discourse of Modernity: Twelve Lectures*, trans. Frederick Lawrence (Cambridge, Mass.: MIT Press, 1987), p. 20.
5 Ibid., p. 265.
6 Zygmunt Bauman, *Culture as Praxis* (London: Sage, 1999), p. xxix. The modern mind is rich in nostalgic notions; nature, culture, and identity are preeminent; "aura" or "memory" are further cases in point.

tus of a project and a postulate."[7] In other words, the discourse on identity indicates a crisis in exactly that which is supposed to be its object. Since this is a feature that will also prove to be a long-term constituent of subjectivity and subjectivization, we may register it under the title of "Bauman's law." While Simmel's law designates a linkage in the processes of rationalization and subjectivization, Bauman's law draws attention to an equally original and hereditary asymmetry between them, thus hinting at the highly precarious status on the side of subjectivization.

The concepts of nature and culture differ in many respects, but they share one characteristic which is decisive for the formation of identity: both are designed to signify what cannot or at least cannot easily be altered, what is supposed to transcend change. The individual is seen to be endowed with innate characteristics, attributes of identity which are irreversibly given by nature: "all that which is mysteriously given us by birth … includes the shape of our bodies and the talents of our minds."[8] Of course, the qualities of culture are not in the same way innate, on the contrary, they are man-made and defined as what distinguishes humans from animals. But the making of culture is a long-term process exceeding the agency of the subject almost to the same extent as the natural conditions of its existence are beyond reach. The individual is born into a family and a larger community whom it has not chosen; it is socialized into a way of life, a system of beliefs, norms, and values, into certain ways of seeing the world, of feeling and behaving, as well as into a language (in the literal and metaphorical sense). The individual may reflect and also act upon all that and even decide to leave its heritage behind, but this is more difficult than changing other aspects of its social existence. I would propose distinguishing between cultural attributes as native (*eingeboren*) versus natural attributes as innate (*angeboren*),[9] yet both classes are equally separate from the principles of modern society.

To place the foundations of identity into the surrogate transcendence of culture and nature, beyond the command of choice and agency, produces two different but interdependent effects. On the one hand, it is evident that nature and

7 Zygmunt Bauman, "From Pilgrim to Tourist – or a Short History of Identity," in *Questions of Cultural Identity*, ed. Stuart Hall and Paul du Gay (London: Sage, 1996), pp. 18, 19.

8 Hannah Arendt, *The Origins of Totalitarianism* (1951), new ed. with added prefaces (New York: Harcourt Brace Jovanovich, 1973), pp. 300ff. Arendt ardently endeavored to keep these matters off the political agenda as a reaction against fascist politics in which the modern effort to substitute the lost roots in blood and soil found its notorious apogee.

9 The gist of both is the same but they differ in degree and value. It is obvious that the binding power of nature over the subject is taken to be stronger than that of culture. On the other hand, the lesser degree of necessity attributed to the cultural "birthmarks" of the subject and the fact that these are products of human agency explains their higher evaluation.

culture impose necessity and constraint on the subject; on the other hand, it is precisely this dependence that allows the subject to escape the grip of society. As a result, the subject is more and other than the sum of social role, place, status, or function. In other words, the subject maintains an *alterity* toward the rules and mechanisms of society, a distance from the "ways of the world," comparable to the religious believer whose liability for the secular realm is limited by his or her obligation to the higher commandments of his or her creed. This alterity toward one (lower-level) order ensuing from an obligation to another (higher-level) order endows the subject with "inwardness" or "depth," from which, at least potentially, resistance against the "world" may spring. As it is widely agreed that "social criticism might require social exile," a "view from outside the walls of the city,"[10] the quality of alterity is pivotal for the formulation of a radical opposition against reality.

Those features of nature and culture that serve to provide identity and stability to the individual subject merge in a concept of collective identity that shares the same linguistic root with *innate* and *native*, namely the concept of *nation*. Under the conditions of modernity and the crisis of traditional foundations of identity which ensues, the nation-state becomes not the only but certainly the most prominent source of individual and collective identity. It is by no means accidental that the idea of the modern nation-state takes its departure at *a* if not *the* crucial moment in the process of modernity, in the American and French Revolutions.[11] The modern idea of the nation shows the same kind of double-edged feature that I have analyzed as typical of the process of subjectivization. On the one hand, it embraces the ideal of autonomy and self-determination, in this case, of a collective body, named the people, whose intention to break free from bondage may be directed against either an *ancien régime* or foreign rule. On the other hand, the idea of the nation embodies the attempt to give direction to this autonomy of the people in a common identity which is beyond choice but which binds the individuals in a *Schicksalsgemeinschaft* (community of fate). The idea of a national community and the sense of allegiance and belonging that it inspires, known as nationalism, are closely linked to the concepts of nature and culture. The identity of the people is

---

10 Seyla Benhabib, "Feminism and Postmodernism: An Uneasy Alliance," *Praxis International* 11, no. 2 (1991), p. 146.
11 "The American Revolution added a further ingredient to the political form of modern society. It asserted the principle of self-determination. Only those states were legitimate in which a people of common *culture* ruled for themselves a common territory. Foreign rule, or rule by an alien elite, as in the Ottoman and Habsburg empires, was unnatural. Only nation-states were *natural political entities*; only they were legitimate" (Entry "Modernization" in *Encyclopaedia Britannica 1999–2000*, www.britannica.com., p. 5).

deduced from nature, that is to say, from blood and soil, descent and territory. In addition to these natural features, identity is derived from culture, a common language, history, custom, and lore. The most important element that the purported "roots" in nature and culture convey to the nation-state is its quasi-transcendence. The nation needs such a transcendent status in order to function as the site of reconciliation and unification, in contrast to the modern civil society, which not only undergoes a constant process of fragmentation and transformation but furthermore is dominated by the dividing principle of competition.[12] The individual as well as the collective subject under the guise of the nation-state must assume a position of alterity if they are to function as sites of identity and orientation.

It is easy to discern a deep incongruity *within* the concept of subjectivity as well as *among* individual and collective identities. The process of modernity as promoting rationalization and subjectivization, for the first time in Western history, privileges the individual subject over the community, the particular over the whole. But as soon as this happens, it is of course consistent that the subject, who is set free to pursue his or her self-chosen aims and ends, must try to define guidelines for this action. The subject unbound from the great chain of being immediately and necessarily asks: "Who am I, where do I come from, where am I going to, and who will accompany me on my journey?" And therefore it is at the very moment of triumph of the unencumbered self that the desire to rid this self again of the burden of individuation and its manifold responsibilities is ignited (Nietzsche's idea of *Zerbrechen der Individuation*). This is also the moment when the priority shifts back from the pole of the individual subject to questions of a collective identity. But whenever and wherever safe ground on which the autonomous decision of the subject might be based comes into sight, or the burden of individual responsibility might be alleviated by a community, the autonomy of the modern subject is perceived as imperiled, and the subject is instantly up in arms against this menace. Craving for guidance, it is at the same time intolerant of any kind of authority or dependence. Accordingly, the modern nation-state wavers between democratic principles and authoritarian structures (and sometimes totalitarian temptations). Modern subjectivity is torn between the impulse to rejoice at the loss of the fetters of origin, tradition, and conventional wisdom of all kinds, on the one hand, and the urge to reestablish

---

12 David Lloyd and Paul Thomas, *Culture and the State* (New York: Routledge, 1998). Lloyd and Thomas name three important aspects of convergence between the concept of the modern nation-state and that of modern culture. "Both are given the role of furnishing sites of reconciliation for a civil and political society that is seen to be riven by conflict and contradiction. Both are seen as the sites in which the highest expressions of human being and human freedom are realized. Both are seen as hedges against the potential anarchy of rapidly transforming societies" (p. 1).

certainty, orientation, and solidarity on the other. This winds up as a no-win situation: each gain of autonomy engenders fear and therefore calls forth a renewed quest for identity, while each effort to settle down on some presumably secure basis is in turn immediately suspected of endangering the hard-won freedom. The subject vacillates between the promise of liberation and the threat of disorientation, it abhors the yoke of tutelage as much as it fears the abandonment of freedom.

Should this seem to be an irresolvably tragic element in the identity-formation of the modern subject, the picture darkens when we take into account one further aspect. The existential conflict between certainty/orientation/solidarity and autonomy is projected onto social and political divisions among different collective subjects. The two inevitable poles of identity-formation, namely, the ambivalence between autonomy and belonging, oscillate at the same time as a dichotomy between self and other. The positive and desirable aspects of identity formation translate into inclusion while the negative and disadvantageous aspects are reflected in exclusion. On the positive side, we identify "us" by way of common characteristics of culture and nature that raise the nation above the rationale and rationality of society and its nexus of efficiency and profitability. On the negative side, we identify "them" as below the societal processes because of specific natural and cultural constraints. "We" are exempt, but "they" are excluded; "we" are above, but "they" are below the level of society; for "us" identity promises belonging, for "them" identity means confinement; "we" are singled out by cultural distinctions, but "they" are marked by natural traits.[13] In short, the desire motivating a critical cultural discourse to raise matters of identity *above* the social process gets entangled in the struggle for power *within* the social and political process.

From early on, some identities, in the first place national identities and, to a lesser degree, class identities, manage to figure on the positive side. Although they do invite polarization between "us" and "them," and although such confrontations are known to have generated disastrously bloody consequences in the course of Western history of the 19th and 20th centuries, these are conceived of as taking place on the same level, on more or less equal terms, so that the competition between identities may take the form of a conflict A vs. B. The rupture is deeper, with repercussions even more devastating, in the cases of ethnicity and gender. Here, one side claims the position of identity but repudiates the right of the other side to make the same claim. In this case, the conflict takes

13 At this point a certain hierarchical element divides the twin concepts of nature and culture. The positive identification is more often based on culture; the negative attribution, legitimating exclusion, refers inevitably to nature.

on the form of A vs. Non-A, confronting a position of identity with a lack of identity. Here the lines of inclusion and exclusion are drawn in a far more rigid fashion. The specifically modern maladies of racism and sexism develop on this ground, that is, on the dark side of the modern quest for identity in nature and culture.

The radically opposed positive and negative aspects of this whole complex of identity politics are perhaps nowhere so intricately connected as in the case of the category of gender. The division of public and private realms in modern society not only reflects the persisting division of labor along the lines of gender difference but, in addition, the modern private sphere of family and intimate personal relationships plays a pivotal role in creating a highly valued sphere beyond the reach of all the effects and side-effects of modernization that are experienced as negative. The private sphere comes to be revered as a "haven in a heartless world," as a refuge of human values expunged from the public sphere, and as the most important resource (birthplace and cradle in the literal sense) of the identity-formation of the subject (*Bildung*). The positive characteristics of the bourgeois private sphere are attributed to women, who are chiefly assigned the duty to inculcate and enact the values and functions of the family. But at the same time, the need to maintain this complex societal construct reinforces the exclusion of women from legal, economic, social, and political rights and participation. The very same reference to nature and culture invoked to solemnize the private sphere as exempt from modern society's war of all against all is used or abused to justify the exclusion of women from everything other than family life. The margin between the boons and banes of identity politics is extremely narrow.

In the long run, however, the denied right of the other generates opposition and leads to the formation of new social movements that struggle against the unequal distribution and unjust divisions that this kind of identity politics implies. Even the most derogatory xeno-identification may be turned into a favorable self-identification to become the nucleus of new forms of identity politics. Notwithstanding substantial differences between movements that revolve around national or class identities and movements taking their departure from the categories of ethnicity/race and gender, the structure of identity politics remains, in principle, the same. The obvious ambiguity of the categories of nature and culture does not diminish their attractiveness as a mainstay of resistance against the conditions of society. And finally, the double dilemma of freedom vs. certainty and inclusion vs. exclusion also persists.

At this point, I will not pursue the historical development of identity politics and their dialectics any further. Instead I shall turn to some still more urgent questions concerning present and future politics of the subject.

"There has been a veritable discursive explosion in recent years around the con-cept of 'identity.'"[14] This dramatically heightened interest in issues of identity has sparked off a widespread debate, giving occasion to recall Simmel's law: "Individuality of being and doing unfolds in the same measure as the social context of the individual is expanding." If this still holds true, we have to understand the "discursive explosion" of recent years as the flip side of an equally dramatic further step in the process of rationalization. The renewed attention paid to identity and identity politics must be perceived against the background of the tremendous progress of *globalization* that we are witnessing today. In a similar vein as rationalization was accompanied by subjectivization, globalization calls forth individualization. In addition, we have perhaps even more reason to assume that Bauman's law is also still valid, according to which we should recognize the increased preoccupation with identity as a symptom of its crisis.

To invoke Simmel's and Bauman's laws means to stress aspects of continua-tion in the long-term process of modernity. Although such aspects are clearly discernible, as the current process of globalization flows from and carries on the longstanding process of rationalization, there are nevertheless significant differ-ences between past and present that have to be taken into account as well. It is important to distinguish between elements of continuity and those of disconti-nuity, for it is as crucial not to mistake old structures for new phenomena as it is necessary not to react in old ways to new exigencies. This involves the much dis-cussed question of a possible transition to a postmodern era or, rather, to a later stage in the ongoing process and project of modernity. While modernity is defined in sharp contrast to a premodern phase of history, by a clear-cut break in the flow of time, as expressed in the metaphor of "revolution," no such rup-ture appears to occur in the present. On the contrary, the process of moderniza-tion is continued and intensified. But it is this very acceleration, the increased speed and extent of modernization, that might induce the transformation into a new stage. The transition from modernity to postmodernity, or from an earlier to a later stage of modernity, does not occur in the form of a break from the pre-vious phase but as its excess.

Among the numerous factors to bring about a real sea change, we have, above all, to consider that the thrust of the current wave of innovation and rationalization is taking place in the fields of genetic engineering and communi-cations technology with effects of commodification in the wings that have mas-sively fueled a new economy. The consequences are so far-reaching that it is no

---

14 Stuart Hall, "Who Needs 'Identity'?," in *Questions of Cultural Identity*, ed. Hall and du Gay, p. 1.

exaggeration to speak of a new level of industrial revolution and a new stage in the evolution of capitalism. The full impact on the future is as yet hardly foreseeable but the relevance for issues of identity and identity politics is obvious enough even now. As major processes of industrialization and commercialization occur in the domains of genetics/reproduction and communication, human nature and culture become the immediate objects of rapid change. Once more the scope of human agency is considerably enlarged, requiring political and social as well as individual decision making and action. Hence the idea of an immutable realm beyond the vagaries of the societal process and immune to historical change, as was once deemed necessary in order to serve as base of identity-building, is no longer tenable. The specifically modern construction of nature and culture as extraterritorial foundations of collective and individual identities has certainly been fictitious right from the outset, but in the light of recent developments, the last glimmer of plausibility is lost. To take these developments seriously means to discern that the paths which served as exits from the identity crisis in earlier phases of the process of modernity are barred today. Furthermore, common definitions of life and death as well as the order of time and space are overturned in ways unheard-of ever before in human history. Previous waves of technological innovation certainly had deep and lasting effects on the realms of culture and nature (this is what the rise of the concepts of the subject and its identity politics was about), but only the recent industrial revolution breaks out in their very heartlands, threatening to overthrow the entire symbolic order of Western thought.

Given the quantity and quality of innovations that separate the current stage of the process of rationalization from preceding waves, it is surprising how much the reactions to this new situation on the part of subjectivity still resemble past patterns. The familiar antagonism, the conflict between the gain in freedom and the loss of certainty, is reinstated or continued. On the one hand, there is again the impulse to see the widening of the circle owing to globalization as liberating. On the other hand, there are again fearful reactions regretting the loss of safe foundations, prompting efforts to reestablish them. The only difference between the present stage and its precedents seems to be that both types of reaction appear radicalized and therefore even more polarized than before.

Under the rubric of a celebratory postmodernism those voices may be summarized who rejoice in the liberating prospects of globalization, including the option to free the self from the constraints which the modern concept of the subject imposed. Transgressing the imprints of national, class, or gender identity in a multicultural global society seems to open up new dimensions of freedom of choice, offering the possibility to willfully, if not arbitrarily, construct, constantly shape, and reshape one's identity according to shifting individual preferences, finally destroying the notorious illusions of imagined foundations in nature and culture. Flexibility and fluidity of identity are acclaimed as new ideals, not least because cultural and historical studies of various stripes have thrown – and rightly so – a very negative light on the history of identity politics, in particular on its involvement with racism and sexism.

This postmodern attitude stands in stark contrast, but actually must rather be considered in close connection to, the opposite stance, which may be summarized under the heading of fundamentalism, if we agree to understand this term in a broad sense. The fundamentalist attitude performs the reverse movement in the desperate but stubborn attempt to reassert or reestablish foundations that are believed to be safe, stable, and untainted by either technological/social progress or postmodern subversion. The scope of such endeavors extends from the promotion of family values in advanced industrial societies to the mobilization of ancient religious visions or indigenous cultures. It is evident that the attitudes of postmodern relativism and fundamentalist essentialism are distributed along certain positional differences and also imply power differentials. Individuals or groups who expect to profit from the progress of globalization are more ready to embrace the postmodern attitude, while those who fear to be on the losing side tend to cling to essentialist alternatives.

Behind the new labels of postmodernism vs. fundamentalism, the contradictory yet circular movement from the triumph of individual freedom to the depression of disorientation and back again is repeated, if only on a larger scale, at higher speed, and with increased volatility among the contrary positions. Basically, there is nothing premodern about essentialism/fundamentalism and there is nothing postmodern about that which comes under this buzzword, nor is there a real contradiction between the two poles. Both alternatives are two sides of a single pattern of reactions to the process of modernity, a pattern that has accompanied this process all along. The fact that both positions now appear as more extreme and their contrast more acute must be read as symptoms of how inadequate *both* have become today. It is high time to break the vicious circle between the notion of a gain of freedom and the search for roots to which the reactions of fundamentalism and postmodernism are still relating. Under the conditions of rationalization/subjectivization, there was both a gain in freedom to rejoice in, as well as a loss of certainty to make up for. Under the continual yet altered conditions of globalization/individualization, however, we have reached a situation of "neither-nor": neither can we hope to compensate the loss of orientation, certainty, or solidarity in a quest for new foundations, nor can we celebrate the freedom we will win.

While this outcome may be more obvious (at least to liberal Western eyes) in the case of the fundamentalist reaction, which becomes bottomless absent the possibility of finding firm ground in nature or culture, as these realms are the main targets of rampant innovation, it is no less pertinent to the opposite case of the postmodern reaction. Only at a very superficial first glance might the current situation seem to favor a further liberation of subjectivity under the guise of individualization. A closer look reveals that the subject who would be able to enjoy his or her liberation from all bonds of identity vanishes in the aftermath of their complete dismissal.

The changes in the structure and character of subjectivity that underlie the transition from the subject to the individual and distinguish the ongoing postmodern process of individualization from the modern process of subjectivization are linked to, but are at the same time obliterated by, a change in the main factor of identity-building. Parallel to the relative retreat of more conventional makers and markers of identity, another powerful player in the game of identity and identity politics comes to the fore: the issue of consumption. The more the subject is set free from traditional bonds and obliged to create and construct its individual identity, the more immediately and invariably it will turn to the marketplace for guidance. The subject begins to "shop for the real self." In the quest for identity, one kind of dependence is replaced by another, but this is to a certain degree concealed by the particular rhetoric of consumption that constantly appeals to the freedom of choice and celebrates the individual as subject of his or her sovereign purchase decision.

Consumption is not exactly a new player in this field, for it has performed the function of "a privileged medium for negotiating identity and status within post-traditional society"[15] ever since Western society began to understand itself a "post-traditional"; this is to say, since the onset of modernity. What is new about the current situation is not that the self dresses and expresses identity by way of acquisition and display of consumer goods, but the immense expansion in what belongs to the sphere of consumption. Not only material articles of all sorts create our lifestyles but, in addition, more and more services, relations, values, concepts, ideas, ultimately the generation of (human) life itself, and social existence as a whole, are colonized by the market. In particular, the entire gamut of inventions and discoveries in the field of the new technologies immediately assume commodity form. This advanced stage of consumer culture is correctly labeled as "hypercommodification," a term being defined as follows: "hypercommodification ... erodes the distinction between commodified and

---

15 Don Slater, *Consumer Culture and Modernity* (Oxford: Polity Press, 1997), pp. 29ff.

noncommodified regions and gives a twist to the commodification of meaning."16

The consequences can hardly be overrated. When the production of meaning is commercialized, the division of functions between the sphere of subjectivized meaning and the rationalized sphere of instrumental reason as the sphere of means is overruled. The distinction between system integration and social integration becomes blurred; social integration tends to be replaced by system integration, meaning and ends tend to be overrun by means. The repercussions are reflected in a coinage such as that of *consumer culture*, forcing together the two worlds of economy and culture that were to be carefully kept apart (or at least distinguished as high and low culture) under the conditions of modernity. In other words, not under the impact of production but under the impact of consumption, capitalism is identified with and as culture. For the first time in its history, capitalism does not spare culture but *becomes* culture.

Under the hegemony of consumer culture, the position of subjectivity is at once "hardened" and "weakened." This double-edged move is not to be confused with the familiar dialectics of win and loss, although it is striking to see a similar form of polarization being recapitulated under altered conditions.

On the one hand, the position of subjectivity is hardened, or, as Alain Touraine puts it, the subject gets locked in an "obsession with identity," as the cleavage between the pole of rationality/the system and the pole of subjectivity/individuality deepens – to the detriment of both: "Without Reason, the Subject is trapped in to an obsession with identity; without the Subject, Reason becomes an instrument of might."17 Touraine regrets the "complete dissociation between system and actors, between the technical or economic world and the world of subjectivity. As our society comes increasingly to resemble a firm fighting for its survival in an international market, there is a widespread obsession with an identity which can no longer be defined in social terms. In poor countries it takes the form of a new communitarianism; in rich countries, that of narcissistic individualism" – the fundamentalist and postmodern positions

16 Stephen Crook, Jan Pakulski, and Malcolm Waters, *Postmodernization: Change in Advanced Society* (London: Sage, 1992), p. 74. "Until the early years of the 20th century ... family, class and community ties and religious affiliation were basic to identity-formation and were relatively non-commodified. In such circumstances a wide variety of goods ... can be sold in association with their 'images.' The limiting condition is that the images must engage with conceptions of self rooted in non-commodified relations" (p. 60). In the course of the 20th century, this undergoes a more or less rapid change: "the images and daydreams which link commodity with identity no longer need to orient themselves to a non-commodified region of meaning. In hypercommodification, commodified meanings become self-referential" (p. 61). "Style follows the erosion of institutionalized cultural authority" (p. 60).
17 Touraine, *Critique of Modernity*, p. 6.

being two sides of the same coin. Touraine's fear: "A complete divorce between public and private life would lead to the triumph of powers defined purely in terms of management and strategy. The majority would react by retreating in to [*sic*] a private space, and that would leave a bottomless void where there was once the public, social and political space that gave birth to modern democracies."[18] The position of subjectivity is hardened, since identity politics applies more and more exclusively to either individual identities or to that of small communities, whereas the notion of a universal public sphere and the idea of a common good recedes into the background.

On the other hand, the position of subjectivity is weakened. With the foundations in nature and culture eroding and the influence of social ties diminishing, the individual is exposed to the (economic) system without mediation or restraint. Without any points of reference in a sphere beyond the reach of the societal process, the subject loses its "alterity" to distinguish it from this process. It must be kept in mind that this does not only affect issues of identity-formation but also concerns the capacity for dissociation from and resistance against a given reality, a capacity that amounts to an important component in the modern understanding of freedom. Together with the constructs of nature and culture, those fields "which offered extraterritorial and Archimedean footholds for critical effectivity"[19] disappear. As a consequence, the individual is devoid of the "depth" or inwardness with which the subject was invested. From this perspective, the position of subjectivity now looks alarmingly feeble. "The managed possession of consumer goods and objects is individualizing, atomizing and dehistoricizing. As a producer ... the worker presupposes others ... As a consumer, man becomes solitary again, or cellular – at best, he[20] becomes gregarious ... The structures of consumption are both very fluid and closed ... The consumer object isolates. The private sphere has no concrete negativity because it is enfolded on its objects, which have none."[21] "A modern world based on pure individual self-interest leaves the individual in a chronically weak condition. Without a binding collective culture, without solidarity, the individual – isolated, adrift on tides of

18 Ibid.
19 Fredric Jameson, *Postmodernism or, The Cultural Logic of Late Capitalism* (Durham, N.C.: Duke University Press, 1991), p. 49.
20 The use of the generic masculine form is particularly misleading in this case as the sphere and the activity of consumption is usually identified with women and femininity (see, e.g., Rita Felski, *The Gender of Modernity* [Cambridge, Mass.: Harvard University Press, 1995]). In overlooking this fact, Baudrillard misses the opportunity to consider the process of the weakening of the subject under the aspect of "feminization."
21 Jean Baudrillard, *The Consumer Society: Myths and Structures* (London: Sage, 1998), p. 85. Such a nostalgic praise of the "concrete negativity" that the bourgeois private sphere offered may appear justified in the present circumstances. But it should not make us forget the extremely high price of social injustice and exclusion that the construct of a secluded private sphere demanded in the past.

momentary desires – is open to manipulation and the most subtle forms of unfreedom."[22] Basically all features attributed to the ideal postmodern identity, such as flexibility, reflexivity, fluidity, versatility, creativity, openness, (self)-irony, are much less achievements of a more enlightened and liberal era that has finally freed the self from the confinement of essentialist subjecthood; they are, instead, to be explained by the exigencies of late capitalism and its concomitant, the hegemony of consumption. However, the weakening or, rather, the adaptation of the subject to the conditions of market society will not bring about the definite end, the "death" of the subject – for one simple reason: the subject is "practically irreplaceable"[23] as consumer. Late modern economy needs the subject position, and it needs the subject in exactly this weak position of the *soggetto debole* that postmodern theory acclaims. Hence, there is little normative input or critical surplus in the plea to keep up a weak subject position for "strategic" reasons, for example, in order to not completely forfeit the subject of movement politics.[24] Market society accomplishes this feat anyway.

For the first time over a long period in Western history, the subject loses its agency and, in particular, its status as agent of resistance against the "ways of the world," against the machinery of a deficient society.

In the end, a negative answer seems to impose itself to my initial question concerning the future of social movements and the development of democracy. And yet, I would caution against an overly pessimistic conclusion.

Keeping in mind the highly problematic character of identity-building on the foundations of nature and culture, I see, in principle, little reason to regret the shift to other ways of resolving these questions. There is no need to be any more critical of identity-formation via consumer culture than with regard to more conventional methods – though there is no reason to be less critical either. The configuration of the subject position has always depended on the formative principles of the respective society and this continues to be the case to the present day. The issue of subjectivity and subject identity must be placed in the context of the shift from the hegemony of politics to the hegemony of economy which began with the fall of the totalitarian regimes of the 20th century.[25] This

---

22 Slater, *Consumer Culture and Modernity*, p. 73.
23 Baudrillard, *The Consumer Society*, p. 83.
24 Cf. Judith Butler, "Contingent Foundations," in Seyla Benhabib, Judith Butler, Drucilla Cornell, and Nancy Fraser, *Feminist Contentions: A Philosophical Exchange* (New York: Routledge, 1995), p. 49.
25 To speak of such a shift does not imply that capitalist economy has not played an immensely important role before, or, on the other hand, that politics in the guise of the nation-state or in any other form ceases to exist.

shift brings about a further step in the process of secularization in the sense that the quest for a transcendental point of reference in which the social order would have to be grounded is abandoned. Under the hegemony of the political, the principle impulse was to substitute a lost transcendent anchorage. In accordance with this intention, the subject was endowed with a quasi-transcendent status and with roots in the extra-societal realms of nature and culture. Capitalist economy instead operates without such a premise, since it does not imply the model of a holistic metaphysical order on which the concept of the political was still molded, but is organized as a self-referential and self-perpetuating mechanism. Such a system has neither need nor use for a transcendental subject position.

However, this loss of the classical locus of resistance "outside the walls of the city" must not necessarily result in the end of social criticism. Above all else, there is an urgent need and a demand for such criticism in view of the anomic features of contemporary society. The world-system of late capitalism is riddled with problems. On the one hand, there are countless forms of psychological and cultural discontent within the privileged centers of consumer culture. On the other hand, there are the infinitely more severe and blatant problems of utter poverty and, still worse, pauperization and exploitation of a growing majority of people all over the world. If the different types of misery, cultural discontent, and social resentment should ever reach a point of intersection, cutting across the lines of social and political divisions as well as divergent "identities," the economic system might prove to be much less stable than it looks today.

Given the need for social criticism, there will be ways to meet this demand. Last but not least, the ideas of freedom and dignity of the human subject as developed in the history of Western thought remain – or, rather, they might yet become – an important weapon in an arsenal of resistance and critique. In order to use this potential, we must not close our eyes to the contingent conditions and limitations of its history. The freedom and dignity of the human subject were never or nowhere reality. We have no paradise to lose but we do have a few past visions to redeem; visions born in the interstices of the errors and horrors of the past.

In one way or another, the politics of the rebellious subject contesting the conditions of the dominant economic system will take on the form of movement politics. This implies the relinking of isolated subjects of consumption into a kind of community. But this community cannot revert to any preestablished common identity. It must at the same time presuppose as well as transgress the individual.

Beyond Diversity:
Cultural Studies and Its Postcommunist Other

Boris Groys

Initially, I had planned to address the relationship between art and politics in modernity. But during these talks, listening to what other speakers had to say, I decided that it would be useful to do so by concentrating in the first place on the present situation in postcommunist Eastern Europe. There are some specific reasons for this choice in the framework of our present discussions – and I would like to begin by trying to elucidate these reasons.

First of all, the topic of this symposium – "Democracy Unrealized" – refers in a very obvious way to the currently dominant discourse describing the victory of the West at the end of the Cold War as the final victory of the forces of democracy over the forces of communism. But the theoretical reflection of this event remains at the same time significantly absent in the context of our present talks. As Okwui Enwezor told me in a private conversation, the postcommunist world, and, specifically, postcommunist Russia, remain a blind spot for today's cultural discourse. And it seems to me that we have reached the point at which we have to ask ourselves: Why?

We have heard already many voices that challenge the claim of democracy's final victory and assert that democracy is still unrealized or even unrealizable. And we can, of course, generally agree with this judgment. But it seems to me very characteristic that all the examples that were used to illustrate this point were – with very few exceptions – related to the noncommunist part of the world as it was divided by the Cold War. All these examples referred namely to the countries of the First World – the countries of the West – or the countries of the so-called Third World that were more or less controlled by the West during the Cold War. And that means that the choice of these examples, being very interesting, stimulating, and fascinating, on the one hand, still tends, on the other hand, to perpetuate on the discursive level the dividing lines of the Cold War that were meanwhile obliterated – or at least transformed – in the field of real political practice. Now, it is, of course, obvious that the concentration on Western countries and on the countries of the Third World which were part of the Western sphere of influence can be easily explained by the mere fact that the

majority of the speakers at this conference have a Western cultural background
– and it seems only natural and legitimate that these speakers are especially
interested in Western topics. But it seems to me that this is not the whole story.
The deeper reason for this blind spot is, actually, theoretical and perhaps – on
an even deeper level – aesthetic. And this deeper reason has in its turn everything to do with the question of the fate of radical politics – and, for that matter, of radical art – in modernity and, specifically, in our time.

I think it is safe to say that the theoretical discourse we have witnessed during these talks has its origin in a certain period of the development of Cultural
Studies. Now, Cultural Studies has some very fundamental difficulties in
describing and theorizing the postcommunist condition. And, frankly, I do not
believe that a simple adjustment of the theoretical framework and vocabulary of
Cultural Studies to the realities of Eastern Europe – without reconsideration of
some of the discipline's fundamental presuppositions – would be sufficient to
make its discourse able to describe and discuss the postcommunist reality. Now,
I will try to explain why such an adjustment seems to be so difficult.

The presently dominant theoretical discourse in the field of Cultural Studies
has a tendency – we have heard it from Stuart Hall – to see historical development as a road that brings the subject from the particular to the universal, from
premodern closed communities, orders, hierarchies, traditions, and cultural
identities toward the open space of universality, free communication, and citizenship in a democratic Modern state. This road of democratization is, at the
same time, the road of modernization. Contemporary Cultural Studies shares
this image with the venerable tradition of the European Enlightenment – even if
the former looks at this image in a different way and, accordingly, draws different conclusions from the analysis of this image. The central question that arises
under these presuppositions is namely the following: How to deal with an individual person traveling along this road – here and now? The traditional answer
of liberal political theory, which has its origins in French Enlightenment
thought, is well known: this person on the road has to move forward as quickly
as possible. And if we see that a certain person is not going fast enough – and
maybe even takes a rest before moving ahead – then appropriate measures must
be taken against this person, because such a person is not only moving too
slowly toward universal freedom but holding up the transition of the whole of
humankind to the state of freedom. But humankind cannot tolerate such a slow
movement because it wants to be free and democratic as soon as possible. That
is the origin of the liberal mode of coercion and violence in the name of democracy and freedom. And it is very much understandable that today's Cultural
Studies tries to reject this kind of coercion and to defend the right of the individual subject to be slow, to be different, to bring its premodern cultural iden-

tity into the future as legitimate luggage that may not be confiscated. And, indeed, if the perfect, absolute democracy is not only unrealized, but also unrealizable, then the way that leads to it is an infinite one – and, being infinite, it makes no sense to force the homogeneity and universality of the infinite future on the heterogeneous cultural identities here and now. Rather, it is better to appreciate diversity and difference, to be more interested in where the subject is coming from than in where it is going to. So we can say that the present strong interest in diversity and difference is dictated in the first place by certain moral and political considerations – namely, by the defense of the so-called underdeveloped cultures against their marginalization and suppression by the dominating modern states in the name of progress. But at the same time, the ideal of progress is not completely rejected by contemporary cultural thought. This thought, rather, strives to find a compromise between the requirements of modern uniform democratic order and the rights of premodern cultural identities situated inside this general order.

But there is also one aspect in all this which I would like to stress. The discourse of diversity and difference presupposes a certain aesthetic choice – I mean here a purely aesthetic preference for the heterogeneous, for the mix, for the crossover. This aesthetic taste is, in fact, very much characteristic of the postmodern art of the late 1970s and '80s – that means during the same time that the discipline of Cultural Studies emerged and developed to its present form. This aesthetic taste is ostensibly very open, very inclusive – and in this sense also genuinely democratic. But, as we know, the postmodern taste is by no means as tolerant as it seems to be at first glance. The postmodern aesthetic sensibility rejects namely everything which is universal, uniform, repetitive, geometrical, minimalist, ascetic, monotonous, boring – everything gray, homogeneous, and reductionist. It dislikes Bauhaus, it dislikes Geometric Abstraction, it dislikes the bureaucratic and the technical: the classical avant-garde is accepted now only under the condition that its universalist claims are rejected and it becomes a part of a general heterogeneous picture. And, of course, the postmodern sensibility strongly dislikes – and *must* dislike – the gray, monotonous, uninspiring look of communism. I believe that this is, in fact, why the postcommunist world remains today a blind spot. Western spectators trained in certain aesthetics and conditioned by a certain artistic sensibility just do not want to look at the postcommunist world because they do not like what they see. The only things that contemporary Western spectators like about the postcommunist – or still communist – East are things like Chinese pagodas, or old Russian churches, or Eastern European cities that look like direct quotations from the 19th century – all the things that are noncommunist or pre-communist, that look diverse and different in the generally accepted sense of these words and that fit well within the framework of the contemporary heterogeneous Western taste. On the contrary, communist aesthetics seems to be *not* different, *not* diverse, *not* regional, *not* colorful enough – and, therefore, confronts the dominating pluralist, postmodern Western taste with its universalist, uniform Other.

But if we now ask ourselves: What is the origin of this dominating postmodern taste for colorful diversity? – there is only one possible answer: it is the market. It is a taste *formed by* contemporary markets, and it is a taste *for* the market. In this respect, it must be recalled that the emergence of the taste for the diverse and the different was directly related to the emergence of new, globalized information, media, and entertainment markets in the 1970s and the expansion of these markets in the '80s and '90s. Every expanding market, as we know, produces diversification and differentiation of the commodities that are offered on this market. Therefore, I believe that the discourse and the politics of cultural diversity and difference cannot be seen and interpreted correctly without being related to the market-driven practice of cultural diversification and differentiation in the last decades of the 20th century. This practice opened a third option for dealing with one's own cultural identity – beyond suppressing it or finding a representation for it in the context of existing political and cultural institutions. This third option is to sell, to commodify, to commercialize this cultural identity on the international media and touristic markets. It is this complicity between the discourse of cultural diversity and the diversification of cultural markets that makes a certain contemporary postmodern critical discourse so immediately plausible and, at the same time, so deeply ambiguous. Being extremely critical of the homogeneous space of the Modern state and its institutions, it tends to be uncritical of contemporary heterogeneous market practices – at least, by not taking them seriously enough into consideration.

Listening to postmodern critical discourse, one has an impression of being confronted with a choice between a certain universal order incorporated by the Modern state, on the one hand, and fragmented, disconnected, diverse "social realities" on the other. But, in fact, such diverse realities simply do not exist – and the choice is a completely illusory one. The apparently fragmented cultural realities are, namely, implicitly connected by the globalized markets. There is no real choice between universality and diversity. Rather, there is a choice between two different types of universality, between two universalities: between the universal validity of a certain political idea and the universal accessibility obtained through contemporary markets. Both – Modern state and contemporary market – are equally universal. But the universality of a political idea is an openly manifested, articulated, visualized universality that demonstrates itself immediately by the uniformity and repetitiveness of its external image. On the other hand, the universality of the market is a hidden, nonexplicit, nonvisualized universality that is obscured by the commodified diversity and difference. So we can say that the postmodern cultural diversity is a pseudonym for the universality of capitalist markets. The universal accessibility of heterogeneous cultural products which is guaranteed by the globalization of contemporary information markets has replaced the universal and homogeneous political projects of the European past – from the Enlightenment to communism. In the past, to be universal has meant to invent an idea or an artistic project that could unite people of different backgrounds, that could transcend the diversity of their already-existing cultural identities, that could be joined by everybody – if he or she would decide to join them. This notion of universality was linked to the concept of inner change, of inner rupture, of rejecting the past and embracing the future, to the notion of *metanoia* – of transition from the old identity to a new one. Today, on the contrary, to be universal means to be able to aetheticize one's identity as it is – without any attempt to change it. Accordingly, this already-existing identity is treated as a kind of ready-made in the universal context of diversity. Under this condition, becoming universal, abstract, uniform makes you aesthetically unattractive and commercially inoperative. As I have already said, for the contemporary taste, the universal looks too gray, boring, unspectacular, unentertaining, uncool to be aesthetically acceptable.

And that is why the postmodern taste is fundamentally an antiradical taste. Radical political aesthetics situates itself always at the *degré zéro* of literary and visual rhetoric, as Roland Barthes defined it[1] – and that means also at the *degré zéro* of diversity and difference. And this is also why the artistic avant-garde – the Bauhaus, etc. – seems to be so outmoded today: these artistic movements embody an aesthetic sensibility for the political, not for the market. I think there can be no doubt about it: every Utopian, radical taste is a taste for the ascetic, uniform, monotonous, gray, and boring. From Plato to the Utopias of the Renaissance to the modern, avant-garde Utopias – all radical political and aesthetic projects presented themselves always at the *degré zéro* of diversity. And that means: one needs to have a certain aesthetic preference for the uniform – as opposed to the diverse – to be ready to accept and to endorse radical political and artistic projects. This kind of taste can be, obviously, very unpopular, very unappealing to the masses. And that is one of the sources of the paradox that is well known to the historians of modern Utopias and of radical politics. On the one hand, these politics are truly democratic because they are truly universal, truly open to all – they are by no means elitist or exclusive. But, on the other hand, they appeal, as I said, to an aesthetic taste that is relatively rare. That is

---

1 Roland Barthes, *Le Degré zéro de l'écriture* (Paris: Gonthier, 1965); English trans. by Annette Lavers and Colin Smith, *Writing Degree Zero* (London: Cape, 1967).

why radical democratic politics presents itself often enough as exclusive, as elitist. One must be committed to radical aesthetics to accept radical politics – and
this sense of commitment produces relatively closed communities united by an
identical project, by an identical vision, by an identical historical goal. The way
of radical art and politics does not take us from closed premodern communities
to open societies and markets. Rather, it takes us from relative open societies to
closed communities based on common commitments. We know from the history of literature that all past Utopias were situated on remote islands or virtually inaccessible mountains. And we know how isolated, how closed the avant-
garde movements were – even if their artistic programs were genuinely open.
We have here a paradox of a universalist but closed community or movement –
a paradox which is truly modern. And that means, in the case of radical political
and artistic programs, we have to travel a different historical road than the one
described by standard Cultural Studies: it is not a road from a premodern community to an open society of universal communication. Rather, it is a road from
open and diverse markets toward Utopian communities based on a common
commitment to a certain radical project. These artificial, Utopian communities
are not based on the historical past, they are not interested in preserving its
traces, in continuing a tradition. On the contrary, these universalist communities are based on historical rupture, on the rejection of diversity and difference
in the name of a common cause.

To illustrate my point, I would like to quote a short but important text by
Kazimir Malevich: "On the Museum," from 1919. At that time, the new Soviet
government feared that the old Russian museums and art collections would be
destroyed by civil war and by the general collapse of state institutions. The
Communist Party responded by trying to secure and save these collections. In
his text, Malevich protested against this pro-museum policy of Soviet power by
calling on the state to not intervene on behalf of the old art collections because
their destruction could open the path to true, living art. After posing several
rhetorical questions such as "Do we need Rubens or the pyramids of Cheops?
Does the pilot flying in the heights of our new awareness need the aging Venus?
Do we need plaster copies of ancient cities borne by Greek columns?," Malevich
comes to the following conclusion:

> Life knows what it is doing, and if it is striving to destroy one must not interfere, since
> by hindering we are blocking the path to a new conception of life that is born within
> us. In burning a corpse we obtain one gram of powder: accordingly thousands of grave-
> yards could be accommodated on a single chemist's shelf. We can make a concession to
> conservatives by offering that they burn all past epochs, since they are dead, and set up
> one pharmacy.

Later, Malevich gives a concrete example of what he means:

> The aim [of this pharmacy] will be the same, even if people will examine the ashes of
> Rubens and all his art – a mass of ideas will arise in people, and will be often more alive
> than actual representation (and take up less room).[2]

For Malevich, the ideas inspired in someone viewing the ashes of Rubens' pictures are certainly not recollections of the burned past, but are instead forward-looking ideas stemming from the realization that a return to the past has become impossible. The sight of the ashes obstructing the way back to their origins is meant to point us – indeed, even compel us – toward the future. Actually, Malevich wrote this short text in a period which saw a widespread surge of enthusiasm for crematoriums in Russian left-wing circles. This fascination with irreparable destruction certainly represents a very traditional line of radical European progressivist thinking. Rousseau had marveled at the burning of the ancient library at Alexandria, a loss which was claimed by him to have opened up the way for a new school of writing. Cremation was viewed as a symbolic rejection of the church's promise of life after death, portrayed in Christian mythology as resurrection from the grave. Anyone willing to make way for the future should also agree to the cremation of his body and the scattering of his ashes. Also in the West, many left-wing intellectuals, particularly Marxists, drew up their wills according to this perspective. In the radically progressive mood that gripped Moscow during the postrevolutionary years, artists and writers in particular were invited to take part in specially organized tours to experience the newly built crematoriums in operation – which also demonstrated in what order and manner the various parts of the body were cremated. These guided tours were very popular, especially among avant-garde artists who were eager to take their friends and lovers with them to such displays. Highly typical in this respect were projects furthering the secondary use of heat emitted during the cremation of corpses, especially for heating public buildings. The inefficiency of Russian crematoriums at that time was cited as the reason why these projects were ultimately discarded. But in any case, the reduction of historical identities and differences to the ashes with their absolute neutrality, uniformity, and complete lack of diversity was seen as a remedy against every nostalgia for and return to origins. By the way, this latter option remains alive in our time. Progress in modern genetics now offers the possibility of reconstructing the genetic code of even the most thoroughly decomposed corpse. On the other hand, as far as we

2 Kazimir Malevich, "On the Museum," in *Essays on Art,* trans. Xenia Glowacki-Prus and Arnold McMillin, ed. Troels Andersen (New York: Wittenborn, 1971), vol. 1, pp. 68–72.

can judge at present, cremation fully erases the genetic code, making it indeed utterly impossible to reproduce the past.

On the political and economic level, the October Revolution effectuated precisely such a complete break with the past, such an absolute destruction of every individual heritage. This break with every kind of heritage was introduced by the Soviet power on the practical level by completely abolishing private property and transferring every individual heritage into the collective property. Finding a trace of one's own heritage in this undifferentiated mass of collective property has become as impossible as tracing the individual incinerated objects in the collective mass of ashes. This complete break with the past constitutes the political as well as artistic avant-garde. The notion of the avant-garde is often associated with the notion of progress. In fact, the term *avant-garde* suggests such an interpretation because of its military connotations – initially, it referred to the troops advancing at the head of an army. The term begins to be used to characterize the radical artistic movement relatively late. To Russian revolutionary art, this notion began to be applied systematically in the 1960s. The Russian artists themselves never used the term *avant-garde*. Instead, they used names like Futurism, or Suprematism, or Constructivism – meaning not moving progressively toward the future but being already situated in the future because of the radical break with the past, being at the end – or even beyond the end – of history, understood in Marxist terms as a history of class struggle, or as a history of different art forms, different art styles, different art movements. Malevich's famous *Black Square*, in particular, was understood as the point zero of art and the point zero of life – and because of that, as the point of identity between life and art, between artist and artwork, between spectator and art object, and so on. The end of history is understood here not in the same way as Francis Fukuyama understands it.[3] The end of history is here brought about not by the final victory of the market over every possible universal, unified political project but, on the contrary, by the ultimate political project, which means an ultimate rejection of the past, a final rupture with the history of diversity. It is the radical, the apocalyptic end of history – not the kind of end-of-history as is described by contemporary liberal theory. That is why the only real heritage of today's postcommunist subject – the real place where it is coming from – is the complete destruction of every kind of heritage, a radical, absolute break with the historical past and with every kind of separate cultural identity. Even the name of the country "Russia" was erased and substituted by a neutral name lacking any cultural tradition: Soviet Union. The con-

3 Francis Fukuyama, *The End of History and the Last Man* (New York: Free Press, 1992).

temporary Russian, post-Soviet citizen is coming from nowhere, from the point zero at the end of every possible history.

Now it becomes clear why it is so difficult for Cultural Studies to describe the way that postcommunist countries and populations entered after the demise of communism. On the one hand, this way seems to be the same old, well-known way from a closed society to an open society, from the community to civil society. But the communist community was in many ways much more radically modern in its rejection of the past than the countries of the West. And this community was closed not because of the stability of its traditions but because of the radicality of its projects. And that means: the postcommunist subject travels the same route as described by the dominating discourse of Cultural Studies – but it travels this route in the opposite direction: not from the past to the future, but from the future to the past; from the end of history, from existing in posthistorical, postapocalyptic time, back to historical time. Postcommunist life is a life backwards, a movement against the flow of time. It is, of course, not a completely unique historical experience. We know many modern apocalyptic, prophetic, religious communities which were subjected to the necessity of going back in historical time. The same can be said about some artistic avant-garde movements and also about some politically motivated communities as we know them from the 1960s. The chief difference is the magnitude of a country like Russia, which must now make its way back – from the future to the past. But it is an important difference. We know that many apocalyptic sects have committed collective suicide because they were incapable of going back in time. But such a huge country as Russia does not have the option of suicide – and has to proceed backwards whatever feelings it has about it.

It goes without saying that the opening of the communist countries has meant for their populations, in the first place, not democratization in political terms but the necessity to survive under new economic conditions dictated by the international markets. And this means already a return of the past, because all communist countries of Eastern Europe, including Russia, had their capitalist past. But until very recent times, the only acquaintance most of the Russian population had with capitalism was above all via pre-revolutionary, 19th-century Russian literature. The sum of what people knew about banks, loans, insurance policies, or privately owned companies was borrowed from reading Tolstoy, Dostoyevsky, and Chekhov at school – leaving impressions not unlike what people felt when they read about ancient Egypt. Of course, everyone was aware that the West was still a capitalist system; yet they were equally aware that they themselves were not living in the West, but in the Soviet Union. Then suddenly all these banks, loans, and insurance policies began to sprout up from their literary graves and become reality; so for ordinary Russians it feels now as if the ancient

Egyptian mummies had risen from their tombs and were now reinstituting all their old laws.

Beyond that – and this is probably the worst part of the story – the contemporary Western cultural markets, as well as contemporary Cultural Studies, require the Russians, Ukrainians, etc., to rediscover, to redefine, and to manifest their alleged cultural identity. To demonstrate, for example, their specific Russianness or Ukrainness, which, as I have tried to show, these postcommunist subjects do not have and cannot have because even if such cultural identities ever really existed they were already completely erased by the universalist Soviet social experiment. The uniqueness of communism lies in the fact that it is the first modern civilization that has historically perished – with the exception, perhaps, of the short-lived fascist regimes of the 1930s and '40s. Up until that time, all other civilizations that had perished were pre-modern; therefore they still had fixed identities which can be documented by some outstanding monuments like Egyptian pyramids. But the communist civilization used only the things that are modern and in everyone's use – and, actually, non-Russian in their origins. The typical Soviet thing was Soviet Marxism. But it makes no sense to present Marxism to the West as a sign of Russian cultural identity because Marxism has, obviously, Western and not Russian origins. The specific Soviet meaning and use of Marxism could function and be demonstrated only in the specific context of the Soviet state. Now that this specific context has dissolved, Marxism has returned to the West – and the traces of its Soviet use have simply disappeared. The postcommunist subject feels itself like a Coca-Cola bottle of Warhol brought back from the museum into the supermarket. In the museum, this Coca-Cola bottle was an artwork and had an identity – but back in the supermarket the same Coca-Cola bottle looks just like every other Coca-Cola bottle. Unfortunately, this complete break with the historical past and this complete erasure of cultural identity are as difficult to explain to the outside world as it is to describe the experience of war or prison to someone who has never been at war or in prison. And that is why, instead of trying to explain its lack of cultural identity, the postcommunist subject tries to invent one – acting like Zelig in the famous Woody Allen movie.

This postcommunist quest for a cultural identity that seems to be so violent, so authentic, and so internally driven is, actually, a hysterical reaction to the requirements of the international cultural markets. Eastern Europeans want now to be as nationalistic, as traditional, as culturally identified, etc., as all the others – but they still do not know how to do this. Therefore, their apparent nationalism is primarily a reflection of and an accommodation to the quest for otherness that is characteristic of the cultural taste of the contemporary West. Ironically, this accommodation to the present international market requirements and dominating cultural taste is mostly interpreted by Western public opinion as a "rebirth" of nationalism, a "return of the repressed," as an additional proof corroborating the current belief in otherness and diversity. A good example of this mirror effect – the East reflecting Western expectations of "otherness" and confirming them by artificially simulating its cultural identity – is the reshaping of Moscow architecture that took place almost immediately after the demise of the Soviet Union.

In the relatively brief period since the Soviet Union was disbanded, Moscow – once the Soviet, now the Russian capital – has already undergone an astonishingly rapid and thorough architectural transformation. A lot has been built in this short time, and the newly constructed buildings and monuments have redefined the face of the city. The question surely is, in what manner? The answer most frequently advanced in texts by Western observers and in some quarters of today's more earnest Russian architectural criticism is that Moscow's architecture is kitschy, restorative, and above all eager to appeal to regressive Russian nationalist sentiments. In the same breath, these commentators claim to make out a certain discrepancy between Russia's embrace of capitalism and the regressive, restorative aesthetics now evident in the Russian capital. The reason most often provided for this alleged contradiction is that, in view of the current wave of modernization and the host of economic and social pressures brought in its wake, these restorative aesthetics are intended as a compensatory measure through their evocation of Russia's past glory.

Without question, the aesthetic profile of modern Moscow is unambiguously restorative; although one encounters a few quotations of contemporary Western architecture, these references are always situated in a historicist, eclectic context. In particular, it is the most representative buildings of Moscow's new architecture that signal a programmatic rejection of the contemporary international idiom. Yet in Russia, as was already mentioned, capitalism is already experienced as restorative, namely as the return from the country's socialist future back to its pre-revolutionary, capitalist past. This in turn means that, rather than contradicting it, restorative architecture is actually complicit with the spirit of Russian capitalism. According to Russian chronology, modernism is a feature of the socialist future, which now belongs to the past, rather than being part of the capitalist past, which is now the future. In Russia, modernism is associated with socialism – and not, as it is in the West, with progressive capitalism. This is not merely because modernist artists often voiced socialist views, but also due to modernism's concurrence with a period when socialism prevailed in Russia – which means, actually, with the entire 20th century. That is why the new Moscow architecture wants to signal the return of the country to pre-revolutionary times, e.g., to the 19th century, by abandoning the modernism of the

20th century. Furthermore, Russians associate modernism above all with Soviet architecture of the 1960s and '70s, which by and large they utterly detested. During these decades, vast urban zones sprung up all over the Soviet Union, stocked with enormous, highly geometrical, standardized residential buildings of a gray and monotonous appearance and entirely bereft of artistic flair. This was architecture on the bottom line. Modernism in this guise is now spurned since it is felt to combine monotony and standardization and embody socialism's characteristic disregard for personal taste. As it happens, similar arguments can be heard today in a like-minded rejection of the oppositional and modernistically inclined dissident culture of the 1960s and '70s, whose proponents nowadays find approval for the most part only in the West. In Russia, the former dissident culture is dismissed for still being too Soviet, in other words, for being too arrogant, intolerant, doctrinaire, and modernist. Instead, the current *cause célèbre* in Russia is postmodernism. Thus, the postmodernist return of 19th-century eclecticism and historicism is currently celebrated in Russia as signaling the advent of true pluralism, openness, democracy, and the right to personal taste – as the immediate visual confirmation that Russian people feel liberated at last from the moralistic sermons of communist ideology and the aesthetic terror of modernism.

But, contrary to this rhetoric of diversity, inclusiveness, and liberation of personal taste, the new Moscow style is, in fact, wholly the product of centralized planning. Today's most representative and stylistically influential buildings have come about on the initiative of the post-Soviet mayor of Moscow, Yuri Luzhkov, and his preferred sculptor, Zurab Tsereteli. As was also the case with Stalinist architecture, which likewise was the result of close cooperation between Stalin and a small coterie of carefully appointed architects, this is an example of a most typically Russian phenomenon – a case, namely, of planned and centralized pluralism. The current Moscow style has distanced itself from the modernist monotony of the 1960s and '70s to the same degree as Stalinist architecture was divesting itself of the rigorism of the Russian avant-garde. The Moscow style is a revival of a revival. But most importantly, this return to popular taste and aesthetic pluralism in both cases ultimately proved to be a state-sponsored mise-en-scène.

The way this kind of controlled pluralism functions is well illustrated by a concrete example, the reconstruction of the Cathedral of Christ the Savior in the center of Moscow, a project which was just recently completed. This rebuilt cathedral is already counted as the most important post-Soviet architectural monument in Moscow today. More than anyone else, Luzhkov has prioritized the reconstruction of the cathedral as the city's most prestigious project. A few historical details should shed light on the implications of this restoration project.

МОСКВА.
Видъ Храма Христа Спасителя.

MOSCOU.
Vue du Temple du Sauveur

Konstantin Ton,
Cathedral of Christ the
Savior (1838–83;
demolished 1931)

The original Cathedral of Christ the Savior was built by the architect Konstantin Ton between 1838 and 1883 as a symbol of Russia's victory over the Napoleonic army; it was demolished on Stalin's orders in 1931. Immediately after its completion, the disproportionately huge cathedral was roundly criticized and ridiculed as monumental kitsch. This original view was shared by all subsequent architectural opinion, which was probably a further reason for the later decision to blow it up – it simply was deemed to be of little artistic value. At the same time, this demolition amounted to an intensely symbolic political act, since in spite of – or rather precisely due to – its kitschy character, the cathedral was immensely popular with the people, as well as being the most vivid expression of the power held by the Russian Orthodox Church in pre-revolutionary Russia. Hence its demolition came as the climax of the anticlerical campaign being waged in the late 1920s and '30s, which is why it has left such an indelible mark on popular memory.

Given its symbolic status, Stalin designed the square that had been cleared by the cathedral's demolition to be a site for the construction of the Palace of the Soviets, which was envisaged as the paramount monument to Soviet communism. The Palace of the Soviets was never built – just as the communist future that it was meant to commemorate was never achieved. Yet the design of the palace, drafted by Boris Iofan in the mid-1930s and, only after numerous revisions, approved by Stalin, is still regarded – justly – as the most notable architectural project of the Stalin era. For although the Palace of the Soviets was never actually erected, the project itself served as a prototype for all Stalinist architecture thereafter. This is particularly conspicuous in the notorious Stalinist skyscrapers built in the postwar years that even now largely dominate Moscow's skyline. Just as official ideology at that time claimed that communism was being

Moskva swimming pool (built 1958; closed 1994),
largest heated open-air pool in the world

Boris Iofan, Palace of the Soviets
(model, variant of original design, 1942–43)

prepared and prefigured by Stalinist culture, Stalin's skyscrapers were assembled
around the nonexistent Palace of the Soviets in order to herald its advent. However, in the course of de-Stalinization during the 1960s, this locale was given
over to build a gigantic open-air swimming pool, the Moskva, in lieu of the
palace; and, like the Cathedral of Christ the Savior, it subsequently enjoyed
enormous popularity. The pool was kept open even in the winter, so for several
months each year vast clouds of steam could be seen from all around, lending
the entire prospect the air of a subterranean hell. But this pool can also be
viewed as a place where Moscow's population could cleanse themselves of the
sins of their Stalinist past. One way or another, it is precisely its memorable
location that makes this swimming pool the most dramatic embodiment of the
"modernist" cultural consciousness of the 1960s and '70s: it represents a radical
renunciation of any type of architectural style, it is like swimming free beneath a
clear sky, the *degré zéro* of architecture.

Following the dissolution of the Soviet Union, the swimming pool was emptied and replaced by an exact replica of the demolished Cathedral of Christ the
Savior. Just how true to the original this copy in fact is has now become a highly
debated and contentious issue in Russia. But ultimately, all that counts is the
underlying intention, which unquestionably is to construct the nearest possible
replica of the demolished church – which functions symbolically as an exact
copy of the historical past, of Russian cultural identity. Far from being a monument to the new Russian nationalism or a symptom of the resurrection of anti-
Western sentiment, the rebuilding of the cathedral was designed to celebrate the
defeat of the Soviet universalist, modernist, avant-garde past and the return to
the folkloristic Russian identity, an identity that can be easily inscribed in the

Reconstructed Cathedral
of Christ the Savior, in
1996 (reconstruction:
1994 – November 1999,
consecrated July 2000)

new capitalist international order. And at first glance, such a symbolic return to national identity seems to be especially smooth in this case: during the entire Soviet period, the site of the cathedral remained, as I said, a void, a blank space – like a white sheet of paper that can be filled with every kind of writing. Accordingly, to reconstruct the old cathedral on its former site, there was no need to remove, to destroy any existing buildings. The Soviet time manifests itself here as an ecstatic interruption of historical time, as a pure absence, as materialized nothingness, as a void, a blank space. So it seems that if this void disappears, nothing will be changed: the deletion will be deleted, and a copy will become identical with the original – without any additional historical losses.

But in fact, this reconstruction demonstrates that the movement to the past – as, earlier, the movement to the future – only brings the country again and again to the same spot. And this spot, this point from which the panorama of Russian history can be seen in its entirety has a name: Stalinism. The culture of the Stalin time was already an attempt to reappropriate the past after the complete revolutionary break with it – to find in the historical garbage pit left behind by the Revolution certain things that could be useful for the construction of the new world after the end of history. The key principle of Stalinist dialectical materialism, which was developed and sealed in the mid-1930s, is embodied in the so-called "Law of the unity and the struggle of opposites." According to this principle, two contradictory statements can be simultaneously valid. Far from being mutually exclusive, "A" and "not A" must be engaged in a dynamic relationship: in its inner structure, a logical contradiction reflects the real conflict between antagonistic historical forces, which is what constitutes the

vitally dynamic core of life. Thus, only statements that harbor internal contradictions are deemed "vital" and hence true. That is why Stalin-era thinking
automatically championed contradiction to the detriment of the consistent
statement. Such great emphasis on contradictoriness was of course a legacy
dialectical materialism had inherited from Hegel's dialectic. Yet in the Leninist-
Stalinist model, as opposed to Hegel's postulates, this contradiction could never
be historically transcended and retrospectively examined. All contradictions
were constantly at play, remained constantly at variance with one another and
constantly comprised a unified whole. So rigid insistence on a single chosen
assertion was counted as a crime, as a perfidious assault on this unity of opposites. The doctrine of the unity and the struggle of opposites constitutes the
underlying motif and the inner mystery of Stalinist totalitarianism. For this
variant of totalitarianism lays claim to unifying absolutely all conceivable contradictions. Stalinism rejects nothing: it takes everything into its embrace and
assigns to everything the position it deserves. The only issue that the Stalinist
mindset finds utterly intolerable is an intransigent adherence to the logical consistency of one's own argument to the exclusion of any contrary position. In
such an attitude, Stalinist ideology sees a refusal of responsibility toward life and
the collective, an attitude that could only be dictated by malicious intentions.
The basic strategy of this ideology can be said to operate in the following manner: If Stalinism has already managed to unite all contradictions under the sheltering roof of its own thinking, what could be the point of partisanly advocating
just one of these various contrary positions? There can ultimately be no rational
explanation for such behavior, since the position in question is already well
looked after within the totality of Stalinist ideology. The sole reason for such a
stubborn act of defiance must consequently lie in an irrational hatred of the
Soviet Union and a personal resentment of Stalin. Since it is impossible to
reason with someone so full of hatred, regrettably the only remedy available is
reeducation or elimination.

     This brief detour into the doctrine of Stalinist dialectical materialism allows
us to formulate the criterion that intrinsically determined artistic creativity during the Stalin era: namely, each work of art endeavored to incorporate a maximum of internal aesthetic contradictions. This same criterion also informed the
strategies of art criticism in that period, which always reacted allergically whenever a work of art was found to be expressing a clearly defined, consistently
articulated, and unambiguously identifiable aesthetic position – the actual
nature of this position was considered secondary. Contrary to the explicit and
aggressive aesthetics of the artistic avant-garde, the aesthetic of the Stalin time
never defined itself in positive terms. Neither Stalinist ideology nor Stalinist art
politics are in any sense "dogmatic." Rather, Stalinist state power acts as an

invisible hand behind the heterogeneity, diversity, and plurality of individual artistic projects – censoring, editing, and combining these projects according to its own vision of the ideologically appropriate mix. Which means that the symbolic void on which the new-old cathedral is built is not such a blank space after all. It is an invisible, internal space of power hidden behind the diversity of artistic forms. That is why, in the present context, it became so easy to coordinate – if not to identify – this invisible hand of Stalinist state power with the invisible hand of the market. Both operate in the same space behind the diverse, heterogeneous, pluralistic surface. Far from signifying a rebirth of Russian cultural identity, the cathedral's copy in the center of Moscow symbolizes a revival of Stalinist cultural practices under the new market conditions.

This example of the revival of Soviet Stalinist aesthetics as an effect of postmodern taste which I have tried to elaborate at some length illustrates a certain point that I would like to make at the end of my presentation. Art is, of course, political. All attempts to define art as autonomous and to situate it above or beyond the political field are utterly naive. But having said that, we should not forget that art cannot be reduced to a specific field among many other fields which are functioning as arenas for political decisions. It is not enough to say that art is dependent on politics. I think it is more important to thematicize the dependence of political discourses, strategies, and decisions on aesthetic attitudes, tastes, preferences, and predispositions. As I have tried to show, radical politics cannot be dissociated from a certain aesthetic taste – the taste for the universal, for the *degré zéro* of diversity. On the other hand, liberal, market-oriented politics is correlated with the preference for diversity, difference, openness, and heterogeneity. In our time, the postmodern taste still prevails. Radical political projects have almost no chance today of being accepted by the public because they do not correlate with the dominant aesthetic sensibility. But the times are changing. And it is very possible that in some near future a new sensibility for radical art and politics will emerge again.

Globalization and Democracy

Michael Hardt and Antonio Negri

And [Jesus] asked him, What is thy name? And he answered, saying,
My name is Legion: for we are many *[et interrogabat eum quod tibi
nomen est et dicit ei Legio nomen mihi est quia multi sumus]*

Mark 5:9

The dominant modern notion of democracy has been intimately tied to the nation-state. To investigate the contemporary status of democracy, then, we should look first at the changing powers and role of the nation-state. Many theorists claim, and many others contest, that the diverse phenomena commonly grouped under the term "globalization" have eroded or even negated the powers of nation-states.[1] Too often, however, this is posed as an either/or proposition: either nation-states are still important or there is a new global order. Both, in fact, are true. The era of globalization has not brought the end of the nation-state – nation-states still fulfill extremely important functions in the establishment and regulation of economic, political, and cultural norms – but nation-states have indeed been displaced from the position of sovereign authority. A focus on the concept and practices of sovereignty helps to clarify this discussion.

We propose the concept of Empire to name our contemporary global arrangement. Empire refers above all to a new form of sovereignty that has succeeded the sovereignty of the nation-state, an unlimited form of sovereignty that knows no boundaries or, rather, knows only flexible, mobile boundaries. We borrow the concept of Empire from the ancient Roman figure in which Empire is seen to supercede the alternation of the three classical forms of government – monarchy, aristocracy, and democracy – by combining them in a single sovereign rule. Our contemporary Empire is indeed monarchical, and this is most apparent in times of military conflict when we can see the extent to which the Pentagon, with its atomic weapons and superior military technology, effectively rules the world. The supranational economic institutions, such as the WTO, the World Bank, and the IMF, also at times exercise a monarchical rule over global affairs. Our Empire, however, is also aristocratic, that is, ruled by a limited

---

1 The most detailed and influential argument that globalization has not undermined the powers of nation-states and that globalization is in this sense a myth is presented by Paul Hirst and Grahame Thompson, *Globalization in Question: The International Economy and the Possibilities of Governance*, 2d ed. (Cambridge, Mass.: Polity Press, 1999).

group of elite actors. The power of nation-states is central here because the few dominant nation-states manage to govern global economic and cultural flows through a kind of aristocratic rule. This aristocracy of nations is revealed clearly, for example, when the G8 nations meet or when the UN Security Council exercises its authority. The major transnational corporations too, in concert and in conflict, constitute a form of aristocracy. Finally, Empire is also democratic in the sense that it claims to represent the global people, although, as we will argue below, this claim to representation is largely illusory. The entire group of nation-states, the dominant and the subordinated ones together, fulfill the primary role here to the extent that they are assumed in some way to represent their peoples. The UN General Assembly is perhaps the most prominent symbol of this democracy of nations. When we recognize that nation-states do not in fact adequately represent their peoples, however, we can have recourse to nongovernmental organizations as the democratic or representative institutions. The functioning of the various different kinds of NGOs as democratic or representative mechanisms is a very complex and important question, which we should not pretend to treat adequately here. In short, Empire is a single sovereign subject that comprehends within its logic all three of these classical forms or levels of rule, the monarchic, the aristocratic, and the democratic. Empire, in other words, is a distinctive form of sovereignty for its ability to include and manage difference within its constitution.

From this perspective, we can see that the functions and authority of nation-states have not disappeared. It is probably more accurate to say that the primary functions of nation-states – the regulation of currencies, economic flows, population migrations, legal norms, cultural values, and so forth – have maintained their importance but been transformed through the contemporary processes of globalization. The radical qualitative shift should be recognized rather in terms of sovereignty. Nation-states can no longer claim the role of sovereign or ultimate authority as they could in the modern era. Empire now stands above the nation-states as the final authority and indeed presents a new form of sovereignty.

We should point out that this is a major historical shift only from the perspective of the dominant nation-states. The subordinate nations were never really sovereign. The entry into modernity for many nation-states was the entry into relations of economic and political subordination that undercut any sovereignty to which the nation might pretend. This shift in the form of sovereignty – from the modern sovereignty located in the nation-state to our postmodern imperial sovereignty – nonetheless effects us all. Even where national sovereignty was never a reality, the passage to Empire has transformed our forms of thought and the range of our political possibilities. In the light of Empire, we have to reconsider and reconceive all the key concepts of political philosophy.

Democracy Unrealized, Democracy Unrealizable This brings us back, first and foremost, to the concept of democracy. The dominant modern notion of democracy was, as we claimed at the outset, based on representational institutions and structures within the bounded national space and dependent on national sovereignty.[2] What was represented in the democratic national institutions was the people, and hence modern national sovereignty tended to take the form of popular sovereignty. The claim that the nation was sovereign, in other words, tended to become identical to the claim that the people was sovereign. But what or who is the people? The people is not a natural or empirical entity; one cannot arrive at the identity of the people by summing up or even averaging the entire population. The people, rather, is a *representation* that creates of the population a unity. Three elements are centrally important here. First of all, the people is one, as Hobbes and the entire modern tradition often repeated. The people can be sovereign only as an identity, a unity. Second, the key to the construction of the people is representation. The empirical multiplicity of the population is made an identity through mechanisms of representation – and here we should include both the political and the aesthetic connotations of the term "representation." Finally, these mechanisms of representation are based on a notion and a condition of measure – and by measure here we mean not so much a quantifiable condition but rather a bounded one. A bounded or measured multiplicity can be represented as a unity, but the immeasurable, the boundless cannot be represented. This is one sense in which the notion of the people is intimately tied to the bounded national space. In short, the people is not an immediate nor an eternal identity, but rather the result of a complex process that is proper to a specific social formation and historical period.

We can simplify this complex situation for a moment and consider only the institutional, political mechanisms of representation, of which the electoral process was at least ideologically the most important. The notion of "one person, one vote," for example, was one of the ideals toward which the various modern schema of popular representation and sovereignty tended. There is no need for us to argue here that these schema of popular representation have always been imperfect and in fact largely illusory. There have long been important critiques of the mechanisms of popular representation in modern democratic societies. It is perhaps an exaggeration to characterize elections as an opportunity to choose which member of the ruling class will misrepresent the people for the next two, four, or six years, but there is certainly some truth in it too and low voter turnout is undoubtedly a symptom of the crisis of popular

---

2 This is the fundamental argument of David Held, *Democracy and the Global Order: From the Modern State to Cosmopolitan Governance* (Stanford: Stanford University Press, 1995).

representation through electoral institutions. We think that today, however, popular representation is undermined in a more basic and fundamental way.

In the passage to Empire, national space loses its definition, national boundaries (although still important) are relativized, and even national imaginaries are destabilized. As national sovereignty is displaced by the authority of the new supranational power, Empire, political reality loses its measure. In this situation, the impossibility of representing the people becomes increasingly clear and thus the concept of the people itself tends to evaporate.

From an institutional, political perspective, imperial sovereignty conflicts with and even negates any conception of popular sovereignty. Consider, for example, the functioning of the supranational economic institutions, such as the World Bank, the IMF, and the WTO. To a large extent, the conditionality required by these institutions takes out of the hands of nation-states decisions over economic and social policy. The subordinate nation-states most visibly, but also the dominate ones, are subject to the rule of these institutions.[3] It is clear that these supranational economic institutions do not and cannot represent the people, except in the most distant and abstract sense – in the sense, for example, that some nation-states, which in some way represent their peoples, designate representatives to the institutions. If one looks for representation in such institutions, there will always inevitably remain a "democratic deficit." It is no accident, in our view, in other words, that these institutions are so isolated from popular representation. They function precisely to the extent that they elude mechanisms of popular representation.

Some of the best liberal Euro-American theorists of globalization do in fact argue that we need to reform the global system and reinforce the mechanisms of democratic political rule, but even they do not imagine that such supranational institutions could ever become representative in any popular sense. One of the fundamental obstacles is the problem of determining what or who is the people in such a conception. One would presumably have to develop a notion of the global people that extends beyond any national or ethnic conception to unite the entirety of humanity. Robert Keohane, for example, one of the leading theo-

---

3 Many authors characterize and lament this shift in decision making from national to supranational institutions as the increasing domination of the economic over the political (with the assumption that the nation-state is the only context in which to conduct politics). Several of these authors invoke the work of Karl Polanyi in the argument to re-embed economic markets within social markets. See, for example, James H. Mittleman, *The Globalization Syndrome: Transformation and Resistance* (Princeton, N.J.: Princeton University Press, 2000), and John Gray, *False Dawn: The Delusions of Global Capitalism* (New York: The New Press, 1998). In our view, it is a mistake to separate the economic and the political in this way and to insist on the autonomy of the political. The supranational economic institutions are also themselves political institutions. The fundamental difference is that these institutions do not allow for (even the pretense of) popular representation.

rists of global democratic reform, finds absurd the notion of a democratization of the supranational institutions in the representational, popular form of "one person, one vote." If that were the case, he reasons, the Chinese and the Indians would overwhelm us![4]

What then does constitute democratic reform in the views of the various leading liberal reformers such as Robert Keohane, Joseph Stiglitz, David Held, Richard Falk, and Ulrick Beck? It is striking in fact how widespread is the use of the term "democracy" in this literature and how universally accepted it is as a goal. One major component of democratic reform is simply greater transparency – Glasnost and Perestroika, perhaps we should understand this as a Gorbachev project for the age of globalization. Transparency itself, however, is not democracy and does not constitute representation.[5] A more substantive notion, which is omnipresent in the literature, is "accountability" (which is often paired with the notion "governance"). The concept of accountability could refer to mechanisms of popular representation, but it does not in these discourses. One has to ask "accountable to whom?" and then we find that the reformers do not propose making global institutions accountable to a global (or even a national) people – the people, precisely, is missing. Rather, the reform would involve making the global institutions accountable to other institutions and especially to a community of experts. If the IMF were more transparent and accountable to economic experts, for example, there would be safeguards against its implementing disastrous policies, such as those dictated by the IMF in Southeast Asia in the late 1990s. What is central and most interesting about the use of the terms "accountability" and "governance" in these discussions, however, is that these terms straddle so comfortably the political and the economic realms. Accountability and governance have long been central concepts in the theoretical vocabulary of capitalist corporations.[6] The notions of accountability and governance seem to be directed most clearly at assuring economic efficiency and stability, not at constructing any popular or representational form of democratic control. Finally, although the term "democracy" is omnipresent in the literature, no global version of democracy in its modern liberal form – that is, as popular representation – is even on the agenda. It seems, in fact, that the greatest conceptual obstacle that prevents these theorists from imagining a global representative schema is precisely the notion of the people. Who is the

---

4 Public discussion at Duke University, October 25, 2000.
5 Joseph Stiglitz, formerly the chief economist of the World Bank, claims that "transparency and public discussion provide a peculiar kind of democracy" ("Globalization and Its Discontents," public lecture at Duke University, March 27, 2001).
6 We are indebted to Craig Borowiak for his analyses of the concept of accountability in the contemporary globalization discussion.

global people? It seems impossible today to grasp the people as a political subject and moreover to represent it institutionally.[7]

We have thought it important to dwell so long on the question of the democratic reform of these institutions not only to take seriously the arguments of
the reformist theorists but also, and more importantly, because this discourse
can be found so widely among various factions of the protest movements against
the WTO, the World Bank, and the IMF. Groups call for greater inclusion and
representation in the decision-making process of the institutions themselves,
demanding, for example, trade union representation or NGO representation or
the like. Such demands may have some positive results, but they ultimately face
insurmountable obstacles. Our argument casts all this on a much more general
plane. If we conceive democracy in terms of a sovereign authority that is representative of the people, then democracy in the imperial age is not only unrealized but actually unrealizable.

Democracy of the Multitude   We thus have to explore new forms of democracy,
forms that are nonrepresentative or differently representative, to discover a
democracy that is adequate to our own times. We have already argued that the
modern notion of democracy is intimately tied to national sovereignty and a
fixed national space, that the modern notion, in short, is founded on measure.
Now we should turn our attention back to explore further the other element in
the equation, the people. The people, as we said earlier, is a product of representation. In modern political theory, the people is most strongly configured as the
product of the founding contractual act of bourgeois society, as all the modern
liberal theorists explain, from Hobbes to Rawls. The contract makes of the population a united social body. This contractual act, however, is nonexistent, mystificatory, and outdated. The contract is nonexistent in the sense that no anthropological or historical fact allows us to assume its reality; rather, the contract
negates any memory of its foundation, and this is certainly part of its violence,
its fundamental denial of difference. The contract is mystificatory, secondly, in
the sense that the people it constructs is presented as equal when the subjects
that form it are in fact unequal; the concepts of justice and legitimacy that

---

7 From this perspective, the project for the construction of a political Europe can appear to some as
  the solution to the puzzle of democracy in the age of globalization. The hypothesis is that the continent can substitute for the nation and revive the mechanisms of representational democracy. This
  seems to us, however, a false solution. Even if one could represent institutionally the European people as a coherent subject, a political Europe is not capable of claiming sovereign authority. Regional
  powers, like nation-states, are merely elements that function within the ultimate sovereignty of
  Empire.

ground it serve only the strongest, who exercise a force of domination and exploitation on the rest of the population. This concept of a people formed through the contract is outdated, finally, because it looks to a society forged by capital: contractualism, people, and capitalism function in fact to make of the plurality a unity, to make of differences an homologous totality, to make of the wealth of all the singular lives of the population the poverty of some and the power of others. But this no longer works: it used to work as long as labor, needs, and desires were so miserable that they received the command of capital as a welcome comfort and a source of security when faced with the risks of the construction of value, the liberation of the imagination, and the organization of society. Today, however, the terms have changed. It is rather our monstrous intelligence and our cooperative power that are put in play: we are a multitude of powerful subjects, a multitude of intelligent monsters.

We thus need to shift our conceptual focus from the people to the multitude. The multitude cannot be grasped in the terms of contractualism – and in general in the terms of transcendental philosophy. In the most general sense, the multitude defies representation because it is a multiplicity, unbounded and immeasurable. The people is represented as a unity but the multitude is not representable because it is monstrous in the face of the teleological and transcendental rationalisms of modernity. In contrast to the concept of the people, the concept of the multitude is a singular multiplicity, a concrete universal. The people constituted a social body but the multitude does not – the multitude is the flesh of life. If on one side we contrast the multitude with the people, on the other side we should contrast it with the masses or the mob. The masses and the mob are most often used to name an irrational and passive social force, dangerous and violent precisely because so easily manipulated. The multitude, in contrast, is an active social agent – a multiplicity that acts. The multitude is not a unity, as is the people, but, in contrast to the masses and the mob, we can see that it is organized. It is an active, self-organizing agent. One great advantage of the concept of the multitude is that it displaces all the modern arguments based on the fear of the masses and even those about the tyranny of the majority, which have so often served as a kind of blackmail to force us to accept and even call for our own domination.

From the perspective of power, however, what can be done with the multitude? In effect, there is nothing to do with it, because the nexus among the unity of the subject (people), the form of its composition (contract among individuals), and the mode of government (monarchy, aristocracy, and democracy, separate or combined) has been blown apart. The radical modification of the mode of production through the hegemony of immaterial labor-power and cooperative living labor – this ontological, productive, biopolitical revolution –

has overturned the parameters of "good government" and destroyed the modern idea of a community that functions for capitalist accumulation, as capitalism imagined it from the beginning.

Allow us a brief parenthesis. Between the 15th and 16th centuries, when modernity appeared in the form of a revolution, the revolutionaries imagined themselves as monsters. Gargantua and Pantagruel can serve as emblems for all the giants and extreme figures of freedom and invention that have come down to us through the ages and proposed the gigantic task of becoming more free. Today we need new giants and new monsters that bring together nature and history, labor and politics, art and invention to demonstrate the new power that the birth of "general intellect," the hegemony of immaterial labor, the new passions of the abstract activity of the multitude provide to humanity. We need a new Rabelais or, really, several.

Spinoza and Marx spoke of the democracy of the multitude or, rather, a form of democracy that no longer has anything to do with the democracy that, along with monarchy and aristocracy, comprise the classical forms of government. The democracy that Spinoza advocates is what he calls an *absolute* democracy – absolute in the sense of being unbounded and immeasurable. The conceptions of social contracts and bounded social bodies are thus completely cast aside. When we say that absolute democracy is outside of the theory (and the mystificatory practice) of the classical forms of government, we mean also, obviously, that any attempt to realize democracy through the reform of the imperial institutions will be vain and useless. We mean, furthermore, that the only path to realize a democracy of the multitude is the path of revolution. What does it mean, however, to call for a revolutionary democracy adequate to the imperial world? Up to this point, we have simply focused on what it is not. It is no longer something that depends on the concept of nation (on the contrary, it is increasingly defined by the struggle against the nation). We have also seen that it is something that does not correspond to the concept of the people and in fact is opposed to any attempt to present as unitary what is different. We need at this point to look to other concepts to help us understand a democracy of the multitude. The concept of counterpower seems fundamental to us when we deal with these new contents of the absolute democracy of the multitude.

Modern Counterpower and the Paradoxes of Modern Insurrection   The concept of counterpower consists primarily of three elements: resistance, insurrection, and constituent power. It is important to recognize, however, that, like the dominant concept of democracy, the dominant concept of counterpower was defined in modernity by the national space and national sovereignty. The effect was that during the modern era – at least since the French Revolution and throughout the long phase of socialist and communist agitation – the three elements of the concept of counterpower (resistance, insurrection, and constituent power) tended to be viewed as external to one another, and thus functioned as different strategies or at least different historical moments of revolutionary strategy. Once the elements were thus divided, the entire concept of counterpower tended to be reduced to one of its elements, the concept of insurrection or, really, civil war. Lenin's political thought is exemplary in this regard. For Lenin, counterpower – that is, in his terms, the dualism of power that consisted of the rise of a proletarian power against the bourgeoisie – could only exist for a very brief period, precisely in the period of insurrection. Resistance, which for Lenin principally took the form of syndicalist wage struggles, had an important political role but it was fundamentally separate from the revolutionary process. Constituent power too tended to disappear in Lenin's vision because every advance of constituent power immediately became an element of the new state, that is, transformed into a new constituted power. What remained of the revolutionary concept of counterpower for Lenin was thus primarily the great force of insurrection or, really, civil war against the dictatorship of the bourgeoisie.

Once we recognize how the modern notion of counterpower was reduced to insurrection, we should look more closely at the conditions and fortunes of modern insurrection. Paradoxically and tragically, even when the modern communist insurrection managed to win, it really lost because it was immediately imprisoned in an alternation between national and international war. Finally it becomes clear that national insurrection was really an illusion.

The Parisian Communards set the model in 1871 for all modern communist insurrection. Their example taught that the winning strategy was to transform international war into civil war – national, interclass war. International war was the condition of possibility for launching insurrection. The Prussians at the gates of Paris not only toppled the Second Empire of Louis Bonaparte, but also made possible the overthrow of Thiers and the Republic. Paris armed is revolution armed! Forty years later, the Bolsheviks too needed the inter-European war, that is, World War I, as the condition of insurrection. And once again the Germans, the national enemy, acted as condition of possibility. The Bolsheviks too transformed international war into civil war.

The tragedy of modern insurrection, however, is that national civil war is immediately and ineluctably transformed back into international war – or, really, a defensive war against the united international bourgeoisie. A properly national, civil war is really not possible insofar as a national victory only gives rise to a new and permanent international war. Therefore, exactly the same condition that makes possible the national communist insurrection – that is, international war – is what imprisons the victorious insurrection or, rather, distorts it into a permanent military regime. The Parisian Communards were caught in this double bind. Marx saw clearly the mistakes of the Commune but did not show that the other options open to them would have equally been mistakes. The choice was either give all power to the Central Committee and march on the bourgeois army at Versailles – that is, become a military regime – or be defeated and massacred. It would not have ended with a victory at Versailles, either. The Prussian and the English ruling classes would not have allowed that. The victory of the Commune would have been the beginning of an unending international war. The Soviet victory only confirmed that double bind. The military victory in Russia, the complete defeat of the national bourgeoisie, only opened an international war (hot and then cold) that lasted for over seventy years.

Insurrection during the cold war operated under the same structure, but only refined the model, reducing international war to its essential form. The cold war fixed the conditions of modern insurrection into a permanent state. On one hand, there was a permanent state of international war that was already coded in class terms. The representational structure of the two opposing powers forced its coding on all new movements. The alternative was also determining in material terms, since an insurrectionary movement could solicit the aid of one of the superpowers or play them off against one another. The formula for national insurrection was ready-made. But also ready-made and ineluctable were the limits of national insurrection. No movement could escape the great cold war alternative. Even insurrectionary movements that did not conceive of themselves primarily in class terms – anticolonial movements in Asia and Africa, antidictatorial movements in Latin America, black power movements in the US – were inevitably forced to be represented on one side of the great struggle. National insurrection during the cold war was ultimately illusory. The victorious insurrection and the revolutionary nation were finally only pawns in the great cold war chess game.

The contemporary relevance that emerges from this brief history of modern insurrection centers around two facts or, really, one fact with two faces. On one side today, with the decline of national sovereignty and the passage to Empire, gone are the conditions that allowed modern insurrection to be thought and at times to be practiced. Today it thus seems almost impossible even to think insurrection. On the other side, however, what is gone is also exactly the condition that kept modern insurrection imprisoned in the interminable play between national and international wars. Today, therefore, when considering the question of insurrection, we are faced with both a great difficulty and an enormous possibility. Let us move back, however, to the more general consideration of counterpower.

A Counterpower of Monstrous Flesh   With the contemporary decline of the sovereignty of the nation-state, it is possible once again to explore the concept of counterpower in its full form and return to its conceptual foundation. Today the relationship among resistance, insurrection, and constituent power has the possibility to be an absolutely continuous relationship, and in each of these moments there is the possibility of the expression of the power of invention. In other words, each of the three moments – resistance, insurrection, and constituent power – can be internal to one another, forming a common means of political expression. The context in which – and against which – this counterpower acts is no longer the limited sovereignty of the nation-state but the unlimited sovereignty of Empire, and thus counterpower too must be reconceived in an unlimited or unbounded way.

Here we are faced with a new imposing and exciting theoretical and political problematic. In our present imperial context, we need to rethink the concepts of resistance, insurrection, and constituent power – and rethink too their internal connections, that is, their unity in the concept and practice of counterpower. When we look across the field of contemporary theoretical production, we can see that we do already have some tools to work with on this terrain. Certainly, Foucault's development of the concept of resistance along with all the work that has followed on his, James Scott's notion of the "weapons of the weak," and all the other work that has emerged on micropolitical resistance should be a foundation for any investigation into this problematic. The great limitation of all this work, however, is that it never manages to discover the internal connection that resistance can have with insurrection and constituent power. Resistance can be a powerful political weapon, in other words, but isolated, individual acts of resistance can never succeed in transforming the structures of power.[8] Today, however, the other two components of counterpower remain completely undeveloped. An insurrection is a collective gesture of revolt, but what are the terms for insurrection today and how can it be put into practice? It should be clear that we can no longer translate insurrection immediately into civil war, as was so common in the modern era, if by "civil" we mean a war within the national space. Insurrection is indeed still a war of the dominated against the rulers within a single society, but that society now tends to be an unlimited global society, imperial society as a whole. How is such an insurrection against Empire to be put into practice? Who can enact it? Where is the internal connection between the micropolitics of resistance and imperial insurrection? And how can we today conceive of constituent power, that is, the common invention of a new

---

8 From our perspective, Félix Guattari, especially in his work with Gilles Deleuze, is the one who has gone furthest to push the notion of resistance toward a conception of molecular revolution.

social and political constitution? Finally, we need to think resistance, insurrection, and constituent power as one indivisible process, the three forged together into a full counterpower and ultimately a new alternative social formation. These are enormous questions and we are only at the very first stages of addressing them.

Rather than confronting them directly, it seems better to us to shift registers and take a different view on the entire problematic. We have to find some way to shake off the shackles of reasonableness, to break out of the common forms of thinking about democracy and society, to create more imaginative and inventive perspectives. Let us begin by looking at the most basic foundation of counterpower where its three elements – resistance, insurrection, and constituent power – most intimately correspond. The primary material of counterpower is the flesh, the common living substance in which the corporeal and the intellectual coincide and are indistinguishable. "The flesh is not matter, is not mind, is not substance," Maurice Merleau-Ponty writes. "To designate it, we should need the old term 'element,' in the sense it was used to speak of water, air, earth, and fire, that is, in the sense of a *general thing* … a sort of incarnate principle that brings a style of being wherever there is a fragment of being. The flesh is in this sense an 'element' of Being."[9] The flesh is pure potentiality, the unformed stuff of life, an element of being. One should be careful, however, not to confuse the flesh with any notion of naked life, which conceives of a living form stripped of all its qualities, a negative limit of life.[10] The flesh is oriented in the other direction, toward the fullness of life. We do not remain flesh, flesh is but an element of being; we continually make of our flesh a form of life.

In the development of forms of life, we discover ourselves as a multitude of bodies and at the same time we recognize that every body is itself a multitude – of molecules, desires, forms of life, inventions. Within each of us resides a legion of demons or, perhaps, of angels – this is the basic foundation, the degree zero of the multitude. What acts on the flesh and gives it form are the powers of invention, those powers that work through singularities to weave together hybridizations of space and metamorphoses of nature – the powers, in short, that modify the modes and forms of existence.

---

9 Maurice Merleau-Ponty, *The Visible and the Invisible*, ed. Claude Lefort, trans. Alphonso Lingis (Evanston, Ill.: Northwestern University Press, 1968), p. 139. Consider also Antonin Artaud's conception of the flesh: "There are intellectual cries, cries born of the *subtlety* of the marrow. That is what I mean by Flesh. I do not separate my thought from my life. With each vibration of my tongue I retrace all the pathways of my thought in my flesh" ("Situation of the Flesh," in *Selected Writings*, ed. Susan Sontag, trans. Helen Weaver [Berkeley: University of California Press, 1988], p. 110).

10 See Giorgio Agamben, *Homo Sacer: Sovereign Power and Bare Life*, trans. Daniel Heller-Roazen (Stanford: Stanford University Press, 1998).

In this context it is clear that the three elements of counterpower (resistance, insurrection, and constituent power) spring forth *together* from every singularity and from every movement of bodies that constitute the multitude. Acts of resistance, collective gestures of revolt, and the common invention of a new social and political constitution pass together through innumerable micropolitical circuits – and thus in the flesh of the multitude is inscribed a new power, a counterpower, a living thing that is against Empire. Here are born the new barbarians, monsters, and beautiful giants that continually emerge from *within* the interstices of imperial power and *against* imperial power itself. The power of invention is monstrous because it is excessive. Every true act of invention, every act, that is, that does not simply reproduce the norm is monstrous. Counterpower is an excessive, overflowing force, and one day it will be unbounded and immeasurable. This tension between the overflowing and the unbounded is where the monstrous characteristics of the flesh and counterpower take on a heightened importance. As we are waiting for a full epiphany of the (resistant, revolting, and constituent) monsters, there grows a recognition that the imperial system, that is, the contemporary form of repression of the will to power of the multitude, is at this point on the ropes, at the margins, precarious, continually plagued by crisis. (Here is where the weak philosophies of the margin, difference, and nakedness appear as the mystifying figures and the unhappy consciousness of imperial hegemony.)

Against this, the power of invention (or, really, counterpower) makes common bodies out of the flesh. These bodies share nothing with the huge animals that Hobbes and the other theorists of the modern state imagined when they made of the Leviathan the sacred instrument, the pitbull of the appropriative bourgeoisie. The multitude we are dealing with today is instead a multiplicity of bodies, each of which is crisscrossed by intellectual and material powers of reason and affect; they are cyborg bodies that move freely without regard to the old boundaries that separated the human from the machinic. These multiple bodies of the multitude enact a continuous invention of new forms of life, new languages, new intellectual and ethical powers. The bodies of the multitude are monstrous, irrecuperable in the capitalist logic that tries continually to control it in the organization of Empire. The bodies of the multitude, finally, are queer bodies that are insusceptible to the forces of discipline and normalization but sensitive only to their own powers of invention.

When we point to the powers of invention as the key to a formation of counterpower in the age of Empire, we do not mean to refer to some exclusive population of artists or philosophers. In the political economy of Empire, the power of invention has become the general and common condition of production. This is what we mean when we claim that immaterial labor and general intellect have come to occupy a dominant position in the capitalist economy.

If, as we have argued, the dominant form of democracy that modernity and European history has bequeathed us – popular, representational democracy – is not only unrealized but actually unrealizable, then one should not view our proposition of an alternative democracy of the multitude as a utopian dream. The unrealizability of the old notion of democracy should, rather, force us to move forward. This also means that we are entirely within and completely against imperial domination, and there is no dialectical path possible. The only invention that now remains for us is the invention of a new democracy, an absolute democracy, unbounded, immeasurable. A democracy of powerful multitudes, not only of equal individuals but of powers equally open to cooperation, to communication, to creation. Here there are no programs to propose – and who would dare still today do such a thing after the 20th century has ended? All the modern protagonists – the priests, the journalists, the preachers, the politicians – may still be of use to imperial power, but not to us. The philosophical and artistic elements in all of us, the practices of working on the flesh and dealing with its irreducible multiplicities, the powers of unbounded invention – these are the leading characteristics of the multitude. Beyond our unrealized democracy, there is a desire for a common life that needs to be realized. We can perhaps, mingling together the flesh and the intellect of the multitude, generate a new youth of humanity through an enormous enterprise of love.

Democracy, Economics, and the Military

Manuel De Landa

"If we are prepared to make an unequivocal distinction between the market economy and capitalism, might this offer us a way of avoiding that 'all or nothing' which politicians are always putting to us, as if it was impossible to retain the market economy without giving the monopolies a free hand, without nationalizing everything in sight? ... As long as the solutions put forward amount to replacing the monopoly of capital with the monopoly of the State, compounding the faults of the former with those of the latter, it is hardly surprising that the classic left-wing solutions do not arouse great electoral enthusiasm. If people set about looking for them, seriously and honestly, economic solutions could be found which would extend the area of the market and would put at its disposal the economic advantages so far kept to itself by one dominant group of society."[1] With these words, the great historian Fernand Braudel concludes his three-volume masterpiece on the economic history of the West. Clearly, he considers the thought expressed in this paragraph to be important enough to serve as a conclusion to his lifelong pursuit of charting the development of the institutions that have shaped the economic life of Europe and its colonies and ex-colonies. But what could he possibly mean by it? How can "capitalism" be unequivocally distinguished from "the market economy" if, according to most theories on the left and right of the political spectrum, the two terms are synonymous? Braudel has two things in mind here, both of which he considers to be important historical discoveries: one is that economic institutions, when examined in concrete historical detail, cannot be said to form an overall system; the other that large economic institutions, forming oligopolies or monopolies, cannot be said to have the same dynamics as networks of small market firms. Moreover, Braudel argues that small firms have always been the source of innovation in the economy, while large ones have been the locus of market power and the manipulation of market forces. I will argue in what fol-

---

1 Fernand Braudel, *The Perspective of the World* (New York: Harper & Row, 1986), p. 632.

lows that both of these ideas, the absence of overall system and the distinction between markets and capitalist corporations, are crucial for an assessment of the compatibility of economic institutions with democratic principles.

Let me first quote Braudel again on these two points. He writes that "we should not be too quick to assume that capitalism embraces the whole of western society, that it accounts for every stitch in the social fabric ... that our societies are organized from top to bottom in a 'capitalist system.' On the contrary, ... there is a dialectic still very much alive between capitalism on one hand, and its antithesis, the 'non-capitalism' of the lower level on the other."[2] This lower level Braudel identifies with the market and he adds that capitalism was carried upward and onward on the shoulders of small shops and "the enormous creative powers of the market, of the lower storey of exchange ... [This] lowest level, not being paralyzed by the size of its plant or organization, is the one readiest to adapt; it is the seed bed of inspiration, improvisation and even innovation, although its most brilliant discoveries sooner or later fall into the hands of the holders of capital. It was not the capitalists who brought about the first cotton revolution; all the new ideas came from enterprising small businesses."[3]

Notice that Braudel is *not* saying that at some point in the economic history of the West, large firms with monopoly power replaced competitive small firms, as if the capitalist system had gone from one stage to another of its development. He is making a much more radical claim: that as far back as the 13th century, big business has coexisted with small enterprises as two very different forms of economic institution, and that the two continue to coexist today. In this regard, and from the point of view of a progressive leftist politico-economic philosophy, the work of Braudel represents a sharp break with past assessments of the role of markets in history. His views are incompatible with those of Marxist historians and closer to the Institutionalist school of economics, the school that began with the work of Thorstein Veblen and Wesley Mitchell, but which today is best represented by the work of John Kenneth Galbraith.

Galbraith, for example, draws a sharp distinction between the world of small businesses, which are mainly price takers and where competition is largely anonymous, from the world of oligopolies, where strategic rivalry is the rule and where prices are managed. Only the former can be said to have any degree of self-regulation, while the latter is, as Galbraith puts it, a "planning system."[4] This phrase means two things. One is that *within* large corporations decision

---

2 Ibid., p. 630.
3 Ibid., p. 631.
4 John Kenneth Galbraith, *The New Industrial State* (Boston: Houghton Mifflin, 1978).

making is not decentralized as it is in true markets, but strongly hierarchical, with decisions about production, investment, or marketing made by professional managers. The other is that *between* corporations, and despite the fact that overt cooperation is forbidden by law in many democratic countries, there are a variety of links that allow these large organizations to coordinate their activities. The most important of these indirect linkages is what Institutionalists call "interlocking directorates," that is, the practice by large banks and insurance companies to place their people on the boards of directors of rival corporations in order to reduce the chance of price wars and other forms of competition that affect profits and control.[5] In this regard, the corporate world, both in its internal as well as external organization, is closer in form to State institutions than to markets.

From the point of view of their impact on democratic principles, the main distinction between these two worlds is summarized in the phrase "market power." In economic textbooks, this phrase is associated with the ability of monopolistic firms to manipulate market forces by, for example, restricting the amount of output of a given product in order to artificially drive up its price. But as studies done by members of the Institutionalist school have clearly shown, this ability to manipulate prices is but one of the many manifestations of the market power that large scale gives to monopolies and oligopolies. A much more direct impact on democratic institutions, for instance, comes from their ability to perform "economic sabotage" of public policies. Well-studied cases include the sabotage by large automobile manufacturers of environmental policies connected with fuel-efficiency standards, using threats of factory closings and large layoffs of workers to get laws adjusted to their benefit. Another example of the degree to which gigantism itself allows some organizations to conduct economic extortion is the forced bailout of failing or mismanaged firms, such as the bailout of Chrysler in the 1980s. In this case, large scale allowed both the privatization of profits and the socialization of losses. Less dramatic examples of corporate extortion include the forceful extraction of a variety of benefits such as tax breaks, low-interest bonds, free land, and cheap electricity, or the erection of barriers to foreign competition, such as quotas, bars, and other forms of protectionism.[6]

These uses of economic power are, of course, very well known, but they have for many years been conceptualized by the Left as examples of the way in which the capitalist system subverts democratic institutions. However, within a concep-

5 See John Munkirs, "Centralized Private Sector Planning," in *The Economy as a System of Power*, ed. Marc R. Tool and Warren J. Samuels (New Brunswick, N.J.: Transaction Books, 1989).
6 See Walter Adams and James Brock, "Corporate Power and Economic Sabotage," in ibid.

tual framework in which "the capitalist system" does not exist, we need to approach these cases in a new light. One possibility is to tackle the question of market power in terms of the distinction between, on the one hand, *economies of scale*, and on the other, *economies of agglomeration*. The basic principle of economies of scale is the production of large runs of more or less homogeneous products, the cost of each replica decreasing as the scale of production increases. By standardizing production, costs can be spread across a large number of identical units and the law of diminishing returns overcome. By contrast, economies of agglomeration involve bringing together, in a particular region or city, a large number of small producers. The efficiencies of this arrangement derive from several sources. First, there are many services, such as accounting and legal services, for example, which large corporations can provide internally but which small firms cannot afford individually. Firms providing these services can move into a agglomerated region to profit from the existence of so many potential clients. Second, and despite the fact that the small firms in question compete against each other, there is a constant sharing of knowledge among them, some of it in the form of shop-talk, some due to the fact that engineers and other knowledge workers move around the region employed first by one, then by another firm.

Well-studied contemporary cases of economies of agglomeration include Silicon Valley and a region in northern Italy called Emilia-Romagna. Though in both cases we have a hybrid phenomenon, that is, they include large organizations operating on economies of scale, the main component in both regions are networks of small producers competing not so much at the level of costs, but *at the level of product design*, and growing not by vertical or horizontal integration, but by *continuous splitting and specialization*. The success of these regional economies, and their proven resiliency to economic downturns, have made them alternative paradigms to corporate capitalism in the eyes of the scholars who have researched them. In particular, these researchers point out that, unlike corporations which internalize not only services but also the production of knowledge in their research and development laboratories, networks of small producers do not internalize but share services and knowledge. This means that no firm can leave the region without also surrendering access to services and to the talent pool that is tied to the region. This is in stark contrast to corporations which, having internalized these external benefits, gain locational mobility as a result. And it is precisely this self-sufficiency and mobility which allows them to close large factories in one place to open them elsewhere, and thus to be able to threaten local governments with the consequences of such a move, not only widespread unemployment but also loss of tax revenue.

Fernand Braudel has shown, with plenty of historical evidence, that these two types of economic dynamics have coexisted for centuries, a coexistence which implies that the economy is a more heterogeneous entity than we thought, and it is this intrinsic heterogeneity that leads Braudel to deny that there is such a thing as a homogeneous "capitalist system." In turn, his assertion of the creativity of the market can now be understood as the belief that economies of agglomeration, and competition in terms of design, are an important source of innovation. From the point of view that concerns us here, the absence of market power and the crucial role played by creativity implies that economies of agglomeration are more compatible with democratic principles than are economies of scale.

This conclusion may be strengthened by analyzing a different aspect of economic power, one which Braudel does not mention but which Michel Foucault has dealt with in his history of discipline and punishment. Foucault has argued for the inclusion of military institutions as part of the history of economic ones, or at least, of that aspect of economic power that involves *control of the labor process* within firms.[7] It has become routine to think of Frederick Taylor, the late 19th-century creator of so-called "scientific management," as the pioneer of labor process analysis, that is, the breaking down of a given factory practice into micro-movements and the combination of these movements into streamlined routines for greater efficiency and centralized management control. But the Dutch commander Maurice of Nassau had already applied these methods to the training of his soldiers beginning in the 1560s. Maurice analyzed the motion needed to load, aim, and fire a weapon into its micro-movements, redesigned them for maximum efficiency, and then imposed them on his soldiers via continuous drill and discipline. As Foucault argues, while the soldiers increased their efficiency tremendously as a collective whole, each individual soldier lost control over his actions in the battlefield. A similar point applies to the application of this idea to factory workers, before and after Taylorism. Collectively workers became more productive, generating the economies of scale so characteristic of 20th-century big business, while simultaneously completely losing control of their individual actions.

Indeed, the very idea of mass production and the industrial discipline it requires is not of bourgeois origin, as Marxist historians would want us to believe when they speak of Fordism, but was born in military arsenals in 18th-century France, and institutionalized as a practice in American arsenals and armories in the early 19th century. The first mass-produced objects were fire weapons with interchangeable parts, and the first workers to bear the brunt of

---

7 Michel Foucault, *Discipline and Punish: The Birth of the Prison*, trans. Alan Sheridan (New York: Vintage Books, 1979).

modern industrial discipline were the craftsmen who worked in those military factories. Recent historians have rediscovered several other cases of the military origins of what were once thought to be civilian innovations. Another important example involves the development of the modern corporation itself in the United States during the 19th century. The first American big business was the railroad industry, which developed the management techniques that many other large enterprises would later adopt. This much is well known. What is not so well known is that military engineers were deeply involved in the creation of the first railroads and that they developed many of the features of management which later came to characterize just about every large commercial enterprise in the United States, Europe, and elsewhere. In the words of historian Charles O'Connell:

> As the railroads evolved and expanded, they began to exhibit structural and procedural characteristics that bore a remarkable resemblance to those of the Army. Both organizations erected complicated management hierarchies to coordinate and control a variety of functionally diverse, geographically separated corporate activities. Both created specialized staff bureaus to provide a range of technical and logistical support services. Both divided corporate authority and responsibility between line and staff agencies and officers and then adopted elaborate written regulations that codified the relationship between them. Both established formal guidelines to govern routine activities and instituted standardized reporting and accounting procedures and forms to provide corporate headquarters with detailed financial and operational information which flowed along carefully defined lines of communication. As the railroads assumed these characteristics, they became America's first "big business."[8]

Thus, the transfer of military practices to the civilian world influenced the lives not only of workers, but of the managers themselves. And the influence did not stop with the development of railroads. The "management science" which is today taught in business schools is a development of military "operations research," a discipline created during World War II to tackle a variety of tactical, strategic, and logistical problems. And it was the combination of this "science of centralization" and the availability of large computers that, in turn, allowed the proliferation of transnational corporations and the consequent internationalization of the routinization of production processes. Much as skills were replaced by commands in the shop floor, so were prices replaced by

---

8 Charles F. O'Connell, Jr., "The Corps of Engineers and the Rise of Modern Management," in *Military Enterprise and Technological Change: Perspectives on the American Experience*, ed. Merritt Roe Smith (Cambridge, Mass.: MIT Press, 1985), p. 88.

commands at the management level. Thus, there is a different sense in which economies of scale, and their militarized production systems, are incompatible with democratic principles.

Foucault has argued that if we are to correctly conceptualize this aspect of Western history, we need to stop viewing the military exclusively in terms of the legitimacy, within democratic regimes, of the monopoly of violence by the State. In particular, the question of Taylorism *lies outside the problematic of legitimacy*. But even if we disregard economics for a moment, the very form which democratic governments adopted in the 18th and 19th centuries was influenced by the military, a fact that should make us pause before using terms like "the State" which, like the term "the Market" or "the Capitalist System," assume more homogeneity than is indeed the case. In particular, democratic institutions followed in their development two distinct projects, one which we may call "unification," the other "uniformization." On one hand, the project of nation-building was an integrative movement, forging bonds that went beyond the primordial ties of family and locality, linking urban and rural populations under a new social contract. On the other hand, and complementing this process of unification, there was the less conscious project of uniformization, that is, of submitting the new population of free citizens to intense and continuous training, testing, and exercise to yield a more or less uniform mass of obedient individuals. In Foucault's own words:

> Historians of ideas usually attribute the dream of a perfect society to the philosophers and jurists of the eighteenth century; but there was also a military dream of society; its fundamental reference was not to the state of nature, but to the meticulously subordinated cogs of a machine, not to the primal social contract, but to permanent coercions, not to fundamental rights, but to indefinitely progressive forms of training, not to the general will but to automatic docility ... The Napoleonic regime was not far off and with it the form of state that was to survive it and, we must not forget, the foundations of which were laid not only by jurists, but also by soldiers, not only counselors of state, but also junior officers, not only the men of the courts, but also the men of the camps. The Roman reference that accompanied this formation certainly bears with it this double index: citizens and legionnaires, law and maneuvers. While jurists or philosophers were seeking in the pact a primal model for the construction or reconstruction of the social body, the soldiers and with them the technicians of discipline were elaborating procedures for the individual and collective coercion of bodies.[9]

9 Foucault, *Discipline and Punish*, p. 169.

It should be clear by now that much historical evidence exists to force us to question the assumption of more or less homogeneous societies undergoing historical change by moving from one stage to another of their development. The very idea that we can break down history into internally homogeneous periods, feudalism and capitalism, for example, or the agricultural, the industrial, and the information ages, has revealed itself to be a myth. But without these homogeneous periodizations, how can we think about history? Does it all become pure heterogeneous and contingent detail without any pattern or structure? The answer is that we do not have to fall into pure contingentism but that we do need to replace many of the ideas we take for granted in order to arrive at a more satisfactory philosophy of history. To begin with, we need to replace the idea of "society as a whole" or of "society as a systematic totality." This idea has several origins. One is the use by sociologists, from Compte and Spencer to Talcott Parsons, of the biological organism as a metaphor for society as a whole. A different source of the idea is Marxism. Karl Marx, of course, had a very different analysis of the matter, replacing the harmonious organic whole with one in which conflict is an integral part, but he retained the idea of an overall system via the notion of a dominant set of production relations. Thus, although Marxism and Functionalism are completely different, they both share what we may call a "methodological holism," that is, both take as their point of departure an assumption of overall systematicity. The danger of rejecting this holism is that we may fall into the opposite trap, the "methodological atomism" of neoclassical economics. Nothing shows this danger more clearly than Margaret Thatcher's assertion that there is no such thing as society, only individuals and their families. Clearly, rejecting holism cannot imply reducing all social processes to the level of individual persons.

An alternative to both holism and atomism is a view which includes wholes but only if it can be demonstrated that these wholes are the result of a specific historical process, or, to use a technical term, only if these wholes can be shown to be *emergent wholes*. We need a view in which, starting from a population of interacting individual persons, several layers of social entities emerge: institutional organizations, cities, nation-states. Each entity would constitute a fully historical being emerging from the interactions of a population of immediately lower-scale entities. Roughly, from the interactions among individual persons, institutional organizations emerge; from the interaction of organizations, individual urban centers emerge; and from urban interactions, nation-states emerge. What this yields is a *social ontology of individual entities each operating at different spatio-temporal scales*, in the sense that, roughly, institutional organizations are larger and last longer than human beings, and cities are larger and last longer than institutions. This implies that even the largest entities, nation-states, are considered individual entities, that is, entities *having the same ontological status* as the others and differing only in scale, so that at no point do we reach the level of a "totality" or of "society as a whole."

Given this new social ontology, human history ceases to be a "single temporal stream," the history of societies or the history of great individuals, and now becomes *a multiple stream, with separate historical processes occurring in parallel at different temporal scales*: a history of individual persons, a history of institutions, a history of cities, and so on. Each level would retain a certain autonomy and call for a different descriptive methodology. A good illustration of historical dynamics at the level of institutional organizations is Michel Foucault's description of the complex institutional ecologies in 18th-century Europe, involving the interactions between hospitals, prisons, schools, barracks, and factories, leading to the development of disciplinary techniques. The level of urban centers may be illustrated by Fernand Braudel's theory of cities as "historical actors," which emphasizes the different roles played by maritime metropolises (Venice, Lisbon, Amsterdam, New York) and landlocked capitals (Paris, Vienna, Madrid). Moreover, besides the idea of a multileveled historical process, treating each level as emerging from interacting populations at the level below allows us to include more heterogeneity in our models of social and historical phenomena. Unlike the "system" paradigm, which imposes a certain degree of artificial homogeneity at the outset, the "nested set of individual entities" paradigm does not have to assume any homogeneity at any level, except contingent uniformities for which a specific historical explanation can be given.

I take this social ontology from the work of Gilles Deleuze, whose philosophy is based on the fundamental notions of "difference" and "heterogeneity." Unlike the negative use of the concept of "difference" in Hegelian philosophy, where differences do enter into the genesis of structure but as the "negation of the negation," Deleuze creates a philosophy where differences are entirely positive. Unlike the negation of the negation which leads to the genesis of totalities, a positive use of difference leads to the quite distinct concept of an "assemblage," an articulation of heterogeneous components where there is no totalization. It is precisely this notion of assemblage that we need in order to properly conceptualize the complex institutional ecologies that Foucault analyzes, or the equally complex urban ecologies analyzed by Braudel. Once in possession of this new idea, we can more easily resist using terms like "the Market" or "the State" and move on to think about these entities as they are, complex assemblages of individual firms of many sizes and dynamics, or complex assemblages of individual governmental agencies and organizations operating with different degrees of autonomy. Given that one crucial characteristic of democratic institutions is that they must respect and articulate personal and ethnic differences, a philosophy which takes heterogeneity seriously and which makes positive differences its cornerstone may be just what we need to assess the future possibilities of democracy.

Democracy De-realized

Homi K. Bhabha

We are witnessing a globalisation of the economy? For certain.
A globalisation of political calculations? Without doubt. But a
universalisation of political consciousness – certainly not.
  Michel Foucault, "For an Ethic of Discomfort" (1979)

In these past, dark days it has been difficult to draw a line between the outrage
and anxiety provoked by the attacks and the ensuing war, and the urgent need
for some more humane and historical reflection on the tragedy itself. After such
knowledge, what forgiveness? The appalling images of death, destruction, and
daring that invaded our homes on September 11 left us with no doubt that
these unimaginable scenes belonged to a moral universe alien to ours, acts per-
petrated by people foreign to the very fiber of our being. But CNN had a sobering tale to tell. While the headline news staggered from one towering inferno to
another, the ticker tape at the bottom of the screen interspersed its roll-call of
the brave and the dead with lists of Hollywood movies – films that had told a
similar story many times before, and new, unreleased movies that were about to
tell it again. What was only an action movie for the longest time turned into
acts of war. Same mise-en-scène, different movie.

I do not want to blast Hollywood, nor to rail against the violence of the mass
media. And I am certainly not suggesting, wistfully, that life follows art because
that only rarely happens. I have chosen to start with the global genre of the terrorist action film in order to question the widely canvassed cultural assumptions
that have come to frame the deadly events. The attacks on New York were a
manifestation of a much deeper "clash of civilizations," we were frequently told.
One night during September, Benjamin Netanyahu developed this thesis to its
logical conclusion and ended up by placing Israel just off the East Coast of
America. The next morning, Deputy Secretary of Defense Paul Wolfowitz
affirmed wide international support for the US from nations that he described
as belonging to the "civilized world" and the "uncivilized world."

Returning to CNN's ticker tape of terrorist movies and special effects, which
demonstrates the futility of framing the event in such a divided and polarized
civilizational narrative. Each of the unimaginable actions we were subjected to
on our TV screens have been repeatedly imagined and applauded in movie
houses across the country by law-abiding Americans, and successfully exported
to other ordinary film-loving folks across the world. However, the decision to

implement and administer a politics of terror, whether it is done in the name of god or the State, is a *political decision* taken by a specific hierarchy of power – even if it is a hierarchy of those who consider themselves powerless. There is no confusing a political act, devoid of legality and humanity, with a civilizational or cultural practice. Ironically, the "clash of civilizations" is an aggressive discourse often used by totalitarians to justify their worst deeds, to induce terror and create debilitating psychoses of persecution amongst oppressed, powerless peoples. When *we* – whoever we may be – use the civilizational argument against *them* – whoever they may be – we are, unwittingly perhaps, speaking in the divisive tongue of tyrants. When the foreign and economic policies of powerful nations are conducted in terms of the civilizational divisions of "them" and "us," nations assume that hawkish, imperialist aspect that provokes a widespread sense of injustice, indignation, and fear. Self-interest and short-term gain are, regrettably, the lingua franca of international politics; diplomacy is part of the ritual of "seduce – and abandon." But we must always remember the decisive effect of the "economies of scale" in these matters. When rich and powerful countries, or less wealthy countries that have acquired regional power and arsenals, play these reckless political games, the lives of ordinary peoples, civilians and soldiers alike, are treated with contempt.

The embattled and embalmed narrative of civilizational clash is often deployed to justify the reckless destruction of civilians who are suspected, by virtue of their culture (considered to be their "second nature"), as being tainted with the "guilt" of their traditions and temperament. Only those societies of the North and the South, the East and West, that ensure the widest democratic participation and protection for their citizens – their majorities and minorities – are in a position to make the deadly difficult decisions that "just" wars demand. To confront terror, out of a sense of democratic solidarity rather than retaliation, gives us some faint hope for the future. Hope, that we might be able to establish a vision of a global society, informed by civil liberties and human rights, that carries with it the shared obligations and responsibilities of common, collaborative citizenship.

What democratic narratives should we turn to in our hour of need, to get beyond the civilizational clash? I have long argued that when faced with the perils and trials of democracy, our lessons of equality and justice are best learned from the peoples of the colonized or enslaved worlds who have harvested the bitter fruits of liberal democracy, rather than from the Western imperial nations and sovereign states that claim to be the seed-beds of democratic thinking. *Democracy Unrealized*, the Berlin platform of Documenta11, invites us to review the challenges of the new Global Order in the *wake* of the Cold War – a wake that hangs like a pallor over many nations devastated by decades of Cold

War rivalry; or failing states that find no comfort in the hollow promises of the multilateral free-market "miracle." Documenta asks us "to question whether the notion of democracy can still be sustained within the philosophical grounds of Western epistemology" and to explore "the potential for revision [and] revaluation" in keeping with the transformations of globalization, so that we may investigate the idea and ideals of democracy as "an ever-open, essentially unfinishable project that in principle has fallen short of its ideals." To pose the crisis of democracy in terms of its unrealized *Ideals* does not adequately challenge the failures of its promise. "Falling short" is often a strategic "necessity" for democratic discourse, which acknowledges failure as part of its evolutionary, utopian narrative. The argument goes something like the following: We fail because we are mortal and bound to history, the faith of democracy lies not in perfectibility but in our perseverance and progress, our commitment to set the highest ideals before ourselves and struggle toward them to revise and reshape our "best selves." Such an internal dialectic of the "unrealized"and the "utopian" encounters the negative instance of "failure" only in order to provide a strange *moral* consolation for itself.

Let me propose, in an affiliative spirit analogous to the platform of Documenta11, an alternate title: *Democracy De-realized*. I use "de-realization" in the sense of Bertolt Brecht's concept of "distantiation" – a critical "distance" or alienation disclosed in the very formation of the democratic experience and its expressions of Equality. I also use *déréalisation* in the surrealist sense of placing an object, idea, or image in a context *not of its making*, in order to defamiliarize it, to frustrate its naturalistic and normative "reference" and see what potential for *translation* that idea or insight has – a translation across genre and geopolitics, territory and temporality. The power of democracy, at its best, lies in its capacity for self-interrogation, and its translatability across traditions in the modern age. If we attempt to De-realize Democracy, by defamiliarizing its historical context and its political project, we recognize not its failure, but its *frailty*, its *fraying edges or limits* that impose their will of inclusion and exclusion on those who are considered – on the grounds of their race, culture, gender, or class – unworthy of the democratic process. In these dire times of global intransigence and war, we recognize what a fragile thing democracy is, how fraught with limitations and contradictions; and yet it is that *fragility, rather than failure or success*, I believe, that fulfills the agenda of the Documenta11 manifesto – the "potential for revision, revaluation of values, extension, and creative transformation to keep in step with 21st-century globalizing processes."

The transformations of our own global century are part of a longer lineage of fraying and fragility that takes us back to an earlier phase of global governance – the colonial empires. With the resurgence of neoliberalism after the Cold War, it becomes especially important to grasp the internal de-realizations of that global ideology, and to delineate its colonial genealogies. For instance, the great British liberal philosopher John Stuart Mill realized that one of the major conundrums of his celebrated theory of democracy consisted in the fact *that he was a democrat in his country and a despot in another country – in colonial India.* What needed to be acknowledged – as Mill *was not able to do* in that great document of modern democracy, *On Liberty* – was the self-contradictoriness of liberal democracy which raged like a war of values in its very soul. Internal to democracy is a struggle between a sincerely held "universalism" as a principle of cultural comparison and scholarly study; and ethnocentrism, even racism, as a condition of ethical practice and political prescription. At the heart of democracy, we witness this de-realizing dialectic between the epistemological and the ethical, between cultural description and political judgment, between principle and power.

Those in the North and the South, in metropoles and peripheries, who have been the victims of Democracy De-realized have their own lessons to teach. For they experience not only the injustice of colonization and slavery, but *know* in some profound way the *ethical impossibility* of perpetuating discrimination, segregation, or global injustice in the modern world. "It is not possible in a modern world to separate people by vertical partitions," W. E. B. Du Bois, the great African-American poet-politician, wrote in 1929. "Who was it that made such group and racial separation *impossible* under modern methods? Who brought fifteen million black folk overseas? ... The world has come together in an organization which you can no more unscramble than you can unscramble eggs."[1] The spatial connectivities and contradictions of the late modern world-picture – reflected in the gargantuan discourses of the "global" – must be placed in a relationship of *ethical contiguity* with the scrambled sites and subjects of racial separation and cultural discrimination. Unless we recognize what is old and weary about the world – those "long histories" of slavery, colonization, diaspora, asylum – we are in no position to represent what is emergent or "new" within our contemporary global moment. What analytic and cultural measures help us to grasp the transformations of global change?

The "new" is only a historic destiny that lives amongst us like the ghost of the future; slender as a leaf of time turning, a sheet of space folding, inscribed on one side by the past, and the other by the present. The announcement of the "new" – as in the New World order, or the new global economy – is almost always the recognition of a turning point in history, the experience of a moment

---

1 "Report of Debate Conducted by the Chicago Forum: Shall the Negro Be Encouraged to Seek Cultural Equality," in *Pamphlets and Leaflets by W. E. B. du Bois,* ed. Herbert Aptheker (White Plains, N.Y.: Kraus-Thomson, 1986), p. 229.

in transition, or in "incubation" as Antonio Gramsci described it.[2] "What exists at any given time [in the name of the new] is a variable combination of old and new," "a *momentary* equilibrium of cultural relations..."[3] Discourses of "incubation" drive us definitionally to-and-fro as we try to derive a critical and epistemological vocabulary from within the global discourse itself. "[The] becoming worldwide [or *mondialisation*] of the world is not the unfolding of a normal, normative or normed process," Jacques Derrida warns us.[4] The contingencies and contiguities of the new cartography of globalism mutate and vacillate, mediate and morph: the North-South axis of the globe shifts to the Global and the Local, and thence to the preferred "southern," postcolonial designation, the Local-Global. For some, globalism is the advent of "disorganized capital" playing to the risk society; for others it is "a fluctuating web of connections between metropolitan regions and exploitable peripheries."[5] Yielding national "sovereignty" to the international regime leaves the compromised nation-state suffering from "social schizophrenia,"[6] its affiliative authority is now metonymically displaced onto the "global city" that reveals the "unbalanced playing field" of the growth of global capital and the claims of marginalized peoples.[7] The territoriality of the global "citizen" is, concurrently, postnational, denational, or transnational. Legal activists and scholars argue productively for what they call "effective nationality," which contests statist discourses of citizenship by emphasizing those articulations of civic/civil life that lie adjacent to the considerations of "formal nationality" and statute law. Indeed, the arguments for a change in the definition of citizenship are based on areas of everyday experience and are better articulated in case law "concerned with a person's connections in fact – their social, political and psychological connections."[8] And finally, according to the legal scholar Larry Lessig, the cyberspace actor is "actually living in two places at once, with no principle of supremacy between ... multiple non-coordinating jurisdictions."[9]

These "non-coordinating jurisdictions," which embody *forms* of global knowledge and practice, are not adequately represented in the scalar measures of

2 *The Gramsci Reader: Selected Writings, 1916–1935*, ed. David Forgacs (New York: Schocken Books, 1998), p. 353.
3 Ibid.
4 Jacques Derrida, *Specters of Marx: The State of the Debt, the Work of Mourning, and the New International*, trans. Peggy Kamuf (New York: Routledge, 1994), p. 78.
5 Allan Sekula, *Fish Story* (Rotterdam: Witte de With, center for contemporary art, and Düsseldorf: Richter Verlag, 1995), p. 48.
6 Manuel Castells, *The Rise of the Network Society* (Cambridge, Mass.: Blackwell, 1996), p. 527.
7 Saskia Sassen, *Globalization and Its Discontents* (New York: New Press, 1998), p. 34.
8 Kim Rubenstein and Daniel Adler, "International Citizenship: The Future of Nationality in a Globalized World," in: *Indiana Journal of Global Legal Studies* 7, no. 2 (2000), p. 546.
9 Larry Lessig, *Code and Other Laws of Cyberspace* (New York: Basic Books, 1999), pp. 193–194.

the gigantic or the increasingly small. The propinquity of jarring jurisdictions – conflictual yet communicative – emerge from the *structure of the global political economy* itself. The economic historian Saskia Sassen describes the process as the "insertions of the global into the fabric of the national … a partial and incipient denationalisation of that which historically has been constructed as the national, or, rather, certain properties of the national."[10] However, all these global discourses represent a double move: the discordant, disseminated sites of the global jurisdiction are, simultaneously, marked by an ethical and analytical desire for proximity. We have to learn to negotiate conflicting social and cultural differences while maintaining the "intimacy" of our intercultural existence, and transnational associations. The uneven and unequal playing field of the global terrain – "partial" and "incipient," neither past nor present but "incubational" – is nonetheless encountered and experienced as living in, and through, a shared historical time of "transition." Where do we turn, as the global world circles around us, to find a critical tradition for our times?

To labor for freedom from an oblique or extra-territorial position contiguous with the State – but discontinuous with many of its aims and institutions – informs the spirit of *minoritarian* representation and humanitarian advocacy. With this in mind, I want to "return" to Gramsci's work on the creation of a *cultural front*, bearing in mind the *partial* "denationalization" of the global condition. A cultural front is not necessarily a political party; it is more a movement or alliance of groups whose struggle for fairness and justice emphasize the deep collaboration between aesthetics, ethics, and activism. A cultural front does not have a homogeneous and totalizing view of the world. It finds its orientation from what Gramsci describes as *"the philosophy of the part* [that] always precedes the philosophy of the whole, not only as its theoretical anticipation but *as a necessity of real life."*[11] Today, as we are offered the stark choices of civilizational clash – between Faith and Unfaith, or Terror and Democracy – it is illuminating to grasp something that demands an understanding that is less dogmatic and totalizing – a philosophy of the part, a perspective that acknowledges its own partiality "as *a necessity of life."* Gramsci's concept of the subaltern takes ethical "survival" as seriously as the challenge to hegemony, which makes him sensitive to our trying times.

The subaltern group is "deprived of historical [dominance] and initiative; it is often in a state of continuous but disorganic expansion, without a necessary party affiliation; and [crucially for the issue of denationalization], its authority

10 Saskia Sassen, "Spatialities and Temporalities of the Global: Elements for a Theorization," *Public Culture* 12, no. 1 (Winter 2000), p. 219.
11 *Gramsci Reader*, p. 337.

may not be able to go beyond a certain *qualitative level* which still remains below the level of the possession of the state."[12] *This would include those who are committed to cultural justice and the emancipatory work of the imagination.* The utopian dream of "total" transformation may not be available to the subaltern perspective, which is nonetheless engaged in both struggle as an active inventory of emancipation, and survival as a mode of forbearance that links the memory of history to the future of freedom. Discourses that champion social "contradiction," as the *a priori* motor of historical change, are propelled in a linear direction toward the terminus of the State. The subaltern imaginary, *deprived of political dominance, and yet seeking to turn that disadvantage into a new vantage point*, has to proceed at an *oblique or adjacent* angle in its antagonistic relation to "the qualitative level of the State." Subalternity represents a form of contestation or challenge to the status quo that does not homogenize or demonize the State in formulating an opposition to it. The subaltern strategy intervenes in state practices from a position that is *contiguous or tangential* to the "authoritarian" institutions of the state – flying just below the level of the State.

It is in this sense that the subaltern group is not a "sub-ordinate" class. It propagates an ethico-political practice in the name of the "human," where "rights" are neither simply universalist nor individuated. The "human" signifies a strategic, translational sign that gives ground *to*, or gains ground *for*, emergent demands for representation, redistribution, and responsibility – claims of the excluded that come "from below the qualitative level of the State"; modes of community and solidarity that are not fully sanctioned by the sovereignty of the State; forms of freedom unprotected by it. Such an "opposition in terms of human rights," Claude Lefort argues, "takes form in centers that power cannot entirely master ... From the legal recognition of strikes or trade unions, to rights relative to work or to social security, there has developed on the basis of the rights of man a whole history *that transgressed the boundaries within which the state claimed to define itself, a history that remains open.*"[13]

For it is in such spaces of "historical openness" that transgress state boundaries that we encounter a form of ethical-political "willing" that confronts the New Global State of titanic economic and political influence with the imperatives of an intellectual-moral community of Rights. Gramsci's concept of subaltern survival and the "philosophy of the part," central to the necessities of everyday life, lead to a practice of inter-national or global history; a *poesis* of imagining the World as an ethical and political project:

---

12 Ibid., p. 351.
13 Claude Lefort, *The Political Forms of Modern Society* (Cambridge: Polity Press, 1986), p. 258.

> One should stress the importance and significance which, in the modern world, political parties have in the *elaboration and the diffusion of the conceptions of the world, because* essentially what they do is to work out the ethics and the politics corresponding to these conceptions and act as it were as their historical laboratory.[14]

What are the conceptions of the world that issue forth from the historical, discursive, and cultural laboratories of contemporary globalization?

"Becoming global" is, in many respects, an aleatory claim rather than an achieved historical condition. Most writings on the *expanse* of globalization emphasize its *excessive* temporality, its acceleration, its intensification, the speeds through which we live in the air, on screen, in the circuits of cyberspace. As the descriptives intensify, I am increasingly drawn to the photographer Allan Sekula's minimalist Zen-like *utterance* "A society of accelerated flows is also in certain key aspects a society of deliberately slow movement."[15] What does this mean for the world as we ought to know it? More than 80 percent of the world's cargo still travels by sea. Large containerized cargo-ships today travel no faster than in the first quarter of the 20th century. Immigrant and refugee smuggling transports take months to deliver their contraband cargo – which may include the 700,000 women and children that are trafficked each year according to the US Justice Department, or the 200 million human beings that are believed to be in the hands of smugglers seeking entry for reasons of economic or political hardship – into the global or transnational world. Immigration and asylum applications can take years to decide – in one recent case, a Sudanese asylum applicant was released after he had been in detention awaiting a decision on his case for six years. Separated or unaccompanied minors who seek asylum as refugees can be held in detention in the US and other parts of the world, without recourse to their families, for anything between six months to a year while their leave to stay is decided.

These "cultural relations" – unequal and uneven – require us to see the antagonisms of the global world in terms of conflictual *contiguities* – rather than social and political "contradictions." The language of contradiction is teleological, it takes a form that totalizes fragments into a holistic system. "Contiguity" as a way of dealing with the "partial or incubational combination of old and new" makes us attentive to the "jurisdictional unsettlement" that marks the life-world of our times. I am, of course, talking in conceptual or metaphorical terms about large patterns of conflict and juxtaposition. But think of the "jurisdictionally unsettled" nature of Truth Commissions, the International Criminal

14 *Gramsci Reader*, p. 335.
15 Sekula, *Fish Story*, p. 50.

Court, or the debate on Reparations: each of these discussions is conducted on complex moral and political grounds that represent the "terrain" of nationhood as an incubatory moment, a transition between the old and the new regime. They are trials of the truth that synchronize the worst excesses of barbarism and the great restraints of civility; justice and injustice are terrifyingly juxtaposed, and, most terrifying of all, they share a contiguous, conflictual border. Their "truths" are neither neatly divisible in guilt or virtue nor are Absolutes available for deliberation. We live in a time of Gramsci's "philosophy of the part." Contiguity, as a critical measure, enables us to evaluate the movement that exists in-between the borderline jurisdictions – national, denational, transnational, post-national – of the global regime.

My own speculations on the ethical and existential "location" of such cultures of "border" living owe something to the work of the psychoanalyst D. W. Winnicott's meditations on the process of "contiguity" as a form of space and time within "the actual world in which the individual lives, which can be objectively perceived."[16] Contiguity, Winnicott suggests, explores a third area of life, in-between the individual and the environment. It is "an intermediate area," or potential space in-between subject and object in which *cultural experience* is located. An area of "intermediate living" is, in Winnicott's words, a *third space* of psychic and social "variability" whose agency and creativity lie in experiences that constellate or "link the past, present and the future." It is the contiguity of these space-and-time frames that constitute the "cultural" as a practice that can both signify and survive the turning points of history and its transitional subjects and objects.

It was through my interest in the "intermediate life" of the global experience – that "third" space somewhere between the old and the new – that I became aware of a kind of contiguous, double horizon that hovered over the global discourse. It was a shuttling back and forth between continuity and contiguity, the tension of the "New World order" surviving in a movement between the dogged persistence of the "national" and the fragile future of transnational/international civil society. Between them emerges "this third space," where the democratic right to have rights, to continually open the debate about the legitimate and the illegitimate, is in tension with the diktat of the Law.

One aspect of this "double-horizon" is created by the foundational narrative of constitutions, laws, policies, legal regulations, and reasoning. *Within that horizon, one takes the world as one finds it and actively sets out to adjudicate it.* This is the important realm of the letter of the Law that the poet W. H. Auden

16 D. W. Winnicott, *Playing and Reality* (London: Tavistock, 1971), p. 103.

so judiciously caught in his famous verse, "Law is as I've told you before… / Law is, but let me explain it once more, / Law is The Law."[17] Such judicial consistency – the phrase comes from Edward Levi's classic *Introduction to Legal Reasoning* – requires that "legal reasoning does attempt to fix the meaning of the word … [so that] subsequent cases must be decided upon the basis that the prior meaning remains. It must not be re-worked."[18] Beyond this legislative interpretation of Law and legality, norm and power – "where the reference [or referent] is fixed" – rises another, contiguous and conflictual horizon of ethical and textual interpretation. It *may not be readily achievable or visible, but it represents a profound commitment to fairness and justice* … This "second aspect" does not signify the "global" as a descriptive condition of contemporary life, but as an ethical or political claim, a wager on the future. For when we use categories like world civilization or global culture, Lévi-Strauss once explained, "We are employing … abstract conceptions to which we attach a moral or logical significance; [as if] we are thinking of aim[s or claims] to be pursued by existing societies; … we must not shut our eyes to the fact that the concept of [global or] world civilization is very sketchy and imperfect."[19]

Such a sketchy, imperfect double horizon sustains a fragile faith in the "making of a world" of fairness that is rendered all the more anxious by the practical impossibility of achieving global justice in any comprehensive sense. For today's world is marked by a denser sense of "jurisdictional uncertainty and unsettlement," of a kind that earlier forms of globalization – colonization or imperialism – had not quite encountered, because slaves and the colonized were not considered, in any full and fair sense, to be part of the civil society or the public world of "nations." Ironically, it is this "jurisdictional unsettlement" that requires that we go beyond the roundelay of "Law is The Law," and embrace a different kind of ethical and poetic justice, that, once again, Auden captures with great insight:

Unlike so many men
I cannot say Law is again,
Nor more than they can we suppress
The universal wish to guess
Or slip out of our own position
Into an unconcerned condition.

17 W. H. Auden, "Law Like Love," in *Selected Poems*, ed. Edward Mendelson (New York: Vintage Books, 1979), pp. 89–90.
18 Edward Levi, *Introduction to Legal Reasoning* (Chicago: University of Chicago Press, 1968), pp. 32–33.
19 Claude Lévi-Strauss, *Race and History* (Paris: UNESCO, 1968), p. 42.

It is the first move of the ethical and aesthetic attitudes to "slip out of our own position" and identify with an-other's condition. Such a slipping out or displacement transforms – or shall I say translates – the very territoriality (and temporality) of our confident claim to being "at home" in our own universe of concern. To be ethically or aesthetically "concerned" requires us to identify with "otherness" or alterity; to relate to what "un-concerns" us and uncannily splits our sense of social sovereignty and moral certainty. Such ethico-political claims to justice and fairness, Claude Lefort argues, are based upon a sense of "symbolic efficacy" and are central to the notion of rights. In an argument that, in some significant respects, follows my description of *the subaltern strategy of contiguity*, Lefort explains how the aspiration and agency of rights makes State power confront its authority and autonomy "according to the criteria of the just and the unjust and not only of the permitted and the forbidden ... Human rights do not attack state-power head on, but *obliquely* ...circumventing it, as it were, it touches the centre from which it draws the justification of its own right to demand the allegiance and obedience of all."[20] It is the oblique movement of the rights discourse, often aspirational and metaphorical in its symbolic efficacy, that drew me to the problem of the double horizon in the making of the world as an imperfect place, "a potential [third] space of intermediate living" – in Winnicott's words – *and none the worse for that.*

The visibility of my doubly horizoned global world picture – aspiration and advocacy, ethics and the law – is nowhere better brought to life than in an image from that fine dissenting work of the global era – Allan Sekula's *Fish Story*. Sekula's project occupies a significant place in my work on the formal invocations of global culture, but I only want to allude to a telling detail on this occasion. For there is a kind of "double horizon" in Sekula's photographic essay of the lifeworld of containerized vessels, which, in his words, "[juggle] a triple funeral: a memorial service for painting, socialism, and the sea."[21] In some of his photographs, you see the partial prow of the container vessel cutting obliquely into the frame of the photograph, almost slicing off a side of the frame, as the container ship with its global goods ploughs its way forward into a horizon, carrying the viewer's eye into the uninterrupted path of "the fluid transnational block of capitalist power ... London ... Hong Kong ... Shenzhen ... Taipei."[22] Sekula's work has been read as a harsh critique of global capitalism in the documentary tradition, the most direct and directive of committed art. What such readings end up commending, congruent with Sekula's critique, is his radical

20 Lefort, *The Political Forms of Modern Society*, p. 265.
21 Sekula, *Fish Story*, p. 48.
22 Ibid.

view of the contradictions of late capitalism. Sekula, I believe, looks beyond that conventional dialectic precisely in the oblique cropping or cutting of the frame as the prow ploughs the global seas. At that oblique angle, *conflictually contiguous* with the ship's forward movement, almost at an anamorphic tilt, lies another kind of horizon that disturbs and diverts – in the political *making* or *poesis* of art – the deadly direction of the "global economy." At times it is the melancholic wake that rises miasma-like, a ghostly shadow hard by the vessel – a kind of memorial wailing or veiling that pulls the eye aside, disturbs the forward look of economic or technological progress. Here there is a kind of straying from the path of the global horizon; the opening up of another kind of reflection in a nonrealistic medium, a semblance of Turner, a stain of steam, and the trace of other ships and other seas. Beside the mourning of Painting, Socialism, and the Sea, there is a space for aspiration and advocacy of rights that de-realizes democracy, as I have described it earlier, a light that dimly seeps through the backlit tilted banked clouds, and breaks up the waves. This "nonrealist" Third Space discloses an oblique, indeterminate movement that is less focused on signifying the determinants of global capitalism and more open to the representation/ enunciation of the "right to have rights" as an urgent and open legal and humanitarian question for those workers on these containerized vessels – often stateless economic and political refugees, a patchwork of minorities – who are the victims of the "jurisdictional unsettlement" of our times. Sekula's containerized vessel now becomes a narrative about the "survival and extension of public space as a political and cultural question … in which it is possible to question [the politics of] Rights on an increasingly broad basis."[23]

Who gives voice to the silence or absence that marks the place where the horizons intersect and intermediate living begins? What material histories emerge from this third space that is neither the Global as the Gigantic nor the local as "smallness"?

Minoritization, now, is not simply that abject condition of being "half-stateless," as Hannah Arendt once described it.[24] Today the identification with minoritarian causes constitutes a form of aspirational activism, committed to an agenda of intercultural and transgroup emancipation. Minorities infrequently subscribe to the apparently utopian or universalist assumptions of democratic progress associated with the founding of the "state" on the culturally transcendent territoriality of the nation. The civic culture and consciousness of the minoritarian citizen, today, is focused, with good reason, on Democracy De-

---

23 Claude Lefort, *Democracy and Political Theory*, trans. David Macey (Minneapolis: University of Minnesota Press, 1988), p. 43.
24 Hannah Arendt, *The Origins of Totalitarianism* (New York: Harcourt, Brace, 1951), p. 275.

realized – on "a regime founded upon the legitimacy of a *debate* as to what is legitimate and what is illegitimate – a debate which is necessarily without any guarantor and without any end. The inspiration behind the rights of man and the spread of rights in our day bears witness to this debate."[25] It is too easy to see minorities as being either antinational or transnational, either domestic or diasporic. More than a mere "grouping" of peoples or a special statistical and legal category, minorities raise this unsettling debate, at the heart of the democratic process, which is not about the legitimacy or implementation of the law, but about what is just and unjust, beyond the letter of the law; and what constitute "rights" beyond the nation-state. The institutions that embody this minoritarian spirit of aspirational activism – NGOs, Truth Commissions, International Courts, New Social Movements, International Aid Agencies, the spirit of Documenta11 itself – live only uncertainly in the shadow of state sovereignty, in the interstices, the in-between spaces, of a new internationalism. The claim to "equality and fraternity" celebrated by national governments, as the basis on which they create their national polities and participate in a world community of free nations, was cynically betrayed in Durban, at the World Congress of Races, when many countries refused to take responsibility for their own discriminatory practices. The unseemly rush to flee from their own historical pasts, like Lady Macbeth fleeing the bedchamber, was only matched by those who stormed out of the Conference chamber as soon as they were confronted with the ongoing injustices of the present. As the *New York Times* reported it, "India successfully lobbied fellow nations to prevent mention of caste and discrimination. Before walking out of the conference over criticism of Israel, the United States objected to any discussion of reparations for the descendants of African slaves. Others refused to consider gays as victims of discrimination."[26]

The making of the minority is central to "achieving a democratic nation" rather than fostering xenophobic and patriotic nationalist myths. The narrative spirit of minoritarian "right" that I am proposing is audible in the recent words of Alioune Tine, a human rights activist from Senegal at the Durban Conference who led a caucus of Africans and blacks in the Americas: "We have never had the opportunity to gather together from every country ... now there is enthusiasm and commitment to remind states to meet their international obligations. That is the next step."[27] In *Development as Freedom*, Amartya Sen supports such an argument, I believe, that human rights and cultural rights must not only, or dogmatically, be seen "in postinstitutional terms as instruments; rather [they may be

25 Lefort, *Democracy and Political Theory*, p. 39.
26 Rachel L. Swarns, "After the Race Conference: Relief and Doubt Over Whether It Will Matter," *New York Times*, September 10, 2001.
27 Serge Schmemann, "The Accord on Racism," *New York Times*, September 9, 2001.

seen] as ... prior ethical entitlements." And he goes on to suggest that "in this sense, human rights may stand for claims, powers and immunities ... [and they may be] supported by ethical judgements, which attach intrinsic importance to these warranties. In fact, human rights may also [accede to] the domain of *potential*, as opposed to *actual*, legal rights. Indeed it is [nccccssary] to scc human rights as a set of ethical claims."[28] For this double and discontinuous horizon of the "world" is part of a larger constitutional shift within nations and across the transnational space, both in aspiration and advocacy.

In the work of W. E. B. Du Bois, I have seen this minoritarian mode of "intermediate living" – an intercultural constitutionalism – turned into a vision of democratic socialism. It is the condition of the minority agent – individual or collective – to take on the challenge of the "contradiction of double aims," to use Du Bois's canonical phrase, and struggle to produce a world-open message. For Du Bois, minoritarian agency is envisaged as an act of enunciation – the slave or the colonized represent their community in the very act of *poesis*, in the making of a "world-opening" message, as Du Bois describes the "voicing" of the marginalized. The burden of the minoritarian "message" is not merely the demand for the respect and recognition of cultural or political differences. This very *aesthetic* act of communication or narration is also an ethical practice "that is complete not in opening to the spectacle of, or the recognition of, the other, but in becoming a responsibility for him."[29] The responsibility of the minoritarian agent lies in creating a world-open forum of communication in which "the crankiest, humblest and poorest ... people are the ... key to the consent of the governed."[30]

For Du Bois, the making of the minority is an affiliative and "translational category of identification"[31] – class, race, gender, national, and regional differences. The claim to political recognition does not require to be underwritten by the authenticity of "racial" groupings or the communal exclusivity or particularism of ethnic experience. Du Bois's central insight lies in emphasizing the "contiguous" and contingent nature of the making of minorities, where solidarity depends on surpassing autonomy or sovereignty in favor of an intercultural articulation of differences. This is a dynamic and dialectical concept of the minority as a *process of affiliation*, an ongoing translation of aims and interests through

---

28 Amartya Sen, *Development as Freedom* (New York: Knopf, 1999), p. 229.

29 Emmanuel Levinas, *The Levinas Reader*, trans. Sean Hand (Oxford: Blackwell, 1989), p. 108.

30 W. E. B. Du Bois, *Darkwater: Voices from within the Veil* (Millwood, N.Y.: Kraus-Thomson, 1975), p. 88.

31 See my "On Cultural Respect," in *The Turn to Ethics*, ed. Marjorie Garber et al. (London: Routledge, 2000), for the distinction between the politics of recognition and the poetics of identification.

which minorities emerge to communicate their messages *adjacently* across communities. This enunciative concept of minoritization is much in advance of the anthropological concept of the minority that is in place in Article 27 of the International Convention on Civil and Political Rights. For Article 27, minorities, in the main, are groups that have existed in a state before becoming beneficiaries of protection. It is their "cohesion" as a minority that has to be protected, for "minorities are conceived [in the article] as social entities wholly sustainable in their separateness."[32] Immigrants and women, for example, have had problems in being recognized by Article 27 because, it is argued, they do not closely approximate to a "jural order with institutions shared by the whole category" and they do not demand the right to sustain their culture "as a fundamental group quality sought to be maintained as an end in itself."[33] Such a strong preference for cultural "holism" prevents the emergence of new, affiliative forms of minoritarian agency and its institutions.

The minoritarian presence is a sign of "intermediate living" within the history of the present, that is neither gigantic nor small, neither global nor local. This subaltern "third force" makes dramatically visible what is involved in regulating the ethical and political borderlands of the global world with its simultaneous, noncoordinating jurisdictions. For the Greeks, legislation and the execution of decisions "[were] political activities because in them [human beings] 'act like craftsmen' and hence *poesis* belongs to the realm of "acting in terms of making, and of its result, the relationship between men, in terms of an accomplished work."[34] And this combination of praxis and *poesis* – of *advocacy and aspiration* in contemporary invocations of the "global" minority and its translational existence, is what I have, so far, explored. But if such is the making – the *poesis* – of a New global World, can it issue forth into a form of *poetry* that invokes the memory of older, earlier globalizations – colonization and slavery – and introduces it into the crafting of our current predicament? The poet Derek Walcott works out the ethics and politics of the contemporary "world" as a terrifying translational tryst with the contiguous, discontinuous languages and cultures that cross and cut in the making of the modern globe. The poet speaks:

> But we were orphans of the nineteenth century,
> sedulous to the morals of a style,
> we lived by another light,

32 Philip Vuciri Ramaga, "The Group Concept in Minority Protection," *Human Rights Quarterly* 15, no. 3 (1993), p. 581.
33 Ibid.
34 Hannah Arendt, *The Human Condition* (Chicago: University of Chicago Press, 1958), pp. 195–196.

Victoria's orphans, bats in the banyan boughs.
Dragonfly, dragonfly
....
caught in the lamp of Giorgione,
dragonfly, in our ears
sang Baudelaire's exhortations to stay drunk,
sang Gauguin's style, awarded Vincent's ear.

I had entered the house of literature as a houseboy,
filched as the slum child stole,
as the young slave appropriated
those heirlooms temptingly left
with the Victorian homilies of *Noli tangere*
This is my body. Drink.
This is my wine......
In the beginning,
all Drunkenness is Dionysiac, divine.

And then one night, somewhere,
a single outcry rocketed in air,
the thick tongue of a fallen, drunken lamp
licked at its alcohol ringing the floor,
and with the fierce rush of a furnace door
suddenly opened, history was here......

Gregorias, listen, lit,
we were the light of the world!
We were blest with a virginal, unpainted world
with Adam's task of giving things their names,
with the smooth white walls of clouds and villages
where you devised your inexhaustible,
impossible Renaissance,
brown cherubs of Giotto and Massacio,
with the salt wind coming through the window,
smelling of turpentine, with nothing so old
that it could not be invented.[35]

---

35 Derek Walcott, "Another Life," in *Collected Poems, 1948–1984* (New York: Farrar, Straus & Giroux, 1986), pp. 219, 221, 294.

The contiguities of our own "incubational" global moment, both old and new, return in those lines that have echoed throughout my talk: "*Nothing so old that it could not be invented.*" This is Walcott's translational claim as he exerts his ethical and political "right to narrate," revising the great frescoes of the "Impossible" Renaissance – whose "originality" it is now impossible to assert *after* the belated task of the translator who inscribes across the "origins" of the Renaissance the history of the middle passage of intermediate living – the unsettled jurisdictions of our cultural and political lives echoed in the disruptions and displacements of Empire. I use the term "right to narrate" to signify an act of communication through which the recounting of themes, histories, and records is part of a process that reveals the transformation of human agency. Such a "right" is not merely a legal, procedural matter; it is also a matter of aesthetic and ethical *form*. Freedom of expression is an individual right; the right to narrate, if you will permit me poetic license, is an *enunciative* right rather than an *expressive right* – the *dialogic*, communal, or group right to address and be addressed, to signify and be interpreted, to speak and be heard, to make a sign and to know that it will receive respectful attention. And that social "relation" – to relate, to narrate, to connect – becomes our jurisdiction and our *juris-dictio*, quite literally, the place from where we speak, from where we engage in the *poesis*, the making, of art and politics.

As I end, let me circle back to the beginning: to the place from where I speak to you today. Fallen towers, falling idols: what has befallen the ideals and the Ideas of global Progress now that the New World is bereft of its towers, its towering ladder without rungs targeted as the symbol of our times? Such days that eerily hollow out the times and places in which we live confront our sense of Progress with the challenge of the *Unbuilt*. The Unbuilt is not a place that you can reach with a ladder, as Ludwig Wittgenstein would put it. What you need once your towers have fallen is a perspicuous vision that reveals a space, a way in the world, that is often obscured by the onward and upward thrust of Progress. Listen to Wittgenstein:

> Our civilisation is characterised by the word "progress." Progress is its form rather than making progress being one of its features. Typically it constructs. It is occupied with building an ever more complicated structure ... I am not interested in constructing a building, so much as in having a perspicuous view of the foundation of possible buildings.[36]

36 Ludwig Wittgenstein, *Culture and Value*, trans. Peter Winch (Oxford: Blackwell, 1980), p. 7.

Neither destruction nor deconstruction, the Unbuilt is the creation of a *form* whose virtual absence raises the question of what it would mean to start again, in the same place, as if it were elsewhere, adjacent to the site of a historic disaster or a personal trauma. The rubble and debris that survive carry the memories of other fallen towers, Babel for instance, and lessons of endless ladders that suddenly collapse beneath our feet. We have no option, *pace* Wittgenstein, but to be interested in constructing buildings; at the same time, we have no choice but to place, in full view of our buildings, the vision of the Unbuilt – "the foundation of *possible* buildings," other foundations, other alternative worlds. Perhaps, then, we will not forget to measure Progress, as it creeps along the ground, from other perspectives, other *possible* foundations, *conflicting and yet contiguous*, even when we believe, in vanity, that we are standing at the top of the tower.

Awaiting The Beautyful Ones

Wole Soyinka

Lest we lose hope entirely, we must never cease to remind ourselves of the miracle of South Africa. Or indeed of lesser zones of optimism, such as the termination of the civil war in Mozambique, a conclusion that might even appear to have been divinely ordered in its timing. That timing enabled a now united nation to cope with the worst flood disaster ever experienced by an African nation within living memory. A flood of epic biblical proportions, no less. Drought, yes – the continent was accustomed to this – but flood, nothing quite like this had ever been visited upon the continent. It was as if the flood was sent to remind warring African nations that there is one potent enemy always lurking round the corner, toward whose control all sensible nations should conserve their forces – Nature. First, a plague of droughts and famine, next the Flood – are we headed for *the fire next time?* This deluge may not have produced a Noah's Ark, but the poignant image that went round the world – one that will remain engraved on many minds till death – that image of the trapped mother who gave birth in a tree, such a portent may be read as a glimmer of potential redemption. It is a picture that should be hung on the office walls of all African political and national leaders, spurring them to reassess their understanding of the purpose of social organization to which all existing resources should be directed – Is it toward the nurturing of life? Or its repudiation in the cause of ego and the desperate consolidation of power?

And there are other spaces of relief – the swift termination of the incipient tyranny of General Guei in Ivory Coast being the most recent, and the most uplifting, since it is one of those rare instances of a successful people's uprising, spontaneous but also, alas, exacting in its toll. And there is the apparent end of the war between the two Congos, the termination of the Eritrean-Ethiopian war, albeit with a most unsatisfactory ending. The dramatic yet tawdry end to the brutal dictatorship of Sani Abacha in Nigeria was another – indeed the oh-so-belated resolve of the Organisation of African Unity to tolerate no more military coups must be reckoned as yet another step on the hard road to optimism. Nor must we forget the collaborative effort now being undertaken to wage war against AIDS – again much much belated, but nonetheless a hint of a new seriousness that offers a glimmer of hope that the present proliferation of ghost towns and villages, wasted by this appalling scourge, may at least be gradually arrested.

However, the title of Ayi Kwei Armah's novel of the late sixties, *The Beautyful Ones Are Not Yet Born*, continues to dominate our awareness of African realities. As if from a corrective, indeed combative, mood to that pessimism, yet another of his fictional works – *Two Thousand Seasons* – narrates a utopia of the past to which the visionary in Ayi Kwei Armah has resorted as a societal idyll for the future, in short, as the path toward a Renaissance of the continent of the black race. This dream of a Renaissance, I have said over and over again, is as old as the history of decolonization, and I mention Ayi Kwei Armah's other book only as a reflection of that dream, a work of fiction that consciously sets out to map a combative project of social reconstruction, based on a carefully conjured, selective past. It is unique in that respect within the corpus of African literature.

This isolated work – isolated in its genre of utopian or, simply, romanticized reconstruction – remains a reference point for the passion that consumed most writers in the sixties and seventies, writers who saw their mission as one of invocation of a past glory, idyll, or model as a means of reconstituting a continent from within. Other novelists, such as Ahmadou Kourouma, Syl Cheney-Coker, Maryse Condé of Guadaloupe do invoke similar histories, but their works evince no interest in proposing them, however selectively, as pointers for the future. They are not used to evoke thoughts of a possible Renaissance. *Two Thousand Seasons*, admittedly rather uneven and sometimes undeveloped in its writing – certainly less accomplished than *The Beautyful Ones* – thus remains our most deliberate, overtly fictional manifesto. What is contained within its rather idealistic pages sums up the social agitation in the breast of most writers – the clear vision of a Renaissance for a continent that has known, in contemporary times, nothing but retrogression. There are of course other novels with a similar mission – Ousmane Sembene's *God's Bits of Wood* is one, and I believe one could describe my own *Season of Anomie* as another. Ayi Kwei Armah's work however does set out, far more self-consciously than the others, to be read as a social manifesto, one that is centered – so early in postcolonial literature – on the liberating principle of democracy, stridently articulated, contemptuously – and even violently – deposing all protagonists of alternative social systems. Therein lie some of its weaknesses as a work of literature however – its unabashed propagandist fervor – but its extract, that democratic and communalistic vision of societal relationships, remains a dream to which one occasionally looks backwards wistfully, as one monstrosity of power after another overtakes the benighted people of a continent.

It was of course a period that was deeply taken with the romance of ideology, of a certain Utopia within grasp, if only the colonial entity could slash the umbilical cord that still attached it to inhuman, exploitative philosophies such as – capitalism. Sacrifices must therefore be accepted, especially a loss of personal fulfillment and individual assertiveness. Even the ability to see and pronounce critically was to be curtailed in favor of the common good, the vision of pan-Africanism or indeed of universal brotherhood. Capitalism was evil, socialism good. Leadership was equated with liberation, opposition or criticism of leadership with neocolonial indoctrination. It would take a while for most writers to begin to recognize that while a change of baton had indeed taken place, with a corresponding change of skin, there really had been no change of heart. By then, of course, power was consolidated. The Cold War had selected and anointed its surrogates on the African continent and their mission was not service to land and people but self-perpetuation and the prodigal exhibitionism that accompanies delusions of grandeur. For the masses of the people, however, it was poverty, social stagnation, and a loss of confidence in their own creative powers, in their innate ability to imaginatively reproduce their existence.

That crisis of poverty and underdevelopment on the African continent cannot be divorced from a distrust, indeed dismissal of cultural antecedents, another casualty of ideological conflicts. This dismissal, or attenuation, of past accumulation of experience resulted in the transplantation of alien developmental strategies that often ended up eroding the traditional economic foundations of society. There is no shortage of African nations whose developmental woes are directly traceable to the negative impact of external values on their cultural usages, the result of new sociopolitical ideas, economic paradigms, and even external cultural norms that come camouflaged in seductive packages, including ideology. Such societies become cultural and developmental pastiches of others, poor cousins and ineffectual mimics. Their normal strategies for the anticipation of, compensation for, and survival in spite of natural disasters are eroded with their cultures. They develop, in fact, a new culture – one of mimicry and dependency. They become helpless, impotent when confronted by the vagaries of nature or disruption of accustomed trading patterns. They especially cannot adapt in times of civil strife.

The psychopathic Marxist regime of Mengistu's Ethiopia is one example. The history of droughts and famines, and the poverty of management strategies, did not commence with that regime, we know, but the consequences were exacerbated most horrendously, owing to the centralist ideology of the Ethiopian Marxist government and its ill-digested, unanalytical collectivization policies. That regime compounded the routine of feudal neglect of the former emperor Haile Selassie, destroyed what was left of the traditional structures of rural society, forced villages into regimented, artificial communities, and thus severed the organic bonds between the cultures of the peoples and their productive strategies. The recent war between Ethiopia and Eritrea has of course relegated to the background the urgency of restitching these broken cultural tissues, of re-creating and reinforcing communities that once survived through an osmotic relationship with Nature, even at its most meager.

Nyerere's Tanzania, during the earlier period of immediate postindependence, was not notably more successful than Ethiopia, but the failure of the economic policies of that nation's socialist experiment did not remotely approach the magnitude of the human disaster that repeatedly afflicted Ethiopia during the same period, and was echoed during the most recent round of mass displacement and starvation. Quite apart from the obvious fact that Tanzania never experiences the severity of drought that seems natural to Ethiopia and Eritrea, the fact is that Nyerere at least attempted to build on the cultural actualities of the peoples that made up Tanzania when he launched his program of *Ujamaa*. It was unfortunate that he did not fully trust that system of self-development and localized economic management and thus preferred to impose on the resourceful intelligence of his peoples, yet again, a textbook economic paradigm from other lands. This only resulted in vitiating the proven efficacy of an ancient, organic process. The creation of new, artificial communities was a disaster, bringing much hardship to his peoples, now deprived of a communally cohering system of productivity that once enabled them to cope with the unexpected. At least, however, Nyerere possessed an unaccustomed leadership integrity and dignity to acknowledge the failure of his well-intentioned experiment.

Most current, and of immediate concern to the rest of the continent, is the regression of Tanzania's neighbor Zimbabwe into a land of fear engendered by state thuggery, whose predictable consequence is the collapse of economic structures and a slow strangulation of civic life. Here, once again, we are confronted by that perennial phenomenon of the African leader who simply cannot bear to be parted from power even in his dotage. One should be forgiven for imagining that surely, especially in that region, after the dismal lesson of Hastings Banda, the temptation to act out those words of egregious arrogance and folly – *l'état, c'est moi* – would have diminished. The contrary is what we are certainly witnessing in the conduct of our once revered revolutionary and liberation warrior Robert Mugabe. Playing the race card with a cynical crudeness, the real victims of his ambition are millions of Zimbabweans who desire change, an opportunity for change, and are entitled to it as equal partners in the struggle for liberation.

Let us not, however, lose sight of some fundamental issues that must be held pertinent to a once settler-colony like Zimbabwe, where a grossly disproportionate few control the largest and richest swaths of farmland in the nation.

Abdul Nasser in his time was compelled to tackle that issue head-on, dispossessing the feudal oligarchy and reinvesting the land among the fellahin. The struggle of the Sandinistas in Nicaragua against a landowning monopoly composed of a few select families is equally historic. Some of the greatest uprisings and consequent civil wars in Mexico have centered squarely on the ownership of land, even right down to contemporary times, with the revolt of the neo-Zapatistas. There is therefore nothing extraordinary or blameworthy in any moves to execute a policy that aims for a more egalitarian apportionment of land and its resources. The question that must be put to Robert Mugabe, however, is this: Just what have you been doing as head of a virtual one-party government in nearly a quarter of a century? Is there no orderly, structured alternative to the unleashing of so-called war veterans on farmowners, their families, and – a majority of the affected who are, however, mostly neglected in Western reporting – African farmhands and managers? That last especially, the farmworkers. In the history of takeover of factories, I have yet to learn of armies of peasants or university lecturers being mobilized to take over the ownership and operations of such factories – no, it is logically the workers themselves. They may be expected to lock out the owners and turn the factory into a cooperative, sometimes retaining the former operatives in management or technical positions in order to ensure continuity in efficiency and productivity. Even Stalin, in his mad race to collectivize land and eliminate all those conveniently designated kulaks, did not send veterans of Russia's revolutionary wars to take over the land. Not that his results were any better, but he appeared at least to have given some thought to structural transfers, which is something totally absent from Mugabe's methodology – if one could call it that, being a violent, chaotic process in response to an ancient history of dispossession, and for the declared intent of the restoration of land justice.

Crude and opportunistic as was Idi Amin's expulsion of Asian businessmen and women from Uganda, Robert Mugabe's political adventurism in his dying days is only another reminder – as if any were needed – that Ayi Kwei Armah's "beautiful ones" are indeed yet to be born, that even when the star of revolutionary beauty appears to have hovered over their nativity, it is extinguished in their maturity, and only the ashes of a spent meteor are left to smother the land in their dotage. We are left to wonder how long the pattern of retrogression must continue to determine the emergence of a beleaguered continent. Stung and humiliated by the clear knowledge that the last elections in Zimbabwe constituted a victory for the opposition – never mind that a vicious campaign of intimidation, murder, and other dismal forms of state terror had succeeded in providing his party a numerical majority – the aging lion has resorted to the most blatant, time-dishonored methods of African dictators who fail to understand that a people must be led in dignity, not dragged on their knees along the pathway to social transformation. Resignations and dismissals of judges have been manipulated at a speed unprecedented in the history of Zimbabwe's judiciary, so that that institution is now packed with Mugabe's creatures, guaranteed to do his bidding and overturn constitutional modes of redress. Free expression has become hazardous, as writers and journalists skeeter around increasingly ill-defined parameters of toleration that recall the darkest days of Idi Amin's Uganda. In vain, his own peers, his brother heads of state in neighboring countries, and with similar revolutionary credentials, attempt to call Fuhrer Mugabe to order – no, he is too far gone on the route to self-apotheosization, indifferent to the price that African nations and peoples continue to pay when forced along this cul-de-sac. A messy end-game is in store for that unlucky nation, the enthronement of brute force as the force of law, and even the possibility of a civil war.

But the opposition remains unbowed, and this gives hope for the future of democracy, not only in that country but to others who watch this dismal, violent saga in sadness and frustration, relating these events to any signs of potential danger within their own countries, and drawing the appropriate lessons for constant vigilance and preparedness. Such apprehensive observers make comparisons also with other nations that have gone through baptisms of fire, such as my own Nigeria, where the once guaranteed assumption of impunity by even military dictators is being subjected to lacerating searchlights, with their explicit warnings to others for the future. Of course, it is not yet over, not even for the Nigerian nation. Some of these generals, these ex-dictators, have yet to understand that their world is gone. Completely shattered. Summoned to appear before Nigeria's version of South Africa's Truth and Reconciliation Commission – named the Oputa Commission on Human Rights Abuses – they insist on clinging to a concept of the immunity of power, both in and out of office. They are caught in a time-warp where they remain oblivious to the fact that such notions were dramatically shattered with the detention of Pinochet in a foreign land, followed by a trial in his own country. Ignored by these Nigerian generals is the even more humiliating status reversal for the once all-powerful Milosevic, the gloating practitioner of ethnic cleansing, who is now standing trial for crimes against humanity.

What the foregoing serves to remind us of is that element that has always defined power – alienation. Alienation from the real world, and a solipsistic immersion in a wished-for world that is totally circumscribed by the limitations of their intelligence. In the Nigerian instance especially, any of these ex-dictators, exercising a modicum of intelligence, observing the processes of the Oputa panel's investigation into abuses of human rights, would immediately realize that they are exposed to very little actual danger from the consequences of their conduct in power. None of them stands the remotest hazard in the nature of the Nemesis that eventually overtook a Pinochet or a Milosevic. In one case, the crime he is accused of having masterminded would be absolutely unprovable – even his most strident accusers privately acknowledge this. For other charge sheets prepared for all these miscreants in power, an appearance, an explication, a plea of extenuating circumstances, and an appeal to the people to forgive and forget past errors – and the odds are on the people's inclination toward reconciliation. The worst of them, to whom a hand of reconciliation would have been unthinkable, is mercifully dead. But now these survivors stand a very real danger of humiliating arrests, and even criminal or civil prosecutions. Personally, I find myself praying that they maintain their acts of defiance to the end, since the panel, having made its stand sternly clear after repeated defiance by the generals, would have no option but to issue warrants of arrest for them. I have already spent blissful hours picturing them in handcuffs, or being caught in violent scenes as a result of sporadic attempts to subject them to citizens' arrests in the midst of one of their social functions, even in those parts of the country that they consider personal bastions of immunity. Somewhere along the murky trajectories of their stay in office, we can only conjecture that they came across the antiquated notion of "the king can do no wrong," forgetting the numerous kings and queens whose ends have fatally given the lie to that notion.

The title of Ayi Kwei Armah's novel, by the way, was taken from an inscription on that ubiquitous conveyance that is variously known in Africa as the *tro-tro*, mammy-wagon, *bolekaja*, etc., inscriptions that have formed the subject of not a few monographs on culture and social mores, as well as coffee-table catalogues. These inscriptions are often taken from proverbs, expressions of traditional wisdoms, sound-bites from the most unlikely sources, wrenched from their original contexts – which may vary from the Bible, Shakespeare, or the Qur'an to Indian or kung-fu films, or even a bit of commercial jingle heard on television and coopted for its pithy sound. Qur'anic inscriptions are also to be found in the Arabic, some with translations, others without. The eclectic appropriation of shorthand quotations and aphorisms for contemporary realities, anxieties, aspirations, and even as a record of events, is very much a feature of popular culture that extends beyond these mobile murals – which is what they are when accompanied by artwork of equally eclectic images, sometimes incongruous, sometimes quite apposite as pictorial illustrations. This process extends into the world of musical lyrics and, of course, popular theater, and functions much in the same way as the works of more sophisticated writers who operate in modern modes of expression or adaptations of the old. I often think that a compulsory exercise for leaders should take the form of a staggered ride through the length and breath of the country in one of these mammy-wagons, that is, changing transportation every fifty miles or so. Not only would they acquire a very real lesson in "how the other side lives" but they might begin to understand that these crude inscriptions are the very definition of the existential reality and worldviews of their companions in those rickety and tumultuous, often fatal contraptions. They would experience the environment over which they preside as "the other side" does, with all the bumps, corrugations, filth, real-life commerce, raucousness, uncertainties, real-time tragedies, and petty triumphs, but above all a resilience that often is the sole surviving element as society itself collapses. They would experience not only "how the other side lives," but how it dies.

Since these leaders are unlikely to accept this therapeutic, even heuristic exercise for the understanding and management of power, perhaps they should simply be compelled to memorize as many of the inscriptions as their brains can accommodate, or else simply recite from a pocketbook of these selections, and meditate on one inscription every day before or after their morning prayers. Maybe even replace their prayers and other spiritual invocations – which appear to have taken the African continent nowhere anyway – with a meditation on a select few, indeed, perhaps just one per day so as not to place them under any mental strain. *No Telephone line to Heaven. Chop small, no quench* or its variant – *Chop small, quench small; Chop big, quench big. The Young shall Grow. The big leaf, falling, cannot dislodge the smaller. Monkey dey work, baboon dey chop. Allah dey! No Condition is Permanent* … ah yes, that especially – *No Condition is Permanent*. You can debate, analyze, reify, or fetishize democracy as long and as elaborately as you like but, place your average citizen in a motor park with lorries filled with dozens of these inscriptions, ask that worker or peasant to point out any single item that accurately defines democracy for him, and the odds are that he will point at that lorry bearing the inscription: *No Condition is Permanent*.

But suppose even this simple reorientation offering is rejected? What other proposals can we offer these leaders toward reconciling the need for their self-fulfillment with the need of the rest of humanity – which is also that of self-fulfillment? The marriage of these two interests is what takes us on the route to that elusive goal called democracy and, having begun this discourse on the platform of literature and the arts, it is in that very direction to which I now turn in exhuming once again my original contribution to this thorny problem. I seize the occasional opportunity to air it, since no one has yet had the courage, or simply the enterprising spirit, to put it to the test. With the retrogressive eruption of the antidemocratic psyche in leadership, such as we witnessed recently in General Guei and, even more alarmingly, in the unfinished business of Zimbabwe, how do we bring a terminal point to this repetitive cycle that continues to lay waste our resources and set back nations in the course of development, sometimes by entire generations?

The last time I spoke on the platform of Documenta – this was in Kassel in 1997 – I explored the many pathways and byways of Ritual, that accommodating mode of rebirth, restitution, exorcism, rehabilitation, rites of passage, etc., etc. – but made no attempt to relate it to contemporary sociopolitical phenomena. Here now is my chance to extend the portals of Ritual toward this critical life-and-death direction.

A Ritual of Power   Now, please pay close attention as I may appear about to shift gears, but I promise you we shall remain firmly on the same terrain. This offering from the Ritualistic arena grows on me all the time, and its presentation, always with newly thought-up variations, has become a ritual in itself whenever yet another power-besotted leader opts to short-circuit our nascent democracies. It also serves to anticipate the question that is often thrown at me and takes the form of: *What do you propose, in practical form? How do you resolve this issue of Power and Freedom, of tyranny and democracy?* There is one obvious answer, which I shall not even discuss, as it will arm my eternal adversaries with the easy accusation of advocating violent resistance which, as everyone knows, is very, very immoral. I mean, I would never dream of advocating such a solution! My unexceptionable answer is therefore derived from my acknowledged field, which is the theatrical. In addition, the new version of this ritual embraces the miracle of modern technology but, first, I must situate this offering accurately – well, as accurately as the analysis of our survivalist political archetypes can be – and clarify the premises on which the ritual proposition has been devised.

My original premise, at the inception of this ritual several years ago, was simply this: that the average dictator, in any culture, is propelled by an incurable death-wish. This was how the idea for my political ritual first took root but, I have since changed my mind. That premise has shifted somewhat and so, naturally, has the ritual format. Mortified by my earlier error, I now make bold to say, with absolute self-assurance, that I have really hit it accurately this time, indeed, that it cannot be faulted by any new analysis of the psychopathology of your representative dictator.

Let us understand quite clearly why my new premise makes sense over and above any other. It requires an understanding of what these men of power really lust after – apart from power, that is. We know all about power already, but then, having killed, tortured, and raped to obtain that power, what makes them desperate to remain – at whatever cost – *terminally* within power? To claim that power is an end in itself simply does not satisfy – there has to be something beyond it, something of great sublimity that eludes the ordinary mind. Thanks, however, to several inspirational sources, I finally stumbled on the answer. The most important of these – I may mention in passing – is the endless cycle of the funeral traditions of the Yoruba, and in particular the *egungun*, that is, the ancestral masquerade.

Earlier, I made what might have sounded a hubristic claim – that my proposal cannot be challenged because it is based on a penetration of the mystery of what lies beyond the lust for power. This implies that the discovery remains in itself unassailable. Let us therefore put that claim to the test by asking the following question: What is it, of all the gratifications open to all the controls that power exercises, what is the one thing that power cannot guarantee to its custodian and monopolist? Wealth? Unlimited access. Sex? Ask and it shall be given. Pomp? Circumstance? Domination? All implicit in the condition of power. Adulation, deification … the list is endless. Only one experience in the province of power remains inaccessible to the holder and that one experience is – let us prolong the suspense no longer – it is to be a live participant at one's own apotheosis; in short, to be a beneficiary of one's own funeral which, in this instance, is nothing less than the funerary ultimate that any mortal can dream of – a state funeral!

Here now are details of our project: Under the supervision of an architect of his choosing, we would construct for each dictator a mausoleum of his dreams. A professional ceremonial or theater director would be engaged to plan, with each, his fantasy funeral. Rehearsals would be conducted with lowered flags, orchestras, horse drawn or motorized carriage – some love the rhythm of those metal-shod hooves, etc., etc., which motorcades cannot provide. Professional mourners and praise-singers would be engaged. Our hero would be free to sleep from time to time in his mausoleum, just to get the feel of it, he would try it for size, savor the color schemes, order alterations, re-award the contract as often as he likes and collect the kickbacks himself – in short, enjoy a unique privilege, one that very few of us – just the occasional crank or two here and there I think – ever experience in our lives. Even I have never undergone this experience, though of course I have been privileged to read and even listen to the broadcast version of my obituary. In contrast to most mortals, our living hero can supervise the writing and personally rehearse the orator for his funeral eulogies. Indeed, he can deliver and record his own oration. He can choose to immortalize his mortality in – virtual reality! He can beam all or any aspect of his obsequies onto vast holographic fields and experience his lavishly decorated coffin being solemnly lowered into a vault of flawless marble, stainless steel, glass, titanium, polished wood, or whatever material he has chosen for his mausoleum. All this he can experience, every year – and even oftener, in its recorded version – in the privacy and safety of his bunker. The populace, I am certain, would require little persuasion to take on a role that anticipates the demise of their tyrant, even if it requires that they put on the composure and weeds of bereavement every year. We propose, in other words, for all our peoples who are afflicted by this pestilence of the sit-tight dictator, a National Day of Internment.

This is necessarily a sketchy – and rudimentary – version of a most elaborate scenario whose details I must preserve for the moment. In another place, I acknowledge the numerous sources of the inspiration for this idea – from traditional cultures to ministers of religion – so that it may not be simply dismissed as some hare-brained notion dreamt up by a delirious dramatist. Needless to say, there are details of this ritual that must be kept secret, just as there are details of any ritual process that can only be revealed to initiates. Also, for fear of plagiarists and copyright bandits, I must preserve for now, details of the translation of this scheme into virtual reality – it opens up such limitless prospects! Dictators do love toys and gadgets – the more technologically illiterate, the more obsessive their attachment – thus it should not be too difficult to seduce them into the technological gratification that is a side-product of exploiting such a medium. A ritual of passage into the ancestral world in virtual reality, with all the emotions of pomp and circumstance, of obsequious mourning by a million population at the touch of a button? What flesh-and-blood dictator could resist such painless apotheosis time and time and time again! Even Christ found himself restricted to only one – and a very simple – resurrection.

To the anticipated question therefore – What practical proposal do I have for this much abused African body that it may preserve itself in democracy, and be free of the boil of dictatorship? – after a lifetime of struggling against this plague, cauterizing it in one limb only to have it erupt in another, I have finally come up with this one unassailable solution: from one end of the continent to the other, let us have – a National Day of Internment!

Democracy between Autonomy and Heteronomy

Ernesto Laclau

In this presentation, we will address the question of the relationship between democracy and autonomy. "Autonomy" is an elusive category: its conceptual specification can involve the operation of very different social logics. The first and most radical way of defining it would be in terms of *self-determination*. An entity is autonomous as far as it does not have to go outside itself in order to be determined in its being. It is in these terms that self-determination, freedom, and infinitude formed, for Hegel, an indissociable whole: true infinitude, as different from a spurious one, involves finding, within itself, the principle of its own determination. And this is the very definition of freedom conceived as autonomy. But this triple equation – freedom, self-determination, and autonomy – involves also the notion that the truly autonomous subject can only be a universal one. As a result, freedom and necessity become, for this universal subject, strictly synonymous. In the classical formulation, freedom can only be the consciousness of necessity. It is only as far as my true self is the universal that nothing is external to myself and that I am really autonomous; anything less than this universal self will be limited by something essentially alien which will be the source of an irreducible heteronomy.

The question that we want to raise concerning democracy is to what extent this ultimate heteronomy is incompatible with freedom – in other terms: to what extent self-determination, conceived as pure universality, is the condition of freedom. We want to suggest that, on the contrary, it is the very failure of a *total* freedom that makes possible the freedoms (in the plural) of contingent and finite subjects. If it could be shown that this is indeed the case, a fully self-determined subject would certainly be impossible; but one would have also to conclude that heteronomy cannot be entirely excluded from the workings of freedom. Freedom would involve an undecidable tension between autonomy and heteronomy and would thus become the name of that very undecidability. The referent of that name, however, would have been displaced: it would no longer be the closure of the gap between universality and particularity, but the very impossibility of that closure. So we will have to explore the different uses to which heteronomy can be put in relation to democracy.

Let us start with the hypothesis that the gap between the universality of the community conceived as a totality and the particularism of a plurality of demands or groups of demands is a constitutive one. If this gap were radically unbridgeable, we would have to conclude that there is no constituency corresponding to the "universal" and that democracy would be impossible. There would be no way of constituting "the people" (*peuple*) and we would just have a civil society conceived as a locus of dispersed demands (the "system of needs," as Hegel called it). In that case, the moment of universality would be transferred to a separate sphere (the State), bureaucracy would become the "universal class," and no democracy (let alone a radical one) would be conceivable. So the very possibility of democracy seems to depend on being able to construct a bridge between the particularism of the demands and the community conceived as a whole – that is, it turns on the possibility of constructing "the people" as a historical agent. There are, however, various ways of conceiving this bridging process. If it is seen as a *necessary* transition from the particularism of the demands to the universality of the community, the emancipation involved in radical democracy would be seen as the movement from the kingdom of necessity to the kingdom of freedom – the latter being conceived as self-determination in the strong sense of radical autonomy. But this is the possibility that we have excluded *ex hypothesi*.

The other alternative is that the bridging of the gap *does* take place, but that the bridge is not a priori inscribed in the nature of the particular demands, for it depends on a contingent process of political construction. In that case, an element of *exteriority* becomes constitutive of the identity of "the people." But if this exteriority is *truly* constitutive, this means that the democratic/emancipatory agent cannot be *entirely* self-determined and that, consequently, its identity will necessarily include an element of heteronomy. We are confronted with the paradoxical situation that autonomy requires its exact opposite – heteronomy – as the condition of its constitution – or, rather, that the couple autonomy/heteronomy is the name of a tension, of a continuum where the conditions for the elimination of one or the other pole of the dichotomy never arise. Democracy, as it were, consists in the negotiation between these two contradictory logics, not in the elimination of heteronomy in the name of a fully fledged self-determination.

The *traces* of this heteronomy can be found in two central aspects of a democratic polity: the double inscription of the identity of the democratic subjects and the emptiness of the place of inscription. Let us start with identity. As we have asserted, there is no concrete demand which finds inscribed, within itself, the conditions of its own universalization. Demands are many – housing, education, freedom of the press, political and economic rights, etc. – and they can be articulated between themselves in a variety of ways. Some of these ways will not be democratic at all – there is no reason why some popular or democratic demands cannot be articulated to authoritarian projects; and, within the field of democratic politics, a plurality of articulating projects will necessarily coexist. (This coexistence is essential if we are going to speak of *democratic* politics.) What is crucial to democratic politics, in terms of what we have called double inscription, is: (1) that the universalization of a demand takes place in terms of *contingent* chains of equivalence[1] with other demands; (2) that, while this universalization will bring about a certain closure, the latter is never total – otherwise a certain articulating content would cease to be contingent and will become necessary, and in that case all possibility of dissent will be excluded and democracy will be at an end.

Let us suppose that a society is experiencing a situation lived as radical injustice: justice, in that case, will be seen as what is present through its very absence; justice will not have a positive content of its own, but certain particular contents will be lived as the *embodiment* of a radical political redress capable of bringing about justice. The overthrow, for instance, of bureaucratic rule in Eastern Europe in the 1980s is a good example. We see here the operation of what we have called double inscription: on the one hand, certain concrete demands are "universalized" when they enter into equivalential chains with other demands; on the other hand, these equivalential chains are the embodiment of something constitutively exceeding them: the empty signifiers "order," "justice," "truth," "revolution," etc. The important point is that the investment of these empty symbols into concrete contents embodying them is a *radical* investment: there is no possibility of moving from one level to the other in terms of a merely logical transition.

The matter could be formulated in terms of Lacanian theory: because the subject is, in a radical sense, the subject of the lack, its relation to a concrete content can only be a relation of *identification*. The universalization achieved through the inscription of a certain demand into chain of equivalences confers a certain power to the subject thus constituted, and in this way endows him with a certain autonomy, but it is an autonomy achieved only at the price of an *identification*. This involves the impossibility of a pure self-determination and is the source of a heteronomy which is always at the heart of autonomy.

If we consider our second aspect concerning the relationship autonomy/heteronomy, similar considerations can be made. The contingent articulation

1 On the notions of equivalence and difference, see Ernesto Laclau and Chantal Mouffe, *Hegemony and Socialist Strategy: Towards a Radical Democratic Politics* (London: Verso, 1985), ch. 3.

between empty universal identity and particular content incarnating the latter is to be found again in the relationship between the empty place of power and the actual force occupying it. This is the very pertinent distinction introduced a long time ago by Claude Lefort. On the difference with the hierarchical societies of the past, where the place of power has a "natural" occupier – where, in our terminology, this is an overlapping between universality and differential particularity – the main change brought about by the "democratic invention" is that this overlapping is unmade: the place of power becomes empty, while its links with its successive occupiers become essentially contingent. I entirely subscribe to this vision of the changes resulting from the democratic revolution. I would only add that the condition of emptying the place of power in the way described by Lefort is that a similar process takes place at the level of the subject: it is because the subject is now split – in the way we described – between particularity and empty universality, that the place of power, in modern democracy, can become empty.

If this conclusion is correct, democracy, as the space of negotiation between universality and particularity, necessarily blurs the boundaries between State and civil society. For Hegel, these boundaries were strict: civil society was the realm of pure particularity, while the universal class was exclusively located in the political sphere. Marx eliminates the latter and transfers the attributes of the "universal class" from bureaucracy to the proletariat, but in this transfer the moment of particularity vanishes: the simplification of class struggle under capitalism leads to a universal subject whose self-determination will not be tainted by any heteronomy. It is only with Gramsci that we see the emergence of a political logic which cuts across the distinction State/civil society and, in that way, makes the interaction between autonomy and heteronomy an integral part of the democratic negotiation.[2] We can add that the undecidability of the game universality/particularity permeates many contemporary debates concerning agency. We have, on the one hand, positions asserting an issue-oriented politics based in cultural diversity, multiculturalism, affirmation of difference, etc. On the other, the insistence that the broader problems linked to emancipatory struggles are abandoned through this emphasis on difference.[3] It should be clear why, in our view, both emphases are unilateral and limited. It is not a question, for us, of denying the radical democratic potential that differential struggles present, but it is not a question either of limiting oneself to the punctual character of those struggles, leaving aside broader strategic considerations. The con-

---

2 Antonio Gramsci, *Selections from the Prison Notebooks*, ed. and trans. Quintin Hoare and Geoffrey Nowell Smith (London: Lawrence & Wishart, 1971), pp. 206–277.
3 This is the position maintained by Slavoj Žižek, among others, over recent years.

struction of contingent chains of equivalence is, in our view, the terrain in which the link between universality and particularity has to be established. The tension between these two polar alternatives – the building up of a universal emancipatory subject, the enlargement of the democratic revolution through the expansion of the equalitarian principles to increasingly larger sections of the population – runs through the whole history of modern democracy.

We have to stress a last point concerning the dialectic between heteronomy and autonomy and its reproduction at all levels of political argument. It concerns the ways of addressing the relationship inclusion/exclusion. As we have seen, an autonomy conceived as strict self-determination cannot leave anything outside itself, it has to reduce anything apparently alien to an internal moment of its self-development. Self-determination has to be all-inclusive. Now, a notion of inclusion conceived this way is not incompatible with *some kind* of exclusion: one which makes the otherness of the other the condition of constitution of the self. The otherness of the other becomes, in that way, an internal moment of a wider totality under which "self" and "other" are subsumed. Their incompatibility is reduced by referring them to a universality transcending both poles of the initial opposition. Hegel was able, in that way, to present "world history" as a purely internal development unified by a cunning of reason which dialectically supercedes and interiorizes all apparent externality. This could not however be, even for Hegel, the totality of the story. For the main line of historical development, as described by him, had to come to terms with the presence of a contingent excess escaping its mastery. Thus, he could not avoid having to speak of "peoples without history." And here we have an exclusion of an entirely different kind: it is an exclusion radically refractory to self-determination, one that the latter cannot retrieve. It involves the emergence of a heterogeneity which threatens the purely internal character of "world history."

Hegel probably thought that the purely marginal character of this social excess was no real threat to his story. And Marx argued along similar lines: the proletariat was part of a world history unified by the category of productive labor.[4] But even in Marx's account, the irreducible remainder was present: it was given by the notion of *lumpenproletariat* as a social excess, without history, living in the interstices of all social formations. The violently dismissive way in which both Marx and Engels referred to the lumpenproletariat is well known. Some of their contemporaries, like Bakunin, took, however, a different view: it was for them the radical exteriority of the lumpenproletariat vis-à-vis the existent system that ensured its revolutionary potential. And some later writers take a similar

---

4 See Peter Stallybrass, "Marx and Heterogeneity: Thinking the Lumpenproletariat," *Representations* 31, no. 1 (Summer 1990), pp. 69–95.

line. Thus, Fanon writes: "The *lumpenproletariat*, once it is constituted, brings all its forces to endanger the 'security' of the town, and it is the sign of the irrevocable decay, the gangrene ever present at the heart of colonial domination. So the pimps, the hooligans, the unemployed, and the petty criminals … throw themselves into the struggle like stout working men. These classless idlers will by militant and decisive action discover the path that leads to nationhood … The prostitutes too, and the maids who are paid two pounds a month, all who turn in circles between suicide and madness, will recover their balance, once more go forward, and march in the great procession of the awakened nation."[5]

We see thus emerging, from within the very logic of construction of the emancipatory subject, the same tension between autonomy and heteronomy that we have pointed out since the beginning of our reflection. Total autonomy would presuppose that only inclusion is ultimately thinkable and that any exclusion is purely transitory or appariential and destined to be finally mastered by the inclusive identitary logic. But it follows that the subject of this logic cannot be any actually existing subject but only a transcendental one (the latter being, of course, the Absolute Spirit, which is not even achievable in the sociopolitical sphere). The second kind of exclusion is, on the contrary, constitutive: the alien opposing it is irreducible to any type of interiorization. Does this mean that we have pure heteronomy and that the possibility of any autonomy has to be discarded? Not at all, for in the very process of opposing something alien one is able to construct the conditions of one's own efficacy within a certain area; one *does* become self-determined in a weak and partial sense. Now, the autonomy thus achieved depends on heteronomy for its emergence in a double sense: firstly, because the autonomy thus conceived is indistinguishable from power, and the latter presupposes something alien over which it is exercised (a power whose object is oneself would not be power at all), and secondly, because it is only through its opposition to a power *external* to itself that the identity of the relatively autonomous entity is constituted. (Going back to Fanon's example: it is only their opposition to colonialism that makes possible the union of the marginals in a new historical actor.)

On the difference with the absolute subject of a total self-determination, the partially autonomous/partially heteronomous identity of the subjects emerging from the second relation of exclusion corresponds exactly with the identity of actually existing social actors. And it is important to realize that these are the only subjects of any possible democracy, the latter involving the presence of irreducible dissent and of a constitutive gap between the particularism of the social

5 Frantz Fanon, quoted in ibid., p. 89.

agents and the universality of the communitarian space. But this gap – without which, as we have seen, there would be no democracy – translates the undecidability which is its necessary corollary to the main categories which have historically structured the discourse of democratic theory. We will discuss its operation in two of these categories, sovereignty and representation, and we will later conclude this presentation by stating the centrality that the notion of hegemony has for a radical approach to democracy.

Sovereignty. It is important to see why sovereignty is a specifically modern category. The notion of an ultimate source of power was certainly not absent from the Ancient World or the Middle Ages – notions such as *summa potestas* or *plenitude potestas* moved certainly in that direction – but on the whole, the limitations of the royal power by natural law, by custom, and by a feudal organization that reduced the king to the role of *primus inter pares* conspired, before the 14th century, against the formulation of a fully fledged theory of sovereignty. (To this, one should add the presence of the two universal powers, the Empire and the Church, which equally limited the sovereignty of the nation states.) The important point for our discussion is that, at the moment of its mature formulation in modern times – for instance, in the Hobbesian principle according to which *auctoritas, non veritas facit legem* – the notion of sovereignty is linked to the absence of limitations in the exercise of power. This means that we are dealing with autonomy in the strong sense of the term discussed above. The State centralization brought about by the absolute monarchies worked in that direction, and democratic theory, at the moment in which it attempted to replace the sovereignty of the king by that of the people, had the whole terrain prepared by centuries of bureaucratic unification.

But a democratic sovereignty has problems of its own, which are not so visible in an authoritarian one. In the case of Rousseau, for instance, we have the whole ensemble of paradoxes linked to the notion of *volonté générale*. The whole question of making possible a will which becomes the locus of a true universality could only be approached by him in terms of homogeneous social actors in small communities, communities that – he was the first to recognize – were every day less compatible with the conditions of the modern world. That is the reason why, from the very beginning, the theory of sovereignty was challenged by opposite approaches which turned constitutionalism into a weapon to prevent the total concentration of power in a single point of the political organism. The American Constitution, for instance, as justified in the Federalist Papers, advocates a loose federation of states which prevents the formation of a strongly centralized juridical structure.

It is easy to see that this opposition overlaps with the two senses of autonomy that we have discussed before. Either we have autonomization of a *particu-*

lar sector against the community as a whole – in which case no subject can truly be a sovereign (and democracy, consequently, identifies itself with a *limitation* of sovereignty), or we have the total autonomy of a fully sovereign power, but in that case such a regime can only be democratic if it overlaps with the homogeneous will of a *volonté générale*. The important point to stress is that these two logics are *ultimately* incompatible: there is no square circle that could bring them together into a logically coherent intellectual mode. The fact that democracy exists in the space of this irreducible tension does not mean, however, that it is impossible, but only that the language game that we call "democracy" consists in negotiating between these two incompatible poles. A society which leans too much toward extreme particularism would not be able to build up any form of global collective representation and collective will – and would be easily manipulated by an administrative power which is not submitted to any political check or challenge. But a society which is exclusively universalistic in terms of the collective identities that it is capable of creating, would have to suppress dissent and would fall into the worst forms of authoritarian unification (*the* Class, *the* Race, *the* Fatherland, etc.). Now, the terrain thus drawn for democratic negotiation is no other than that of an autonomy contaminated by heteronomy, for it will be the negotiation of social agents who are *less* than the "universal class."

Representation. We have asserted that a certain universalization – which stops short of full self-determination – is a condition of democracy. How is that universalization, however, achievable? We have already given some elements to start answering that question. Two central dimensions should be taken into account. The first is what we have called equivalential relations: a social identity universalizes itself when it enters into an equivalential relation with other identities. And identities are structured around demands. A demand which remains closed within its own particularity without establishing equivalences with other identities can never become political. Politics supposes negotiating connections between demands and constituting wider social identities as a result of those connections.

But there is a second and equally important connection. Wider popular identities are organized around equivalential chains. But it is not enough to enumerate the links of the chain in a purely additive exercise: it is also necessary to *name* the chain, to *signify* it as a whole. The symbolic unity of "the people" is crucial in any process of political construction. The *means of representation* of these collective ensembles, however, are only the particular links constituting the chain. This requires that some of these links become split from their own particularities and that, without ceasing to be particular, they become the signifiers of a certain overflow of meaning. "Socialization of the means of production," for instance, is a technical way of running the economy, but in the social-ist discourses of the beginning of the 20th century it signified a much wider project of human emancipation, equivalentially embracing demands coming from a variety of fields. Without this bringing together of demands through naming those wider ensembles, there would be no possibility of universalization.

This has, however, an important consequence: there is only universalization through representation. The idea of a purely self-transparent autonomy should be resolutely discarded. Why? Firstly, because no autonomy could exist except by making the subject more universal – which is only achievable through the expansion of the equivalential chains. A demand closed with its own particular-ity, far from being autonomous, would be reduced to a hopeless heteronomy: it could not constitute any power and it would be unable to establish any war of position in the negotiation of the tension autonomy/heteronomy. Secondly, as we have seen, the condition of the equivalential chain becoming a wider collec-tive ensemble is the representation of that ensemble by a particular signifier whose identity is split between its own particularity and its wider representative function. This is the operation that Gramsci called "hegemony." But if the wider (more universal) identity requires being represented by a universal equiva-lent – what in my terminology I have called an empty signifier[6] – this means that there are no social identities except through a process of representation. Representation is not a subsidiary relation, one that completes an identity con-stituted outside and previous to the process of representation, but is inscribed in the originary construction of social identities. The process of representation and the process of formation of social identities is actually one and the same process. And here we find again the dialectic between autonomy and heteronomy: no autonomy can exist except through the equivalential universalization of demands and the power relations that the latter involves (this is the autonomous moment); but no universalization can take place except through representation (this is the heteronomous moment). Representation involves a double move-ment between representative and those who are represented, in which both sides contribute something to the representative process without being possible to assign any ultimate priority to either side.[7]

Hegemony. Let us recapitulate. We have argued in this paper that some of the stark oppositions that have dominated social and political theory for a long while are simply the result of making a choice for one extreme of opposition and presenting the other as its strict antithesis. We have maintained, on the contrary,

6 See my essay "Why Do Empty Signifiers Matter to Politics?," in *Emancipation(s)* (London: Verso, 1996).
7 See my essay "Power and Representation," in ibid.

that in most cases the two extreme opposites, far from rejecting each other, con-
taminate each other, so that it is only by focusing on their processes of mutual
subversion that new language games can be designed which take into account
the historical possibilities for democratic theory and practice that those *apparent*
blind alleys actually open.

The center of our analysis was the relation between autonomy and heteronomy. We tried to show that the strict identification between autonomy, freedom, and self-determination leads to a situation in which: (a) such identification does not correspond to any possible subject; and (b) that it is only by
articulating autonomy and heteronomy in their tense relation that it is possible
to develop more complex strategic games that open the way to actual democratic interactions. The same can be said of other couples of traditionally antagonistic concepts – some of which we have referred to briefly – such as universality and particularity, power and emancipation, inclusion and exclusion, etc.

Central to our concern has been the category of "power" which, in our view,
points to the terrain in which the negotiation between most of our dichotomies
takes place. To go back to autonomy/heteronomy: for a subject who is less than
the Absolute Spirit to be autonomous involves the construction of *a power relation*, something which makes possible autonomy as a result of a relation of
forces which, however, presupposes the moment of heteronomy. The same can
be said of all other oppositions. And this leads us to the question of hegemony,
which is for me the basic category of political analysis. I have defined "hegemony" as the process by which a certain particularity assumes the representation
of a universality which is incommensurable with it. We have here an undecidable terrain between universality and particularity. We are not simply in the terrain of pure particularity, which would involve straight domination; but we do
not have pure, uncontaminated universality either. What we have is a mutual
subversion between universality and particularity which creates the field of a
tension which cannot be overcome. As in the cases of power/emancipation,
inclusion/exclusion, and autonomy/heteronomy (but perhaps they are not *different* cases), it is this logic of undecidability which is at the root of the political
productivity of the notion of hegemony. As Kant writes in the *Critique of Pure
Reason*: "Much is already gained if we can bring a number of investigations
under the formula of a single problem."[8]

---

8 *Immanuel Kant's Critique of Pure Reason*, trans. Norman Kemp Smith (London: Macmillan, 1985),
   B 19, p. 55.

In Search of Dynamic Republicanism for the 21st Century

Zhiyuan Cui

J. G. A. Pocock published his monumental study on "the Machiavellian Moment and Atlantic Republican Tradition" in 1975.[1] The field of history of political thought in the English-speaking world has been profoundly transformed ever since. In the vivid words of Joyce Appleby, "the recent discovery of republicanism as the reigning social theory of eighteenth-century America has produced a reaction among historians akin to the response of chemists to a new element."[2] However, most of the debates triggered by Pocock's seminal work focused either on the relative importance of liberalism and republicanism[3] or on the difference between humanist and jurist modes of discourse in early modern times.[4] These debates, though very important in their own right, neglected the potential of republicanism as an institutional alternative to both "capitalism" and "socialism." I propose to explore in this brief paper the potential of republican thought for our institutional innovations in the 21st century.

Why have I chosen this topic?

The justification for my choice is twofold. The first is textual, the second political. The textual justification is that Pocock himself has hinted that republicanism can be viewed in contrast to "capitalism" and "socialism," though not exactly in these terms; the political justification is my engagement with the current ideological debates in China, which lends a sense of urgency to the search for institutional alternatives to both "socialism" and "capitalism" as these terms

---

1 J. G. A. Pocock, *The Machiavellian Moment: Florentine Political Thought and the Atlantic Republican Tradition* (Princeton, N.J.: Princeton University Press, 1975).

2 Joyce Oldham Appleby, *Liberalism and Republicanism in the Historical Imagination* (Cambridge, Mass.: Harvard University Press, 1992), p. 277.

3 Isaac Kramnick's *Republicanism and Bourgeois Radicalism* (Ithaca, N.Y.: Cornell University Press, 1990) is a representative critique of Pocock's "republican" thesis. Pocock's review of Kramnick's book is his most thoughtful response to the critics; see Pocock's review in *Eighteenth-Century Studies* 25, no. 2 (Winter 1991–1992), pp. 219–227.

4 Richard Tuck devotes the first chapter of his new book on international law to a critique of Pocock's view of the relationship between humanist and jurist modes of thought; see his *The Rights of War and Peace: Political Thought and the International Order from Grotius to Kant* (New York: Oxford University Press, 1999), p. 12.

are traditionally defined and used in today's global ideological discourse. After the tragedy of September 11, this search becomes ever more critical, since the distorted elements of truth in Islamic fundamentalism reflect the frustrations felt by people with regard to conventional "capitalism" and "socialism," as vividly illustrated in the letter sent by Khomeini to Gorbachev in January 1989.[5]

Pocock's interest in republicanism as an alternative to "capitalism" can be gleaned in his characterization of the role of property in the republican vision: "The citizen possessed property in order to be autonomous and autonomy was necessary for him to develop virtue or goodness as an actor within the political, social and natural realm or order. He did not possess it in order to engage in trade, exchange or profit."[6] Clearly, this republican vision of property is quite different from the conventional definition of "capitalist" property, which emphasizes unrestricted transfer and accumulation as the crucial feature of property ownership. Pocock even states that "Bourgeois ideology," as a matter of historical fact, "may never have fully won" its struggle for existence.[7]

Pocock's interest in republicanism as an alternative to "socialism" can be seen in the last chapter of *The Machiavellian Moment*, where he argues that "The quarrel between civic virtue and secular time has been one of the main sources of the Western awareness of human historicity."[8] "Socialism," in Pocock's view, represents a static moral polemic against the historical change along the "capitalist" road. To be sure, Pocock acknowledged that republicanism shared this static vision with socialism. However, from his argument that "republican theory" is an "early form of historicism," I assume that what Pocock really wants is to develop a dynamic version of republicanism for modern and postmodern times.

On the political motivation behind my choice of topic, I would like to emphasize that the dichotomy of capitalism versus socialism is more confusing than illuminating in understanding the current sea change in China. Can we say that today's China is moving toward "capitalism," as seems to be the consensus of the Western Left and Right? The answer depends on what we mean by "capitalism." Deng Xiaoping once said, "we do not know what socialism is." In fact, we might add, "we also do not know what capitalism is." In his monumental

5 Khomeini states the following in his letter: "of course, it is possible that due to incorrect methods and wrong actions of the former communist strongmen regarding economics, the grass might seem greener in the Western world. However, the truth lies elsewhere. If at this juncture you wish only to undo the blind economic knots of socialism and communism by taking refuge in the bosom of Western capitalism, not only will you not have cured any of the ills of your society; on the contrary …" (cited in Bobby Sayyid, *A Fundamental Fear: Eurocentrism and the Emergence of Islamism* [London: Zed Books, 1998], p. 131.)
6 J .G. A. Pocock, *Virtue, Commerce and History* (Cambridge: Cambridge University Press, 1985), p. 103.
7 Pocock, *The Machiavellian Moment*, p. 461.
8 Ibid, p. 551.

work on the history of modern civilization from the 15th to 18th century, Fernand Braudel confessed that he might have written the entire book without using the word "capitalism."[9] Indeed, the word "capitalism" seems too broad to be useful for analyzing today's China.[10] Should we say the corporate shareholding system is inherently "capitalist"? If so, how do we make sense of the historical fact that J. S. Mill argues for the General Act of Incorporation with limited liability for shareholders in front of the British Parliament in 1850 on the basis of its supposed capacity to promote workers' cooperatives?[11]

After all, American "legal realism" in insisting that "ownership" is not a single right, but a "bundle of rights"[12] which can be rearranged to regulate changing social relations.[13] The vocabulary of "bundle of rights" makes it possible to break away from the Stalinist conception of socialist ownership as having only two possible types, namely, "state ownership" and "collective ownership." The Chinese Communist Party's 15th Congress did exactly that by allowing cross-stockholding between state shares, legal-person shares, and individual shares. It opens up the possibility of enlarging and democratizing the stakeholders of the bundle of property rights in corporations. Of course, it also leaves room for corruption and misappropriation of public assets. In a sense, we are witnessing today a Chinese "Augustan" age.[14] It is here that both hope and danger for China lies.

I am still in the early stages of working out the institutional innovations required by a dynamic republicanism. But to give a hint of the kinds of institutions I am thinking of, let me take the example of the republican vision of property as the basis of autonomy and security. Obviously, in today's world, both in China and the West, it is impossible to revive the Harrington type of landownership as the basis for individual autonomy. This vision of landownership was a

---

9 Fernand Braudel, *Civilization materielle, économie et capitalisme, XVe–XVIIIe siècle*, The Chinese translation (Beijing: Sanlian Bookstore, 1993), vol. 2, p. 234.

10 Indeed, as increasingly being realized by scholars, "capitalism" is not a useful analytical concept for studying Western history either. For instance, Ellen Meiksins Wood argues that "the eighteenth-century French bourgeoisie was not a capitalist class" (in her "Capitalism or Enlightenment?," *History of Political Thought* 21, no. 3 [2000], p. 413).

11 Mill reasoned as follows: when owners' liability is unlimited, only rich people can afford to do business; the regime of limited liability would encourage workers to form their own cooperatives to compete in the market on a safer footing.

12 By separating ownership into its constituent parts, i.e., a "bundle of rights" such as income right, use right, control right, and transfer right, legal realism demonstrates that ownership does not imply any pre-political, absolute or fixed set of rights. See Morton Horwitz, *The Transformation of American Law, 1870–1960* (New York: Oxford University Press, 1992), pp. 145–169.

13 The former president of Austria, Karl Renner, has written the best synthesis of Marxism and legal realism. See his *Institutions of Private Law and Their Social Functions* (London: Routledge & Kegan Paul, 1949).

14 See chapter 13 of Pocock's *The Machiavellian Moment* on the Augustan debates over land, trade, and public debt. The similarity with contemporary China cannot be missed.

static version of republicanism to begin with. However, we could introduce a modern and dynamic version of Harringtonian property: the "social dividend."

The idea of the "social dividend" is first proposed by James Meade, a British economist who won the Nobel Prize in 1977. In Meade's program, every citizen is paid a tax-free social dividend according to the citizen's age and family status but without any other conditions.[15] Two basic reasons for instituting the social dividend are: (1) the promotion of equality by providing everyone with the same basic unconditional income; (2) the reduction of risks by providing some part of income that is unaffected by variations required by flexibility in the labor market. The intuitive core of the idea of a social dividend lies in the attempt to replace the demand for job tenure by an enhancement of the resources and capabilities of the individual worker-citizen.

One of the advantages of a social dividend over the conventional social-democratic policy of a "conditional benefit" is that the former improves the incentives of the recipient for accepting low-earning jobs. This may look counterintuitive at first sight, because an "unconditional social dividend" seems not to reduce the incentive to accept low-wage jobs (in comparison with conditional benefits based on unemployment). However, Meade nicely demonstrates that intuition to be wrong with the following simple example: "a recipient of a Social Dividend of 80 supplemented by a Conditional Benefit of 20 will have an incentive to take outside earnings so long as those earnings after deduction of Income Tax are greater than 20; but if he or she had relied for the whole 100 on a Conditional Benefit, there would be no incentive to accept any outside earnings less than 100."[16]

How could the regime of social dividend be financed? In the context of today's Western world, Meade envisions five stages of reform to the tax system, the final stage being socialization of 50 percent of national assets as a source of revenue for financing the social dividend. However, he argues that "the government plays no direct part in the management of the partnership enterprises or other private concerns the capital of which it owns indirectly. There is a free and very vigorous competitive capital market and Stock Exchange on which private individuals and institutions freely deal in respect to the 50 percent of the real assets of the community which they own. The government invests its ownership of the other 50 percent of the community's real assets in competitive unit trusts and similar competitive investment institutions which merge the government's fund with the private funds in the search of a high yield on the funds so employed."[17]

15 J. E. Meade, *Liberty, Equality and Efficiency* (New York: New York University Press, 1993).
16 Ibid., p. 152.
17 Ibid., p. 157.

Obviously, this mechanism of financing a social dividend almost amounts to a revolution in the West, because as Meade himself emphasizes, "at present in the typical capitalist economy the State far from being a new owner of capital assets in fact is often on balance a debtor to the private sector of the community."[18] In light of this fact, I will not discuss the feasibility of instituting a social dividend in the West.[19] But I cannot help pointing out to the people of post-communist countries, especially China: Hey, here is your comparative advantage in institutional innovation!

The trick of history is this: given the failure of privatization to generate broad public support, the pace of its implementation remains slow in China. As a result, many firms' assets are still partly in state hands. At this juncture, if the Chinese people decided to pursue James Meade's program of the social dividend, the chance of its success would be greater than in the West. Would the Chinese people do it? The real constraint is not material. It is spiritual in nature: Will the people and the leaders of China and other postcommunist countries have the courage and the vision to establish new institutions so far unseen in the world? It is here that a fertile field for the development of a dynamic republicanism for the 21st century may be found.[20]

So far, I only use the example of a "social dividend" to illustrate how we might transform the republican vision of property as the basis of autonomy and security into a workable institution under contemporary conditions. The limit of time does not allow me to discuss many more issues of dynamic republicanism, such as the relations between republicanism and empire/globalization, and between republicanism and "mixed constitution."[21] I only hope I have aroused your interest in searching for alternatives to the conventional versions of "capitalism" and "socialism" and, in this search, you might consider republicanism as a tentative starting point.

---

18 Ibid.

19 It is interesting to note that, according to official estimates, the US government's public debt will be fully redeemed by 2012. If the fiscal surplus continues after public debt retirement, the US government would have no choice but to start acquiring stock claims on the private sector. In other words, something similar to the Chinese "state shares" would appear in the US stock markets. To prevent this from happening is the main reason why Alan Greenspan supports Bush's tax cut plan. See Ronald McKinnon, "The International Dollar Standard and the Sustainability of the U.S. Current Account Deficit," *Brookings Papers on Economic Activity*, no. 1 (2001), p. 238.

20 It is encouraging in this context to read Pocock's argument against New Zealand's privatization methods. See his "Deconstructing Europe," in *The Question of Europe*, ed. Peter Gowan and Perry Anderson (London: Verso, 1997).

21 See Sheldon Wolin, *Tocqueville Between Two Worlds* (Princeton, N.J.: Princeton University Press, 2001) for a sophisticated analysis of the relationship between republicanism and democracy in modern Western history.

Liberal Democracy and Its Slippages

Harbans Mukhia

Let me at the outset express a sense of very great honor at the invitation extended to me to conclude this magnificently conceived series of lectures on the problematic and the problems of liberal democracy. Some of the scholars who have participated in this series, and others who have been unable to do so for a variety of reasons, have at one time or another been a kind of role model for many of us; to find myself now placed in their ranks is a privilege that far exceeds any that I have yet been accorded.

It also gives me a reason and an opportunity to engage in a measure of self-questioning by enabling me to look at my own location in a "third world" society. I must ask myself whether such location is the only vantage point available to me today for looking at problems that are increasingly transgressing boundaries laid down by history. The easiest course open to me would be to blame imperialism, colonialism, and neocolonialism, etc., for hindering the universalization of democracy and its implementation in large parts of Asia, Africa, and Latin America with some persuasive reasoning. I hope to avoid that course because I always find it less than satisfying, at least for myself, for it looks at the world from a static rather than a dynamic stance. A half century ago, when a large part of the world was still reeling under colonial dominance, I would have happily held it responsible for all the ills of my society. Today, when the possibility of unprecedented growth by developing societies through their own initiatives and efforts compressed in a couple of decades has been demonstrated to be patent, blaming someone else for our own failure seems to me to amount to an alibi. I would, instead, endeavor to confine myself to the parameters of the problematic constituted for this series of lectures: to look at various joints in the conception of liberal democracy that makes its whole project unrealizable, therefore unrealized in full measure.

The Search for Equality: Diverse Histories   Let me begin with the simple enough proposition that the quest for democracy is premised upon the quest for liberty and equality. Both liberty and equality are centered on the individual; it is the liberty of the individual from constraints imposed by the state, society, and the community and it is the individual's equality with other individuals irrespective of the status derived from birth, class, or any other social benchmark that is liberal democracy's goal. When the French Revolution created perhaps the most evocative and the most enduring of all slogans comprising three most powerful words – *liberté, égalité, fraternité* – the energy embedded in these words was perceived to have had universal resonance. The ideal of liberty and equality being inscribed went far beyond the boundaries of France and French society. It encompassed what it perceived were universal human aspirations. It has remained democracy's abiding goal.

In some profound ways, the French Revolution saw itself self-consciously and aggressively making a break with history by setting itself apart from it and in assuming the representation of universal human egalitarian and therefore democratic aspirations. The 14th of July 1789 was not yet another day in history when yet another king and queen were overthrown and were soon done away with; this was seen to constitute the beginning of a major turning point not merely in the future of France or Europe, but of the whole of humanity. In one of the emphatic breaks with history, the Revolution was to declare that "feudalism stood abolished from this day …"[1] Such a brash "abolition" of history also created several sources of tension, which has not yet found a resolution.

Indeed, if the French Revolution created this tension self-consciously and assertively, the same could be said, though in a milder form, about the entire gamut of political and social thought in Europe, centered on the question of equality and the individual, manifest and mediated through democracy and through the rapidity of historical change. The celebration of "progress" in history in Europe, encapsulated in the notion of linear time, counterposed to its antithesis, changelessness symbolized in cyclical Oriental time, was central to most 19th-century thinking in Europe. From the Magna Carta onward to the English Civil War, on the one hand, and the evolution of the theory of social contract on the other, the roots of liberal democracy have remained firmly located in European soil even as the tree has branched out far and wide. The universal validity of liberal democracy, rooted in the European soil, seems to me to be based upon the negation of urges for equality in a much wider segment of human history and in varied forms that have been around for much longer than the past couple of centuries in Europe.

---

1 Decree August 5 and August 11, 1789, passed by the Assemblée Nationale. See Michel Vovelle, *La Chute de la monarchie, 1789–92* (Paris: Editions du Seuil, 1972), p. 173.

In some important ways, human history has been a site for the repeated assertion of egalitarian urges which have at times manifested themselves in religious, and at others in secular ideologies. Historians have seen the rise of Buddhism in the sixth century B.C. in the foothills of the Himalayas as a movement of protest against the Brahmanical Hindu orthodoxy which was predicated upon social inequalities derived from one's birth. Renunciation of wealth, status, and power by the initiates, the ordained monks, was the high-water mark of the assertion of complete equality in the common assembly, the *sangha*. Renunciation, as opposed to deprivation and short of an armed uprising, has been in every religion the most powerful form of protest against the high and the mighty, against unequal access to resources whether economic, cultural, or spiritual. And I would like all of us to appreciate the force of renunciation as a mode of asserting equality not only by those who are deprived of wealth and power but by those who actually possess it in ample measure. The search for equality is thus a humane quest which has as much appeal for those at the higher rungs of the social order as for those perpetually rendered unequal by that same order; it is, then, not always a quest by those born into misery. The fact that Buddhism made the *sangha* the exclusive preserve of men and thus did not envisage gender equality need not persuade us to underrate the strength of the egalitarian urge that has made it such an indelible presence in our common human history. In modern India, it still remains an inviting form of search for social equality for those who are at the lower rungs of the caste hierarchy.

In Islam too, in one face of it, the mystic, *Sufi* face, protest against distortion of the egalitarian ethos of Islam by the Muslim State, normatively if not always empirically, found expression in the renunciation of wealth and power and the creation of a distance between the sources of wealth and power and the Sufi order which was the site of protest. In the history of Islam, the time of the Prophet Muhammad and the first four of his caliphs, Abu Bakr, Usman, Umar, and Ali, is universally constructed as the golden age, when piety and truth prevailed and an egalitarian ethos permeated the community, even though the reality was that three of the four caliphs had been assassinated in internecine feuds within the community. As Islam spread out of Arabia and brought under subjugation vast territories with varied histories, piety, truth, and equality became the first casualties. The conquest of Iran, with its age-old structures of imperial grandeur and governance, came as the turning point when equality became completely inconsistent with the governance of huge empires. The State was thus perceived as the chief agency of the distortion of Islam, when conquest and subjugation of the conquered people became the driving force. In protest against this distortion, the Sufis adopted the mode of renunciation of all worldly possessions and cherished penury in lieu of wealth, humility in lieu of power, and love in lieu of subjugation. Developed to its apogee in medieval Iran and India, Sufism became a universal phenomenon in the Muslim world and is still a living force in many regions, even as its protest against the State has greatly subsided. In the history of Sufism, the Sultan/*darvish* (Ruler/renouncer) dichotomy has been normatively a durable one, though it has not been short of shared spaces between them. Even as the Sufi's renunciation is an individual act, its association with protest against the institutions of distortion of egalitarian ethos, especially the State, has always evoked larger societal reverberations.

Several religious expressions, especially those centered on a monotheistic imaging of God, such as Christianity, Islam, and Sikhism, have been instrumental in major social upheavals, primarily moved by their egalitarian appeal to those denied equality in the social set up in which they were located. The concept of social equality is innate to the notion of monotheism, in which a single God being the creator of all humanity also cares for everyone in equal measure and is equally accessible to all. Indeed, in some extremely powerful ways, monotheistic religious identity establishes equality among believers by becoming the single cementing bond and displacing other internal cleavages, such as those of wealth, status, caste, etc. This is one of the chief motivating forces of what tends ultimately to merge in what we call religious fundamentalism. Osama bin Laden is an extreme example of this merger; there are many other more moderate examples. In present-day India, the unfolding of the ideology of Hindu nationalism by the ruling political party, the Bharatiya Janata Party (BJP), blends two contradictory motivations: the lower castes in the Hindu community experience an upward mobility when appeal is made to their Hindu rather than their caste identity; and this is cemented through the identification of all Hindus with the very modern phenomenon of nationalism. Those at the receiving end of social cleavages experience an upward mobility through these bonds, and those at the higher rungs experience a sense of "nobler meaning" in dedicating, or even sacrificing, their lives for the shared religious community than merely seeking a materially well-appointed life for themselves. The number of highly educated, qualified, and successful professionals who get involved in what are perceived as acts of terror, at times inspired by religious fervor, as on September 11, at others by the desire to change the world into a better one through violent revolution, has often surprised liberal commentators everywhere. Che Guevara and Fidel Castro were cult figures for youth around the world in the 1960s; for the liberal establishment of the US, they were anarchic terrorists, even if the term was then not in use. For, they defy all basic assumptions of liberal democracy which are centered on the supremacy of the individual to the exclusion of other commitments. To the "terrorist," the other commitments are his own medium of establishing "democracy" of the faith in opposition to the privileging of the individual, including himself. Is liberal democracy equipped to resolve this tension in any other manner except through a head-on collision with it, as it is doing in Afghanistan today, playing out its assumption of the inevitability of its ultimate triumph the world over?

Indeed, this assumption itself poses a fascinating paradox. For, even as liberal democracy is posited upon secular values of nondiscrimination among citizens on the basis of their religious identity, its assumption of inevitable ultimate triumph seems to derive heavily from theological lineages, especially the theology of proselytizing religions, such as Christianity and Islam. A proselytizing religion, or for that matter any proselytizing ideology such as Marxism, must predicate itself upon the assumption of its possession of the finality of truth and its ultimate triumph. Both Christianity and Islam operate on this assumption. So, indeed, does liberal democracy.

The positing of universal validity of all the values of liberal democracy and its ultimate triumph is also derived from a second lineage, that of natural science mediated through 19th-century positivism. In assuming that social dynamics are as capable of reduction to a given mode of reasoning and to universal validation as the study of natural phenomena in the disciplines of natural sciences, positivism sought to erase the fundamental distinction between the study of the natural and the social: in one, the facts are given, objective and verifiable (and falsifiable) from the outside; in the other, facts are constantly culturally constructed, thus subject to mutation through human intervention and open to variable and ever changing validation. If universal validity is fundamental to one, variation and contentious diversity is the very lifeline of the other. Diversity, with a much longer history and a much wider spread of reach behind it, is threatened by the rather brief and rather provincial history of universal validity of liberal democracy.

The most recent experiment with the realization of social equality was that of Marxian socialism. Its failure and its disastrous results should constitute no deterrent to recognizing its value as an important part of the intellectual legacy of humankind.

In all these experiments, the individual identity has been subsumed, indeed subordinated, to the identity of the community. This too has been one of the means of achieving equality, by not allowing anyone to rise above the entire community's identity – religious community in other cases, the Party in the case of Marxian socialism. Liberal democracy, on the other hand, privileges the individual and ensures ever growing withdrawal of mechanisms of control over the individual, whether the family, the state, the church, or the nation.

Clearly then, "equality" and therefore "democracy" has been open to several forms of appropriation in human history. Privileging the Western liberal notion of democracy underscores its triumphal premise, which in turn creates enormous tensions vis-à-vis other forms and makes it extremely vulnerable. Its innate ambition of hegemony places it in an interminable conflict with a plurality of patterns of historical development across the globe, each with a legitimate claim to "democracy," and presumes its overarching presence in the ever changing global scenario. Huntington's vision of a "clash of civilizations" is one expression of that tension; the ground reality of events since September 11 is another.

A second source of tension lies in the universalist premise of liberal democracy and its innate hegemonic ambition within a given nation and between nations. The chief instrument of the realization of democracy has been periodic elections. The universal adult franchise, itself with a very brief history of no more than six or seven decades in the most advanced democracies of the West, is the medium which normatively ensures equality to all citizens. However, incapable as the instrument is of establishing a decisive democratic superiority of a majority vote of say 51 percent over a rival vote of 49 percent, the history of electoral democracies almost the world over has in any case been witness to rule by governments elected by a minority vote. What then would be the measure of democratic legitimacy of such regimes, which seem to form the rule rather than the exception?

Much more important, however, is the qualification introduced in the project of these lectures: far from being value-neutral in terms of a range of options in the realization of democracy, liberal democracy has integral links with the market and capitalism. The supremacy of the market and of capitalism's hegemony is liberal democracy's alter ego, as it were, and the assumption of its ultimate triumph is at work here too. The further assumption that the market is a great equalizer would find favor only with a group of economists and sociologists; history, especially of the past couple of centuries, points to the contrary lesson which has demonstrated the market as the instrument of differentiation and hegemonization within societies and between them. It impedes, rather than promotes, equality and democracy; it creates encompassing inequalities. It was the driving force of imperialism and colonialism for nearly two centuries before the Second World War. It has also been the field where the state has intervened decisively and used force to remove obstacles to market expansion within a nation and globally.

In this overarching ambience of tension between diverse landscapes of democracy and the search for a hegemonic and universal concept, can one merely describe the state of things and leave it at that? Valuable as the plea for plurality may be considered, what if eruption of tensions between competing visions takes drastic forms as it did on September 11?

The events of September 11 and after are the most recent and the most explosive in their impact; these have been preceded by innumerable other events in the same genre but not of the same dimensions. What appears common among all these is a perceived tension between Western cultural hegemony and indigenous traditions, whether religious or other. Iran's Islamic Revolution under the leadership of Imam Khomeini was the previous major episode in this unfolding scenario, though the manifestation of tension there was entirely localized. Is a clash between these visions of society inevitable? Perhaps yes, to the extent that each is marked by the idea of triumph, which necessarily implies intolerance of the other. But, there is too in each of the varied traditions, whether religious or more broadly cultural, a very strong presence of tolerance of difference; and there is the force of the history of coexistence. The vision of increasing and almost forced uniformity globally as much as locally, which is the foundation of liberal democracy, poses an enormous threat to tolerance of difference and lends strength to resistance in many forms. The Afghan case is particularly illuminating. Through its long history of conversion to Islam, it has never ever been known for intolerance of other religions; indeed, in all popular images in stories – such as Rabindranath Tagore's short but celebrated story "Kabuliwala"[2] – and in films, the Afghan male, usually the only Afghan character, always comes across as simple, fiercely loyal to whomever he owes loyalty, and very humane, his Islamic profile almost always remaining in the shadows, virtually unnoticeable. The Taliban image has no more than two decades of history behind it and came about in response first to Soviet communism's threat and more recently Western, more specifically US attempts to isolate Afghanistan from the rest of the world, first having abetted and armed the Taliban resistance, including its strong, aggressive Islamic profile.

Short of the threat of hegemonic uniformity, it is possible to envision a greater degree of tolerance of plurality everywhere. Both Christianity and Islam, the two most populous religious communities on earth, were fired by the proselytizing zeal for a few centuries after their birth; for long the zeal has reached its plateau in both and there is little evidence of attempts by either at bringing the world to its heels either before the altar or in the courtyard of the mosque. Tol-

---

2 "Kabuliwala" is a colloquial Bengali word for "the man from Kabul." In the story, Rahmat, the Kabuliwala, is a petty hawker who brings some small things from Afghanistan to hawk in Calcutta. He develops special affection for a young girl in a (Hindu) writer's family because she reminds him of his own daughter back home. He gets arrested for assaulting a customer in a fit of rage because the man had cheated him. When he is released from prison, he heads straight for the child's home, carrying small gifts for her. This however is the day of her wedding and she cannot recognize him standing before her. Kabuliwala is heartbroken, struck with the thought, what if his own daughter too failed to remember him! *Collected Works of Rabindranath Tagore* (in Bengali), vol. 7 (Calcutta, 1961), pp. 133–140.

erance of difference has become part of the existence of all communities and groups. The triumphal zeal of Marxian socialism, the chief proselytizing ideology of the modern age, too dissipated very quickly after the initial couple of decades. Those of us who grew up in the mid-1950s would remember Khrushchev's fervent call for "peaceful coexistence" between different regimes, even as Mao Zedong was screaming that "socialism was inevitable" for all of humankind. These two visions became the sore point of tension within the socialist world.

We might also ponder another paradox: the flag bearers of liberal democracy in the world we inhabit today, the US and the UK, have also installed and sustained the most outrageously dictatorial regimes over a major part of the globe. Iran was well on its way to becoming a mirror-image liberal democracy in the 1950s under Mossadegh, who, in his perception of his own nation's interests, nationalized the production of oil, when the US-UK combine overthrew him and installed a caricature of Westernization in the form of the Shah. This laid the basis of the Islamic Revolution under a little known cleric then in exile in Paris, Ayatollah Khomeini. The Taliban would probably have had a marginal, virtually anonymous existence but for the support extended by the US in its battle against the Soviet regime. The recent history of many governments in Asia, Africa, and Latin America testifies to the same story of frontline liberal democracies turning bastions of support and sustenance to the most authoritarian regimes, where one would have expected an air of celebration at the advancement of democracy in any part of the world.

The point here is not to take delight in the irony of the situation, but to ask a basic question: What part of the universalizing ambition of liberal democracy operating in one part of the world yet has space for dislodging liberal democratic regimes in other parts and installing utterly authoritarian ones in their place? The supremacy of "national interests" of states in a position of dominance, like the US, would be a quick and a good explanation, for sure. But clearly, when "national interests" come into conflict with the universal and indivisible legitimacy of liberal democracy, what conceptual flaw allows the "national interests" to drive a hole into it? And, what are its sources of strength that might allow it to place restraints on regional interests on behalf of universal values?

Let me conclude my first plea here: the positivist assumption of the objectivity and the finality of one universal vision, with triumphal underpinnings implicit in it, which lies at the base of liberal democracy, needs to be scrutinized very critically and space for the plurality of visions and their mutual tolerance needs to be enlarged exponentially where historical and cultural experiences of all segments of humanity become part of the process of a shared but diversified human future. We also need to evolve a large range of institutional forms for realizing democratic aspirations, with electoral democracy being just one of them.

The Search for Alternatives to Personal Acquisition   Let me now turn to my second plea. One of the premises of equality and democracy is economic equality, not in the sense of ensuring the same level of income or economic resources to all citizens, but more in the sense of minimizing economic disparities between regions, groups, families, and, in the end, individuals. The great French historian Marc Bloch once movingly remarked: Can a small man ever be free? It is equally important to note that the only brief time in human history when humanity experienced equality of resources – and even gender equality – was in the early period of the hunting-gathering stage, which in a sort of idyllic image came to be referred to as "primitive communism" in Marxian literature. In the first edition of the *Communist Manifesto* in 1848, its authors Marx and Engels had declared that "The history of all hitherto existing society is the history of class struggle." Engels later amended this in 1888 after Marx's death five years earlier, and the statement now read "all *written* history is the history of class struggle."[3] This was a clear and succinct admission that prior to *written* history, that is, prior to the division of society into distinct and antagonistic classes, humanity had experienced the state of "communism" when equality at all planes, including gender equality, had prevailed, even though it was primitive inasmuch as nature rather than humankind or society had ordained it. This was the part of the hunting-gathering stage when the concept even of private possession, far lower in scale than private property, had not yet evolved. The egalitarian experience of this stage encompasses the whole of humanity, and its universality therefore is unique, never replicated again. I believe it is perhaps the dormant universal memory of this experience that erupts again and again in different segments of humanity in a variety of modes as manifestations of egalitarian urges. It was the same idiom of communism, now socially created through the development of technology and therefore at the point of culmination of "progress," that Marx and Engels envisaged as the end of history.

However, Marx and Engels committed a major error in reducing the great complexity of human behavior to a single base, i.e., the economic infrastructure.

---

3 Note by Engels to the English edition of 1888. David Fernbach, ed., *Karl Marx: The Revolutions of 1848, Political Writings*, vol. 1 (Harmondsworth: Penguin Books, 1973), note 13, pp. 67–68. In the note, Engels briefly explains the dissolution of "the primitive form of society everywhere from India to Ireland," the beginning of differentiation and the rise of antagonistic classes. For details he refers us to his *The Origin of the Family, Private Property and the State* (first published 1884).

The assumption remained fundamental to Marxism that once the economic infrastructure changed, mediated through class struggle, every aspect of human behavior – culture, politics, religion, philosophy, everything – would change to keep in correspondence with the economic transformation. In his celebrated Preface to *The Critique of Political Economy*, Marx had repeatedly emphasized the correspondence of the "superstructure" to the base. As economic infrastructure evolved from one stage of development to the next in a linear movement, from Primitive Communism to Slavery to Feudalism to Capitalism, etc., the political, social, and philosophical realms must also keep changing *in correspondence* with the moving infrastructure. "The religious world is a reflex of the real world," Marx had declared in volume 1 of *Capital*.[4] Two worlds were being constructed here: the real world, namely, that of the economy, and its reflex, that of religion and culture. If the real world had an objective existence, the reflex could make no such claims and it must change keeping pace with the "real world," as its reflex. When after Marx's death Joseph Bloch wrote to Engels and inquired with a touch of complaint whether he and Marx hadn't gone overboard in underwriting the economy as the sole moving force of all social progress, Engels' response of September 21, 1890, became a classic rejoinder by Marxists around the world to all further questions in this genre. Yes, Engels conceded, Marx and he had had to go all out to place emphasis on the economy because so gross had been its neglect by Idealist philosophers, their "adversaries." "We make our history ourselves," he asserted, "but in the first place, under very definite assumptions and conditions. Among these the economic ones are ultimately decisive. But the political ones, etc., and indeed even the traditions which haunt human minds also play a part, although not the decisive one."[5] The repeated emphasis on the economy as the ultimate determinant of the state of society's being established it as the irreducible premise of Marxism. The search for the ultimate determinant – the last instance – teleology thus greatly simplified what by any stretch would be an extremely complex process.

Indeed, any kind of totalizing explanation that seeks to ground it on a determinist base remains an inadequate explanation of the very multisided and very complex human behavior. I have no problem with a totalizing explanation without a determinist base to it. This is possible if we do not seek a last-instance explanation, if we do not construct a permanent structure of causal hierarchy. The *Annales* historiography developed in France, of which Marc Bloch along

---

4 Karl Marx, *Capital*, vol. 1 (Moscow: Progress Publishers, 1954), p. 79.
5 Karl Marx and Frederick Engels, *Selected Works in Three Volumes*, vol. 3 (Moscow: Progress Publishers, 1970), pp. 487–489. Engels uses various synonyms for "the ultimate determinant" in the letter such as "the *ultimately* determining element" (emphasis in original), "finally … necessary," "in the last resort," etc.

with his friend Lucien Febvre was the founder, seems to me to have overcome this problem of constructing a total history without a permanently structured causal hierarchy, by exploring moving conjunctures of causal explanations. It is possible to conceive of several others.

However, having said that, it is important to recognize that Marxism did question one of the basic assumptions underlying human history – that personal, or individual, acquisition of wealth is the only possible driving force of economic production. He recognized the tension between social production and individual acquisition, and he envisaged an alternative to it in the abolition of private property and the complete socialization of production and distribution of wealth. The recently collapsed socialist regimes, whose establishment had been inspired by Marxian theory, did seek to construct an alternative system of economic production where the driving force was not individual acquisition. The collapse of these regimes has been seen as a reinforcement of the earlier assumption of the exclusive validity of Capitalist ethos as the motive force of economic production and the end of history with this ultimate triumph.

I would like to make a plea for recognizing the value of this alternative even in its utter, indeed disastrous failure. In positing all history as the history of class struggle, Marx was basically seeking the end of history in a sense the very opposite of the meaning that has now been invested in the phrase by Francis Fukuyama, clearly delighting in the ironic turn. If Marx's denial of the self for society as the motor of economic production has proved disastrous, he had also visualized technology increasingly displacing human labor, and gradually human intervention in the process of economic production altogether. All human history has been marked by the production of subsistence as well as surplus through labor. Forms of human labor and its organization have come into conflict with technology, forcing it on to the path of development. This in sum is the class struggle. The class struggle will end with technology having developed to the extent of rendering human labor unnecessary for producing subsistence and surplus and therefore rendering its question of labor for subsistence irrelevant. Classes and class struggle would reach their terminal point then, for there would be no need or space for private possession, much less of private property. It is then that human beings would be able to realize their innate finer faculties. As Marx had put it somewhat poetically in *The German Ideology*, it is "in the communist society where nobody has one exclusive sphere of activity but each can become accomplished in any branch he wishes; society regulates the general production and thus makes it possible for me to do one thing today and another tomorrow, to hunt in the morning, fish in the afternoon, rear cattle in the evening, criticize after dinner just as I have a mind, without ever becoming hunter, fisherman, shepherd or critic."[6] All the tensions of history, of class struggle, would cease in the state of communism, the end of history as we have known and experienced it so far, and the beginning of real human history.

Present in this dreamlike scenario is a great deal of the Christian vision of the paradise, where human beings will not have to labor for their subsistence, where there will be eternal peace and no tension. Indeed, a great many of the premises of Marxism, or for that matter much of modern rationalist thought, can be traced back to medieval Christian theology. But if we leave that question aside for the moment, Marx's vision of technology increasingly taking over the processes of production from human beings is no longer a wild dream, and we are witness to the progress of technology doing precisely that, if bit by bit, inch by inch. If progress of technology appears somewhat tardy, a good part of it can become explicable in terms of the Marxist argument of social relations of production – here the compulsive nature of individual acquisition – standing in the way, though surely this cannot be the sole explanation.

But my basic point is: Should the disastrous experience of Marxian socialism in our times terminate our search for an alternative – or perhaps alternatives – to personal acquisition as the exclusive guide to economic and social development? I do not have the competence to suggest what the alternative(s) could be and I do not think it possible for me or anyone else to think up one on the spur of the moment. But my plea is that we do not foreclose such possibilities and do not constrict human imagination, which is a resource far greater and far more valuable than all the wealth it has created in history. Marx did imagine one that failed. It is important to cherish our failures as much as our successes, a lesson that Capitalism does not allow us to learn. That, I think, is its chief limitation.

6 Karl Marx and Frederick Engels, *The German Ideology*, in Marx and Engels, *Collected Works*, vol. 5 (Moscow: Progress Publishers, 1976), p. 47.

Arquitectos Sin Fronteras–España (ASF-E) is a nonprofit, nongovernmental development organization. Founded in 1992 by a group of architects and technicians who had previously collaborated with other NGOs, ASF-E is an association of people who participate on a volunteer basis in architecture, infrastructure, and planning projects in which the main goal is the economic and social development of the area concerned. ASF-E focuses on cooperation for development rather than emergency aid, and is active in developing countries in Africa, Central and South America, Asia, and Europe. **Marta Calsina** is the president of Arquitectos Sin Fronteras. **Elsa López** is a member of ASF-E's Fourth World Committee.

Upendra Baxi is currently Professor of Law at the University of Warwick, UK. He was formerly Professor of Law at the University of Delhi (1973–96), where he also served as Vice Chancellor (1990–94). Baxi has sought to contribute to renovation of legality in ways that empower the impoverished; he initiated social action litigation (mislabeled "public interest litigation") before the Supreme Court of India. He is currently completing a *People's Report on Human Rights Education*. His most recent publication is *The Future of Human Rights* (2002).

Born in India, **Homi K. Bhabha** is Anne F. Rothenberg Professor of English and American Literature and Language at Harvard University in Cambridge, Massachusetts. His publications include *Nation and Narration* (1990), *The Location of Culture* (1994), and a special issue of the periodical *Critical Inquiry* entitled "Front Lines/Border Posts" (Spring 1997). A regular contributor to *Artforum* magazine, Bhabha is currently working on a new book, *A Measure of Dwelling: A History of Cosmopolitanism*. He has delivered a number of distinguished lectures, including the DuBois Lectures at Harvard University and the Amnesty Human Rights Lecture at Oxford University.

Akeel Bilgrami is the Johnsonian Professor of Philosophy at Columbia University, New York, where he has taught since 1985. He has served as chairman of Columbia's Philosophy Department and has held visiting positions at Yale, Oxford, Jawaharlal Nehru University (New Delhi), and Australian National University. In winter 2000 he held the Radhakrishnan Chair in India. A frequent contributor of articles in both scholarly and journalistic venues, Bilgrami's books include *Belief and Meaning* (1992), *Self-Knowledge and Intentionality* (2002), and *Politics and the Moral Psychology of Identity* (2002).

Stefano Boeri is an architect and urban planner, and a lecturer at the universities of Milan and Genoa. As a founding member of Multiplicity, a research group on contemporary urban conditions, he co-organized the project "Uncertain States of Europe" (USE) for the exhibition *Mutations*, presented at arc en rêve centre d'architecture in Bordeaux (2000–2001). With photographer Gabriele Basilico, he published *Italy: Cross Sections of a Country* (1998), an eclectic atlas of the Italian urban landscape. His office is involved in many projects in port cities on the Mediterranean, including Genoa, Naples, Salerno, and Trieste.

A pioneer of cultural studies in Italy, **Iain Chambers** was born in Macclesfield, UK. He is presently Professor of the History of English Culture at the Istituto Universitario Orientale, Naples. He is the author of *Migrancy, Culture, Identity* (1994) and *Culture after Humanism* (2001), and co-editor of *The Post-colonial Question: Common Skies, Divided Horizons* (1996).

Born in China, **Zhiyuan Cui** is presently a Visiting Research Fellow at the East Asian Institute, National University of Singapore. He has taught in the Department of Political Science at the Massachusetts Institute of Technology and the Department of Economics at the People's University of China in Beijing. He is co-author (with Adam Przeworski et al.) of *Sustainable Democracy* (1993), edited the Roberto Mangabeira Unger reader, *Politics: The Central Texts* (1997), and has contributed chapters to several books on transformation in the former socialist countries of Eastern Europe. His book *Wrestling with the Invisible Hand* is forthcoming from Harvard University Press.

Manuel De Landa was born in Mexico City and has lived in Manhattan since 1975, where he began a career as an independent filmmaker. In 1980, he acquired an industrial-grade computer and became a programmer and computer artist, writing his own software for several years. He is the author of *War in the Age of Intelligent Machines* (1991), *A Thousand Years of Nonlinear History*

(1997), and *Intensive Science and Virtual Philosophy* (2002), as well as many philosophical essays published in various journals and collections. He is an Adjunct Professor in the School of Architecture, Columbia University, New York.

Demokratische Offensive, an association of various antiracism and civil-society initiatives, was founded in 1999 in Vienna, immediately after the election that made the FPÖ (Austrian Freedom Party) the second largest party in Austria. **Isolde Charim** is a journalist and lecturer in philosophy at the University of Vienna; **Gerald Eibegger,** a former literary and artistic director, is currently a collaborator on the project Netzwerk Innovation. **Robert Misik** is a journalist and foreign affairs editor at the Austrian newsmagazine *Format.* **Rudolf Scholten** was Austrian Minister of Science, Art, and Transportation (1990–97) and, since 1997, has been a member of the managing board of Österreichische Kontrollbank AG.

Born in Argentina, **Enrique Dussel** is Professor of Philosophy and Latin American Studies at the Universidad Autónoma Metropolitana and Professor of Church History and Theology at the Instituto Teológico de Estudios Superiores, both in Mexico City. Internationally renowned for his contributions to liberation theology, he has taught as a visiting professor at many universities. Among his more than fifty books are *The Underside of Modernity: Apel, Ricoeur, Rorty, Taylor, and the Philosophy of Liberation* (1996), *Ética de la liberación en la edad de la globalización y de la exclusión* (1998), *Etica della comunicazione ed etica della liberazione* (1999), and *Towards an Unknown Marx: A Commentary on the Manuscripts of 1861–63* (2001).

Boris Groys was born in East Berlin. Before emigrating to the Federal Republic of Germany in 1981, he was a researcher at the universities of Leningrad and Moscow. Since 1994 he has taught philosophy and aesthetics at the Hochschule für Gestaltung (School for Design) in Karlsruhe, and was Rector of the Academy of Fine Arts Vienna in 2001. His many publications include *The Total Art of Stalinism: Avant-garde, Aesthetic Dictatorship, and Beyond* (1992), *Über das Neue: Versuch einer Kulturökonomie* (1992), *Die Erfindung Rußlands* (1995), *Logik der Sammlung: Am Ende des musealen Zeitalters* (1997), and *Unter Verdacht: Eine Phänomenologie der Medien* (2000).

Stuart Hall, a leading figure on the British left, was born in Jamaica and studied at Oxford. He then worked at the Centre for Contemporary Cultural Studies at the University of Birmingham, where he made groundbreaking contributions to the field of cultural studies. Since 1979, he has been a professor in the Sociology program at Open University, Milton Keynes. Author of many books and articles, his publications include *Resistance through Rituals: Youth Subcultures in Post-war Britain* (1976), *Policing the Crisis: Mugging, the State, and Law and Order* (1978), *Questions of Cultural Identity* (1996), *Stuart Hall: Critical Dialogues in Cultural Studies* (1996), *Visual Culture: The Reader* (1999), and *Different: A Historical Context* (2001).

Michael Hardt is Associate Professor of Literature and Romance Studies at Duke University, Durham, North Carolina. He is the author of *Gilles Deleuze: An Apprenticeship in Philosophy* (1993) and co-author, with Antonio Negri, of *Labor of Dionysus: A Critique of the State-form* (1994) and *Empire* (2000).

Cornelia Klinger is a Permanent Fellow in Gender Studies and Political Philosophy at the Institut für die Wissenschaften vom Menschen (Institute for Human Sciences) in Vienna and teaches Philosophy at the University of Tübingen, Germany. She has written a wide range of articles on feminist philosophy, German idealism, and the political and aesthetic theories of Romanticism. She is co-editor of *Continental Philosophy in Feminist Perspective: Re-reading the Canon in German* (2000) and author of *Flucht, Trost, Revolte: Die Moderne und ihre ästhetischen Gegenwelten* (1995).

Born in Argentina, **Ernesto Laclau** studied at the University of Essex, Colchester, where he is Professor of Political Science at the Centre for Theoretical Studies in the Humanities and Social Sciences. His current research topics include theory in comparative perspective, the discursive construction of social antagonism, and deconstruction and politics. He has authored and co-authored many books, including *Hegemony and Socialist Strategy: Towards a Radical Democratic Politics* (1985), *New Reflections on the Revolution of Our Time* (1990), *The Making of Political Identities* (1994), *Emancipation(s)* (1996), and *Contingency, Hegemony, Universality: Contemporary Dialogues on the Left* (2000) with Judith Butler and Slavoj Žižek.

Born in Vienna, **Oliver Marchart** teaches media and cultural studies at the Institut für Medienwissenschaften (Institute for Media Studies), University of Basel. He has published scholarly articles in many venues. His books include *Neoismus: Avantgarde und Selbsthistorisierung* (1997) and *Das Ende des Josephinismus: Zur Politisierung der österreichischen Kulturpolitik* (1999); he is the co-editor of *Laclau: A Critical Reader* (2002).

Chantal Mouffe is Professor of Political Theory at the University of Westminster in London. She has taught and researched in many universities in Europe, North America, and Latin America and is a member of the Collège International de Philosophie in Paris. She is the editor of *Gramsci and Marxist Theory* (1979), *Dimensions of Radical Democracy: Pluralism, Citizenship, Community* (1992), *Deconstruction and Pragmatism* (1996), and *The Challenge of Carl Schmitt* (1999); the co-author with Ernesto Laclau of *Hegemony and Socialist Strategy: Towards a Radical Democratic Politics* (1985); and the author of *The Return of the Political* (1993) and *The Democratic Paradox* (2000). She is currently elaborating a nonrationalist approach to political theory and engaged in research projects on the rise of right-wing populism in Europe and the limits of the Third Way.

Born in India, **Harbans Mukhia** is Professor of History and Rector, Jawaharlal Nehru University, New Delhi. In the 1970s and '80s, he worked on the theoretical and empirical premises of feudalism in a comparative perspective. His 1981 essay, "Was There Feudalism in Indian History?" (*Journal of Peasant Studies*), launched an international debate, published as *Feudalism and Non-European Societies* in 1985, and later as *The Feudalism Debate* (1999). In 1988–90, he co-edited (with Maurice Aymard) *French Studies in History*, a multivolume collection of the works of Annales historians for publication in India. Other books include *Perspectives on Medieval History* (1993), and *Religion, Religiosity, and Communalism* (co-editor, 1996).

Sean Nazerali is a Canadian/British citizen who has been living and working in Central Europe for the past seven years. He co-founded the only Romani school in the Czech Republic, the Romská Stredni Skola Sociální (Romani Secondary School of Social Work) in Kolín, and is a political advisor to the president of the International Romani Union, the oldest and most widely recognized Romani organization in the world.

Antonio Negri has served as a member of the Italian parliament and held a chair in political science at the University of Padua. After living in exile in France for nearly fourteen years, he is currently serving a prison sentence in Italy for his political activism in the 1970s. He is the author of over twenty books, the most recent of which are *Insurgencies* (1999), *Empire* (with Michael Hardt) (2000), and *Kairos, Alma Venus, Multitudo: Nove lezioni impartite a me stesso* (2000).

Bhikhu Parekh is Centennial Professor at London School of Economics and Political Science. In addition to his academic work, he is active in British public life. He was a member of the Rampton/Swann Committee of Inquiry into the Educational Problems of Ethnic Minority Children (1978–81), and Deputy Chairman and Acting Chairman of the Commission for Racial Equality (1985–90). He was appointed to the House of Lords in March 2000, and chaired the Commission on the Future of Multi-Ethnic Britain, whose report was published in October 2000. Parekh has authored several books, including *Hannah Arendt and the Search for a New Political Philosophy* (1981), *Marx's Theory of Ideology* (1982), *Colonialism, Tradition, and Reform: An Analysis of Gandhi's Political Discourse* (1999), and *Rethinking Multiculturalism: Cultural Diversity and Political Theory* (2000).

After working for many years as a journalist for major US newspapers, **Mark Potok** became the director of publication and information at the Southern Poverty Law Center (SPLC) in Montgomery, Alabama. He is also the editor of the Center's *Intelligence Report* and oversees its Klanwatch Project.

Florian Schneider is a writer, filmmaker, and media activist based in Munich. As one of the founders of the „kein mensch ist illegal" (no one is illegal) network, he is involved in numerous online and offline activities around the issues of borders, migration, and media.

Playwright, poet, novelist, and political activist, **Wole Soyinka** was born in western Nigeria. In 1967, while serving as director of the drama school at Ibadan University, he was arrested for writings sympathetic to secessionist Biafra and imprisoned for twenty-seven months, twenty-two of which were spent in solitary confinement. This was not the first or last time Soyinka would be harassed by the authorities, which led to periods of exile from his homeland. Soyinka has published many works of drama, fiction, poetry, and political criticism, including *The Interpreters* (1965), *Madmen and Specialists* (1971), *A Play of Giants* (1984), *Requiem for a Futurologist* (1985), *The Open Sore of a Continent* (1996), and *The Burden of Memory, The Muse of Forgiveness* (1998). His controversial prison memoir, *The Man Died*, was published in 1972. Soyinka was awarded the Nobel Prize for literature in 1986, the first African writer to be honored by the Nobel Committee. He is currently Professor of Comparative Literature at Emory University in Atlanta, Georgia, and Director of Literary Arts at the University of Nevada.

Immanuel Wallerstein is the founder and director of the Fernand Braudel Center for the Study of Economies, Historical Systems, and Civilizations, and Distinguished Professor of Sociology at the State University of New York, Binghamton. He is the former president of the International Sociological Association (1994–98), and is affiliated with the Maison des Sciences de l'Homme in Paris. Author of countless publications, beginning with his earliest scholarly interest in Africa's struggle for independence to pathbreaking work on the modern world-system and structures of knowledge, Wallerstein's recent books include *After Liberalism* (1995), *Historical Capitalism, with Capitalist Civilization* (1995), *Utopistics, or, Historical Choices of the Twenty-first Century* (1998), and *The End of the World as We Know It: Social Science for the Twenty-first Century* (1999).

Ruth Wodak is Professor of Applied Linguistics at the University of Vienna, director of the Wittgenstein Research Center "Discourse, Politics, Identity," and a research professor at the Österreichische Akademie der Wissenschaften (Austrian Academy of Sciences). She is also director of the Austrian National Focal Point for the European Monitoring Centre on Racism and Xenophobia (EUMC). Her fields of interest are sociolinguistics, psycholinguistics, discourse analysis, and gender studies. She is the editor of the journal *Language and Politics* and has authored/co-authored many works, including *Disorders of Discourse* (1996), *Gender and Discourse* (1997), *The Discursive Construction of National Identity* (1999), *Discourse and Discrimination* (2000), *Methods of Critical Discourse Analysis* (2001), and *The Haider Phenomenon* (2002).

Slavoj Žižek was born in Ljubljana, Slovenia. He has been a researcher at the Institute for Social Sciences at the University of Ljubljana since 1979, and has taught at many academic institutions in the United States as a visiting professor. A prolific writer, many of his works examine phenomena of popular culture, film, and new media through the lens of psychoanalytic theory. Recent publications include *The Abyss of Freedom* (1997), *The Ticklish Subject: The Absent Centre of Political Ontology* (1999), *Enjoy Your Symptom! Jacques Lacan in Hollywood and Out* (2001), *Did Somebody Say Totalitarianism?* (2001), and *Welcome to the Desert of the Real* (2001). In 1990, he was a candidate for the presidency of the Republic of Slovenia. He currently directs a research group at the Kulturwissenschaftliches Institut (Institute of Cultural Studies) in Essen, Germany.